The Complete Guide to Tractor-Trailer Operations
Fifth Edition

by

Mike Byrnes and Associates, Inc.
Publishers

Associate Member

Associate Member

3rd Printing

Published by:

Mike Byrnes and Associates, Inc.
www.bumper2bumpertruckbook.com
P.O. Box 8866
Corpus Christi, TX, 78468-8866
355 Keewaydin Lane
Port Aransas, Texas 78373

Other publications by Mike Byrnes and Associates:

BUMPER TO BUMPER, La guía completa para operaciones de autotransporte de carga

EL GLOSARIO, the BUMPER TO BUMPER Spanish-English Glossary of Trucking Terms

BUMPER TO BUMPER, The Diesel Mechanics Student's Guide to Tractor-Trailer Operations

Barron's How to Prepare for the Commercial Driver's License Truck Driver's Test (written by Mike Byrnes and Associates, published by Barron's Educational Series, Inc.)

Easy CDL Exam Review, Easy CDL Hazardous Materials Endorsement Review and *Easy CDL for Hot Shot Trucking* apps for the iPhone and iPad (written by Mike Byrnes and Associates, published by StudyByApp.com)

This publication is designed to provide accurate and authoritative information regarding the subject matter covered. It is sold with the understanding that the publisher is not engaged in rendering legal, accounting, or other professional service. If legal advice or other expert assistance is required, the services of a competent professional should be sought. Further, the publishers accept no responsibility for injuries or damages resulting from the use or misuse of information contained herein.

ISBN 0-9621687-6-9
ISBN13 978-0-9621687-6-5

Table of Contents

Contents

Acknowledgments

Mike Byrnes and Associates, Inc., specializes in publications for truck driver training and related occupations and concerns. Our staff represents over 55 years of truck driving and driver training experience and an equal amount of professional writing and editing experience. We offer publications that address all skill levels: pre-employment or entry-level, on-the-job trainee, and refresher. We pride ourselves on producing materials that are easy to read.

Our publications are written with the goal of meeting industry standards for training set by the Department of Transportation and other professional associations.

BUMPER TO BUMPER, The Complete Guide to Tractor-Trailer Operations, is our original text on truck driving and related activities. It was first published in 1988. For this edition we wish to acknowledge the people who cared enough about making *BUMPER TO BUMPER* the most thorough textbook on truck driving and gave us their comments and suggestions. Specifically, we wish to thank Michael V. Green, HDS Truck Driving Institute; Jay Shelly, Center for Transportation Safety, Inc.; John Rojas, Del Mar College; Wade Murphree, Chuck Wirth and Earl Peterson, American Institute of Technology; Anita Kerezman; Gene Breeden, A-1 Truck Driver Training; Greta Nord and Pete Nagel, Western Pacific Truck School; Denver Hamrick, Hamrick Truck Driving School; Bonnie Trown, United Truck and Car Driving School; Rick Dalton, Salt Lake Community College, Brick Kepler, Professional Drivers Academy; Harold Durbin, College of Instrument Technology; Jordan Hatch, College of Eastern Utah and Bud Williams, IITR Truck Driving School for their help and support.

To Jerry Bateman, Don Lowe, and Bob Taylor, thanks for being there.

As this edition was in progress, Mike Byrnes passed away. This book was his idea in the first place and so we formally dedicate this edition to him. He left a legacy of enthusiasm for and dedication to excellence in truck driver education. We continue on in that tradition, guided by his principles and concern for you, the student.

Figure 1-4 used by permission. Technology provided under contract to Heavy Vehicle Electronic License Plate, Inc. (HELP, Inc.) by Lockheed Martin IMS, Inc.

Preface

Those in trucking like to explain how important the industry is to the American economy and way of life by saying "If you have it, a truck probably brought it." Look around you now, right where you sit, and you'll begin to see the truth of that statement. There are few industries in America today that touch so many people in so many ways, every day. There are few workers who keep the nation's lifeblood pumping as do this country's truck drivers. Every year, increasingly better drivers, and more of them, are needed.

There are and always have been easier jobs than driving a truck. In the early days drivers struggled with slow, awkward equipment and bumpy roads. Today it's the challenge of keeping up with ever-changing technology, regulations, crowded roads, and crowded schedules. But none of those have ever been quite enough to keep people like you from climbing up into that cab.

Maybe it's the draw of the open road or the special satisfaction of being able to depend on your own knowledge and skills. Perhaps it's the thrill of being responsible for thousands of dollars of equipment and cargo. Or maybe it's the pride that comes from doing a good job in spite of a few obstacles, a job that means an awful lot to an awful lot of people. One or all of these may be the reason you chose to learn to drive a truck instead of push a pencil, pound a calculator, or something a little less challenging.

We've been involved in training people like you for almost 30 years, preparing them for a long, profitable, and satisfying career. This book sprang from a need we experienced throughout the years we have been involved in the training of over-the-road drivers. That need was for a textbook to accompany training programs such as the one you're in now.

In publishing this fourth edition, our goals are the same when we first published this book in 1988. We wanted to offer a textbook that was complete, covering everything you must know to have a good shot at success in your chosen field. We wanted something that was well-illustrated. It had to have all the forms and charts we found ourselves referring to in class, the ones that you need to see and know how to use. It had to have crisp, clear technical drawings to help you become familiar with your equipment.

We wanted the book to be thorough and accurate, and then we wanted something more. We wanted it to be easy, even enjoyable for you to read and use. We wanted you to get more out of it than just a good knowledge of equipment or how to do logs. We wanted you to be able to get the feel of the truck driver's job.

Take a moment now to scan the Table of Contents. You may be wondering why we included some of the topics we did. Chapters on equipment, driving maneuvers, and map reading probably seem appropriate enough. But why did we include a chapter titled "Your Future in Trucking" or one on the driver's life or continuing education? It's because we wanted you to finish the book with the knowledge that the professional driver's job today is bigger than just getting the vehicle from Point A to Point B.

The need for such expanded training is more critical than ever. Transportation safety experts along with Department of Transportation officials continually reemphasize that entry level drivers must know far more than simply what's required to obtain a Commercial Driver's License.

BUMPER TO BUMPER goes beyond the basics of inspection, driving, and transporting cargo to give you complete familiarity with industry terminology, the mechanical components of tractors and trailers, and the science of safe driving. You'll learn how to take care of the cargo, the equipment, the customer – and yourself. You'll begin to develop the good habits, attitudes, and safety skills that make you a valued employee. All this helps you get the kind of training that will satisfy the concerns of transportation industry leaders.

To be successful today you must know more, do more, have a broader view of your responsibilities than drivers of the past. The trucking industry doesn't stand still, never has as you'll learn in Chapter 1. That's why this fourth edition was necessary. In it we've updated information to reflect changes in the regulations, equipment, and the economy. You shouldn't stand still either. Make it a point to learn something new about your job and your industry every day.

In *BUMPER TO BUMPER*, you are getting the work of writers with a wide range of experience in the trucking industry: employers, managers, drivers, owner/operators, and mechanical experts. You're also benefitting from the expertise of people experienced in the education and training of drivers. We have developed training courses for some of the largest driver training institutions in the country. We've brought all this knowledge and experience together for you in one volume.

We hope *BUMPER TO BUMPER* makes your training easier and more enjoyable. If you have comments about the book, we'd love to hear them, be they criticisms or compliments. Just write to us at

BUMPER TO BUMPER
Mike Byrnes and Associates
P.O. Box 8866
Corpus Christi, TX 78468-8866
mbapub@aol.com

If you have a question or would like a reply, please say so in your letter and be sure to give us your address.

HOW BUMPER TO BUMPER IS ORGANIZED

We know you are eager to start this book and get into your training. Before you do, though, we hope you will read just a few more pages of introduction. We organized the book and put certain features in it to make reading easier. If you know about them, you should get more out of your reading.

FINDING YOUR WAY AROUND

The chapters in *BUMPER TO BUMPER* are grouped around different aspects of trucking. For instance, the first chapter serves as an introduction to the industry. Chapters 2 through 11 are technical subjects that have to do with the power unit. That's followed by chapters 12 through 14, on the trailer. The next group, chapters 15 through 32, deal with professional driver requirements and activities. The last three chapters, 33 through 35, deal with employment and continuing education.

BUMPER TO BUMPER can be used with almost any type of truck driver training curriculum. All you have to do is match the subject matter of your course outline to the subject matter of the chapters in this book. You don't have to read the chapters in the order in which they are listed. Each chapter can stand on its own. You don't have to worry that you'll miss out on something if you skip around.

The Table of Contents tells you the page number on which each chapter begins. Use the Table of Contents to go right to that part of the book you want to read or review. We've also indexed *BUMPER TO BUMPER* for your convenience. The Index guides you to the location of material that deals with a particular subject. Say you want to find what the book has to say about the engine. Look up "engine" in the Index. Then go to the page or pages that are listed. Each one of those pages will have some material on the engine.

THE STRUCTURE OF THE CHAPTERS

You'll find that essential topics, words, and key phrases are highlighted using **bold** type. So are the topic headings. Along with the lists of words with "bullets," these form a visible outline of the chapter. Use this outline to help focus your reading.

Scan the chapter by reading just the highlighted words before you actually read all the way through. This will give you an overview of what the chapter is about.

Then form mental questions about the subject matter you're about to read. Write these questions down. As you go through the chapter, read with an eye towards finding the answers. When you're done, look at your list of questions again. You should be able to answer all of them easily. If not, again scan the highlighted words for just that material which will answer the question.

Using this method, the material will fall into place more easily and stick with you longer. This "outline" will also help you when you return to the chapter for review. Scanning the words in bold may be all you need to do to recall the material.

Often, a picture can say it better than words, so *BUMPER TO BUMPER* includes many charts, technical illustrations, and graphs. They're numbered by chapter. For instance, the first illustration in Chapter 4 is numbered 4-1, "4" for Chapter 4 and "1" for first illustration, and so on.

ABOUT THE QUIZZES

You'll notice there are quizzes at the end of each chapter. They are designed to test your knowledge of the material presented in *BUMPER TO BUMPER*. Your instructor may have you take these quizzes and turn them in for a grade. Even if you are not assigned the quizzes, you should take them. They will help you measure your comprehension and progress.

If you're taking these quizzes on your own, as open book tests, be sure to read the next section, Getting the Most in the Least Study Time. It includes valuable tips for answering the types of questions you'll find in this book. Then, to check your work, see your instructor for the answer key.

GETTING THE MOST IN THE LEAST STUDY TIME

Well here you are hitting the books—again. If you've been out of school for some time you may be less than crazy about the idea. We want to assure you that this time around things will be different. You'll probably do better and enjoy your studies more now than you did in grade school. As an adult learner, your strong desire to succeed and your interest in the subject will help. Plus, *BUMPER TO BUMPER* is written in a practical, economical way so you don't have to read anything you won't use in your chosen career.

Still, if you don't have all the time in the world to study, you might appreciate some tips that will help you get the most in the least amount of time.

HAVE A PLAN OF ACTION

Your first step is to have a plan of action. When and where are you going to work on your studies? You'll have the easiest time of it if you work when you are alert, relaxed, and free of distraction. Try to study at the same time every day or week. That helps make studying a habit.

Set yourself a goal, say, so many pages a session. Make this a reasonable goal. If you set your goal too high, you'll just feel bad when you fail to meet it. Instead, commit yourself to something doable. Then keep track of your progress. You'll feel an extra measure of accomplishment when you see how well you are coming along. If you fall behind, you'll know to step up the pace so you don't have to cram it all in under pressure. Cramming is not a good learning method.

Find a good place in which to read where the noises of television, stereo, and radio, not to mention other people, will not distract you. Read at a steady even pace with few interruptions. Have drinks, snacks, or supplies you'll need while you read in place before you sit down.

Work for about 45 minutes at a time. Then stop, stretch, or walk around the room. This will give you the little mental break you need to keep from getting tired. Then go for another 45 minutes. Alternate good, focused study with short breaks and in no time you will have met your goal for the session.

TEST FOR SUCCESS

The final quiz is also a type of learning aid. You may not have thought of a test this way before but that's what it is. Answering questions helps you measure how well you understood what you read. If you can't answer some of the questions, you know just what parts you should review.

Here are some tips for answering the types of questions you'll find in *BUMPER TO BUMPER*.

TRUE/FALSE. Read the statement. Is the whole statement true? If so, select answer choice A, True. If any part of the statement is false, select answer choice B, False.

FILL IN THE BLANK. You're given a statement with some words missing. Fill in the blank with the word or words that will complete the statement and make it true.

MULTIPLE CHOICE. This is similar to fill-in-the-blank except that some answers have been suggested. Only one of the choices is true. Here's how to go about finding which one.

Read the statement, filling in the blank with the material in the first answer choice, A. Does it make a true statement? If so, answer choice A is the correct choice. If not, ask yourself "why not?" Your response might lead you to the right answer choice. If this doesn't work, try the statement again, this time with the material in the next answer choice, B. Keep working through all the answer choices until you find the one that makes a true statement out of the question.

MATCHING. In these questions, you're asked to match items in one group with items in another group. Each item from one group will match one and only one other item from the other group.

TEST YOUR OBSERVATION SKILLS

Being observant is an important skill for a professional driver. Each chapter offers you a chance to test your observation skills. Special illustrations open each chapter. These illustrations picture something unusual. At some point in each chapter, you'll be asked questions about the illustration. You can check the answers at the back of the book, where you can also chart the development of your ability to be observant.

CHAPTER 1

YOUR FUTURE IN TRUCKING

Opportunities in the Trucking Industry

Welcome to the start of your career as a professional driver in the trucking industry. Regardless of what attracted you to trucking, you may not fully realize the size of the field you are about to enter, or the number of opportunities it holds for you.

The trucking industry **employs more people than any other private industry in the United States,** over nine million men and women. People of every age, background, race, and religion are involved. About two million of these workers are drivers. This book will prepare you to be one of those drivers.

Of course, the trucking industry employs **many kinds of workers** besides drivers. For instance, dispatchers are needed to send trucks to the right destination with the right cargo. Freight handlers and loading dock and warehouse workers load and unload trucks. Mechanics repair and maintain trucks. Other shop workers fuel them and service the lights and tires.

Trucking companies have many office workers, billing clerks, customer service clerks, and computer operators. Truck makers employ engineers and factory workers in their plants. Suppliers that make the engines and tires and other parts also offer employment opportunities.

So you see, the trucking industry is one of the biggest industries in the country. It is a dynamic, growing industry. It fills a transportation need. It provides door-to-door fast freight service to almost every town in the United States. Often it is the only freight service to thousands of communities.

The trucking industry receives no subsidies from the government. It pays its own way. In fact, federal and state governments collect about nine billion dollars in taxes and fees each year. You can be proud you have chosen the trucking industry for your career!

Jobs in the Trucking Industry

Trucking keeps getting bigger and bigger. It **grows with the country**. As the number of people in the country grows, so does the trucking industry. More people means more products are used and must be shipped. That calls for more people in trucking.

fig. 1-1
The trucking industry employs far more people than just drivers.

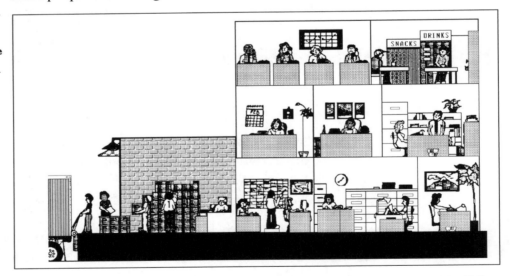

Food is one of the most important goods hauled by trucks. Fuel and building supplies are more in demand by more people. Clothing and furniture, medical supplies, and toys have to be hauled from city to city. Autos and machinery can be added to the list. Thousands of items are hauled by trucks.

Everything you use is hauled by a truck at some point or other. It can be the raw material that is hauled to a plant by truck. It can be the finished product that is shipped by truck to a warehouse. Trucking has become an important part of the American economy. It grows with the nation's economy.

Because it keeps on growing larger and larger **more workers are needed every year.** The industry needs workers of every kind, from the city pickup-and-delivery driver to the King of the Road, the long distance interstate over-the-road driver, from the person who answers the phone to the sales manager, from the billing clerk to the office manager, from city and line dispatchers to operations managers.

We're not done yet! There are still many more types of workers needed to support the industry. For instance, there are the mechanics in the shop. Other shop employees are the tire workers, lubrication, and fuel island attendants. Most terminals have dock workers. These are employees that unload and load freight. Some may be trained to drive and handle forklifts, some to operate a dock crane. Dock workers can specialize in handling certain freight such as 20-foot rolls of carpeting. Others will be trained to handle frozen commodities or certain hazardous materials. Some will wear protective clothing. Certain lead workers and dock foremen use two-way radios on the job.

Workers are needed to move trailers in and out from the dock. They are called hostlers, or yard hostlers. They drive a special tractor called a yard goat. This tractor will have a fifth wheel that lifts the trailer with hydraulic or air pressure. There is a walkway from the driver's door to a platform at the rear. The yard hostler can remove a trailer from the dock without setting foot on the ground!

TRUCKING INDUSTRY JOB DESCRIPTIONS

When you think "trucking," you probably think **"over-the-road driver."** But as you're beginning to see, there's more, much more. Many **pickup and delivery (PUD) drivers** start their career as over-the-road or OTR drivers. Some OTR drivers grow weary of the road, being away from home and family, and become PUD drivers after a long over-the-road career. A good yard hostler may have an opportunity to become an OTR driver.

Modern PUD drivers are highly specialized workers. They must be able to drive anything from a straight truck to a tractor-trailer unit. They use two-way radios and mobile telephones. They can assist a shipper in filling out bills of lading. They know how to collect COD, cash on delivery money. They can handle an Order Notify delivery. They know how to load "haz mat," hazardous materials.

Many PUD drivers are called driver-salesmen because they are trained to work with the sales staff. They ask the shipper for more shipments. They point out extra service their company offers. They secure more business by being friendly and cooperative.

Whether OTR or PUD, drivers depend on the **dispatchers.** Dispatchers are the backbone of any trucking company. They send the right truck with the right driver to the correct destination. City, or PUD, dispatchers often answer the phone hundreds of times a day. They may wear special phone headsets so they can keep their hands free to operate their computers, write down pickups, and answer the two-way radio. They talk to drivers and hostlers who come to their window to report.

They work closely with **sales and operations** people. Most of the phone calls they receive are from customers ordering a pickup. Dispatchers ask what kind of freight is being shipped and where it is going. They enter the details in the computer. Then the pickup is assigned to a PUD driver. City dispatchers are fast and pay attention to details. They must know how to talk to customers as well as PUD drivers on the road.

OTR dispatchers handle heavy duty long haul loads. When a trailer is loaded and ready to go, dispatch takes over. Dispatchers have a list of ready tractors and drivers that changes all the time. They match tractors and drivers with each load. Their job is to get each load moving to a correct consignee or to another terminal. A typical load may be dispatched from Florida to a terminal in Canada or from New York to Los Angeles.

In addition to calls from customers, these dispatchers receive calls from drivers on the road. They talk to drivers who have vehicle breakdowns, or drivers who are unloading and need another load. They monitor a computer screen that displays the location of trucks tracked by satellite. OTR dispatchers are trained to handle every type of problem possible. They must know whom to inform about a customer complaint, or what to do in an accident.

Large trucking companies with many terminals will also have another type of dispatcher. A separate unit called Central Dispatch will be in charge of all movement of OTR haul equipment. Central dispatchers keep a balance of trucks and trailers at each terminal. Nothing moves without their OK.

Safety Department employees make sure the company operates within safety guidelines. There are many federal and state agencies that look after employee protection. Some agencies also look out for the public's safety. The **safety inspectors and directors** must be aware of all the thousands of rules that govern safety in trucking. Safety employees make surprise visits to terminals looking for hazards. They watch dock workers, hostlers, and shop and yard employees and follow truck drivers on city streets and on highways. They hold meetings to raise awareness about safety and conduct training and complete the required reports. They work with all other departments to make sure safety rules are followed.

In spite of all the best training and equipment, accidents still occur. The Safety Department gets all the facts of each accident. An accident investigator is sent to the scene. This person's job is to collect all the facts. The driver and any witnesses are asked questions about what happened. Photos are taken and drawings are made. The investigator's report will allow the company to take action so another accident does not happen. Working closely with government agencies and insurance companies, the investigator helps the safety department achieve its goals.

Office and clerical jobs make up a large part of any trucking company. It seems there are about two clerks for every driver. Customer service clerks answer questions from customers. They must be polite and know everything possible about trucking. Customers call to ask where their shipments are. This is called tracing shipments. They call to report loss or damage. They call to ask about errors in billing. They call to report that a driver was extra helpful, or was careless or rude. Customer service people have to be able to solve a problem so the customer is still happy with the service.

Another office job is the freight bill clerk. This person "cuts" (prepares) a freight bill for each shipment. The freight bill is usually typed on a special keyboard that is part of a master computer program. The freight bill format will show up on a monitor screen. The clerk will type in the details from a bill of lading that has been rated (assigned a price for the shipping service). Other billing clerks process freight bill invoices that are sent to the customer.

There are many other clerks in a trucking office. There are claims clerks, over, short, and damage (OS&D) clerks, and general clerks. There are receptionists and secretaries. The accounting department has special collection clerks. The maintenance department has record-keeping clerks, and so on. There are many employment opportunities for those who prefer an office job to driving.

As people get more experience, they are promoted into more qualified jobs. A billing clerk can become an office manager. A customer service clerk or a PUD driver can become a sales person for the company. A city dispatcher can become an OTR dispatcher and then be sent to the central dispatch office. A mechanic may be promoted to shop manager. Other promotions could lead to purchasing or maintenance positions. A rate clerk can become a traffic manager.

Trucking almost always **promotes from within** the industry. Because it is a highly specialized industry it must draw on the experienced, qualified workers who are available. Many terminal managers started as dock workers or PUD drivers. Many OTR long distance truck drivers started as yard hostlers. Driver trainees not old enough to begin careers as interstate drivers can always begin as local city drivers. The basic experience can be very rewarding later.

fig. 1-2
This carrier's organizational chart shows how the different jobs in trucking are related.

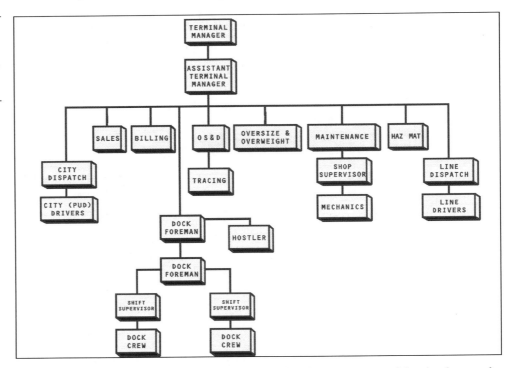

As you can see, there are many varied employment opportunities in the trucking industry. The trucking industry grows with the country. It increases in size every year. It is tied closely to the economy and population growth. When more goods are shipped, more trucks and drivers are needed. Your future in trucking is as secure as the future of our great nation.

Advances in the Trucking Industry

What will the future bring to trucking? Which way is the industry leaning? What are the trends? In predicting the future, we can learn from the past. We know that **advances in communications** have brought more efficient service. Drivers are in constant contact with their dispatchers. They can use two-way radios, mobile telephones, fax machines, and toll-free numbers to call in often. Truck stops offer fax services for drivers on the road. Satellite communications help dispatchers to track the movement of a truck and its load. Little precious time is lost checking on the status of the driver and the load.

Electronic advances are playing a larger part in the make-up of the truck itself. Some cabs have less wiring because sensors transmit signals to the dashboard instruments. Electronic fuel injection meters fuel more efficiently into the engine.

Onboard **computers** can produce a trip report within minutes of arrival, showing fuel use, idling time, and other important information. The same computer can pinpoint problems that affect economy or wear and tear.

fig. 1-3
Trucks on the road can now be tracked by satellites.

An electronic device placed in a truck can send signals to a satellite. The satellite can then return these signals to a computer in the terminal. In this way, the computer can track the truck and show on a screen where the truck is at any time. The dispatcher and driver can communicate instantly, by voice or electronically.

Brake by wire, also called electronic braking system (EBS), is a promising advancement in improved braking systems. Because air brake lines are so long, air brake balancing can be a problem. EBS may be a solution.

Drivers can fuel up at stations without even needing an attendant. An electronic card, like a credit card, activates the fuel pump. After the fuel is dispensed, the charge is billed to the driver's company.

Other advances are **new designs in trucks** to reduce wind drag. Extra wide and extra long trailers were authorized for use on the interstate a few years ago. Trucks using the interstate highway system are no longer subject to varied state laws as long as they fall into the federally mandated length laws.

The **roads themselves have improved** right along with the trucks. Highway designs have hit new highs. New stretches of highways are designed to keep the driver alert and awake. Special surfaces allow rain to run off and make for better and safer stops. Many on- and off-ramps are now lighted with nonglare lamps. Safety rules have been rewritten. Hazardous material handling has been tightened up. The result has been greater safety for all those using the public roads, truck drivers and motorists alike.

These are some of the changes and advances we have seen. What are the trends?

Based on the advances of the past, the trends appear to be in the following areas:

- improved and longer-lasting equipment
- faster and more accurate communications
- greater efficiency and more economy
- improved highway designs
- larger loads
- more emphasis on safety

Better Drivers

Trucks and highways can always be upgraded, but how about drivers? If there is any trend in the area of "drivers," it's toward demanding **more and better qualified** truck drivers on the nation's highways. Why?

Since the Motor Carrier Act of 1980, when trucking was deregulated, many new truck operators entered the industry. Trucking accidents went up almost 20 percent.

Most of the increase was tied to the truck driver. Unethical truck drivers carried several states' driver licenses in hopes that bad driving records would get lost in the shuffle. Drivers used legal and illegal drugs and alcohol to battle fatigue and stress. Some drivers carried two or more log books and drove as many as 100 hours a week. Others cut corners by driving unsafe vehicles. Still others used one or more false names because their license was already suspended in a state.

These are just some of the reasons the public began calling their elected representatives for help. They demanded action to take the bad driver off the road. They wanted to feel safe again when they drove alongside an 18-wheeler. They wanted to bring back the super driver, the competent, honest professional who would stop and help a motorist in trouble.

The Commercial Motor Vehicle Safety Act was passed in 1986 partly in response to this demand. The goal of the CMVSA is expressed in the Federal Motor Carrier Safety Regulations (FMCSR) Subpart A, Section 383, item 1. This states "The purpose of this part is to help reduce or prevent truck and bus accidents, fatalities, and injuries by requiring drivers to have a single commercial motor vehicle driver's license and by disqualifying drivers who operate commercial motor vehicles in an unsafe manner."

The regulations in FMCSR 383 contain the guidelines for the **Commercial Driver's License** program. These regulations require commercial motor vehicle drivers to have certain knowledge and skills. Drivers show they have these skills by passing one or more tests. Then they receive a commercial driver's license (**CDL**). The **"single driver's license"** part of the regulations means drivers can no longer hide a bad driving record by holding several licenses.

Employers are required to **check the employment records** of new hires as far back as 10 years. Present employees must notify their employer and home state in writing when they receive a violation or suspension. There are federal penalties involved for persons convicted of criminal acts and traffic violations, such as driving under the influence of drugs or alcohol (DUI). It is a serious offense to conceal or hide the truth about past records.

The CDL program was a huge success in getting bad drivers off the road. Drivers' bad records come back to haunt them. Past employers are contacted about how a certain driver performed, all in an attempt to identify drivers with poor driving records. The law requires trucking companies to conduct pre-employment and random **drug tests** and look for alcohol use. Abusers are offered a chance to recover in a rehab program. Good drivers are in short supply. At the same time, they are in demand because of increased need.

Commercial drivers must have the required knowledge and skill. They must have clean records. They must lead clean lives.

OBSERVATION SKILLS TEST

Being observant is an important skill for a professional driver. This is one of many exercises that will test your observation skills, or help develop them if they are weak. This chapter started with a large illustration. Without looking at it again, try to recall everything you can remember about it. Then turn to the Observation Skills Test Grid at the back of the book to see how you did. There you'll find instructions on how to chart the development of your observation skills. **Hint:** Something important is missing from the picture.

Young people seeking to enter the industry must be taught just how serious the problem has become. They must say no to drugs, no to alcohol, no to drag racing on public roads. They must value and preserve their safe driving record from the first moment they get behind the wheel–any wheel! They have to shape up or they will have no chance for a future as commercial drivers.

Your Future in Trucking

The drivers of the future may someday be in constant contact with their dispatcher. As you have seen, satellite tracking is being used to locate trucks and plot trucks' progress. Some systems offer near-instant satellite link to a dispatcher.

Tomorrow's drivers will operate trucks that have become lighter and more streamlined. They'll be able to carry larger payloads. Advances in alternative fuels will have you burning compressed natural gas (CNG) or liquefied natural gas (LNG) in your truck engine. More efficient engines will mean less fuel used, more economy. Highways will be the safest yet, with improved lighting and surfaces. You will have the advantage of intelligent vehicle highway systems such as collision avoidance systems, electronic message boards, and automatic toll collection. The present emphasis on safety will extend further into the jobs of hauling hazardous materials and commercial long distance driving, minimizing the risk to the driver. You will operate trucks with an automatic vehicle identification (AVI) system. A truck with AVI can be weighed automatically while in motion at highway speeds. AVI is pictured in Figure 1-4. These improvements mean your job will be safer, more rewarding, easier in some respects, more demanding in others.

**Figure 1-4
An AVI system at work.**

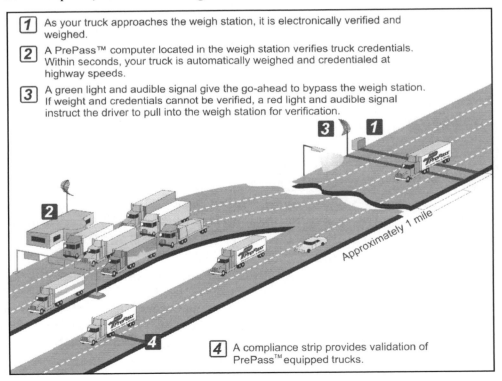

1. As your truck approaches the weigh station, it is electronically verified and weighed.

2. A PrePass™ computer located in the weigh station verifies truck credentials. Within seconds, your truck is automatically weighed and credentialed at highway speeds.

3. A green light and audible signal give the go-ahead to bypass the weigh station. If weight and credentials cannot be verified, a red light and audible signal instruct the driver to pull into the weigh station for verification.

Approximately 1 mile

4. A compliance strip provides validation of PrePass™ equipped trucks.

Either way, you have unique opportunities before you. You'll be in demand by an industry that needs your skills and dedication if it is to continue to grow. You have the chance to develop into a well-trained, safety-minded professional driver.

In fact, your role as the guardian of commercial vehicle safety is protected by the federal government. If you become aware of an actual or potential violation of a federal motor carrier safety regulation, you should report it. The Federal Motor Carrier Safety Administration provides a toll-free hotline phone number for this. It is 1-888-DOT-SAFT (or 1-888-368-7238). "Whistleblower" protection laws provide that your employer may not penalize you for doing this. Your employer may not discharge, discipline or discriminate against you regarding your pay, terms or privileges of employment if, in relation to a violation of a commercial motor vehicle safety regulation you:

- filed a complaint
- began a proceeding
- testified in a proceeding related to a violation of a commercial motor vehicle safety regulation
- will testify in a proceeding
- refused to operate a commercial motor vehicle because:
  - □ such operation would have violated a federal safety or health regulation
  - □ you had reasonable apprehension that you or someone else would have been seriously injured or impaired if the unsafe vehicle had been operated and you asked your employer to correct the unsafe vehicle and the employer refused.

You may also make complaints regarding violations online using a secure system at http://www.1-888-DOT-SAFT.com.

Opportunities, challenges, rewards—It's all part of your future in trucking. So let's get on with it!

Chapter 1 Quiz

1. The trucking industry employs more people than any other private industry in the United States.
   A. True
   B. False

2. Federal and state governments pay about nine billion dollars in taxes and fees each year to support the trucking industry.
   A. True
   B. False

3. A yard goat is _____.
   A. a slang term for a driver trainee
   B. a special tractor used by hostlers
   C. just one type of cargo hauled by OTR drivers

4. Many PUD drivers start their career as over-the-road drivers.
   A. True
   B. False

5. Drivers never get involved in sales.
   A. True
   B. False

6. Over-the-road drivers work with dispatchers, but city PUD drivers don't.
   A. True
   B. False

7. Advances in communications such as _____ have made for more efficient pickup and delivery.
   A. telephone deregulation
   B. touch tone phones
   C. mobile phones and satellite comunnication

8. Today's trailers are shorter and narrower than older trucks, to save on fuel.
   A. True
   B. False

9. Which is **not** a future trend of the trucking industry?
   A. improved highway designs
   B. larger loads
   C. reduced demand for drivers

10. Deregulation of the industry made it even easier to get several different driver's licenses from different states.
    A. True
    B. False

DASHBOARD AND GAUGES

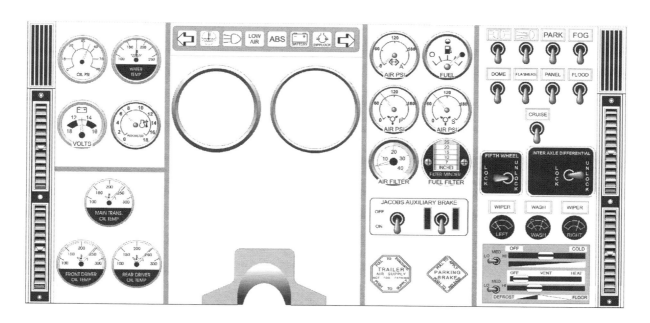

Getting into the Truck

The previous chapter gave you a good general knowledge of the trucking industry. It got you into the industry. In this chapter, we're going to get you into the truck. You'll begin to learn more of the specifics you'll need to do your job as a driver. We'll go inside the tractor to take a look at the dashboard. You'll get a basic introduction to the components of the dashboard and to the systems those components monitor or control.

The first thing you will notice when you actually get into the truck and sit behind the wheel is **the dashboard.** The dashboard is also called a dash or instrument panel. Figure 2-1 on the next page shows you an example of the gauges, switches, lights, and controls you'll find on a modern dashboard.

The dash houses a variety of **gauges and warning lights.** Some of these **monitor** the operating condition of **the engine.** Others **monitor** the operating condition of the engine's **auxiliary systems.** Each gauge and warning light has its own function.

Besides gauges and warning lights, there are also switches and controls on the dash. The **switches and controls** are used to **operate the vehicle.** An example

fig. 2-1
On a dashboard, you'll find components clustered according to their function.

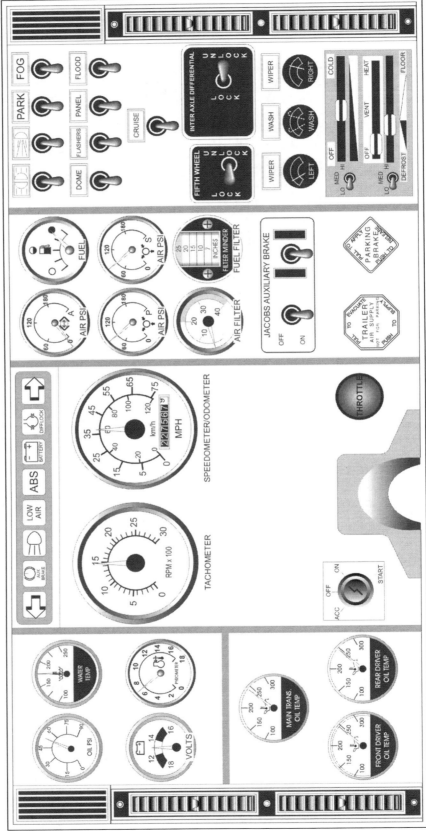

of these is the parking light switch. When you activate this switch, you turn on the parking lights.

On the instrument panel or dash, gauges, lights, switches, and controls are grouped together in clusters. These clusters are called **instrument clusters.** Figure 2-1 illustrates this.

Be aware, though, that all instrument panels are not the same. They all have very nearly the same gauges, switches, lights, and controls. They all tend to cluster these components, though not necessarily in the same way. They all tend to place the components used most often closer to the driver. However, you should note that the **arrangement of the clusters differs from truck to truck,** too. That is why you must become familiar with the dash of a truck before you drive it.

> OBSERVATION SKILLS TEST
> Speaking of becoming familiar with the dash, did you familiarize yourself with one at the start of this chapter? What did you notice about it? Turn to the Observation Skills Test Grid at the back of the book to see just how well you "learned" that particular dashboard.

Using Figure 2-1 as a guide, let's take a quick look at the instrument panel to find out what's there and exactly where it is. Then, we'll look at each component more closely and you'll learn what each one does.

Dashboard Components

Let's start at the far left of the illustration. The first thing you'll see is an **air conditioning vent.** You'll be happy to know that tractors are very comfortable.

Next to the vent you'll notice four gauges. These four gauges make up **the engine cluster.** From left to right, the two on top are the oil pressure gauge and the engine coolant temperature gauge. The two on the bottom from left to right are the voltmeter and the pyrometer. You'll learn what a pyrometer is later in this chapter.

Below the engine cluster is a small cluster that we'll call **the unit cluster.** It includes gauges that tell you the temperature of various parts of your tractor. Most often, there will be a transmission temperature gauge and two rear axle gauges, one for the forward rear axle and one for the rear rear axle.

Next, at the top center of the dash, we have **the warning lights cluster.** Sometimes these lights are accompanied by buzzers to make sure you know there is a problem you must attend to immediately.

We'll call the gauges and controls behind the steering wheel **the steering wheel cluster.** Here you'll find the ignition switch, the tachometer, the speedometer/odometer, and the throttle.

Next, moving from left to right, is another series of gauges. Those on top are **the brake application gauge,** and the fuel gauge.

Under this is **the air supply pressure gauge.** The left gauge shows the air pressure in the primary system. The right gauge shows the air pressure in the secondary system. The large cluster below the air gauges is made up of:

- the air filter gauge
- the fuel filter gauge
- the system parking brake knob
- the auxiliary brake controls
- the trailer air supply knob

On the top right side of the dash is **the lights cluster.** It includes all the light switches except the dimmer switch, which may be on the turn signal stalk or on the floorboard. You'll learn more about this switch later in this chapter.

Below the lights cluster is **the controls cluster.** We call it that because it consists of the controls that haven't fit into any other cluster. Here you'll find the fifth wheel lock control, the inter-axle differential control, the windshield wipers, and the heater and air conditioning controls.

Next to the lights cluster and the control cluster is another air conditioning vent.

That ends our get-acquainted tour of the dashboard. Now we'll focus on each cluster and tell you what each gauge shows and what each control and switch does. Then we'll take a quick look at the controls in the rest of the cab, including the pedals on the floor of the cab, the trailer brake hand control valve, and the transmission control lever.

The Engine Cluster

THE ENGINE OIL PRESSURE GAUGE

This gauge **tells you the oil pressure in the engine.** When the oil is cold, the gauge will show a high reading. After the engine has warmed up, the reading should return to normal. Measurements are displayed in pounds per square inch gauge (psig), which most people simply refer to as pounds per square inch or psi.

Always check this instrument after starting the engine. Oil pressure should come up in a few seconds. **If no pressure shows, stop the engine at once.** You can ruin the engine by running it with no oil pressure.

When the engine is running at normal temperatures and the oil is hot, the normal idle pressure runs from 10 to 20 psig and the **normal operating pressure runs from 30 to 75 psig.** The oil pressure gauge in Figure 2-1 is at 55 psig. That means our truck is running in the normal range. You should always check the operator's manual provided by the manufacturer showing specific gauges.

THE WATER TEMPERATURE GAUGE

This gauge is usually marked "Temp," "Water Temp," or by a symbol or icon. **It shows the engine cooling system temperature.** The gauge displays measurements in degrees. A typical gauge will have a range of 100 to 250 degrees Fahrenheit.

fig. 2-2
The water temperature gauge tells you the temperature of the engine coolant.

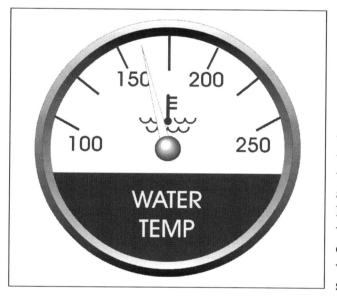

In **normal** operation, the gauge may read between 165 and **185 degrees Fahrenheit.** The gauge may read higher if you are pulling a heavy load up grade or operate the truck in hot weather. If the temperature goes above the safe limit, the high engine temperature warning light will come on. In some cabs, a warning buzzer will sound, too.

THE VOLTMETER

This gauge **shows the charge condition of the battery.** The voltmeter is identified by the word "Volts" shown on the lower portion of the gauge. There is often a diagram of a battery as well as the word "Volts."

The voltmeter has a colored band divided into three segments. Each of these segments indicates a different battery condition. The left-hand red segment indicates an undercharged battery. The middle green segment indicates normal battery condition. The right-hand red segment indicates an overcharge condition. The gauge pointer indicates which condition the battery is in. If the voltmeter indicates a continuous undercharging or overcharging condition, there is probably a malfunction in the charging system. Report this condition to Maintenance. The voltmeter in Figure 2-1 is in the normal range.

THE PYROMETER

The pyrometer **tells you the engine exhaust temperature.** Because it shows changes in the exhaust temperatures almost as soon as they occur, this gauge is a very good indicator of how hard the engine is working. The safe temperature range will be shown on the dashboard next to the gauge or on the gauge. Stay within that range. High exhaust temperature indicates inefficient engine operation. It can damage the turbocharger and other engine parts.

The Unit Temperature Cluster

Unit temperature gauges monitor temperature in the various components of the truck. Some of these parts are in **the transmission** and the rear axle differentials. Some trucks have a gauge for **the forward rear axle differentials** and a gauge for **the rear rear axle differentials.** These gauges are usually clearly marked for the component they monitor.

- main
- front driver
- rear driver

Like the engine temperature gauge, the unit temperature gauges display measurement in degrees. A high temperature reading will alert you to problems in that particular part. If the temperature is high, you should stop the truck before damage occurs.

Oil temperatures in transmissions normally range from 180 to 250 degrees Fahrenheit. The normal range for axles is from 160 to 250 degrees Fahrenheit. Use these ranges as guidelines only. Your best source of information is the operator's manual and your experience of what normal temperatures are for your vehicle. If the temperature goes higher, you need to do something.

The Warning Lights Cluster

As with all the gauges, controls, and switches in this chapter, the **placement of the warning lights cluster varies from truck to truck.**

This cluster is often called the telltale panel. Each individual warning light will be clearly marked. Some of these warning lights tell you a control is working. Some tell you a control or gauge is not working. Some of them tell you there is a problem that demands your immediate attention.

To get to know these warning lights, let's begin at the left and move toward the right. We've included the identifying symbols.

- the left hand turn signal (L.H.)

- the water temperature warning light (WATER)

- the high beam light (H.B.)

- the low air pressure warning light (AIR)

- anti-lock brake system (ABS)

- battery

- differential lock warning light (D.L.)

- the right hand turn signal (R.H.)

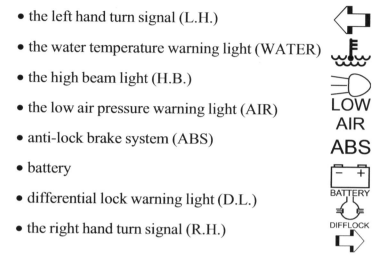

The **turn signal indicator lights** should come on whenever you use the right or left turn signal. If they don't come on, that's a warning something is wrong. It could be the warning light or the signal itself. Check it out. Your turn signals are important safety tools because they let other drivers know what you plan to do. Also, it's illegal to drive without them.

The water temperature, low oil pressure, and low air pressure warning lights should not come on. If they do, that's a warning something is wrong. The **water temperature warning light** will come on if the water temperature in the cooling system gets too high. The **low oil pressure warning light** will come on when the oil pressure is too low. The **low air pressure warning light** will come on if the air pressure in the braking system drops **below 60 psig.** The **low water level warning light** will come on if—you guessed it—the **water level is low.** These warning lights often have buzzers that sound, too. As you can see, they are really back-up systems for the gauges.

The high beam and differential lock lights are **reminders.** The **high beam light** reminds you the high beam is on. The **differential lock light** reminds you the differential lock is in the locked position. You'll learn about the differential lock control later in this chapter.

When you start up the truck, the lights on the warning light cluster should come on for a few moments to show they are working, then go out. If you have a light that doesn't come on, check to see if it is in fact broken. If you have one light that stays on after the others go out, you should check for problems in that system before you drive the truck.

The Steering Wheel Cluster

THE TACHOMETER

A tachometer (also called a tach) **shows engine crankshaft revolutions per minute** (rpm). A tachometer can be mechanical or electrical.

The tachometer **tells you when it's time to shift gears.** To determine the engine rpm, you multiply the number shown on the tachometer by 100. For example, 15 on the tach means 1,500 rpm.

The number of revolutions per minute an engine can turn differs from engine to engine. An average high horsepower diesel only turns up to 2,100 rpm. The range of the engine may go from 500 rpm (idle speed) to 2,100 rpm. The typical operating range is even shorter. Stay within the operating range for good engine performance.

Engine speeds in most engines are **governed.** This means that the number of rpm the engine will make in any gear is limited. If you want to see how many rpm your engine is turning, just look at the tach. This is called "driving by the tach." You'll learn more about using the tach in Chapter 16, Putting the Truck in Motion.

fig. 2-3
The speedometer gauge is combined with an odometer.

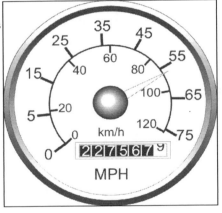

THE SPEEDOMETER/ODOMETER

The speedometer **shows truck speed in miles per hour** (mph). It may be mechanical or electrical. Inside the speedometer is an odometer. The **odometer keeps track of the total miles** the truck is driven. Mileage is shown in miles and sometimes tenths of miles.

THE IGNITION SWITCH

The ignition switch **turns on the truck electrical systems and turns the engine over so it can start.** Your truck may have a starter button you push in, or the starter may take a key. When the key is straight up and down, the switch is off. When the key is turned to the left, the accessory circuits are on. By turning the key to the right (on) position, the accessory and ignition circuits are turned on. By turning the key to the far right (start position), the starter switch is engaged.

Release the key as soon as the engine turns over. After a false start, do not operate the starter again until the engine has stopped completely. Let the starter cool for 30 seconds before trying again.

THE HAND THROTTLE

The hand throttle is a kind of accelerator on your dash. It can be **pulled out to set a specific engine speed,** or rpm. You could use the throttle in extremely cold weather to keep the engine warm when idling. You might also use it to get engine speed up and deliver more power to operate a power take-off (PTO) device. You'll learn about PTOs later in this chapter.

CRUISE CONTROL

The **cruise control acts much like the hand throttle,** but as the name implies, you will use the cruise control after you reach highway speeds. A switch turns the cruise control on and a second switch or button is used to set the desired cruise speed.

The Fuel Cluster

THE FUEL GAUGE

The fuel gauge **indicates the fuel level** in the supply tanks. Most fuel gauges are electrically operated. The fuel gauge is connected to a sending unit in the supply tank. Some trucks use more than one fuel supply tank. If your truck does, be sure to check the fuel level in all tanks before assuming you're out of fuel. The fuel gauge in Figure 2-1 shows the tank is full.

THE FUEL FILTER GAUGE

This gauge **indicates the condition of the fuel filter.** It is marked "Fuel Filter." It has a colored band divided into two segments. The left segment is white. The middle and right segments are red. It also has numbered markings. You have a clogged fuel filter if the needle reads in the red range.

The Brake Cluster

THE AIR PRESSURE GAUGE

This gauge is used on trucks equipped with air brakes and is identified by the word "Air" on the lower portion of its face. (Because the vehicle has a dual air braking system, there will be a gauge for each half of the system. Such a vehicle might have two gauges, or one gauge with two needles.) One gauge will be marked as the primary (P) or as (1). The other gauge will be marked as secondary (S) or (2). The air pressure gauge shows a reading in pounds per square inch gauge (psig). It indicates **psig available in the reservoirs for braking power.**

Use the air pressure gauge to check the operation of the air compressor. It is an important safety indicator. The **normal** gauge reading **is 100 to 120 psig.**

The pressure will vary in this range because of compressor operation and brake application.

Don't drive a truck with air brakes **until** the gauge reads **at least 100 psig.** Should the pressure drop below 90 pounds when you are driving the truck, stop immediately. If you don't, your brakes may come on automatically if the pressure drops much further.

LOW AIR PRESSURE WARNING DEVICE

All trucks with air brakes also have a **low air pressure warning device.** The device must be easily seen or heard, and it's usually a light or a buzzer. Sometimes it's both. It gives a continuous warning whenever the air pressure drops below a safe level, usually 60 psig. The warning won't stop until the air pressure exceeds 60 psig.

THE AIR BRAKE APPLICATION GAUGE

Not available in all trucks, this gauge **shows the amount of pressure applied to the brakes.** Naturally, a heavy brake application will cause a higher reading than a light brake application. When the brakes are released, the gauge pointer should return to zero.

THE ENGINE AIR FILTER GAUGE

This gauge **indicates the condition of the air filter.** It's marked "Air Filter." If the gauge reads in the red area, you have a clogged air filter. A clogged air filter should be cleaned or changed right away. It's important to keep the air filter clean because a clogged air filter restricts air flow. Restricted air flow interferes with the operation of the engine.

THE AUXILIARY BRAKE OR ENGINE RETARDER

Some trucks use engine retarders **to help the service brakes slow the truck.** The controls needed to operate the retarder are located on the dash. Our example in Figure 2-1 shows controls for the Jacobs auxiliary brake, also called the Jake Brake. Auxiliary brakes will be discussed in Chapter 22. You'll learn when and how to use them.

THE TRAILER AIR SUPPLY VALVE KNOB

The trailer air supply valve controls the tractor protection valve (TPV) which is usually under the left rear of the cab. The trailer air supply valve supplies air to the trailer. The TPV **prevents the loss of tractor air pressure in a trailer breakaway.** If the trailer air lines break, the TPV automatically shuts off the air supply to the trailer. This unit was designed to function automatically. However, it can be operated manually.

fig. 2-4
The trailer air supply controls the tractor protection valve which protects the tractor brake air supply in case of emergency.

The trailer air supply valve knob is labeled, colored red, and eight-sided, like a stop sign. It has two positions, normal and emergency. When it is in the normal position, the service and emergency brakes of both the tractor and the trailer are functional. However, if there is a large air loss from the trailer, the TPV will close automatically and the knob will pop out to the emergency position. This closes the air lines leading to the trailer which automatically set the trailer brakes, and protects the air in the tractor from loss. If the air in the tractor is lost, the tractor service brakes cannot work and the emergency brakes will come on.

You should manually pull this control knob out to the emergency position whenever you couple or uncouple a trailer. You should also pull it out when you bobtail (drive your tractor without a trailer). Once a trailer is coupled to the tractor, return the trailer air supply valve knob to the normal position. The control should be in the normal position whenever a trailer is coupled to the tractor.

THE PARKING BRAKE VALVE

This control knob is labelled, colored yellow, and diamond shaped. It should be applied when you park your rig. It **applies the parking brakes for both the tractor and the trailer.** To apply this brake, pull the knob out. To release, push the knob in.

THE TRACTOR PARKING BRAKE VALVE

On trucks equipped with this optional valve, this control knob is labelled, blue in color, and round in shape. It **applies the tractor parking brakes only.** To apply the tractor parking brakes, pull the knob out. To release the tractor parking brakes, push the knob in. You'll use these brakes when coupling or uncoupling.

The Lights Cluster

From left to right, the light switches listed below are in the lights cluster on the dashboard shown in Figure 2-1. Light control switches can be **toggle switches** (levers that pivot), **rocker (flip) switches,** or **push/pull buttons.** Each switch will be clearly marked to indicate which lights it controls. Remember that dashboards differ from truck to truck. Your truck will probably have a lights cluster. It may not have all the light switches listed here, or it may have many more.

- headlights switch
- clearance lights switch
- parking lights switch
- fog lights switch

- dome light switch
- emergency flashers switch
- panel lights switch
- flood light switch

You'll often find the emergency flasher control (usually with the turn signal flasher), the dome light, and the panel light switches closer to the steering wheel. In Figure 2-1, the headlights and clearance lights switches are labeled with a symbol or icon. These icons are used on many dashboards to designate the headlights and the clearance lights. You will learn how these lights, the parking, fog, and emergency lights, must be used as you read the following chapters. The dome light lights the inside of the cab. The panel light lights up the dashboard. The flood light is used at night when you need to check your load on the road or in an emergency.

The Controls Cluster

THE FIFTH WHEEL LOCK
This control is used **to lock the fifth wheel in position.** It allows you to unlock the fifth wheel in order to slide the fifth wheel back and forth to distribute the weight better. You'll learn all about sliding fifth wheels in Chapter 23.

THE INTER-AXLE DIFFERENTIAL LOCK
If your rig has dual rear axles it may have an inter-axle differential and you'll have an inter-axle differential control. The inter-axle differential **allows the front axle to turn at a different speed than the rear axle.** When the control is set at the unlocked position, the inter-axle differential lets each axle shaft and wheel turn at a different speed than the others. The control should be set on the unlocked position unless the road surface is slippery and traction is poor. Then the control should be put in the locked position, locking the front and rear axles so power will go equally to both rear axles. Do not run on dry roads with the inter-axle differential in the locked position. You could damage it. You'll learn more about inter-axle differentials in Chapter 7, on the drive train.

THE WINDSHIELD WIPERS
Truck windshield wipers are operated by air or electricity. Usually, **wipers have two controls, one for each wiper.** To turn the wiper on low speed, the knob is turned to the first position to the right. To operate the wiper on high speed, the knob is turned to the second position to the right. To turn the wiper off, the knob is turned all the way to the left.

Some air wiper systems use one control knob for both wipers. It's located on the dash. Others have one control knob for each wiper. To turn the wipers on, turn the knobs to the right. To turn the wipers off, turn the knobs to the left. Wiper speeds are controlled by the position of the knobs.

There is a **separate knob for the windshield washers.** In Figure 2-1, it's located between the wiper controls.

THE AIR CONDITIONING CONTROLS

Cab temperature is easily controlled in modern trucks. There may be up to nine air outlets in the cab and two in the sleeper. It may be hard to believe there is enough room in the cab for such a large dashboard and so many other cab controls. Fan speed controls include low, medium, and high. Controls are included for cooling, heating, and defrosting.

The Rest of the Cab

That finishes our tour of the dashboard. So, we'll leave the dashboard and tour the controls in the rest of the cab. Let's start with the pedals on the cab floor.

THE ACCELERATOR PEDAL

You'll find the accelerator on the floor of the cab under the steering wheel. You **use your right foot** to operate this pedal and **control engine speed.** When you depress the pedal, the speed of the vehicle increases. As you let your foot off the pedal, the speed decreases. If you take your foot off the pedal, the engine idles.

THE BRAKE PEDAL

You'll find the brake pedal just to the left of the accelerator. It's also called a **foot valve** or **treadle valve.** You **operate** this pedal **with your right foot.** When you depress the brake pedal, all the brakes are applied.

THE CLUTCH PEDAL

To the left of the brake pedal is the clutch pedal. You **use your left foot** to operate the clutch pedal. When you depress the clutch pedal, the clutch is disengaged. When you release the clutch pedal, the clutch is engaged. Depressing the clutch pedal all the way to the floor engages the clutch brake, which is covered in Chapter 16.

fig. 2-5
The controls on the floor under the steering wheel are, from right to left, the accelerator, the brake pedal and the clutch pedal.

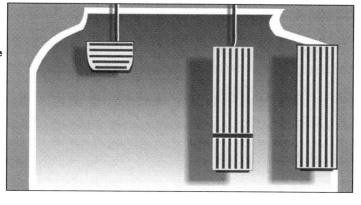

THE DIMMER SWITCH

The dimmer switch is combined with the turn signal which is mounted on the steering column below the steering wheel. It controls the high and low beams on the truck's headlights. Low beams should be used when driving in traffic. High beams should be used on open roads when there is no oncoming traffic and no traffic closer than 500 feet in front of you.

THE TRAILER BRAKE HAND CONTROL VALVE

This lever is usually located on the steering column. It **operates the trailer brakes only.** To engage the trailer brakes, you move the handle down.

THE TRANSMISSION SHIFT CONTROL LEVER

Transmissions differ from truck to truck. However, the transmission shift control lever most often **extends through the cab floor.** It's always on the right-hand side of the driver. You'll learn more about transmission levers in the next chapter.

THE POWER TAKE-OFF (PTO) LEVER

The power take-off lever is really a knob, although it's often called a lever. And, there are two of them. You'll find them on trucks such as winch trucks, snow blower trucks, and dump trucks equipped with power take-off units (PTO). If your truck has a PTO, you will use the knob or switch to connect the PTO to the transmission. Then use the second knob or switch to control the mechanism being powered by the PTO.

Chapter 2 Quiz

1. Gauges and warning lights on the dash monitor only the operating condition of the engine.
    A. True
    B. False

2. As you look at different truck dashboards, you will find similar gauges, knobs, and switches laid out in _____ patterns.
    A. identical
    B. confusing
    C. different
    D. unidentified

3. The needle on the water temperature gauge will point to _____degrees when the engine has reached normal operating temperature.
    A. 225-250
    B. 200-225
    C. 165-185
    D. 100-150

4. You have started the engine. If the oil pressure does not come up within seconds, you should _____.
   A. not be too concerned. It's probably a faulty gauge.
   B. think that an extremely heavy grade of oil is taking a long time to thin out and register.
   C. go have breakfast and check again when you finish.
   D. shut off the engine at once.

5. The low air pressure warning light will come on if the air pressure in the system drops below _____psig.
   A. 120
   B. 100
   C. 90
   D. 60

6. The term given to limiting the number of rpm your engine is able to turn is called _____.
   A. slack adjusting
   B. cruise control
   C. governed speed
   D. locking the differential

7. All trucks with air brakes have _____.
   A. an air brake application gauge
   B. a low air warning device
   C. an engine retarder
   D. a tractor parking brake valve

8. The primary and secondary air pressure gauges show the psig available in the reservoirs for braking power.
   A. True
   B. False

9. When in the out or emergency position, the red trailer air supply valve prevents the loss of tractor air pressure by closing _____.
   A. off the wet tank reservoir
   B. the tractor protection valve
   C. the primary air system reservoir
   D. the relay valves to the trailer's brake chambers

10. The dash-mounted parking brake valve knob is diamond shaped and red.
    A. True
    B. False

CHAPTER 3

TRANSMISSIONS

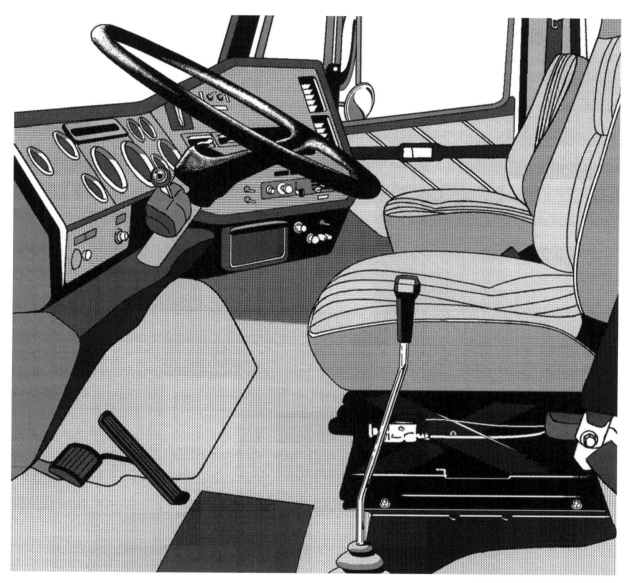

What Is a Transmission?

The truck engine is the component that produces the power to move the vehicle. The force of combustion causes pistons to move up and down. Then this movement of the pistons is changed to a circular motion by the crankshaft. We go into how and why in Chapter 6. The transmission gets this circular motion to the wheels. It's an **assembly** of gears and shafts that transmits the power from the engine through the driveline to the driving axles, the wheels, and the tires.

The circular motion produced by the engine is measured in revolutions per minute (rpm). The wheels of the truck also rotate, of course, but you don't normally measure that in rpm. An engine can operate efficiently only within a rather small rpm range. Yet the wheels have to be able to travel through a broader range of speeds than that. This is another important function of the transmission. It expands the limited range of speeds the engine can turn at into the **wider range of speeds** needed by the wheels to move your truck down the road. This allows the engine to stay in the narrow rpm range where it can operate efficiently and produce the most power (torque) while the truck's wheels can go from barely moving to highway speeds.

Transmitting Force

In the case of a vehicle transmission, the turning of the engine is what makes the vehicle's wheels turn. How does the transmission get the force from the engine to the wheels? We said the transmission was an assembly of gears and shafts. Let's explore how this assembly transmits power. We'll look at the gears first.

Take two gears, A and B, both the same size. They have the same number of teeth, and the same amount of space between the teeth. Now let's mesh them and apply a force to one gear, turning Gear A through one revolution. As the teeth of Gear A press on the teeth of Gear B, Gear B also moves. When Gear A completes one revolution, so has Gear B. What we have just done is to transmit a force acting on Gear A to Gear B.

fig. 3-1
Simple transmission of force.

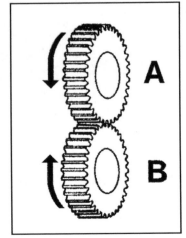

That was simple. Let's make it a little more interesting. We'll use gears of different sizes. A gear is sized by how many teeth it has. A gear with 12 teeth is larger than a gear with eight teeth (assuming, of course, that the space between the teeth is equal on both gears). Let's mesh those gears and apply a force to the smaller gear, A. When our smaller gear, A, has made one complete revolution, Gear B has only made two-thirds of a revolution. Only eight of its teeth have been contacted by the eight teeth of Gear A. To move Gear B all the way around, we have to move Gear A one-half turn more so four more of Gear A's teeth will move the last four of Gear B's.

fig. 3-2
The small gear, A, will have to make more than one complete revolution to turn Gear B once.

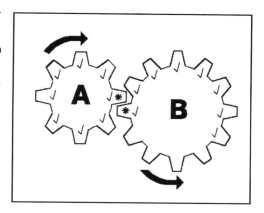

Why is this important? To answer that question, we have to make two statements about force. One is that, to get a certain amount of work done with a small gear will take more time than with a larger gear. You've just seen a simple demonstration of this with our large and small gears. To make large gear B go all the way around, small gear A had to make more than one complete turn (took more time). If Gear A were the same size or larger than Gear B, it would have moved Gear B through one revolution in less time. So here's our second statement about force: **the least speed is produced when a small gear turns a larger gear.**

This **difference in size between one gear and another** is called **gear ratio.** A gear ratio always describes the gear doing the driving acting upon the gear being driven. So, a gear ratio of 5:1 means a small gear is going through five revolutions to turn a larger gear once. If the larger gear were turning the smaller gear, the ratio would be 1:5.

Still don't see why this is important? Recall that at the start of this chapter, we said that the engine has a limited range of rpm compared to the wheels. We had to find some way to get the wheels to turn at more and different speeds than the engine is capable of doing. We use the principle of gear ratio to do this. You can see from our discussion that **different ratios** would **result in faster or slower speeds.** With the right combinations of small gears and large gears, an engine can drive the wheels at different rates of speed and operate very efficiently under many conditions. How much speed is produced depends on which gear is engaged, or turning the other gear.

You might see this better if we introduce some shafts to connect the engine and wheels. For the purposes of this demonstration, we're going to oversimplify, and leave out some very important components of a true transmission. We'll put them back in later in the chapter.

Look at Figure 3-3, on the next page. We've got a shaft coming out of the engine. At the end of our engine shaft, we have a gear. At the other end of our assembly, we have a wheel, and it, too, is connected to a shaft with a gear on the end. If we turn on the engine, the speed of the turning engine will be transmitted to the engine shaft, and to the gear that's attached to it. If we mesh the two gears, the engine shaft gear will turn the wheel shaft gear, which will turn the wheel shaft, and finally, the wheel itself. In a very simple way, we have transmitted the turning of the engine to the wheel to make the wheel turn.

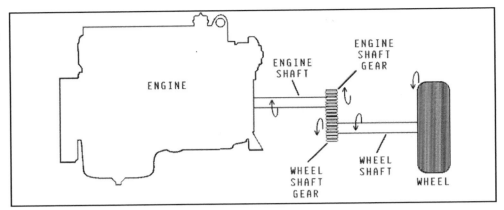

fig. 3-3
Using gears and shafts to transmit the turning of the engine to a wheel.

EXPANDING THE RANGE OF SPEED

Let's look at what different gear ratios (different combinations of gears) at the same engine speed will get us. Let's take a very small engine shaft gear turning a very much larger wheel shaft gear, say a 17:1 ratio. Here we have the least speed. Speed, if you think about it, is how far you can go in a given amount of time. If our wheel were moving forward across a surface, instead of spinning in space, it would cover a distance. The longer it takes the wheel to make a revolution, the longer it takes to cover that distance. Our gear ratio tells us that large wheel shaft gear is only going to make one revolution for every 17 times the engine shaft gear turns. The wheel will be turning quite slowly, taking a long time to go a distance. In other words, it's moving at low speed.

Now let's take another gear ratio, 5:1. Remember, the engine speed hasn't changed. Now our wheel shaft gear turns once for every five revolutions of the engine shaft gear. The wheel's turning faster, so it covers the same distance in less time. We have more speed.

Last, let's look at a gear ratio of 1:1. The gears are the same size. As you've probably guessed by now, this gives us the most speed of our three combinations.

In a vehicle, these different combinations meet different needs. To get a vehicle going from a standstill, it takes a lot of power. At the same time, you want very little speed. If the wheels were turning very quickly, the vehicle would lurch into motion. You'd have a jackrabbit start. The 17:1 gear ratio will get the truck into motion, at the low speed desired.

At the other extreme, a 1:1 gear ratio is well suited for traveling at highway speeds. In order to go 50 miles per hour, the wheels must turn very fast. The 1:1 gear ratio yields the most speed of our three combinations.

If we had all three combinations in one vehicle, we would have three speeds: slow, medium, and fast. Our engine, within its limited rpm range, would be able to drive the wheels through a wide range of speeds. Clearly, though, our basic transmission, pictured in Figure 3-3, will not work. We need a way to connect three different gear combinations to the engine and wheels in a way that lets us use just one at a time. Fortunately, this has already been invented.

Shifting Gears

The input shaft (sometimes called the clutch shaft) of the transmission is more or less what we've been calling the "engine shaft." It's connected to the engine through the clutch, which we'll discuss in more detail later in this chapter. The output shaft is roughly equivalent to what we've been calling the "wheel shaft." It's connected to the wheels through the drive shaft and drive axle. The input and output shafts are in line with each other and together are called the mainshaft.

Transmitting the power from the input shaft to the output shaft is the counter-shaft. It's called that because it turns in a direction opposite (or counter) to that of the engine. The input shaft has only one gear which drives the countershaft. Both the output shaft and countershaft have gears of various sizes on them.

SLIDING GEARS

There are basically two ways to achieve different gear combinations in to-day's truck transmissions. In the sliding gear transmission, different sized gears slide along the output shaft. The output shaft is grooved, or splined, along its length. The core of the output shaft gears has ridges that mesh with the output shaft grooves so that if an output shaft gear is turning, the output shaft turns with it. The output shaft gears can slide along the length of the out-put shaft. On the other hand, the gears on the countershaft are fixed. They do not slide on the shaft. If a moving countershaft gear meshes with an output shaft gear, the countershaft gear will turn the output shaft gear and the output shaft itself. Gears are changed by sliding one output shaft gear out of mesh with a countershaft gear, and sliding a different output shaft gear into mesh with another countershaft gear. That is to say, **only one pair of gears is in mesh at any given time.**

Look at Figure 3-4 (A), which pictures the in-line input shaft-output shaft type of assembly. Starting from the left, note the input shaft gear, rotating with the input shaft. It meshes with the countershaft drive gear, which gets the counter-shaft turning (remember, the countershaft gears are fixed on the shaft). The shifter yokes at the top of the picture have selected low gear, putting the low output shaft gear in mesh with the low countershaft gear. Note the very small countershaft gear in comparison with the larger output shaft gear. The low countershaft gear drives the low output shaft gear, and that turns the output shaft. This will turn the drive shaft and wheels. Since we have such a high gear ratio, the wheels will turn slowly.

In Figure 3-4 (B), the shifter yokes have selected second, taking the countershaft and output shaft low gears out of mesh and putting the countershaft and output shaft second gears in mesh. Note the two gears are more equal in size. The gear ratio is smaller than in low gear, so we will get more speed.

fig. 3-4
Shifting from low (A) to second gear (B) with sliding gears.

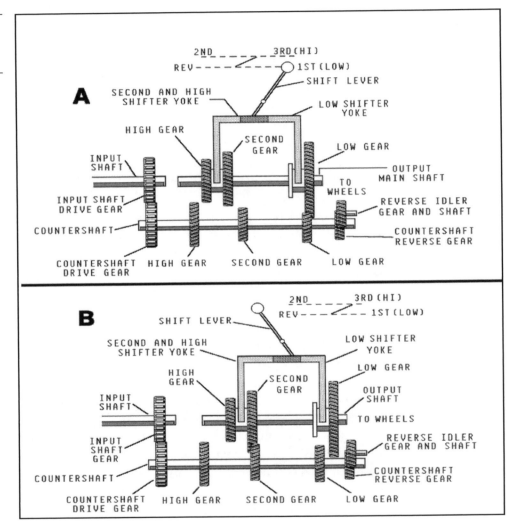

SLIDING CLUTCH

In the sliding clutch type, the gears on the output shaft are floating. They are not fixed to the shaft. All combinations of gears are in mesh at the same time (so this is sometimes called constant mesh transmission). But if none of the output shaft gears is locked into place on the output shaft, no power is transmitted. A mechanism called a sliding clutch or shifter collar causes one output shaft gear to lock onto its shaft. Since this gear is in mesh with a countershaft gear, that gets the shaft turning. The effect is that although **all the gear sets are in mesh at the same time, only one is working.**

Look at Figure 3-5, which shows first gear engaged. From left to right, you see five sets of meshed gears: drive, third, second, first, and reverse. Note the gear ratios. A large countershaft gear is driving a smaller output shaft gear in third, the second gears are fairly similar in size and in first, the small gear is driving a larger gear. All the gears are in mesh, as we said, but only one set, first gear, is engaged. Note the position of the shift collar. This collar can also engage the reverse gear, by moving the shift lever left. Moving the shift lever to the left causes the shifter yoke to move to the right.

fig. 3-5
First gear engaged by shift collar in sliding clutch transmission.

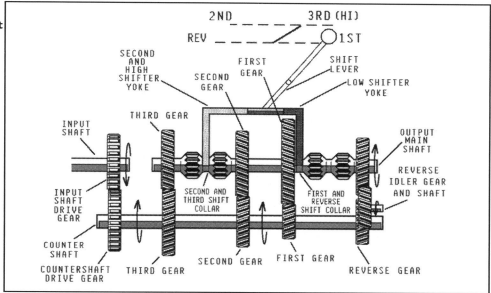

REVERSE

How do we get the wheels to turn in the opposite direction? A reverse idler shaft and gear serve this purpose. The reverse idler shaft gear does not slide on its shaft. The reverse idler gear and countershaft gear are always engaged, so they always turn together. When reverse is needed, the input shaft gear, in mesh with the countershaft gear, turns the countershaft. The countershaft gear, in mesh with the reverse idler shaft gear, turns the reverse idler gear. The reverse idler shaft gear turns the output shaft gear, and the output shaft turns. Putting in this extra gear, the **reverse idler shaft gear,** is what **reverses the motion.** Look at Figure 3-5, and trace this reversing in the constant mesh transmission. Figure 3-6, on the next page, shows how reverse works in sliding gear transmissions.

In reverse, the reverse idler shaft turns counterclockwise, the countershaft turns clockwise, and the output shaft turns counterclockwise. This makes the wheels turn backwards, causing the truck to back up.

That's the basic idea behind the transmission of power and the right kind of speed from the engine to the wheels. In the trucks that you'll drive, it's a little more complex than what we've described. We've described only three forward gear combinations and one reverse. But once you understand the three-speed, you can work out the principle behind whatever you'll be driving.

OBSERVATION   SKILLS   TEST

How closely did you observe the illustration that began this chapter? What did you notice? **Hint:** something's out of place and something's missing. Turn to the Observation Skills Test Grid at the back of the book to see how you did.

If your truck is going to be faced with many different challenges in terms of load weight, grade, road conditions, and running speeds, you may want to have a wide choice of gear ratios to achieve a high degree of operating efficiency. If your driving task is fairly simple, you might not need so many options. In Chapter 16, we give a few examples of why you might or might not need a wide choice of gears.

fig. 3-6
Reverse in a sliding gear transmission.

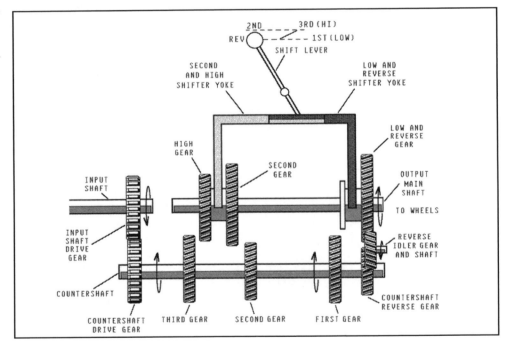

Features of Heavy Truck Transmissions

Here are some other features of heavy truck transmissions that we should explore:

- multiple countershaft
- ranges and splitters

MULTIPLE COUNTERSHAFT

Truck transmissions have more than one countershaft. Figure 3-7 shows the different number of countershafts used and their locations in the transmission.

fig. 3-7
(A) Single countershaft
(B) Twin countershaft
(C) Triple countershaft.

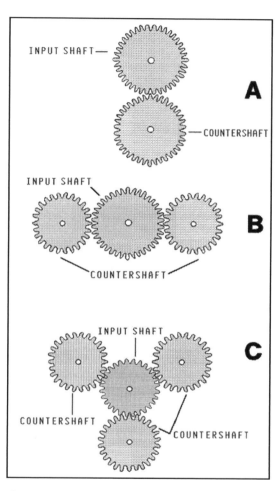

The operating principle of a multiple countershaft transmission is the same as a single countershaft unit. The main difference is the **multiple countershaft** unit **spreads out the force** that acts **on the countershaft.** Over time, it is this force, and the work it causes the countershaft to do, that causes the shaft to wear out. When you let out the clutch, the work load is taken up by more than one countershaft. Each countershaft has to do less work, bear less force. You can see that dividing this power would increase shaft and transmission life.

RANGES AND SPLITTERS

Truck transmissions differ from three-speed transmissions in that they use **compound transmissions.** That means they use more than one transmission. Compound transmissions **increase the number of gear ratios.** The more gear ratios you have in higher gears, the quicker you can get to highway speed. This **improves engine efficiency.**

The first compound transmission was the **auxiliary transmission,** which is two transmissions, one behind the other. This combination of transmissions (sometimes called a twin stick or Brownie) is rarely used anymore, but it did lead to the development of modern range control and splitter transmissions. With both these types, there is one transmission box and one gear shift with a range control and/or splitter control.

Ranges

The **range control offers** you **a high range and a low range** of the gears you have. You recall we said you might want more than three gear ratio options. If you wanted nine gear ratios, you might assume you add six more combinations of gears. Range control on a transmission lets you have more gear ratio options with fewer than an equal number of gear combinations. Keeping the need to add hardware to a minimum keeps down the total weight of the vehicle. And, it keeps the transmission from becoming mechanically complicated.

The range control transmission comes in several speeds. For example, the **seven-speed** transmission has a four-speed main transmission with a high and low range. So, why doesn't the range control make this transmission into an eight-speed? You might think that if you start out with four gears, and add a second range, your total would be eight. Instead, when you use this model and go from low to high range, you do not shift from fourth low to first high. Rather, you shift from fourth low to second high. The seven-speed transmission is not pictured here, but the same holds true for other transmissions with ranges. The **nine-speed range control** is a five-speed main transmission. The range control does not make it ten. When you shift from low range to high range, you go from fourth low to fifth high (see Figure 3-8).

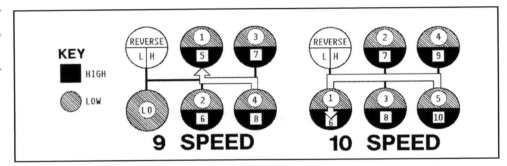

However, with the **10-speed range control,** you do shift from fifth low to first high which is really sixth gear (see Figure 3-8). How will you know which is to be the case in the truck you're about to drive? Well, you could memorize all the different transmissions and ranges available. But that's not really necessary. Somewhere inside the truck, you should find a shift pattern for the transmission which will describe what to do. It may be on the dashboard, or on the sun visor. Make checking this shift pattern part of your familiarization routine.

Splitters
The **13-speed transmission** is a five-speed main transmission with high/low range and a splitter control. The splitter has the effect of putting another gear between each of the gear combinations in high range, thus doubling the available combinations in that range. Here's how it adds up. There are five gear ratios in low range plus four gear ratios in high range. The splitter makes eight gear ratios out of the four in high range. Eight plus five equals 13. You'll find an illustration of the splitter control itself in Chapter 16, Putting the Truck in Motion.

Automatic Transmissions

Most of today's trucks used for heavy duty applications have manual transmissions installed in them, so we've focused on that type. But automatic transmissions are available. In some respects, they're easier to drive.

Chapter 3 Quiz

1. The transmission is _____ that transmits the power from the engine through the driveline to the driving axles, the wheels, and the tires.
   A. a set of levers
   B. a two-part device
   C. a range control
   D. an assembly of gears and shafts

2. In the sliding gear transmission, the _____ gears slide on their shaft.
   A. output shaft
   B. countershaft
   C. drive shaft
   D. reverse idler shaft

3. The _____ always turn together.
   A. countershaft gear and the reverse idler gear
   B. countershaft and the main shaft
   C. input shaft and the output shaft
   D. reverse idler shaft gear and the input shaft

4. A gear ratio always describes the gear doing the driving acting upon the gear being driven.
   A. True
   B. False

5. The input shaft and the output shaft are never parallel to each other.
   A. True
   B. False

6. The most speed is produced with a _____ gear ratio.
   A. 17:1
   B. 5:1
   C. 1:1
   D. 0:17

7. A transmission with a range control will always have a splitter.
   A. True
   B. False

8. A five-speed main transmission with a range control and a splitter will have _____ speeds.
   A. 5
   B. 8
   C. 13
   D. 15

9. The main advantage of multiple countershafts is they _____.
   A. help obtain highway speeds faster
   B. increase transmission life
   C. increase the number of available gear ratios
   D. increase the weight of the transmission

10. Truck transmissions are available in automatic as well as manual.
    A. True
    B. False

CHAPTER 4

AIR BRAKES

Your Brakes Are Your Best Friend

You learned in Chapter 3 that the transmission is the part of your truck that turns engine power into the torque that will make your wheels turn and move your vehicle down the road. Now that you understand what makes your truck go, you need to understand what makes it stop: the brakes.

You must be familiar with the parts of **your brake system** and how the system works **so you can use and inspect the brakes properly.** If you can do this, you can pass the CDL Air Brake knowledge and skills tests. (If you don't pass the tests, you'll have an air brake restriction on your license. With this restriction, you won't be allowed to drive a vehicle with air brakes.)

The ability to use your brakes properly could save your life and the lives of others. A three-year study conducted by the Office of Motor Carriers (OMC) showed that **brake failures are the leading mechanical cause of accidents.** The ability to detect problems with your brakes during inspections will ensure that the brakes will be there when you need them. When you're driving an 80,000 pound rig down the road at 50 mph, your brakes are your best friend. In this chapter, you'll learn how to treat them right.

The Basics of Brakes

The most basic thing you can learn about any system is its purpose. The purpose of the brake system is to slow, stop, and park the vehicle, of course. But you may not realize that it's not enough just to stop a heavy duty truck. If damage and injury occur during a braking procedure, it can hardly be called a successful stop. By the time you begin your first job as a driver, you will have learned how to **slow, stop, and park your vehicle in a predictable, controlled way.**

The **basic parts** of the brake system are **the service brake and the emergency or spring (parking) brake.** All heavy duty highway trucks and trailers manufactured after 1975 must have both.

You control the service brake system with the brake pedal. Chapter 2 introduced this tractor control. The emergency or spring brake system comes into play when you park or if the brake system air pressure drops below 45 pounds per square inch (psi). This would happen if an air line breaks. If it does happen, the spring brake becomes an emergency brake that automatically brings the truck to a stop.

The basic theory of braking includes four factors: friction, heat, weight, and speed.

fig. 4-1
Friction between the brake lining and the brake drums slows the wheels and stops the truck.

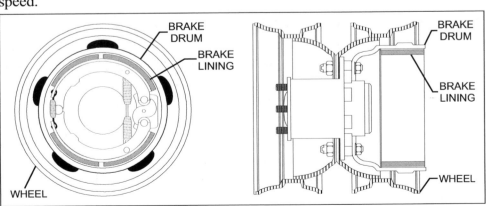

Friction between the brake linings on the brake shoes and the brake drums stops the truck. Varying the amount of air pressure applied to the brakes changes the amount of force the brake shoe applies to the brake drum, and the amount of friction that's created. Since the brake drum is bolted to the wheel, if the drum slows, so does the wheel. This is how you control the slowing and stopping of the truck.

As you probably know, **where there's friction, there's heat.** Applying more air pressure means creating more friction, bringing the truck to a stop sooner. But it also means creating more heat. Repeatedly applying and releasing the brakes, known as pumping or fanning the brakes, also means creating more friction and more heat. If brakes are applied with a great deal of force or too often, **heat** can **build up.** This **can cause poor brake performance,** or what is known as brake fade.

Weight affects how much energy it takes to stop. **The more the truck weighs, the more energy it takes to stop.** If you double the weight, the energy needed to stop is also doubled. The more energy it takes, the more air pressure is needed. More air pressure means more friction means more heat, and we're back again to causing brake fade.

To come to a safe stop, you must have more than good brakes. You must **have enough stopping distance.** You don't come to an immediate stop the minute you hit the brake pedal. Your vehicle travels some distance before stopping. This is the stopping distance. Three things make up stopping distance: perception distance, reaction distance, and braking distance.

Perception distance is **how far your vehicle travels from the time your eyes see a hazard until your brain registers** the need to stop. This takes about three-fourths of a second. At 55 mph perception distance is about 60 feet. **Reaction distance** is **how far the vehicle travels from when your brain registers the need to stop until your foot actually presses the brake pedal.** This usually takes another three-fourths of a second, or 60 feet at 55 mph. **Braking distance** is **how far the vehicle travels until the brakes bring it to a complete stop.** At 55 mph on dry pavement with good brakes, you'll travel about 170 feet. **Total stopping distance** at 55 mph under good conditions **is 290 feet.** Add to this **brake lag, the distance you travel before your brakes actually apply.** You could travel as much as 32 feet from the time you press the brake pedal until the brakes apply. There's little you can do to shorten this total stopping distance. To stop safely, you must always give yourself at least 290 feet. Often, you'll need more.

Speed affects how long it takes to stop the truck. If you double your speed from 20 to 40 mph, it takes four times the distance to stop. Technically, the effect of speed is geometric. That means as you go faster, the relative time it takes to stop does not stay the same. It multiplies. For example, if you double your speed from 30 to 60 mph, it will take you not twice as much, but six and one-half times the distance to stop. However, it's enough to know that doubling your speed quadruples your stopping distance.

The Air Brakes

Air brakes are **operated by compressed air.** So the parts of the system must be designed to maintain a supply of compressed air, plus direct and control its flow. These parts must also be designed to use the energy of compressed air to apply the brakes.

In this section, we're going to take a close look at the parts that perform these tasks. First let's list them to get an idea of the scope of the material we'll be covering. The numbers in the list below match those in Figure 4-2.

- the compressor (1)
- the air governor (2)
- the air dryer (3)
- the alcohol evaporator (3)
- the air reservoir system (4)
- the system protection valves (5)
- the operational control valves (6)
- the warning devices
- the gauges
- the brake chambers (7)
- the slack adjusters (8)
- the brake drums
- the braking mechanism
- the glad hands (9)
- the stop lights

Many of these components have subparts. For instance, there are five system protection valves. You can see this is a complicated system. Once you know the parts, where they're located, and what they do, you'll be on your way to being able to use and inspect the system properly.

THE COMPRESSOR

The compressor is a machine that draws in the air around it, **pumps** that **air into a smaller space to increase its pressure,** and then pumps it into the air reservoir system where it is stored in air tanks until it is needed. The engine provides the power for the compressor, so it is usually mounted on the side of the engine. Compressors can be gear- or belt-driven, and may have their own oil supply or be lubricated with engine oil.

THE AIR GOVERNOR

Located on the compressor, the air governor controls when the compressor will pump air into the reservoir system. It **regulates the amount of air pressure in the system.** When pressure reaches the cut-out level (around 120 or 125 psi), the governor stops the compressor from pumping air into the tanks. When the pressure in the tank falls to about 100 psi, the governor signals the compressor to cut in (begin pumping air into the tanks again).

fig. 4-2
A typical dual air brake system for a tractor-trailer.

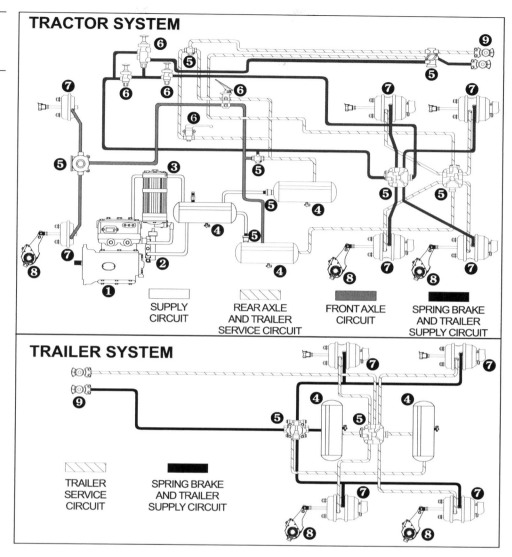

THE AIR DRYER

When the air leaves the compressor, it flows through the air dryer. This **cleans and removes moisture and vaporized oil from the compressed air.** When you compress air, you also heat it up. As it cools off, any moisture in it condenses. Also, small amounts of oil from the compressor are vaporized and travel out of the compressor with the air. When the compressed air cools, this oil also condenses. The result will be a sludge that can clog and corrode valves if it's not removed from the system. In cold weather, this sludge can freeze in the lines and the valves. The air dryer does a pretty good job of removing this condensed moisture and oil. But the dryer doesn't get it all. You'll need to finish the job. We'll tell you how later.

THE ALCOHOL EVAPORATOR

Some vehicles have an alcohol evaporator. Putting alcohol in the air brake system keeps the moisture in the compressed air from freezing. Ice in the system could cause brake failure.

THE AIR RESERVOIR SYSTEM

From the air dryer, the compressed air goes to the reservoir system, which **stores the air until it is needed.**

The first tractor reservoir tank in a dual circuit air brake system is called **the main supply tank, or the wet tank.** A **second tank** called the primary holds compressed air for **the rear axle supply.** A **third tank** called the secondary holds compressed air for **the front axle supply. Both** these tanks are **also called dry tanks.** Wet tank and dry tank simply refers to how much condensed moisture and oil might still be found in these tanks. You can see the tractor air reservoirs and the **front and rear axle trailer reservoirs** in Figure 4-2.

There are three types of valves in the air reservoir system: safety valves, check valves, and air tank drain valves.

Safety valves protect the air tanks by **releasing excess pressure** if the air governor fails. Safety valves are usually set to open at 150 psi. If the safety valve releases air, that's a sign something is wrong.

Check valves allow air to flow in one direction only. All air tanks must have them. If there is a leak in a supply tank or in the air compressor discharge line, these valves prevent loss of pressure in the rest of the system. Check valves are placed in the lines going into the tanks.

An **air tank drain valve** is located at the bottom of each supply tank. The petcock, or draining mechanism, on these valves **must be opened manually so moisture can drain from the tanks.** Many new systems have spit valves or automatic moisture ejectors which can also be opened manually. From what you already know about the damage and problems condensed moisture and oil can cause in a brake system, you can see how important it is that the tanks be drained **daily.** There is, in fact, no more important maintenance you can do. If your tractor-trailer is equipped with automatic moisture ejectors, make sure you check them for proper operation weekly.

Let's take a minute now and look at an explanation of how the service air brake system works. The spring or parking brakes work differently. You'll learn how those work later in this section.

The compressor draws in surrounding air, compresses it, and pumps it to the air dryer. The air dryer removes moisture from the compressed air, which then flows into the air reservoir system. When you operate one of the air control valves (the foot valve or the hand valve), the compressed air flows to the brake chambers. In the brake chambers, the compressed air moves the service brake linkages that press the brake shoes and linings against the brake drums. You'll get a more detailed look at how things work in the brake chamber later in this section.

THE SYSTEM PROTECTION VALVES

Four types of valves provide various kinds of protection in air brake systems.

- quick release valves
- relay valves
- tractor parking valve
- parking brake valve

Quick release valves are found near the brake chambers. When you apply the brakes, the air passes into the brake chambers. That compressed air applies the brakes and continues to apply them. Once you release the brakes, that air must be released very quickly so the brakes will release. The **quick release valve lets** this **air escape very quickly from the brake chamber.**

Air brake systems on tractors that have **dual air brake systems,** as in Figure 4-2, and on trailers, **use relay valves.** The relay valve functions somewhat like a quick release valve in that it causes the air to be delivered into the brake chamber more quickly. With a relay valve, pressure is stored not only in the supply tanks but also in the lines that go up to the relay valve. When you apply the foot valve, a signal in the form of air pressure is sent to the relay valve. The relay valve opens and sends the air pressure to the brake chambers immediately. When you release the brakes, the relay works just like a quick release valve by immediately exhausting the air from the brake chamber. You can see why tractors and trailers with long service brake lines benefit from the use of relay valves. The length of time it takes for the relay valve to detect increased air pressure after you depress the foot valve is the brake lag discussed on page 43.

fig. 4-3
This is the type of brake chamber you'll find on tractor drive wheels and trailer wheels. The front steering axles will have only the service brake chamber.

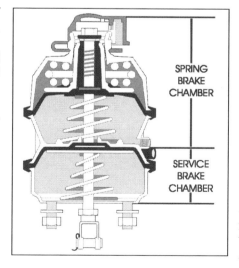

SPRING BRAKE CHAMBER

SERVICE BRAKE CHAMBER

Emergency or **spring brakes** are required on all heavy duty highway vehicles manufactured since 1975. You'll find spring brakes on all the trailer wheels and on at least one set of tractor drive wheels. They are **both parking and emergency brakes.** Figure 4-3 shows you how the spring brake rides on the back of the service brake air chamber.

The service brake part of the brake in Figure 4-3 works in the way we've already described. This is how the spring brake works. The **pressure that applies this brake** is **provided by a spring.** The spring is **held back (the released position) by air pressure.** When you apply the parking brakes, you **release that pressure and the spring presses forward** to apply the brakes.

The spring brakes are applied by pulling out the parking brake valve. All air brake systems have this valve. It's used to park the tractor and the trailer when they are coupled. It's a yellow push-pull diamond shaped knob that you'll find on your dashboard. It's pictured in Figure 4-4.

fig. 4-4
Dash mounted push-pull air control valve knobs. The trailer air supply knob is red, the parking brake knob is yellow.

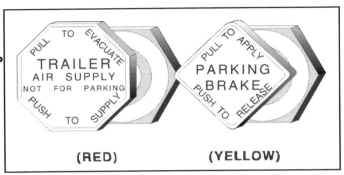

When you apply the parking brakes by pulling out the yellow knob, you intentionally release air pressure from the spring brake chambers. However, in an emergency, **if the brake system air pressure drops to a range betwen 20 and 45 pounds per square inch (psi),** the spring brakes will automatically apply, bringing the truck to a stop. The parking brakes become emergency brakes. At the same time, the red trailer air supply control knob and the yellow parking knob on your dashboard will pop out automatically.

To release the parking brakes and recharge the system, you must push the parking brake and the trailer air supply knob back in. When the system recharges, the spring in the spring brake chamber is pushed back and held back by air pressure.

Never push the brake pedal down when the spring brakes are on. This is called "compounding." The combined force of the springs and the air pressure could damage your brakes. However some trucks are equipped with a compounding valve that would prevent the added pressure from damaging the chambers. Your safety supervisor or operator's manual can tell you if your vehicle is equipped this way.

Rarely, you'll find a tractor with a **tractor parking only valve** for use when you're coupling and uncoupling. We discussed this control in Chapter 2, also. It's a push-pull blue round knob.

OBSERVATION SKILLS TEST

Recall the illustration that began this chapter. Turn to the Observation Skills Test Grid at the back of the book to see if you noticed all the important features of the picture.

THE OPERATIONAL CONTROL VALVES

These controls are the brake pedal, the trailer hand valve control, and the tractor protection valve that works with the trailer air supply control.

The **brake pedal** is also called a treadle or foot valve. It **operates a valve that supplies air pressure** to both the tractor's and the trailer's service braking system.

When you press on the treadle, air pressure is sent through the air lines to the relay valves. Then the air is near the brake chambers being held back by the relay valves. When the relay valve senses the surge of air pressure, it opens and air speeds into the service brake chambers. When you release the treadle, the air exhausts through the quick release valves and the brakes are released. This applying and releasing lets some compressed air escape out of the system and reduces the air pressure in the tanks. Then pressure must be built up again. This is why fanning the brakes leads to brake failure. You exhaust the compressed air faster than the compressor can replace it.

Your tractor may have a **trailer hand valve.** It **operates the trailer brakes only,** letting you control the amount of air directed to the trailer brakes. This **must never be used as a parking brake.** The brakes will hold only if there is air pressure in the trailer air tank. When that leaks away, the brakes will release. You can use the trailer hand valve to set the trailer service brakes when coupling or uncoupling, or to test the trailer brakes.

The **tractor protection valve (TPV)** works with the trailer air supply control. That's the push-pull, red knob on your dashboard. You see one in Chapter 2. The TPV's job is to protect the tractor air supply in case of air pressure loss in the trailer's air lines. The TPV itself is located at the point under the tractor's frame where the flexible air lines that go to the trailer are connected by the glad hands. The valve **separates the tractor air supply from the trailer air supply.**

If anything goes wrong with the trailer system that causes it to lose air pressure below around 20 to 45 psi, a spring in the trailer air supply valve on the dashboard pops the red knob out. This action sends a signal to the tractor protection valve. It then closes off the air supply to the trailer. This has two effects. One, it **protects the tractor air supply from loss,** ensuring that the tractor's service brakes will work. Two, because the trailer is losing air pressure and no more is coming from the tractor, the **trailer emergency brakes activate.** So, the trailer spring brakes apply and you have control over the tractor service brakes. This lets you bring your rig to a controlled, safe stop. All this happens automatically, but only after you have been warned by the low air pressure warning devices, which you'll learn about next.

The tractor protection valve can also be operated manually by pulling out the **trailer air supply control.** This shuts off the air supply to the trailer and puts on the trailer emergency brakes. To resupply the trailer brakes with air, simply push the red knob in.

THE WARNING DEVICES

Two devices warn you of **low air pressure**: the **warning light** and the **warning buzzer.** Your truck will have at least one of them. They are located in the cab.

Some older vehicles have a low air pressure warning device called a **wig wag.** This is a signal flag that drops down from the top of the cab into the driver's view when the air pressure gets too low. You can't reset it until you restore the air pressure to a safe level.

If the pressure in any one of your service air tanks drops below 60 psi while the ignition is on, these devices will go off. **If a low air pressure warning device goes off, pull your vehicle off the road at the first safe place you find to stop.** Do not resume driving until the problem has been corrected.

THE GAUGES

All vehicles with air brakes have a **pressure gauge** connected to the air tank, so you can see how much pressure there is in the tank. A dual air brake system

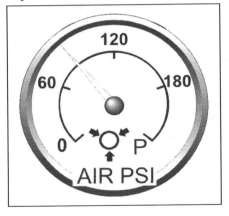

fig. 4-5
The primary air pressure gauge.

has a gauge for each tank, the primary (marked P) and the secondary (marked S), or one gauge with a separate needle for each tank.

Your vehicle may be equipped with an **application pressure gauge.** This shows how much air pressure you are applying to the brakes when you depress the brake pedal. If you see you need increasingly more pressure to get the same braking effect, you should suspect brake fade.

THE BRAKE CHAMBERS

The brake chambers, or pods, hold some of the parts that make up the service brakes. They are listed below.

- air inlet
- a diaphragm
- a push rod
- a return spring
- a clevis assembly

Pressurized air enters the brake chamber at the air inlet. The air then pushes against the **diaphragm.** The diaphragm **pushes** the **push rod** which is **connected to the slack adjuster** which is **connected to the braking mechanism.** You can see the push rod in both Part A and Part B of Figure 4-6. The **return spring returns the diaphragm to its proper position** once the quick release valve has released the pressurized air from the chamber. The **clevis assembly** provides a mechanism for **attaching the slack adjuster to the push rod.**

fig. 4-6
Part A shows the parts of a service brake air chamber. Part B shows the parts of the braking mechanism (foundation brakes).

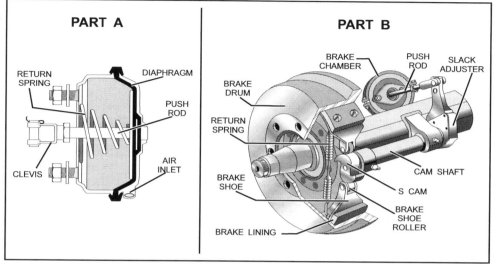

Besides the brake chamber, a slack adjuster, a brake drum, brake shoes and linings, a brake camshaft, and S cam make up a service brake. You know in general how service brakes work. As we cover each of these parts, you'll learn more specifically how they work. As you learn about each part, find it on Figure 4-6. Do this each time you read about a new part. Study the figure to see how the parts fit together and work.

THE SLACK ADJUSTERS

Slack adjusters **adjust the brakes** to **make up for brake lining wear.** A slack adjuster is a lever arm attached to the push rod of the brake chamber at the clevis assembly. You can see the clevis assembly on Part A of Figure 4-6. You can see the slack adjuster on Part B. Its job is to adjust the travel of the push rod. The camshaft is attached to the slack adjuster. The camshaft rotates with the slack adjuster. This rotation turns the S cam which forces the lining against the brake drum.

Slack adjusters can be adjusted manually or automatically. Hand adjusted slack adjusters have an **adjusting nut.** To adjust this type you must have special training and certification. Part 396.25 of the Federal Motor Carriers Safety Regulations (FMCSR) states the qualifications you need to inspect, maintain, service, and repair brake systems of commercial motor vehicles. Part 396.25 also is specific about the push rod travel for the variety of makes and sizes of brake chambers used on tractors and trailers. It is important that you read and understand the sections that pertain to brakes in the FMCSR. When you pass the air brake knowledge and skills test for a CDL you are qualified to inspect the air brake system.

Automatic slack adjusters make an adjustment automatically whenever the brakes are applied. They sense the distance the push rod travels each time and keep the brakes in constant adjustment. The FMCSR requires that commercial motor vehicles manufactured on or after October 20, 1994, be equipped with automatic slack adjusters. This is because of the difficulty of keeping manual slack adjusters in proper adjustment at all wheels at all times. Often, only one or two brakes are in proper adjustment. Then they do all the work and the brakes that are out of adjustment fail to contribute to the braking effort. Repairs made to automatic slack adjusters must be done by certified personnel according to FMCSR Part 396.25. The company you drive for will also have policies that direct you if you detect problems with push rod travel on the equipment you drive.

fig. 4-7
A typical brake drum showing the friction area.

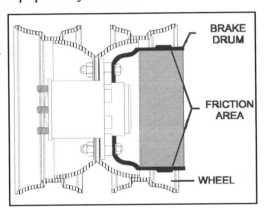

THE BRAKE DRUMS
Brake drums are made of iron or steel. They are bolted to the wheels, so the wheel and the drum rotate together. The **inside surface** of a brake drum **should be smooth and uniform.** If there are scores or ridges cut into the surface more than half the width of the friction area, the brake linings may not make complete contact with the drum. That could result in poor brake performance. See Figure 4-7.

THE BRAKING MECHANISM
The braking mechanism, which consists of the brake shoes, the brake linings, the brake camshaft, and the S cam, is found **inside the drum.** You can see this in the cutaway view in Figure 4-6 Part B. It is the action of the brake shoes pushing the brake lining against the brake drum surface that produces friction and stops the vehicle.

THE BRAKE SHOES AND LININGS. Each brake drum contains two brake shoes with attached linings that are made of metallic mineral fiber. Linings must be secure on the shoes and free of oil or grease. They should be no thinner than one-quarter of an inch at the thinnest point.

THE BRAKE CAMSHAFT. The brake camshaft is attached to the slack adjuster. The **slack adjuster converts** the **pushing motion of the push rod into the twisting motion** of the brake camshaft. The brake camshaft **turns the S cam.**

THE S CAM. The S cam is part of the brake camshaft. As the brake camshaft twists, it turns the S cam. This action **pushes the brake shoes and linings against the brake drum.**

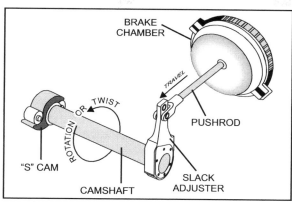

fig. 4-8
Applying the service brakes extends the push rod travel. That moves the slack adjuster which rotates the cam shaft and the S cam, which spreads the brake shoe apart.

Now you know enough to take a close look at how the service brakes work. You press on the treadle. This sends a signal to the relay valve. The relay valve opens and air enters the brake chamber through the air inlet. The pressurized air pushes the diaphragm. The diaphragm pushes the push rod. The push rod pushes the slack adjuster. The slack adjuster twists. This twisting action turns the brake camshaft, turning the S cam, as shown in Figure 4-8. The turning S cam pushes the brake shoes and linings against the brake drum. This creates friction which slows and stops the turning of the brake drum. Because the brake drum is attached to the wheel, the wheel also stops turning. When you release the treadle, the signal to the relay valve stops. The relay valve closes the air inlet and quickly exhausts the air from inside the brake chamber.

WEDGE BRAKES AND DISC BRAKES. Instead of S cam brakes, your vehicle may have **wedge or disc brake**s. In a wedge brake, the push rod pushes a wedge between the end of two brake shoes. The wedge pushes the shoes apart and against the inside of the brake drum. A disc brake has a power screw instead of an S cam. Air pressure acting on the diaphragm pushes the slack adjuster. The slack adjuster turns the power screw. The power screw clamps the disc between the brake lining pads of a caliper.

THE GLAD HANDS
Glad hands are the **coupling devices** on the ends of the air lines on the back of your tractor and on the front of your trailer. These lines **connect the service and emergency brakes of your trailer to the tractor air supply system.** They must be connected properly. Often they are color-coded. In that case, the service brake air line is colored blue and the emergency brake air line is colored red. The coupling device is a snap-lock type, similar to a radiator cap. When you're bobtailing, you can connect the hoses to the couplers on the back of the cab provided for that purpose. These couplers are often called **dummy couplers.** They **protect the lines and keep water and dirt out.** If your tractor doesn't have dummy couplers, just connect the lines together and secure them to the back of the tractor.

STOP LIGHTS
Although they don't help you stop your vehicle, your stop lights are part of the brake system. Air pressure works a switch that turns on the stop lights when you step on the brake. This tells drivers behind you that you are stopping or slowing.

Anti-lock Braking System

Advancements in electronics have been put to use to improve the braking system you just read about. **Before anti-lock braking systems (ABS), a hard brake application would often result in wheel lockup.** In Chapter 19 we discuss wheel lockup and skids. **Anti-lock braking systems do not shorten stopping distance** but they **do prevent wheel lockup** and reduce the chance of a skid or jackknife.

fig. 4-9
Basic parts of an anti-lock braking system.

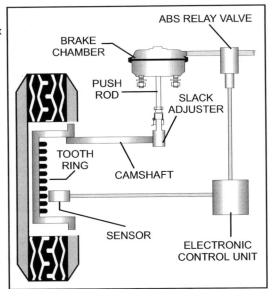

A microcomputer called **the electronic control unit (ECU)** is the brain of the ABS system as shown in Figure 4-9. The ECU constantly **receives signals from** sensors and a toothed ring located at the drum of **each wheel.** The sensors and toothed ring constantly measure wheel speed. During a brake application if a wheel tries to lock up, the sensor sends a signal to the ECU. The **ECU transmits electrical pulses to an ABS relay or modulating valve at each wheel which automatically apply, hold, or release** brake chamber pressure up to as many as five times per second. This prevents wheel lockup. You'll find ABS on all tractors manufactured after March 1, 1997, and all new trailers manufactured after March 1, 1998.

Another feature that can be installed with the ABS system is **an automatic traction control system (ATC).** The ATC system uses the sensors and toothed rings at the wheels, and a separate ECU for this system modulates the engine's throttle. This **helps keep wheels from slipping or spinning out during acceleration.** Wheel spin-out is discussed further in Chapter 19.

Brake by Wire

Another improvement in the air brake system is **the electronic braking system (EBS),** also known as brake by wire. The EBS system **uses a sensor at the brake pedal to measure braking demand.** The brake pedal signal is transmitted to yet another electronic control unit which calculates the air pressure needed to fill that demand. The ECU then electronically signals relay valves at each axle to provide the air pressure needed to meet the demand calculated by the ECU. The electronic signal sent by "wire" is much faster than the air signal you read about in the discussion of the basic air brake system on pages 43 and 47. The brake by wire system greatly **reduces the**

time it takes for brakes at the wheel to respond to the driver's pressing the brake pedal. In other words, it reduces brake lag. More than that, it ensures that braking force is evenly distributed among all the wheels by monitoring wheel sensors already installed in the system for the ABS.

If there is a failure in the EBS system, the brakes revert to normal dual air brake system operation.

Emergency Brake Situations

You know now what happens when the spring brakes are automatically activated because of an emergency situation. You also know what happens when the tractor protection valve activates. In this section, we're going to look at the emergency situations that call for the activation of these brakes.

If the trailer breaks away from the tractor, the air hoses for both the service and the emergency brakes will break away from the trailer. This will activate an immediate application of the tractor protection valve to protect the air pressure in the tractor. You need that air pressure to bring your tractor to a safe stop. A **trailer breakaway** will also activate the trailer emergency brakes and this will bring the trailer to a stop. Trailer breakaways are very, very rare. What is more likely is that one of the air lines will rupture.

If **a service brake air line ruptures,** nothing will happen until the brakes are applied. Then air will escape from the damaged service line instead of going to the trailer brakes. Should this happen only the tractor's brakes will work to slow the vehicle. You will notice the absence of the trailer's brakes. Repeated pumping or application of the service brake will reduce the air pressure. When the pressure falls below about 45 psi, the emergency brakes apply automatically and bring the vehicle to a stop.

If **an emergency brake air line ruptures,** there will be an immediate and rapid loss of pressure in the emergency brake lines. The tractor protection valve will activate, as will the trailer emergency brakes, just as if there had been a trailer breakaway.

If **the discharge line from the compressor to the main supply tank ruptures,** there will be a loss of air from this tank. The one-way check valve between the main tank and the dry tanks will prevent the loss of air from those tanks. When the main air tank air pressure drops below 60 psi, a low pressure switch will activate a warning device. There should be enough air pressure left in the tank to bring the vehicle to a stop. There will be enough for a limited number of brake applications.

Testing Your Brake Systems

What **causes** emergency brake situations? **Rarely, a road hazard** will rupture an air line. For instance, you might run over a two-by-four that could then flip up and rupture a line. The more likely and **most frequent** cause of emergency brake situations is **poor maintenance.**

What follows are **four tests** that will help you **make sure your air brake systems are functioning properly** before you need to rely on them. **Check your owner's manual for the readings and responses that you should expect.**

Testing the Compressor
This procedure **tests pressure build-up time, the low pressure warning indicator, and the air governor.**

- Open the petcocks and drain the wet air tank first. Then drain the dry air tanks until the gauges read zero and close the petcocks.
- Start the engine and run it at operating rpm. The compressor should start to fill the tanks.
- Watch the low air pressure warning device. If the warning stops before pressure reaches 60 psi, it needs to be adjusted.
- In a vehicle with a dual air system, pressure should build from 85 to 100 psi within 45 seconds. If the build-up takes longer, there's a problem somewhere. In older vehicles with single air systems, the pressure should go from 50 psi to 90 psi within three minutes with the engine at an idle speed of 600-900 rpm.
- Keep filling the tanks until the governor stops the compressor. If the governor continues filling the tanks above 120-130 psi, the governor needs to be adjusted.
- With the parking brake released (to avoid compounding), push and release the brake pedal until pressure in the system falls to just below 100 psi. If the governor is adjusted properly pressure should begin to rise again.

Report the results of failed tests to the Maintenance Shop. See that all indicated adjustments are made before you take your rig on the road.

Testing Air Loss Rate
With these simple steps, you can **test the brake system's ability to hold air pressure.**

- When the pressure is fully built up, typically 125 psi, turn off the engine, chock the wheels, release the brakes, and let everything stand for one minute.
- Notice the reading on the pressure gauge and start timing.
- After one minute, note the pressure again.

The pressure should not have dropped more than two psi per minute for the tractor only. If you are coupled to one or more trailers, the pressure should not have dropped more than three psi per minute. If the pressure drop is greater, something is wrong. Find out what is wrong and see that it's fixed before you drive your rig.

- Next, press hard on the brake pedal and wait for one minute.
- Note the reading on the pressure gauge and keep pressing on the brake pedal. After one minute, note the pressure again.

If you're testing your tractor only, the pressure drop should not be more than three psi per minute. If you're testing a tractor-trailer combination, the drop should not be more than four psi per minute. For a double-trailer combination, it should not be more than six psi per minute.

Testing the Emergency System
These two steps **test your low air pressure warning device and your spring brake emergency application.**

- With air pressure at about 90 pounds and the engine off, push and release the foot brake until the low air pressure warning comes on.

If the warning device fails to come on below 60 psi, get it adjusted before you drive your rig. The warning should come on before the spring brakes are automatically applied.

- Continue pushing and releasing the foot brake until the spring brakes apply automatically.

Spring brakes should apply between 20 and 40 psi. If they apply above 45 psi, something is wrong.

Testing the Parking and Service Brakes
These tests will help determine if the parking and service brakes work properly.

- With the parking brake on, put the vehicle in a low gear and gently try to move the vehicle forward. If the parking brake works properly, the vehicle should not move.
- With normal air pressure in the system, release the parking brake and move the vehicle forward slowly. Check to see that the vehicle stops evenly when the brake pedal is firmly pushed and that nothing "feels" unusual.

Chapter 4 Quiz

1.   Brake failures _____.
     A.   are the leading mechanical cause of accidents
     B.   are most often caused by road hazards
     C.   often lead to trailer breakaway
     D.   are most often caused by brake fade

2.   The purpose of the service brake system and the emergency brake system is to _____.
     A.   slow, stop, and park your vehicle
     B.   prevent breakaway trailers
     C.   slow, stop, and park the vehicle in a predictable, controlled way
     D.   prevent the loss of air pressure from the tractor's braking system

3.   The four factors of the basic theory of braking are heat, weight, speed, and _____.
     A.   air pressure
     B.   how many trailers you're pulling
     C.   moisture content in the wet tank
     D.   friction

For questions 4 through 8, please fill in the blanks in the illustration below with the correct labels.

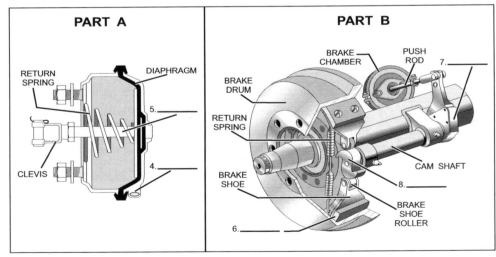

9.   "The slack adjuster twists. This twisting action turns the brake camshaft, turning the S cam." The quoted text is part of the explanation of how the wedge brakes work.
     A.   True
     B.   False

10. If _____, nothing will happen until you apply the brakes.
    A. the trailer breaks away
    B. a service brake air line ruptures
    C. the discharge line from the compressor to the main supply tank ruptures
    D. a spring brake air line ruptures

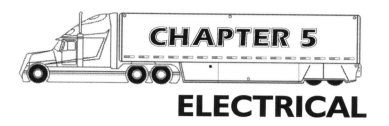

CHAPTER 5

ELECTRICAL

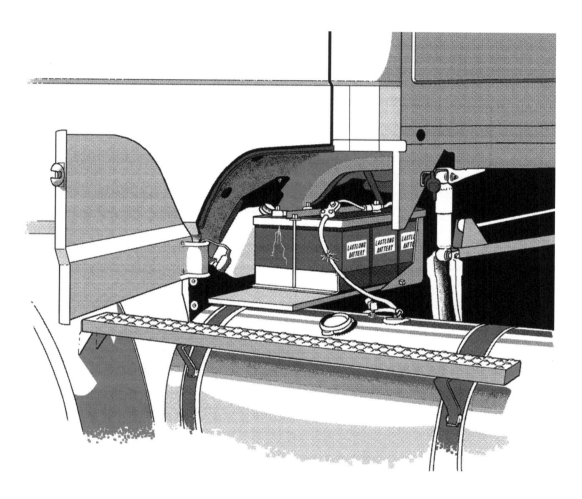

The Power Behind the Power

Of course, the power that runs your truck comes from the engine, but the fact is that **the power behind that engine power is electrical power.** You can't even start your truck without a starting circuit. You can't keep it going for long without a charging circuit. You can't run your lights without a lighting circuit and your dashboard instruments won't work without an instrument circuit.

As you can see, electrical systems in diesel trucks serve many necessary functions. They can also be quite complicated. Unless you understand the electrical system, it just looks like a maze of wires. But understand it you must, if only to bail yourself out of an electrical problem some dark night on a deserted highway.

The first step in understanding the system is to understand some of the basics of electricity.

The Basics of Electrical Current

An electron is a tiny particle of matter that carries a negative charge of electricity. **Electrical current is produced by electron flow.** All matter contains electrons, but some matter conducts electricity better than other matter.

To be a good conductor of electricity, the matter must have a large number of electrons that can be set in motion easily. Copper wire is a good conductor of electricity. Rubber is not a good conductor. That is why rubber is used as an insulator around copper wire.

Insulated **wires bring the current to the parts that need electricity** to operate. **Terminals are** the **connecting devices.** They are found on the ends of the wires and on the electrical components used to connect the wires to the parts. There is also a main terminal from which the wires originate and which contains all the system circuit breakers and fuses.

Pressure gets the electrons flowing. **Voltage is** another name for **electrical pressure.** Alternators or generators produce voltage. The term **amperage** or amps refers to the specified **amount of electric current** that is produced and carried by the wires.

The electrons flow through electrical circuits. A **circuit is a continuous path** basically made up of wire (the conductor), a source of power that drives the current around the circuit (the batteries and alternator or generator) and the devices that use the electricity (your radio and lights, for instance). This type of circuit is called a complete or closed circuit. **For current to flow, there must be a closed circuit.** For a circuit to be closed, all the components in that circuit must be grounded. That means there must be a wire or a conductor to bring the electrons back to where they started.

There are two other kinds of circuits: the open circuit and the short circuit. Electricity will not flow to its destination in either of these types of circuits and that usually means trouble.

An **open circuit** occurs when the normal **flow of electrical current is stopped.** A number of conditions can cause this. However, corroded connections and broken wires account for most open circuits. Open circuits account for most electrical problems.

A **short circuit** occurs when the electrical **current bypasses part of the normal circuit.** This means that instead of flowing to a light bulb, for instance, the current stops short of its destination and flows back to the battery. Shorts happen when the insulation has come off a section of a wire and it touches something outside the normal circuit, like another wire or part of the frame. Then the current takes the shortest route back to the source, using the other wire or frame to complete the circuit. It never does make it to the light bulb.

fig. 5-1
A short circuit will keep current from getting to the device it's meant to operate.

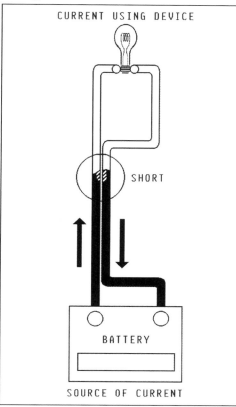

Any of these conditions can cause a short circuit.

- Two wires rub together until the insulation wears away and the bare wires touch each other.
- The wires in an electrical coil (like the starter winding) lose their insulation and touch each other.
- A wire rubs against the frame or other metal part of the truck until the bare wire touches another piece of metal.

During regular inspections, keep your eyes open for frayed or broken wires.

Circuit breakers and fuses protect the circuit from short circuits and from current overloads. A current overload happens when a circuit gets more current than it can handle. A short circuit is usually the cause of an overload. This is what happens. Turning on the lights, the starter motor, or radio "uses" (actually, slows down) the flow of the electricity. But if there is a short circuit, the bulb is not lit. The motor or the radio won't work. There is nothing to "use" the flow of current. This means there is more current in the wire than the wire can handle by itself and it will overheat and damage itself. Fuses or circuit breakers are placed in each circuit to prevent this.

Here's how they work. Fuses are rated by their amperage carrying capacity. In other words, they can handle only so much current. By design, this is even less than the wire can handle. If there is an overload, the **fuse will blow and open or break the circuit before the wire can be damaged.** When the circuit is open, current can no longer flow. Once a **fuse** is blown, it **must be replaced.**

Circuit breakers are also rated by their amperage carrying capacity. A circuit breaker used on a circuit will have the same amperage carrying capacity as the circuit. If there is more current load than the circuit breaker can carry, the circuit breaker opens and breaks the circuit. Once **a circuit breaker** has opened, it usually **resets automatically.** This is an advantage circuit breakers have over fuses.

A Truck's Basic Electrical System

Wires, circuit breakers, fuses, components, and terminals make up the circuits in your truck. There is one main terminal block that contains all the circuit breakers and fuses. From this terminal block, wires run out in bunches to connectors. At the connectors the wires split and go to other connectors or to parts that need electricity to operate.

All the wires in your truck's electrical system are color-coded. Color coding makes it easier to trace a wire from one connector to another and to components. You'll learn more about color coding and tracing wires later in this chapter. Right now, we're going to look at the basic component of the truck's electrical system: the battery system.

THE BATTERIES
Most trucks have a basic 12-volt electrical system. Many of the system's parts are the same as the ones in the humble family car. One of the major components is the battery system. **Batteries convert stored chemical energy into electrical energy** and then supply power to the rest of the electrical system.

Major battery parts are a case, a number of individual cells, cell connectors, and two terminal posts. See Figure 5-2 on the next page.

The **two posts on the top part of the battery** are called main battery terminals or battery posts. The **positive (+) post is the larger** one. The other is the negative (-) post. The battery **cables** are **connected to** these **posts.**

The vent caps are also on the top part of the battery. Gases build up when the battery charges. The **vent caps let** these **gases escape.** You will remove the vent caps to check the battery's liquid level.

Batteries are dry-charged, wet-charged, and maintenance free. The dry-charged battery has no electrolyte solution in it when it leaves the factory. The dealer adds the electrolyte solution to the battery upon selling it. The wet-charged battery has the electrolyte solution already in it when it leaves the factory. With these types of batteries, you must check the level of the solution as part of your preventive maintenance. The maintenance free battery does not usually require this periodic maintenance.

fig. 5-2
The components of a typical battery.

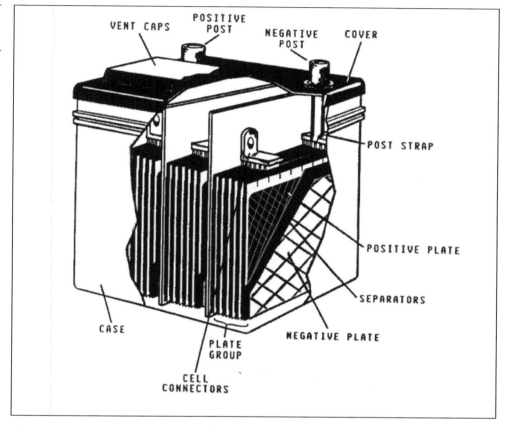

Good maintenance practices will extend a battery's life. Make sure the cable connectors are not corroded. If they are, clean them or replace them. To **prevent corrosion, keep the exterior of the battery clean. Coat the battery terminals with** a high temperature **grease,** petroleum jelly, or a terminal protector.

Check and **replace any cables that are frayed, worn, or cracked.** Check to **make sure the battery connections are tight.** Unless you have a maintenance-free battery, **check the electrolyte level regularly.** Check the hold-down bars to make **sure the battery is snug.** This keeps it from being damaged by vibration.

WORKING SAFELY WITH BATTERIES

The electrolyte solution is acid and very dangerous. Electricity is always dangerous. So here are some important safety practices you should use around batteries to avoid serious injury.

- Never put your face directly over the battery when you are working on or around it.
- Disconnect the battery ground strap before you begin any electrical or engine work.
- Connect the ground strap last when you install a new battery.
- Disconnect the battery cable before fast charging the battery.
- Never use a fast charger as a booster to start the truck.
- Never hook up the battery backwards.
- Do not lay metal tools or other objects on the battery.
- Keep sparks and fires away from batteries. Gas from the electrolyte can catch fire.
- Use only distilled water to refill the battery.
- Avoid spilling the acid electrolyte solution. It will burn your skin.

The battery is the power source for a truck's electrical system. It supplies power to start the engine. Then the alternator or generator supplies power to charge the battery and to run the truck's systems. Older trucks may have generators. Newer trucks have alternators.

We'll talk about these two components later. Right now, let's take a look at the starter. The battery's main job is to supply power to the starting circuit.

OBSERVATION SKILLS TEST

Good observation skills will help you keep your electrical system working at top notch level. Did you notice any problems in the illustration that began this chapter? Go to the back of the book and check your answers on the Observation Skills Test Grid.

The Starting Circuit

The starting circuit supplies electrical power to the starter motor, or starter. The **starter's job is to crank the engine.** That's why the starting circuit is also called the cranking circuit.

PARTS OF THE STARTING CIRCUIT
The parts of the starting circuit are listed below.

- the ignition switch
- the starting switch
- the starting circuit wiring
- the battery
- the starter motor

The **ignition switch opens and closes the circuit between the battery and starting switch,** which lets electrical current flow to the starter motor (the starter). When you turn the key all the way to the right, the ignition switch is in its "start" position. That action completes a circuit between the battery and the starter. After the truck's engine has started, the ignition switch goes back to the "run" position. This breaks the circuit between the battery and the starter.

The **starting switch opens and closes the starter circuit.** It's installed between the battery and the starter. The solenoid starting switch is the one used in most starting circuits. The purpose of the **solenoid switch** is to **control the starting motor.**

It takes only a small amount of current to close the solenoid switch. That means light, low amperage wires can be used to lead to this switch. The batteries are usually mounted close to the solenoid. That way the heavy, high amperage cables to the solenoid can be very short. The shorter heavy duty wires are better, especially on cold days when the starter needs to draw a lot of current to get the engine started. With shorter wire, there is less resistance and more current flow. That means short, heavy duty wires from the batteries to the solenoid will result in faster, more reliable starts.

There are two commonly used types of starting circuits: the 12-volt and the 24-volt. The 12-volt circuit connects all the batteries in parallel. The batteries are connected positive to positive and negative to negative. Figure 5-3 shows the components of a 12-volt starting circuit. In this circuit, the **voltage is kept at a constant 12 volts.**

fig. 5-3
A 12-volt starting system includes the batteries, the ignition switch, the starter solenoid, the starter motor, and the engine flywheel.

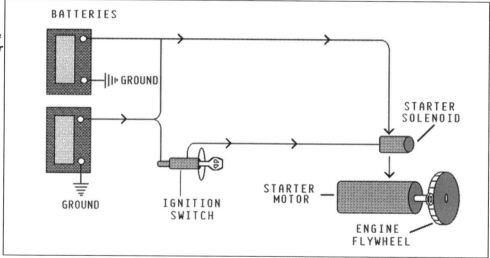

The 12-volt starter circuit works like this. You turn the key to the start position on the ignition switch. Current flows directly from the battery to the starter. The starter then engages and cranks the engine flywheel.

Some heavy duty diesel engines need more starting power. So they use a 24-volt starting circuit **with a 24-volt starter.** These starters supply faster engine cranking speeds. The **normal voltage is 12,** but the voltage does not stay at a constant 12 volts. It's **increased to 24 volts for the purpose of cranking the engine.**

You may wonder how a 24-volt starter could be used with a truck's basic 12-volt electrical system. The series-parallel switch makes this possible. Figure 5-4 shows a typical 24-volt starting circuit. In View A, the batteries are connected in series for starting. They are hooked up positive to negative. In this way, the starter motor is supplied with 24 volts. In View B, the engine has started and the series-parallel switch has changed the circuit to a 12-volt parallel system.

fig. 5-4
(A) Batteries connected in series for starting and (B) batteries connected in parallel for normal use.

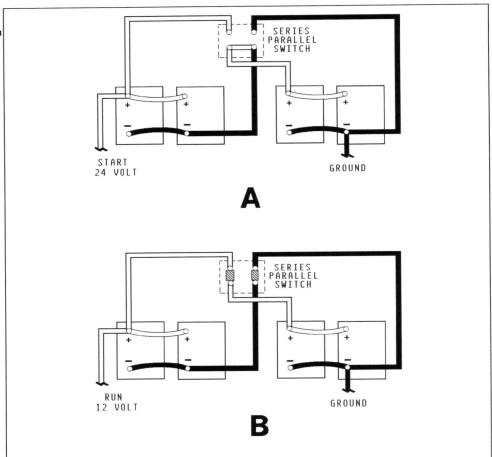

The Charging Circuit

Once the engine has started, an **alternator supplies the power that keeps the battery charged and runs the truck's systems.** The charging circuit is very important. It replaces the current that starting the engine uses up. Older trucks had generators while newer trucks have alternators. Whichever your truck uses, the circuit it's in is called the charging circuit (which makes sense since it charges the batteries).

While the engine is running, a belt from the engine crankshaft drives the alternator. The alternator then produces electricity to run all the other electrical circuits and to keep the battery charged. When the engine is not running, the battery provides the energy for circuits that need electricity. The lights, radio, and other instruments get their electrical power from the battery when the engine is not running.

THE ALTERNATOR

The components of the alternator charging circuit are listed below.

- the battery
- the regulator
- the alternator
- the ammeter or voltmeter
- the ignition switch

The **alternator** does the same job the generator does, but it's **lighter, cheaper** to build, and it **produces more current at low speeds.** In fact, the alternator can produce almost maximum current even at very slow engine speeds. This is important to drivers who work in heavy city traffic. Figure 5-5 shows an alternator charging circuit.

fig. 5-5
Alternator charging circuit.

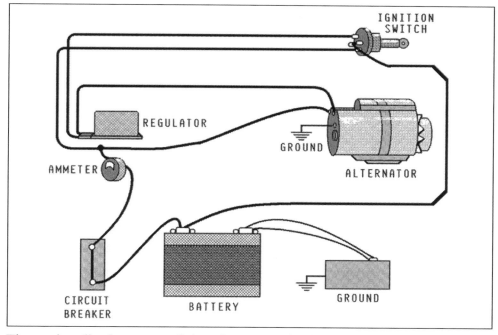

The major disadvantage of the **alternator** is that it **produces alternating current.** "Alternating" means the voltage is continually changing back and forth from positive to negative. Direct current is the only type that can charge the battery.

This problem is overcome by using **silicon diodes** to **change the alternating current into direct current.** These diodes act as one-way valves for electricity. They permit electricity to flow in only one direction and will stop it if it tries to go the other direction. So when the electricity comes to the diode, it is going back and forth. When it leaves the diode, it's going in only one direction.

The alternator has a voltage regulator that controls the amount of current it puts out. This alternator regulator has two electromagnets. One stops excessive voltage output. The other stops excessive current output.

The Lighting and Instrument Circuits

Another circuit in the electrical system is the lighting circuit. The **lighting circuit is composed of circuit breakers, fuses, and the wiring that connects to the various lights** on the truck. These lights include:

- the headlights
- the backing lights
- the turn signals
- the interior lights

- the parking lights
- the brake lights
- the emergency flashing lights
- the auxiliary lights

The **instrument circuit consists of the battery, the alternator, gauges and switches** on the dashboard, **and the connecting wiring.** The gauges and switches vary from truck to truck.

Tracing the Wires

First of all remember never to work with an electrical circuit unless you know what you're doing. You can make things worse. Having said that, we can assure you there are some things you can do and should do. You should know the basics of how your truck's electrical system works. You should be able to do simple, minor troubleshooting. To do this, you need to know about wiring and wiring diagrams.

Electrical systems use various sizes of wire. Wire is sized according to its diameter, or thickness, not including the insulation. Wire size is shown in terms of gauge, which is a series of numbers ranging from 0000 to 36. The larger the gauge number, the smaller the wire. For example, a No. 1 gauge wire is larger than a No. 36 gauge wire.

Larger wire has more current carrying capacity than smaller wire. Take the wire that goes from the battery to the starter. It is a heavy cable. Because of its size, we determine that it carries a heavy load.

Each **wire is color-coded.** This makes it easier to identify wires when you troubleshoot an electrical system. The **wiring diagram** for each truck and trailer **shows the color code** and the sizes of the wires. Although each manufacturer uses its own color coding system, most use red for power wires and white for ground wires.

fig. 5-6
So you can understand the symbols used, the wiring diagram will include a symbol chart similar to this one.

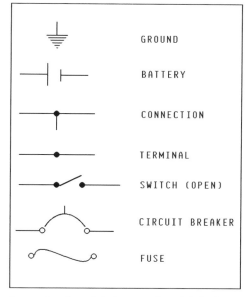

GROUND

BATTERY

CONNECTION

TERMINAL

SWITCH (OPEN)

CIRCUIT BREAKER

FUSE

Wiring diagrams **trace the flow of electrical current.** All wiring diagrams have the same basic information. They all use the same symbols to designate electrical parts. See Figure 5-6. When an electrical device fails, you can use the wiring diagram to figure out which wires might be involved.

You will use a wiring diagram to do simple troubleshooting. You might need to do this in some on-the-road situations, for instance, if your clearance lights suddenly go out. If that happens, here's what you should do in the order in which you should do it.

- Most circuit breakers reset automatically, and you can hear them click on and off. Check the circuit breakers and fuses. If the breaker is off, reset it. If the fuse has blown, the glass window will be darkened, or you'll be able to see the broken metal ribbon inside. Replace broken fuses.
- Check the bulbs. If the bulbs are bad, they will have darkened. Or you'll be able to see the broken filament or hear it rattling around inside. Replace bad bulbs.
- If the breaker trips again or the fuse blows again, check for loose connections or broken wires.
- Using your wiring diagram, follow the clearance light wires from the main terminal toward the lights.
- If you find a loose connection, tighten it.
- If you find a broken wire, twist the ends together and wrap with electrical tape. Turn off the switch controlling that series of wires before you reattach the wires.

You can use the same basic procedures to solve many other simple electrical problems.

When you fix a broken wire on the road, it is only a temporary fix. Get it taken care of properly as soon as you arrive at your destination.

The Current Path

Taking what you've learned about the electrical system, let's trace the path of current through a truck's electrical system. The path begins at the battery. When the ignition switch is turned to the start position, the current flows from the battery to the starter. The starter cranks the engine. After the engine has started running, current flows from the alternator back to the battery to replace the current used to start the engine and to the other parts that need electrical power.

Chapter 5 Quiz

1. _____ refers to the specified amount of electric current that is produced and carried by the wires.
   A. Voltage
   B. Electronics
   C. Amperage
   D. Resistance

2. _____ circuits account for most electrical problems.
   A. Open
   B. Closed
   C. Complete
   D. Short

3. Circuit breakers and fuses protect the circuit from _____.
   A. overloaded circuits
   B. closed circuits
   C. open circuits
   D. complete circuits

4. Most trucks have a basic 24-volt system.
   A. True
   B. False

5. The starter's job is to_____.
   A. supply electrical power to the ignition switch
   B. crank the engine
   C. operate the starter switch
   D. operate the alternator

6.   The 12-volt circuit connects all the batteries in parallel.
      A. True
      B. False

7.   Once the engine has started, the _____ supplies the power
      that keeps the battery charged and runs the truck's systems.
      A. series-parallel switch
      B. engine
      C. 24-volt system
      D. alternator

8.   The _____ uses a voltage regulator that has two separate
      electromagnets.
      A. alternator
      B. 12-volt battery system
      C. generator
      D. starter

9.   Wire is sized according to its length.
      A. True
      B. False

10.   The bulb in the picture to the right is not lit up. Why?
      A. The current (wire) is not connected to the
          source (battery).
      B. The switch has not been turned on.
      C. The fuse has blown.
      D. The current is overloaded.

LIGHT BULB

FUSE

CURRENT

BATTERY

CHAPTER 6

ENGINES

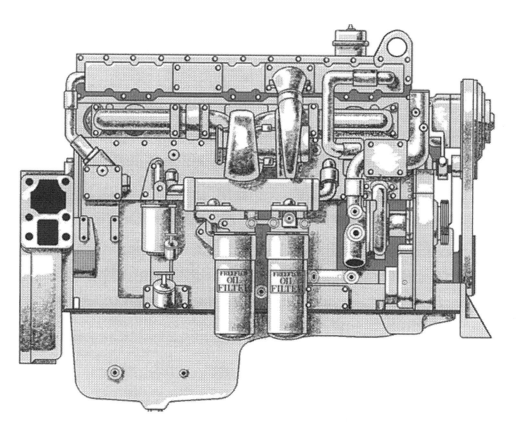

The Heart of the Truck

In this chapter, you'll learn about the heart of the truck—the engine. You'll learn about the parts, the principles of operation, and the auxiliary systems.

In terms of operation and parts, the **diesel engine** in the truck you will drive is **in some ways like the gasoline engine** in a family car. Both are internal combustion engines. Both use air and fuel in the combustion process. How the air and fuel mixture is ignited is one of the main differences between diesel and gas engines. Diesel engines depend on heat created by air compression for ignition. You'll see how later in this chapter.

Diesel and gasoline engines have many similar parts. They both have pistons and valves, for instance. However, **there are differences.** Diesel engine parts are placed under greater stresses than the ones in gasoline engines. These stresses are higher temperatures and compression pressures. To withstand these stresses, diesel engine parts must be stronger.

Diesel engines also usually have higher maximum torque and higher compression ratios than gasoline engines. They **are more efficient.** They turn slower and last longer. They need servicing less often. That is why the diesel engine is relied on to provide economical power whenever a job calls for an engine high in horsepower and reliability.

The Engine Parts

Before you learn about the principles of engine operation, you need to know more about its parts. Then we can talk about how these parts work together to produce power.

The main parts of the diesel engine are :

- the cylinder block
- the pistons
- the connecting rods
- the crankshaft
- the valve train

and all the smaller components that comprise these parts. We're going to look closely at each of these parts.

THE CYLINDER BLOCK

As you can see in Figure 6-1, the **cylinder block** consists of many smaller components. It **contains the cylinder bores** (or piston holes), the **water jackets,** the **oil passages,** and the top half of the **crankcase.** The lower half of the crankcase is an oil pan that is bolted to the bottom of the block. One feature of engine design is the number of cylinder bores used. Diesel engines may have four, six, or eight cylinders.

Notice the cylinder bores in Figure 6-1 on the next page. These bores go down into the engine block. The pistons, which you'll learn about next, fit into these bores. In some types of blocks, the pistons run directly in the bores. In other types, **liners** are used. Then the liner can be replaced if the cylinder bore becomes scored or worn. Scoring occurs when the piston scrapes the cylinder during movement. It's much less costly to replace a liner than to repair the bores or replace the block.

Dry liners can be used with this type of engine design just described. The cylinder bores are made larger and then the liners are press-fitted into the

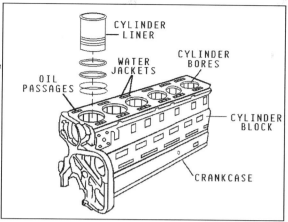

bores and held there by friction. However, diesel engines are usually designed to use wet liners, and wet liners are preferred because they are easier to replace and cool faster.

To understand the difference between the wet liner and the dry liner, you first need to know about the **water jackets.** The water jackets are the spaces in the block that surround the cylinder bores with coolant to carry away some of the engine heat. Dry liners are very thin and simply fit inside enlarged cylinder bores. Wet liners are much thicker and actually form the outer parts of the water jackets.

Cylinder blocks that use wet liners are basically hollow inside. The block has a shoulder at the top of each cylinder bore. The edges of the liners slip down over these shoulders, hold the liners in place, and form a seal at the top of the liner. The bottom of the liner has an O-ring that makes a seal between the liner and the block. The coolant then flows between and around the liners.

THE PISTONS

The arrangement of the pistons is a major factor in engine design. There are two types of engines based on piston arrangement: the V-type engine and the in-line engine. With the **V-type half the cylinders and pistons are on one side** and the **other half are on the other side.** The engine we use in our illustrations in this chapter is an **in-line** engine. In this engine, the **cylinders** are **all in a straight line.**

Diesel engine pistons are designed to be very **durable.** They **must withstand high compression pressures** of around 900 psi **and temperatures** of around 1,000 degrees Fahrenheit. Depending on the weather, pistons can be exposed to very cold temperatures, too.

Pistons are usually made of malleable iron or aluminum. Aluminum pistons are lighter than iron ones, which reduces the load on the engine bearings and crankshaft. Aluminum pistons conduct heat better than iron ones; in fact, they cool off two times faster. Vibration has less of an effect on aluminum pistons.

Aluminum pistons do wear out faster than iron ones, and they cannot withstand heat as well as iron pistons. However, their ability to resist scoring and the other advantages we've listed far outweigh these disadvantages. Aluminum pistons and piston parts are built heavier to compensate for faster wear, and special rings are used to reduce the negative effects of heat. A nickel iron alloy is used for piston ring inserts because it expands at the same rate as aluminum, but is stronger and wears better under heat. Also, heat treated steel bands are used in the crown of the piston. These bands add strength and increase piston life.

Let's take a close look at the two major parts of the piston: the crown (top) and the rings.

Pistons have formed crowns or flat crowns. **Diesel engines** most often **use formed crown pistons** because they create better air turbulence for combustion. Air turbulence is the swirling of the air in the combustion chamber. This helps mix the fuel sprayed into the cylinder with the air. Good air turbulence means **more complete combustion.** It also makes for more even cylinder pressure and cleaner emissions.

The two types of piston rings are compression rings and oil rings. **Compression rings** are usually made of cast iron and are often chrome plated to cut down on scoring and decrease wear. Installed near the top of the piston, they **make the piston fit the cylinder wall** so that compression is created and maintained. In other words, they keep the compressed air in the cylinder from escaping and thus **maintain compression pressure in the combustion chamber.** Many pistons only use one or two compression rings; however, some designs have several rings.

Oil rings are usually very thin, made of cast iron, and can come in one or two pieces. Most use an expander which forces the oil ring against the cylinder wall. **Oil rings spread oil along the sides of the cylinder** so there is always a film of oil between the piston and the cylinder as the piston moves up and down. This both serves **to cool the engine** and to **prevent scoring** of the cylinder walls. On some piston designs, these rings are installed right below the compression rings. On other designs, more oil rings are installed below the piston pin. You'll learn about the piston pin when we talk about connecting rods. Figure 6-2 on the next page shows you both the piston and the connecting rod in relation to the cylinder block.

As we said, oil is used **to keep pistons cool.** Engines use one of three methods to do this: circulation, splash, or spray. Most diesel engines use the spray method. Oil is sprayed through a jet in the block. This **oil is sprayed on the underside of the piston head.** To provide better cooling, the bottom of the piston heads are finned, which also adds strength to the piston.

Because the piston slides up and down the cylinder 2,000 times or more a minute at full speed, all pistons and cylinders will eventually wear out, even with good lubrication. However, you can prolong the life of your pistons and cylinders or cylinder liners. Here's how.

- Change the oil frequently. This removes impurities that could build up in the oil, score the cylinder walls, or cause the oil to lose some of its lubrication ability.
- Keep the air filter clean. If dirt from the air gets into the cylinder, it may score the cylinder walls.
- Don't overheat the engine. When metal heats up, it expands. That means the cylinder bore size will decrease while the piston size increases, decreasing the clearance between the piston and the cylinder. The piston may scrape hard against the cylinder, damaging both parts.

THE CONNECTING RODS

The piston is connected to the crankshaft by the connecting rod and the connecting rod is connected to the piston by the piston pin. You can see this in Figure 6-2.

fig. 6-2
The piston and connecting rod parts fit together and then go inside the cylinder liner.

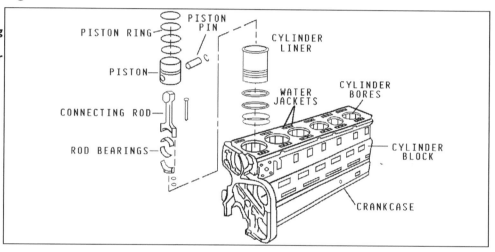

Connecting rods are made of forged steel. They **transfer the piston's up and down motion to the crankshaft's rotary, or turning, motion.** The two types of connecting rods are the I-beam and the tubular. The type used depends on engine design. The main parts of the connecting rod are the piston pin and the bearings.

The **piston pin connects** the top end of the **connecting rod with the piston.** Piston pins are made of chromium steel and come in various diameters (sizes). The size of the pin used depends on the load it has to carry.

Wherever you have moving parts in an engine, you'll find bearings. The **connecting rod bearings** are the thin wall type. They reduce friction, **protect the crankshaft and the connecting rod from excessive wear,** and ensure that the crankshaft and connecting rod turn freely. These bearings have holes in the center through which oil flows to lubricate and keep parts cool.

THE CRANKSHAFT

The crankshaft is forged or cast heat-treated steel. The crankshaft is the **main shaft** of the diesel engine. Its rotating motion is used to drive the **truck's wheels.**

Crankshafts have drilled **oil passages** and so does the cylinder block. The crankshaft passages line up with holes in the connecting rods and main bearings. Crankshaft holes are used to **supply lubrication** to the crankshaft bearings and the pistons. The **crankshaft bearings** are the main bearings of the engine. They **reduce friction** and ensure that the crankshaft turns freely.

The **flywheel** is connected to one end of the crankshaft. It does three jobs. When you start the engine, **the starter engages it** to start the crankshaft turning. It **forms one face of the clutch.** As the engine runs, it **dampens** the **vibration** of combustion.

fig. 6-3
Now we've added the crankshaft and its parts and the camshaft and its parts.

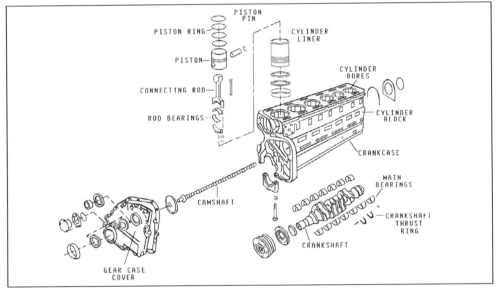

THE VALVE TRAIN

The **valve train** is that series of parts which **operates the intake and exhaust valves.** First let's look at the parts; then we'll describe how they work.

Each cylinder has at least one intake and one exhaust valve. **Intake valves let air into the cylinders.** The **exhaust valves let burned gases out** of the cylinders after combustion. Two-stroke cycle engines have no intake valves. They use intake ports instead.

Because valves are exposed to high temperatures and pressures, they are made of special alloys, usually in two pieces. The valve head and face make up one piece; the fillet and stem make up the other piece.

The valve head rests on the valve seat. Many engines use replaceable valve seat inserts. These inserts are used so seat life can be lengthened. It is important that valve seats be installed properly. If they are not, a valve leak could occur.

The valve guide keeps the valve in alignment with the valve seat. Valve springs pull the valves closed.

The **camshaft** is a straight steel shaft on which there are a number of bearings and cams. Each cam has a **cam lobe,** or bump, on it. Each cam rotates as the camshaft turns.

fig. 6-4
The purpose of the valve train is to open and close intake and exhaust valves.

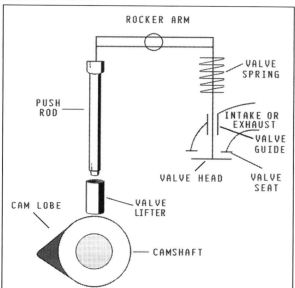

The push rod is just that—a straight rod. One end sits on top of the valve lifter or cam follower which sits on top of the camshaft. The other is connected to a **rocker arm.** The rocker arm acts like a teeter-totter to **open and close valves.** It works like this. The camshaft turns and the cam lobe contacts the push rod, pushing it up. The push rod pushes one end of the rocker arm. The other end pushes the valve down, opening it. As the camshaft continues to turn, the lobe moves on and the push rod returns to its normal position. The rocker arm rocks back and the spring under the valve pulls it back into place.

Principles of Operation

As we discussed in Chapter 5, the starter cranks the engine and gets the crankshaft turning. The turning crankshaft pushes the pistons down in the cylinders. While the pistons are moving down, air is pulled into the cylinders. Then, as the pistons start to move up again, the air intake stops. The moving pistons squeeze the air in the cylinders into a smaller and smaller space. As the air is being compressed, it also begins to heat up. By the time the pistons reach the top of the cylinders, the air will be very hot.

When the pistons get near the Top Dead Center (TDC) of the cylinders, the fuel is injected into the cylinders. The hot compressed air ignites the fuel. This is called combustion. The temperature and pressure increases as the fuel burns. The pressure forces the piston down and the connecting rod transfers this downward thrust to the crankshaft. The turning force is transferred to the engine flywheel. In Chapter 3 we show how this force then goes through the clutch and the transmission where it's turned into torque that is transmitted to the wheels through the drive train.

THE TWO-CYCLE AND FOUR-CYCLE ENGINES

The method used to obtain power is a feature of diesel engine design. Some engines use the two-stroke cycle for power. Other engines use the four-stroke cycle. However, both use the compression/combustion method just described to make power. The term stroke refers to the up and down movement of the piston.

In a **two-stroke cycle engine** the piston makes two strokes in its combustion process: the **compression stroke** and the **power stroke.** With the power stroke, the piston moves down the cylinder. Combustion has already taken place. As it gets close to the bottom, the exhaust valves open and the intake ports are uncovered. Two-stroke cycle engines use intake ports instead of intake valves. After the ports are uncovered, air is forced into the cylinder by the supercharger. The exhaust gases are pushed out by the forced air. While this is going on, the piston is still moving down the cylinder.

When the piston gets to the Bottom Dead Center (BDC) of the cylinder, it begins its upward, or compression stroke. While the piston continues upward, the exhaust valve closes. Forced air continues to enter the cylinder until the piston's upward movement covers the intake ports. The remaining air is compressed. Just before the piston reaches Top Dead Center (TDC), the fuel is injected and combustion occurs, starting the process over again.

As the name implies, the **four-stroke cycle engine** uses four piston strokes: **intake, compression, power, and exhaust.** On the intake stroke, air enters the cylinder as the piston moves down. As the compression stroke starts, the intake valve closes and then the piston moves up the cylinder, compressing the air. The piston continues up until just before it reaches TDC. Fuel is then injected into the cylinder and combustion takes place. The high pressure caused by combustion forces the piston down the cylinder for the power stroke. As the piston reaches BDC, the exhaust valve opens. The piston moves up the cylinder again, pushing out the burned gases through the exhaust valve for the exhaust stroke.

Each of these engines has advantages and disadvantages. The **two-stroke engine is able to produce more power from a smaller engine.** This is because it only requires two strokes to get one power stroke. The four-stroke engine needs four strokes for each power stroke. So in effect each piston provides twice as much power in a two-stroke engine. This means the engine can be built smaller and still provide the same power output as a larger four-stroke engine. The disadvantage of a two-stroke is that it **is less efficient** than the four-stroke engine. This is mainly because the two-stroke **requires a supercharger that** is driven by the engine. This **uses some power that could go to the wheels. Four-stroke engines usually use a turbocharger that** is driven by the exhaust gases and so **does not rob any power from the engine.**

Auxiliary Systems

Just learning about the engine is not enough. A driver must know about the other vehicle systems that work with the engine. These are referred to as auxiliary systems. The electrical system covered in Chapter 5 is one of the auxiliary systems. The rest of this chapter will discuss the other auxiliary systems.

COOLING

All engines have some type of **cooling system** that **controls the engine's temperature and prevents overheating.** Two types of cooling systems are the air cooling system and the liquid cooling system. The **liquid cooling system is** the one **most often used.**

The parts that make up the liquid cooling system are listed below:

- the radiator
- the radiator cap
- the fan and fan belt
- the water pump

- the thermostat
- the engine water jacket
- the water hoses
- the coolant

The radiator, the largest component in the cooling system, consists of an upper and lower tank, a core, a filler cap, an overflow tube, and connections for water hoses. The coolant absorbs heat as it travels through the cylinder block. **In the radiator,** the **coolant releases heat** into the surrounding air.

To fill the radiator, you pour coolant into the filler neck of the upper tank. An overflow tube on one side of the filler neck lets excess water or pressure escape. The radiator cap fits on the filler neck. The radiator cap seals the radiator and provides a way to release excess pressure. Inside the cap is a spring-loaded seal. If the pressure gets too high the pressure overcomes the spring and raises the seal. This allows water and pressure to flow out. When the pressure drops, the spring pushes the seal back in place and stops the flow. The pressure cap allows the coolant to reach a higher boiling point.

You'll find the fan and fan belt behind the radiator. The fan belt drives the fan.

There are two types of fans. One type starts turning as soon as the engine is turned on and continues to turn until the engine stops. The second type is the **clutch fan.** It's thermostatically operated. This means the fan **doesn't begin turning until the engine temperature reaches the clutch fan's preset temperature.**

The first type of fan uses the most power from the engine because it is always turning whether the engine requires cooling or not. This is why the other type is used. It saves power and increases fuel economy. The savings can be great because the engine fan on a big truck can use up to 25 horsepower.

The **water pump moves the coolant through the cooling system.** The thermostat controls engine temperature. The thermostat fits into a housing in the water jacket.

The water jacket is found in the engine head and cylinder block and consists of passages around cylinders and valves through which the coolant flows.

The **water hoses connect the cooling system components.** They are also called radiator hoses.

Most of the **coolant is 50 percent water and 50 percent antifreeze** plus chemical additives. Most manufacturers recommend distilled water and low silicate ethylene glycol or propylene glycol antifreeze.

Now let's look at how all these parts work together to cool the engine. Look at Figure 6-5 as we discuss this process.

fig. 6-5
The radiator and its parts work together to control engine temperature and prevent overheating.

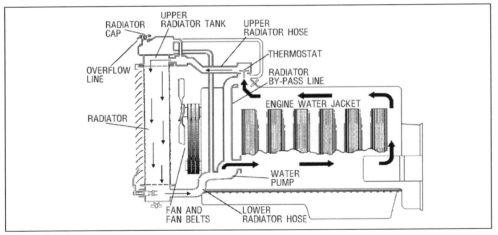

When you start a cold engine, the thermostat is closed. The coolant in the water jacket begins to circulate around the cylinders and valves. As it circulates it flows past the thermostat. **When the coolant reaches the thermostat's preset temperature,** around 180 degrees Fahrenheit, the **thermostat opens the passage to the radiator** and **directs** some of the **coolant to** flow through the **radiator to cool off the coolant.**

The hot coolant leaves the engine through the upper water hose. It goes through the hose into the top tank of the radiator and down through the radiator's core. The forward motion of the truck and the **fan pull air in through the radiator and cool the coolant.**

When the coolant reaches the bottom tank, the water pump draws the coolant through the lower water hose. The coolant passes through the water pump and is forced through the water jacket. Then the process begins again.

The whole idea of the thermostat is to direct the flow of the water. When the water is below about 180 degrees Fahrenheit, the thermostat directs the water to flow only through the block and pump, without going through the radiator. Then as the water temperature increases to about 180 degrees Fahrenheit, the thermostat opens and permits some water to flow into the radiator. The thermostat continually opens and closes slightly to direct the flow of the coolant and thereby control engine temperature.

THE FUEL SYSTEM

The **fuel system delivers the fuel to the engine.** The parts of the fuel system are as follows:

- the fuel tank
- the fuel filter or filters
- the fuel pump
- the fuel lines
- the fuel injectors
- the fuel

The **fuel tank holds the fuel** and the **filter cleans it** before it reaches the fuel pump. The fuel system on a diesel engine is a precision piece of equipment with very close tolerances and small holes. If dirt, gum, or water gets into the system, damage or at least poor performance will result. Fuel with this kind of sludge in it will plug up the system. You can see why there are sometimes two filters.

The **fuel pump delivers the fuel to the engine.** The two types of fuel pumps are the constant volume type and the metering type. **Fuel lines carry the fuel from the pump to the cylinders.** The fuel **injectors spray the fuel into the combustion chambers.**

Let's examine two grades of diesel fuel. **Grade 2 diesel fuel** is the **most widely used.** It's a little less costly and thicker than Grade 1. The only advantage to Grade 1 is that the temperature has to drop much lower for No. 1 fuel to thicken or jell than it would for No. 2. But this does not make up for the risk you can run using such a thin fuel. Its thinness means it doesn't do as good a job of lubricating as No. 2. That means more wear. Grade 1 also does not produce as much power. Performance suffers.

During the winter, refineries change the mix of No. 2 diesel so it will stay fluid at colder temperatures. Also, the fuel stations will mix Grade 1 and 2 to achieve the same end. You would use Grade 1 fuel only if you were running in below zero degree temperatures. Trucks designed to run in such cold weather will use fuel heaters and additives to keep No. 2 diesel from jelling.

Let's trace the flow of the fuel through the fuel system. The fuel leaves the fuel tank and runs through the fuel lines to the check valve. From there, it flows through the filter and into the fuel pump. The pump forces it through the fuel lines and into the fuel injectors. The injectors spray a measured amount of fuel into the cylinders.

THE LUBRICATING SYSTEM

The **lubricating system cleans, cools, and oils the engine's moving parts.** It helps the piston rings seal the combustion chamber and **reduces wear on metal parts** by keeping a thin film of oil between them.

Lubricating systems differ depending on the make and model of truck, but they all consist of the components listed below.

- the oil pan
- the oil filters
- the oil

- the oil pump
- the oil cooler

You'll use the type of oil recommended by the manufacturer of your engine. Diesel engine oils are readily available. The oil must be changed according to the manufacturer's directions, or more often.

fig. 6-6
A typical lubrication system for a heavy duty truck.

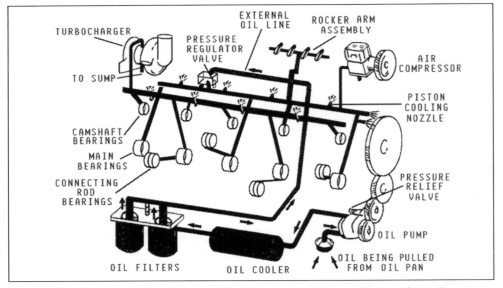

Changing the oil is one of the **most important** things you can do **to improve the performance and lengthen the service of your engine.** The oil gets dirty largely because of the by-products of combustion. But the residue of un-burned fuel on the cylinder walls also mixes with the oil. This tends to dilute the oil so it doesn't lubricate as well. Coolant can ruin oil very quickly. If you notice a light foam in the oil or an increased amount of oil on the dipstick, change it immediately and check the cooling system. You may have a slight internal leak.

The oil pan holds the oil. The **oil pump,** under pressure, **pumps the oil from the oil pan through the oil cooler.** After leaving the cooler, the oil moves **through the filters.** Oil filters strain out metallic particles and dirt from the oil. The filtered oil then goes **through the lubricating lines into the engine.**

Some parts, like crankshaft bearings and camshaft bearings, get oil under direct pressure from the oil pump. Others, like the cylinder walls and pistons, have oil sprayed or splashed over them. Most engines use both direct pressure and splashing in their lubricating system.

THE EXHAUST SYSTEM
The **exhaust system provides an outlet for engine heat, burned gases, and other waste products.**

The parts of a typical exhaust system are the exhaust manifold, the exhaust pipe, and the muffler. The **exhaust manifold receives the exhaust gases from the cylinders.** From the exhaust manifold, these **gases pass through the turbocharger, the exhaust pipe, and into the muffler.** The muffler's job is to reduce exhaust noise.

SUPERCHARGERS, TURBOCHARGERS, AND AFTERCOOLERS
Both **superchargers and turbochargers** are blowers used by both two-stroke and four-stroke cycle engines to **increase engine power by packing more air into the cylinder.** Both help to make an engine burn cleaner and cooler.

Let's look at superchargers first. A **supercharger is** a **mechanically driven** blower. An accessory shaft from the engine drives the supercharger. The supercharger both **provides pressurized air to the cylinder and forces exhaust gases out** of the cylinder. This is used primarily on two stroke engines.

The **turbocharger is** a supercharger that is **driven by the exhaust gases.** A turbocharger is more efficient because no power is drawn off the engine to run it.

Many diesel truck engines have an **aftercooler** located between the turbocharger and the intake manifold. An aftercooler is a heat exchanger. It **takes the hot air leaving the turbocharger and cools it before it goes to the engine.** This **increases power** because cooler air is denser and more oxygen can be packed into the cylinder. That means more fuel can be burned and that means more power from the engine.

OBSERVATION SKILLS TEST

Recall the illustration that began this chapter. Then turn to the Observation Skills Test Grid at the end of the book and answer the questions you find there.

Chapter 6 Quiz

1. The main part of the engine is the _____.
   A rocker arm
   B. valve
   C. cylinder
   D. cylinder block

2. Installed near the top of the piston, the oil rings make the piston fit the cylinder wall so that compression is created and maintained.
   A. True
   B. False

3. The _____ dampens the vibration of combustion and is engaged by the starter when you start the engine.
   A. crankshaft
   B. flywheel
   C. camshaft
   D. connecting rod

For Questions 4, 5, 6, and 7, fill in the blanks in the figure below to identify

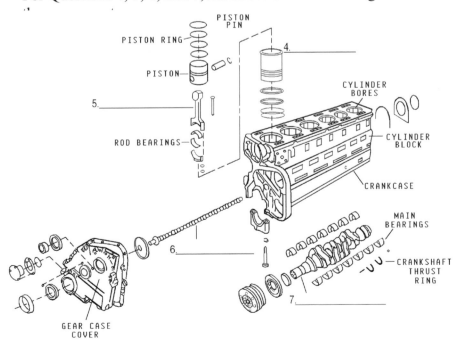

For Question 8, fill in the blank in the figure below.

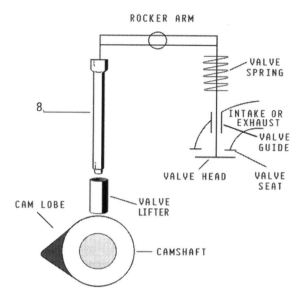

9.   The job of the _____ system is to control the engine's temperature and prevent overheating.
      A. lubricating
      B. turbocharging
      C. fuel
      D. cooling

10.   The oil gets dirty largely because of _____.
      A. the by-products of combustion
      B. dirt left in the engine from the manufacturing process
      C. coolant leaks
      D. the practice of mixing Grade 1 and Grade 2 fuels

CHAPTER 7

DRIVE TRAIN

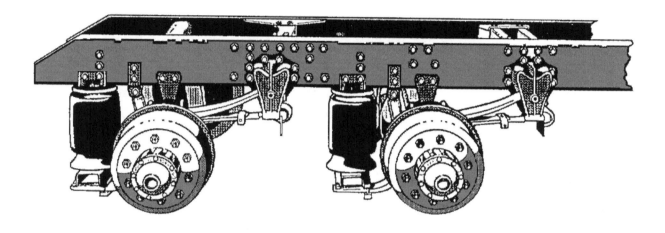

From the Engine to the Wheels

That's what the drive train is, everything from the engine to the wheels that actually makes the truck move. So, the drive train is made up of the engine,

- the clutch
- the transmission
- the drive shaft

- the differential
- the inter-axle differential
- the axles

and the wheels. The engine was covered in the last chapter and the transmission in Chapter 3. In this chapter, you'll learn about the rest of the drive train up to the wheels. You'll learn about the wheels in Chapter 9. We'll also cover the axles, the frame, and suspension systems.

The Clutch

The clutch is the component that **connects or disconnects the engine from the transmission and the driveline.** When the clutch is engaged, the power produced by the engine is transmitted through the clutch to the transmission. When the clutch is disengaged, the power flow stops at the flywheel. The clutch provides the driver with an easy way to shift gears.

The clutch is made up of the clutch housing, the flywheel, the clutch disc (or discs), the pressure plate, the release assembly, and the controls. The clutch forces plate surfaces together under pressure.

The **pressure plate** assembly is bolted to the flywheel. It provides the necessary force to **keep the clutch plate in constant contact with the flywheel** while the clutch is engaged.

The clutch disc or discs consists of a smooth disc or discs, or plate, a facing material attached to the disc surface, and a splined hub. The clutch disc is also called the driven plate assembly, the clutch plate, and the driven disc or discs. It's attached to the transmission input shaft with the splined, or grooved, shaft.

A single-plate clutch is one that has only one driven disc activated by the cover assembly. A **dual-plate clutch** has two driven discs separated by a smooth surfaced center plate. The dual-plate clutch greatly **increases the amount of engine torque the clutch is able to absorb and transfer to the transmission.** Dual-plate clutches are used with heavy duty truck engines.

fig. 7-1
The friction disc type clutch is the type most commonly used with manual transmissions.

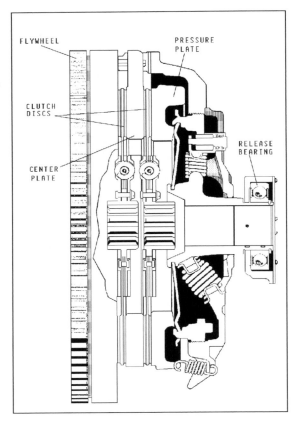

We will discuss the **friction disc clutch,** the type most commonly used **in trucks with manual transmissions.** It is shown in Figure 7-1. The major components of this clutch are the flywheel, the clutch disc or discs, the pressure plate assembly, and the clutch release bearing. The flywheel is attached to the engine's crankshaft. It is the driving member of the clutch.

The **clutch release assembly** includes the release bearing assembly and the clutch release mechanism. When the clutch pedal is pressed, the release fingers rotate and pull on the release bearing. This forces the release bearing against the clutch release levers. The release members move the pressure plate to the rear of the clutch assembly, **disengaging the clutch.** See Figure 7-2 on the next page.

Let's look at the clutch controls. The clutch control you'll use most often is the **clutch pedal** in the cab. This activates the clutch linkage between the pedal and the **release mechanism** on the clutch.

fig. 7-2
A clutch release mechanism. Depressing the clutch pedal moves the pressure plate to the rear of the clutch assembly.

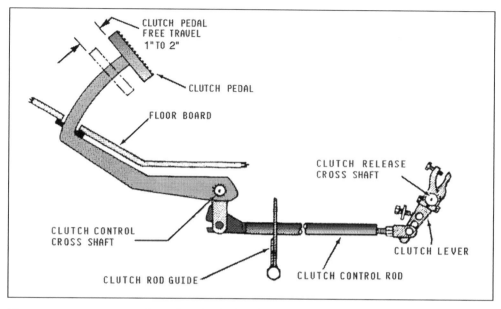

There are two types of mechanical clutches: the direct and the cable operated. **Direct clutch controls** are made up of a manually operated assembly of levers, rods, and springs that connect the pedal to the clutch release mechanism. The arrangement of the **mechanical linkage** components varies. **Conventional tractors use the direct control** because the pedal is physically close to the clutch.

Cable operated clutch controls use a cable to **replace part of the linkage. Cabovers sometimes use a cable** because it's several feet from the clutch to the pedal. Also, the cable provides a way for the linkage to flex when the pedal tilts up with the cab.

HOW THE CLUTCH WORKS

Now that we know the basic components of a clutch, let's see one in action. First of all, the driver **pushes down on the clutch pedal** to disengage the clutch so the gears can be shifted. This **activates the clutch release assembly** which **separates the pressure plate from the clutch plate.** This means that the **power from the engine is also separated from the transmission.** After the driver has made the shift, the **clutch pedal is released.** The **pressure plate** is now forced against the **clutch plate,** which is forced against the **flywheel.** That means that all three parts will **rotate as a unit.** The engine's **power is now being transmitted by the clutch to the transmission** gears. The gears cannot be shifted when there is power on the gears.

There's more on the operation of the clutch in Chapter 16.

The Driveline

The driveline consists of all the components that connect **the transmission to the differential.** The driveline **transmits the engine's torque from the transmission to the differential.** You'll learn about the differential next. Right now, look at Figure 7-3. You can see that the main components of the driveline are the drive shaft, the universal joints, and the flanges or yokes. How many drive shafts and universal joints are used on a truck depends on the wheelbase length, the types of transmission and rear axle combination, and what auxiliary equipment is used. Now let's look at each component individually.

fig. 7-3
The driveline consists of the drive shaft, universal joints, and yokes or flanges.

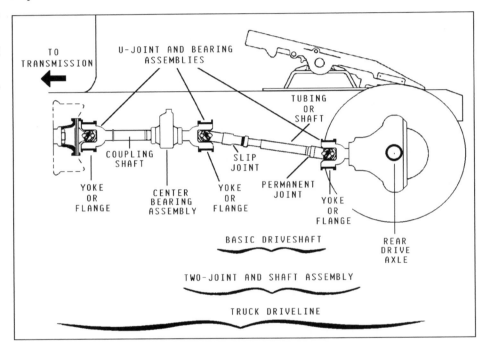

DRIVE SHAFT

Most drive shafts are made of hollow steel tubing because such tubing provides maximum torque-carrying capacity at minimum weight. The hollow shaft is the strongest and it has a great resistance to twist.

The drive shaft spins three to four times faster than the wheels or tires, which means the drive shaft must be exactly balanced. At the factory, drive shafts are dynamically balanced and permanent weights are attached to prevent vibration.

The **basic drive shaft** assembly is a **dual U-joint and shaft assembly,** which is a drive shaft with a universal joint at each end. The principal parts of this dual U-joint and shaft assembly are the slip joint, the tubular shaft, and the permanent joint, as you can see in Figure 7-3.

The U-joint is a flexible coupling used to transfer the rotary motion between one rotating shaft and another while allowing for changes in the driveline operating angle. This is necessary because the differential moves up and down when the truck goes over bumps causing the angle between the transmission and the differential to change. U-joint is short for universal joint. These connectors are also referred to as "Cordon Joints."

The slip joint provides a way for the drive shaft to change its length slightly while operating, thus making up for the movement of the rear axle and the suspension.

In other words, the **U-joint allows a change in the angle between the transmission and the rear end.** The **slip joint permits a change in length.** Both these actions are needed because the rear end moves up and down in relation to the transmission.

The **center bearing assembly supports the driveline** when two or more drive shafts are used. The **coupling shaft** is an extension shaft used to **connect the transmission output shaft to the differential on long wheelbase tractors,** because the distance is too great for a single shaft. A center bearing assembly connected to the truck's frame is usually used to support the coupling shaft.

The Differential

There are two types of differentials. One is called simply the differential. It divides the drive axle in half and allows each half to spin independently. The other is the inter-axle differential. It divides the two axles and lets each turn independently of the other.

THE DIFFERENTIAL

The axle differential is a gear mechanism that does two main jobs. It **transmits power** from the drive shaft to the axles. It splits the drive axle in half and then **lets each axle half turn at a different speed than the other.** This means that each wheel can rotate independently of the other under certain conditions. Take cornering, for example. When you corner, the outside wheel must rotate faster than the inside wheel. Figure 7-4 on the next page shows you how the differential operates when you turn a corner. Without the differential, you'll drag at least one set of tires around the corner. That will mean you'll wear out your tires very quickly.

Before we explain the differential and how it works, let's take a minute to clear up a couple of common misunderstandings. First, a differential does not divide the drive power equally between the wheels. Second, it does not send all the power to the wheels that have the most traction.

What a differential does do is send **all the power to the wheels with the least traction.** That means if you jack up one side of your drive axle, start up your tractor, and engage the clutch, your tractor will just sit and spin. The same thing can happen if just one set of wheels is on a patch of ice and you try to start the truck moving.

There are several types of differentials, but the major components of a typical differential are the drive pinion gear, the ring gear, and four spider gears. These parts are enclosed in a differential case that is mounted at the center of the drive axle housing.

The drive pinion gear is connected to the end of the drive shaft and it drives the ring gear. The four spider gears are attached to the ring gear and mesh with gears on the ends of the drive axle halves. Each spider gear is free to rotate. Each axle gear meshes with all four spider gears. So the **power is transferred from the ring gear through the spider gears and into the axle halves.**

When both wheels turn at the same speed (traveling in a straight line), drive pinions rotate with the spider gears. However, the spider gears do not revolve because both wheels are turning at the same rpm. In other words, **both axle halves revolve at the same speed.**

When your **truck makes a turn,** the **inner wheels** begin to **slow down.** As one axle half begins to spin at a slower speed than the other, the **spider gears** begin to **rotate, allowing** the **axle halves to spin at different speeds** and letting you make a turn without scrubbing your tires. In other words, the spider gears that are attached to the axle shaft of the inner wheel slow down, too, and begin to rotate in a direction that adds speed to the opposite spider gears and the outer wheel.

Another way to look at this is to say that the spider gears have acted as balancing levers. To illustrate this, let's say that the vehicle is traveling at a constant speed going into a curve. The inner wheels slow to only half of the vehicle speed. The differential increases the speed of the outer wheels to twice the vehicle speed. The differential has transmitted the decrease in speed of the inner wheels to the outer wheels as a proportionate increase in speed.

fig. 7-4
When you turn a corner, your differential will let your outer drive wheels turn faster than your inner drive wheels.

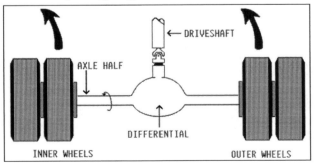

The types of gears and gear teeth used in differentials are the hypoid, amboid, and spiral beveled. The most common type of ring-and-drive pinion gearing used in differentials are the hypoid and amboid. See Figure 7-5. The hypoid is used mainly on the forward axle of the tandem drive. The amboid is often used on the rear axle of a tandem drive assembly.

fig. 7-5
Most trucks use hypoid gearing because it provides quieter operation and strong torque-carrying capacity.

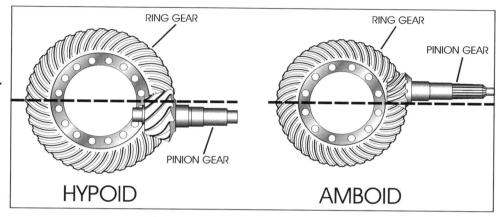

RING GEAR

RING GEAR

PINION GEAR

PINION GEAR

HYPOID

AMBOID

THE INTER-AXLE DIFFERENTIAL

The inter-axle differential is **used on tandem rear-drive axle trucks.** It's also called a power divider.

The **tandem assembly** on trucks with tandem rear-drive axles has two parts: the front rear axle and the rear rear axle. Both of the axles are called drivers.

When a tractor has two drive axles, a differential and the inter-axle differential are housed together in the differential case assembly on the front rear axle. Another differential is mounted on the rear rear axle. A short drive shaft connects the drive unit of the front rear axle to the drive unit of the rear rear axle.

In terms of function, the inter-axle differential is really just another differential. It does the same thing the axle differential does, but between two axles rather than between two axle halves. It is needed because just as the inside and outside tires rotate at different speeds sometimes, so do the front and rear axles. The inter-axle differential **compensates for slippage, mismatched tires between axles, and cornering.** It can also be used to improve traction when trying to couple to a loaded trailer and when adjusting sliders.

The main difference between the differential and the inter-axle differential is that the inter-axle differential can and should be used **when you encounter slippery road conditions.** Chapter 2 shows that there is a control in your cab that lets you **lock the inter-axle differential** and there is a warning light that reminds you when it is locked.

With normal road conditions, the inter-axle differential should remain unlocked. Along with the front rear differential and the rear rear differential, the inter-axle differential provides the capability for each set of wheels to spin independently of the others. In this way, you eliminate tire scrubbing when you take curves or make turns.

However, with slippery road conditions, you should lock the inter-axle differential. This forces the axle halves on the front rear differential and the rear rear differential to turn together. This doubles your traction on a slippery road surface because it ensures that power will go to each axle. Now for your tractor to spin out, two wheels (one on each axle) will have to spin. If the inter-axle was not locked, one wheel could spin and you would lose traction. Figure 7-6 shows you what we mean.

fig. 7-6
The large black arrows show you where the power goes on a slippery road surface when the inter-axle control is locked.

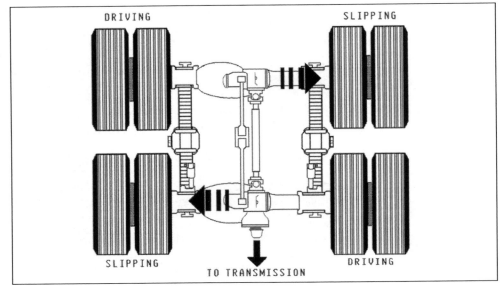

The Axles

Truck axles can be divided into two categories: **drive axles** (also called live or power axles) and **non-drive axles** (also called dead or non-power axles). The three main parts of a drive axle are the axle halves, the axle housing, and the differential. One job of the differential is to transmit the torque from the drive shaft to the drive axles.

Axles are also labeled by their position on the truck: front or rear. Front axles are either drive or non-drive steering axles. The most common is the non-drive front axle. Its construction is an I-beam crossmember mounted between pivot centers. Front axles are rated by their weight carrying capacity, normally 12,000 pounds.

Many trucks have one drive axle. Many are equipped with two rear drive axles, one behind the other. This is the tandem arrangement we discussed when you learned about inter-axle differentials.

The Frame

The frame is **the foundation of the truck.** The truck body, engine, drive train, steering system axle, wheels and tires, brake assemblies, suspension system, and other components or assemblies are all directly or indirectly mounted on the frame or suspended from it.

The major parts of the frame are the side rails and crossmembers. The **side rails carry the load.** A number of crossmembers are bolted or riveted to the side rails. These crossmembers stabilize the frame. They also support the engine, transmission, cab, and other heavy components. **For added strength, gusset plates** are welded or riveted at the points **where the crossmembers are joined to the side rails.** The gusset plates are actually angular pieces of metal.

Frames are made of steel or aluminum. Brackets and hangers are bolted or riveted to the frame to support shock absorbers, springs, fenders, and running boards.

OBSERVATION SKILLS TEST

Did you carefully study the illustration that began this chapter? Are your observation skills improving? Turn to the Observation Skills Test Grid at the back of the book and see how you're doing.

The Suspension System

The suspension system serves many purposes. It **supports the weight of the vehicle,** keeping the frame from resting directly on the axles. The suspension also **provides a smoother ride** for the driver and the cargo. **It absorbs the shocks** and jolts of traveling over the road's surface and **keeps the wheels and tires from bouncing on rough terrain.** It also helps maintain proper frame alignment. Thus, the suspension system protects the wheels and tires from undue wear.

Two common suspension systems are the leaf spring and air ride. There are a variety of leaf spring and air ride suspensions for the different positions of the axles on tractors and trailers. Each suspension, spring or air, has a load rating based upon the number of pounds it can safely support. A single axle suspension will generally be designed to support less weight than that of a tandem axle. Heavy-duty suspensions are designed to handle much more weight for off-road trucks, tractors, and trailers involved in heavy-duty applications such as construction, mining, and forestry.

THE LEAF SPRING SUSPENSION

The leaf spring suspension is made up of two or more long **metal strips,** or leaves, that are **shackled together with clamps.** Typically the leaf springs are bowed with the outer ends of the spring curved upward connecting to shackles or hangers on the frame of the vehicle. The middle of the leaf spring connects to the axle or a center beam between two axles. **As weight from the vehicle pushes downward on the hangers, the springs' outer ends are forced downward.**

The number of leaves on each assembly will vary depending upon the type of metal they are made of and the amount of weight they must bear. **The weight the springs must bear depends on the axle position on the vehicle and the type of hauling the tractor or trailer will be doing.** The fewer the leaves and the more flexible they are, the more road shocks and bumps can be absorbed. This contributes to a smooth ride for the driver and the cargo.

Taper Leaf Suspensions

Taper leaf springs are used on single and tandem axles of tractors. They **are the most often used suspension on the steering axle** of on-road tractors because they are light, inexpensive, and provide for a smooth ride. They have metal strips of equal length that are thinner at their ends than at their center. A typical steering axle taper leaf spring suspension might use two or three long, flexible leaves. See Figure 7-7.

fig. 7-7
Front and rear suspensions: (A) taper leaf (B) multi-leaf.

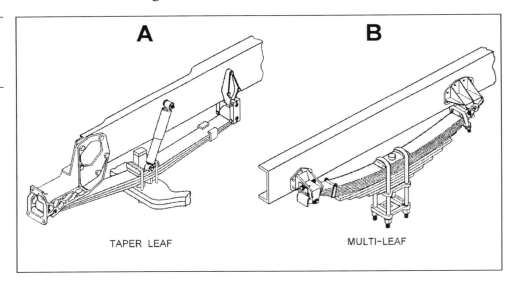

A

B

TAPER LEAF

MULTI-LEAF

Multi-leaf Suspensions

Multi-leaf springs use many leaves and are common on drive and tandem axles of tractors and trailers. They are bigger and heavier than taper leaf springs and **are often used for heavier loads.** Because of their many leaves, multi-leaf suspensions are also much stiffer than taper leaf springs which makes for a rough ride, particularly when there is an empty load.

THE AIR RIDE SUSPENSION

Air ride suspensions are designed for all types of axles and are common on tractors and trailers. The air suspension system consists of a rubber-fabric bag that holds air. The top of the bag is attached to a metal plate that is connected to the vehicle frame. The bottom of the bag rests on the suspension assembly (see Figure 7-8). **A height control valve adjusts the amount of air in the bag.** When weight is put on a tractor or trailer axle, the height valve automatically opens and compressed air flows into the air bag supporting the weight of that axle, raising the tractor-trailer to its unloaded height. When weight is removed or the cargo is unloaded, the valve exhausts air from the bag, keeping the tractor and trailer balanced and level at all times.

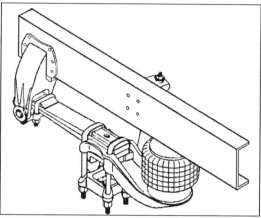

fig. 7-8
An air ride suspension gives a smoother ride than a leaf-type system.

Electronic vans (trailers) used to haul very sensitive electronic equipment were some of the first trailers equipped with air ride suspensions. Over the years most other types of trailers have been equipped with air suspension.

So why use an air suspension? **Air suspensions are comfortable** to ride in **and** they **keep the cargo safe.** The air suspension maintains the following at all times:

- the correct vehicle height
- precise wheel alignment
- excellent riding comfort

Spring Suspension with Torque Rods

Figure 7-9 shows a typical tandem axle spring suspension using torque rods. Torque rods transmit torque and braking effort to the truck's frame. When you put a heavily loaded truck into motion and when you brake, the axles tend to turn forward or backward. This is called "axle wind up." **Torque rods absorb and transmit the effect of axle wind up to the frame and correct alignment is maintained.** As the driver you must realize the importance of correct alignment. Start and stop the vehicle as gently as possible to help reduce the stress on the suspension system.

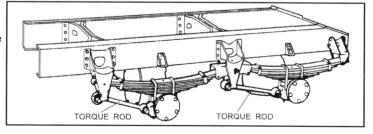

TORQUE ROD   TORQUE ROD

fig. 7-9
Torque rods absorb and transmit the effect of axle wind up to the frame and help maintain correct alignment.

Chapter 7 Quiz

1. The _____ is the mechanical component that allows the engine to be connected to, or disconnected from, the transmission.
    A. inter-axle differential
    B. differential
    C. clutch
    D. driveline

2. When you press down the clutch pedal, you _____.
    A. engage the clutch, which allows power to flow from the transmission to the differential
    B. disengage the clutch, thereby stopping power flow at the flywheel
    C. engage the clutch, thereby stopping power flow at the flywheel
    D. disengage the clutch, which allows power to flow from the transmission to the differential

3. _____ refers to all the individual components that connect the transmission to the differential.
    A. Driveline
    B. Power train
    C. Drive shaft
    D. Drive train

4. The air ride suspension system constantly adjusts itself as you load and unload to maintain correct vehicle height.
    A. True
    B. False

5. The _____ is a flexible coupling used to transfer the rotary motion between one rotating shaft and another while allowing for changes in the driveline operating angle.
    A. flange
    B. yoke
    C. short coupled joint
    D. U-joint

6. The _____ is a gear mechanism that transmits power from the drive shaft to the axles. It splits the drive axle in half and then lets each axle half turn at a different speed than the other.
   A. driveline
   B. differential
   C. drive train
   D. inter-axle differential

7. The _____ does the same thing the axle differential does, but between two axles rather than between two axle halves.
   A. U-joint
   B. transmission
   C. inter-axle differential
   D. clutch

8. The three main parts of the _____ axle are the axle halves, the axle housing, and the differential.
   A. drive
   B. front
   C. non-drive
   D. driveline

9. The _____ is the foundation of the truck.
   A. driveline
   B. frame
   C. inter-axle differential
   D. pinion shaft gear

10. The weight of the vehicle is supported by the _____.
    A. frame
    B. wheels
    C. drive shaft
    D. suspension system

CHAPTER 8

STEERING

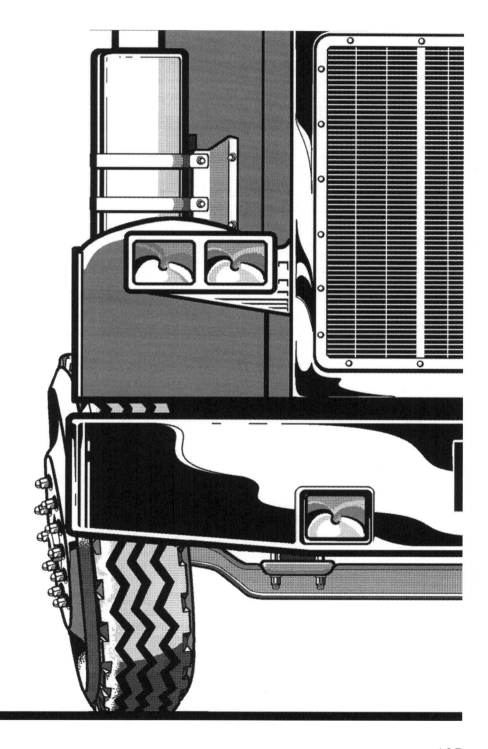

How the Wheel in Your Hands Controls the Wheels on the Road

The early chapters in this book describe how the truck goes and how it stops. They show how the engine's power, the power that gets you where you want to go, moves through the transmission and the drive train to the truck's wheels and tires. What controls that power are the steering components. In this chapter, you'll learn about the types of steering and the steering components. You'll also learn about alignment, or what keeps the steering components working properly.

The **steering system enables the tractor to change direction and get around corners.** A good steering system **provides precise rolling, without slipping,** when you turn a corner or negotiate a curve. In this chapter, we're not going to talk about how to turn corners. That's covered in the chapter on driving techniques. Instead you'll learn about what happens when you turn the steering wheel. In other words, you'll learn how the wheel in your hands controls the wheels on the road.

Steering Components

The wheel in your hands is the steering wheel. It controls the steering wheels on the road that are connected to the steering axle. Between the steering wheel and the steering axle are the components that make steering possible. Figure 8-1 on the next page shows the basic steering components and how the steering action flows through the system. Refer to it as you proceed through the following discussion.

The steering system starts with the **steering wheel,** which is **connected to** the **steering column** by a spline or shaft and held by a nut. The steering wheel transfers the driver's instructions to the steering system, allowing you to control the tractor's direction.

As you turn the steering wheel, the column turns in the same direction. This **turning motion** continues **through the U-joint to the steering gear shaft.** From there the motion continues **through another U-joint to the steering gear box.** The **steering gear box,** also called the steering sector, **changes the rotating motion** of the steering column **to the back and forth,** or reciprocating motion, of the Pitman arm. The **Pitman arm** is a lever attached to the steering gear box. The **drag link** joins the Pitman arm and the steering arm.

The steering arm is the first steering component that is part of the **steering axle.** The steering, or front axle, does two jobs. It **carries a load** just like other

fig. 8-1
These components make up all types of steering systems, whether manual or power.

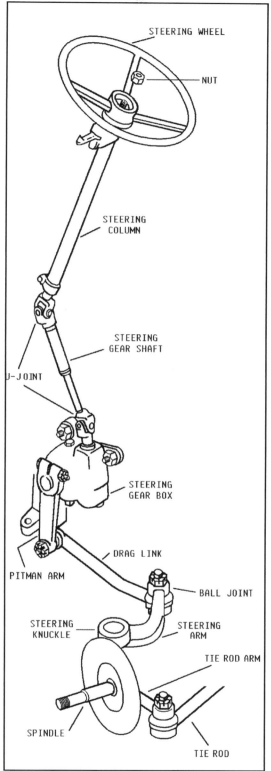

STEERING WHEEL

NUT

STEERING COLUMN

STEERING GEAR SHAFT

U-JOINT

STEERING GEAR BOX

PITMAN ARM

DRAG LINK

BALL JOINT

STEERING KNUCKLE

STEERING ARM

TIE ROD ARM

SPINDLE

TIE ROD

axles. In addition, however, it **steers the truck** and so it has different components and looks different. Steering axles use an I-beam construction. The components of the steering axle are listed below.

- the steering arm
- the steering knuckles
- the spindles
- the tie rod arm
- the tie rod

The **steering arm turns the front wheels left and right** when the Pitman arm pulls it back and forth. The steering arm is connected to the **steering knuckle,** which is a moveable connection between the axle and the wheels that **lets the wheels turn left or right.**

There is a steering knuckle at the end of each axle. The steering knuckles are very important because they contain the seals, bushings, and bearings that support the weight of the tractor. The steering knuckles transfer motion to the tie rod arm and the tie rod.

The spindles are the parts of the steering axle knuckles that are inserted through the wheels.

A tie rod **holds both wheels in the same position. As the left** wheel turns, the right wheel moves in the same direction. In addition, the **kingpin,** which is contained in the steering knuckle, **allows each wheel to have its own pivot point.** As you can see in Figure 8-2 on the next page, the spindle, or stub axle, on which the wheel rotates is attached to the kingpin.

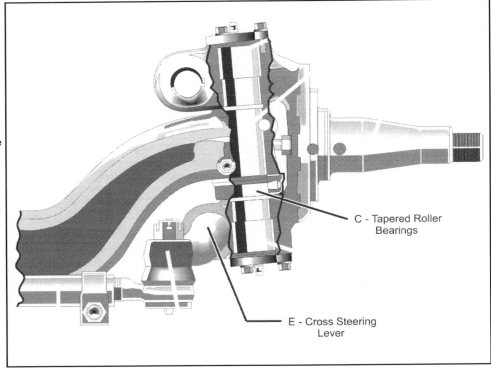

fig. 8-2
The steering knuckle includes the kingpin (A), the bushings (B), and the tapered roller bearings (C). The steering knuckle is attached to the spindle (D) and to the cross steering lever (E). A ball joint (F) connects the cross steering lever to the tie rod (G).

C - Tapered Roller Bearings

E - Cross Steering Lever

Types of Steering

The two types of steering are manual and power. In this chapter, we'll focus on manual steering because the manual system is the basis for the power system. So, if you know the manual system there are just a few things you need to know about power systems.

As you've just learned, the **manual steering system multiplies steering wheel effort** through gears and mechanical linkage. Just imagine the strength you would need if you got down on the ground, grabbed the wheels, and tried to move them with 12,000 pounds of load resting on them. The steering system "multiplies" the fairly small effort you exert at the steering wheel into this greater force needed to move the front wheels. At the same time, the **motion** at the steering wheel **is reduced** at the front wheel. In other words, you may turn the wheel completely around two or three times to make your front wheels move through only a few degrees of a circle.

Power steering systems go this one better. **Power steering systems use hydraulic pressure to assist** the mechanical linkage in making the turn. This way even less effort comes from your arms.

When hydraulic pressure is used to assist steering, the steering gear box is replaced with a hydraulic unit. A hydraulic pump is added to the engine to supply the pressure used to help turn the wheels. So, when you turn the steering wheel to the right, the hydraulic valve senses this. A valve opens and the pressure of the oil is used to help turn the wheels to the right.

Alignment

When you **align** the steering system, you **put** the **components at** the **right angles to maintain** assembly **balance.** Keeping the steering system in alignment is essential to safe and proper operation of the truck.

As a driver, you will probably never perform steering system repairs or alignments, but you must know when a system needs repair or alignment. **Improper alignment leads to excess wear** on both the steering components and on the tires. The next chapter covers tires and wheels in detail. What you need to know now is that improper alignment can very quickly ruin a tire that may cost as much or more than $350.

Four angles that affect alignment are listed below.

- toe in
- toe out
- caster
- camber

If any of these angles is out of alignment, problems will result. Another angle that affects steering is the turning angle. We'll cover that angle in this chapter, too.

TOE IN AND TOE OUT

Picture a steering axle with wheels and tires mounted. To understand toe in and toe out, think of the fronts of the tires as the toes and the backs of the tires as the heels. **Toe in** means **the distance between the toes of the tires is less than the distance between the heels** of those tires. **Toe out** means the **distance between the toes of the tires is greater than the distance between the heels** of those tires.

Too Much Toe In or Toe Out

Not only does too much toe in or toe out make the truck **hard to steer,** it also **causes the tires to wear** rapidly and unevenly. If you notice that the edges of your tires look like feather edges or like the teeth of a saw, have your alignment checked. **Feathered or saw-toothed tire edges** that point inward often indicate too much toe in. Feathered or saw-toothed edges that point outward often mean too much toe out.

Excessive toe out can be caused by a bent tie rod. If it is bent, it may need to be replaced. Usually the toe in can be adjusted. To do this, a mechanic will usually adjust the threads on the tie rod end of the steering linkage.

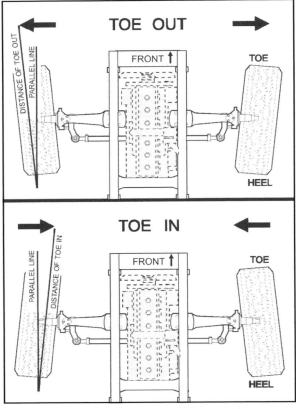

fig. 8-3
Too much toe in or too much toe out makes the truck hard to steer.

Proper Toe In and Toe Out

You do, however, want a little toe in. It will balance the camber. What's camber? We'll talk about that next.

CAMBER

Camber is the position of the top of the tire. When there is **zero camber,** the top of the tire sits directly over the bottom of the tire. If you were to draw a dotted line from the top of the tire to the bottom, it would be a vertical line. When there is **positive camber,** the tire leans slightly away from the body of the truck. So would your imaginary line. When there is **negative camber** the tire leans toward the body of the truck. Negative camber is also called reverse camber.

If you draw a line from the top to the bottom of a tire that has positive or negative camber, it will create an angle when compared to the straight line of zero camber. This angle is called the positive or the negative **degree of camber.** Figure 8-4 on the next page shows you what we mean.

Improper Camber
Improper camber causes road shocks, uneven tire wear, and steering wander. If you feel it in the steering wheel every time your front tire hits a bump, you are experiencing road shock and you probably have a problem with degree of camber.

Too much or too little camber causes uneven tire wear. **Too much camber wears away tread on the outside edge** of the tire. If there is **too little camber,** the **inside edge will be smooth.**

Steering wander occurs when a tractor pulls to one side on a flat road. It's most often caused by uneven camber. That is, **one tire has more or less camber than the other.** The truck usually pulls to the side with the highest positive camber.

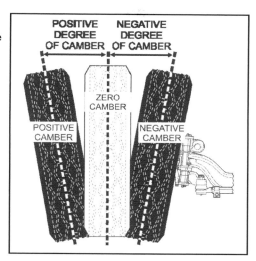

fig. 8-4
Degree of camber can be positive or negative.

Uneven camber is caused by using:

- different sized tires
- improperly inflated tires
- unevenly worn tires

Improper cambering can also be caused by:

- worn steering knuckles
- knuckle pins that are not in correct position
- worn kingpin bushings
- bent axles

Camber cannot be adjusted like toe in. To correct an improper camber, the mechanic must find the cause and repair or replace the part.

Proper Camber

Remember that **all the alignment angles work as a unit.** When your steering components are properly aligned, your tractor maneuvers easily. Just as proper alignment calls for a little toe in, it also calls for a little positive camber. Positive camber causes the wheels to pull away from the tractor, and a little toe in will balance that.

OBSERVATION SKILLS TEST

Recall the illustration that began this chapter. What did you notice? Go to the Observation Skills Test Grid at the back of the book now and see how your observation skills are improving.

CASTER

Caster is the position of the tire in relation to the steering knuckle kingpin. Look at Figure 8-5 on the next page. When there is **zero caster,** you can draw a line through the center of the steering knuckle kingpin and that line will hit the ground at the center bottom of the tire. When there is **positive caster,** a line through the center of the kingpin hits the ground in front of the center bottom of the tire. When there is **negative caster,** a line drawn through the center of the kingpin will hit the ground in back of the center bottom of the tire.

Positive Caster

You have probably noticed in your car that the steering wheel will try to come back to a straight ahead position after you turn a corner. This is caused by **positive caster.** Caster makes the front wheels more stable, especially as the wheels **return to a straight ahead position after turning a corner.** It also curbs the wheels' natural tendency to move from side to side at the back as the vehicle moves.

Too much positive caster :

- makes steering hard
- increases road shock
- can cause wandering at high speed
- can cause a chattering sound in your power steering.

Improper Caster

Zero or too much negative caster causes the **front** to **shimmy** and wander at low speeds. At high speeds, it causes front end instability. With zero or negative caster, the wheels will be slow to straighten after negotiating a turn or curve.

Proper Caster

Just as **both wheels should have** equal, or even, camber, both should have **equal caster.** If you have **uneven positive caster,** your **vehicle will pull toward the side** that has the least caster.

fig. 8-5
Caster is the position of the tire as it relates to the steering knuckle kingpin.

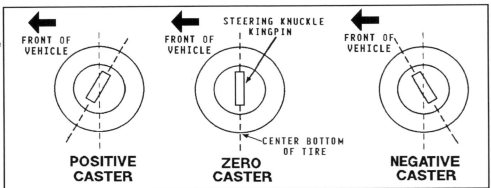

Incorrect caster will not affect tire wear, so you can't rely on looking at your tires to tell you about caster. Caster is usually made with a tapered caster plate placed between the suspension springs and the axle. The caster angle is corrected by replacing the caster plate with a plate that will provide the proper caster. For proper alignment, caster should be slightly positive.

THE TURNING RADIUS

Toe in, toe out, camber, and caster affect how easily your vehicle can make turns and curves. They affect the handling of the truck on straightaways too. Toe in, toe out, and camber affect tire wear. **Turning radius is the size of the circle your tractor makes while turning around.** It is determined by the length of your tractor and the maximum angle the wheels can be turned. The turning radius is the distance from the center to the outside tire marks of a circle made by a turning tractor.

The turning radius **determines** the **maneuverability** of the tractor. The turning radius is determined by the turning angle. The **turning angle** is the **number of degrees to the right or left that the front wheels can be turned from a straight ahead position.**

fig. 8-6
Turning radius and turning angle affect the maneuverability of the vehicle.

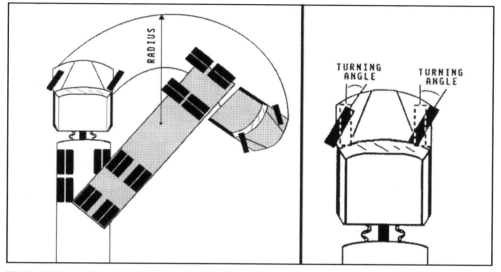

THE SET-BACK FRONT AXLE

A cabover tractor tends to have a tighter turning radius than a conventional model mainly because the tractor design calls for a shorter wheelbase. A recent development in tractor design allows for a set-back front axle on conventional tractor models. Figure 8-7 shows you a comparison of a conventional tractor with a regular front axle and one with a set-back front axle. These may be offered as an option or as an entirely different model.

fig. 8-7
A regular front axle is set back about 30 inches from the front of the tractor while a set-back axle is set back about 46 inches.

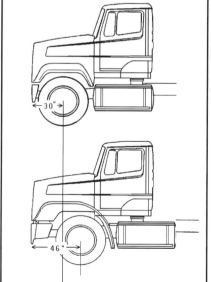

To allow for this set-back axle on conventional tractors, design changes were made to the hood, the steering linkage, the front suspension mounts, and the front bumper.

The set-back front axle results in several advantages. The front axles can carry a heavier load, increasing the payload. You ride more comfortably because the set-back axle lets the suspension system work better. Maintenance is easier because the engine compartment is more open and easier to get to.

But the advantage to notice here is that the set-back axle narrows the turning radius by as much as 26 percent. This is because the set-back axle tightens the steering angle and shortens the wheelbase. Because of improved clearances between the steering components and the tires, set-back wheels can make a turn that is

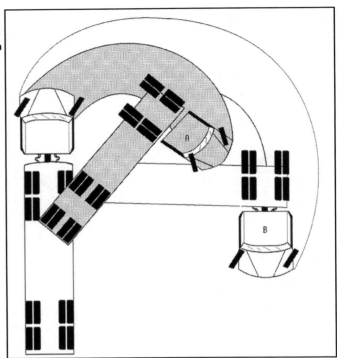

fig. 8-8
The set-back front axle of Tractor A leads to a much tighter turning radius than the conventional front axle of Tractor B.

up to 7½ degrees tighter than conventional wheels. Add that to the 16-inch shorter wheelbase and you have a greatly improved turning radius.

This greatly improved turning radius means **maneuverability is greatly improved.** This is a real boon in any tight driving situation like city loading docks and heavy in-town traffic.

STEERING GEOMETRY

Steering geometry refers to how your truck responds to its steering system. It refers to all the angles of alignment you've just learned about and how they work together to improve the maneuverability of your truck and to protect your tires from undue wear. It includes how the movement of the steering wheel is changed to the left or right movement of the wheels of your tractor.

Keeping the steering system in good mechanical condition is very important to safe, efficient tractor operation. The signs of improper alignment you've learned about in this chapter will warn you of problems in your steering geometry. Those signs are:

- difficulty steering
- front end instability
- feathered edge tire wear
- chattering in the power steering
- increased road shock
- saw-tooth tire wear
- steering wander
- shimmy

Difficulty straightening out after negotiating a turn or curve, tread worn away on the inside or outside edges of your tires, and an improper turning angle are also signs of steering problems.

These signs tell you that repairs or adjustments are needed. You will probably not make these repairs or adjustments yourself, but it is your responsibility to see that the signs are reported to Maintenance. In some cases, it may also be your duty to make sure needed repairs or adjustments are made.

Chapter 8 Quiz

1. The power steering system uses air pressure to assist steering.
   A. True
   B. False

2. _____ describes a steering axle assembly wherein the distance between the toes of the tires is less than the distance between the heels of those tires.
   A. Caster
   B. Toe in
   C. Toe out
   D. Camber

For Questions 3 through 6, please label the unlabelled steering components in the figure on the right.

3. _____
4. _____
5. _____
6. _____

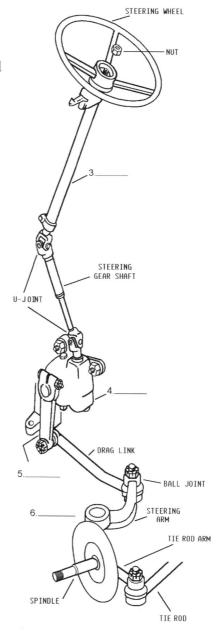

7. _____ describes a steering axle assembly wherein the distance between the toes of the tires is greater than the distance between the heels of those tires.
   A. Caster
   B. Toe in
   C. Toe out
   D. Camber

8. _____ describes how the tire leans in relation to the truck.
   A. Caster
   B. Toe in
   C. Toe out
   D. Camber

9. _____ is the position of the tire in relation to the steering knuckle kingpin.
   A. Caster
   B. Toe in
   C. Toe out
   D. Camber

10. A tractor with a set-back axle _____.
    A. has a faulty alignment
    B. has a tighter turning radius
    C. requires power steering
    D. uses a steering sector instead of a steering gear box

CHAPTER 9
TIRES AND WHEELS

If It Goes, It Probably Has Tires and Wheels

The engine's power goes through the drive train to the wheels and finally to the very surface of the tires. Not only does the engine's power end up there, but so does the weight of your rig and your cargo. You can see the importance of the 18 tires on the typical rig. They

- provide proper traction
- dampen vibration
- absorb road shock
- transfer braking force to the road surface

as well as transfer driving force to the road surface.

BASIC CONSTRUCTION

Now that we know what tires do, let's look at how they are built. There are many different tire designs, but the basic principle of tire construction is the same.

Tires are made up of plies, bead coils, beads, sidewalls, tread, and the inner liner. Plies consist of **separate layers of rubber cushioned cord** and make up **the body of the tire.** All of the **plies** are **tied into bundles of wire called the bead coils.**

Bead coils form the **bead,** which is **the part of the tire that fits into the rim** and **secures the tire to the rim.** Bead coils provide the hoop strength for the bead sections so that the tire will hold its shape when it's being mounted on a wheel.

The **sidewalls** are **layers of rubber covering** which **connect the bead to the tread.** Sidewalls protect the plies in the sidewall area. The **tread** is the part of the tire that **contacts the road.** Treads are designed for specific applications. Some applications require that the tread provide extra traction. Others call for a tread designed for high-speed use. The **inner liner** is the sealing material that **keeps the air in the tire.**

TUBE OR TUBELESS

Tires can either be tube type or tubeless. **Tubeless tires weigh less,** have fewer components, and have a slower rate of pressure loss from punctures. Tires constantly flex when they are in use and this flexing creates heat, which leads to breakdown. With fewer parts to flex and create heat, tubeless tires **last longer.** Tubeless tires are less dangerous to repair because they have a single rim instead of a split rim.

Now that you have learned the basics of tire construction, let's move on and discuss the different types of tires. The three basic types are the bias ply, the belted bias ply, and the radial. Each type is available with tube or tubeless construction, although radials are usually tubeless.

fig. 9-1
The components of the tubeless and tube-type tires.

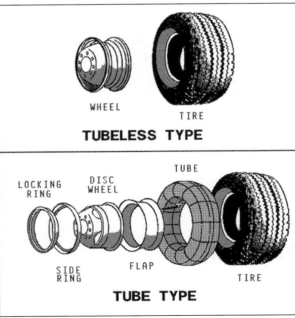

WHEEL

TIRE

TUBELESS TYPE

LOCKING RING

DISC WHEEL

TUBE

SIDE RING

FLAP

TIRE

TUBE TYPE

BIAS PLY TIRES

Let's look at the bias ply first. In Figure 9-2(A) on the next page, you can see the bias **plies** running at a **crisscross** or bias **angle.** This **makes the sidewall and tread rigid.**

Figure 9-2(C) is the **belted bias** ply tire. Like the bias ply tire, its **plies cross at an angle.** However, an **extra layered belt of fabric or steel is placed between**

the plies and the tread. The belts **make** the **tread** of this tire **more rigid** than the bias ply tire. The tread will last longer because the belts reduce tread motion when the tire is running.

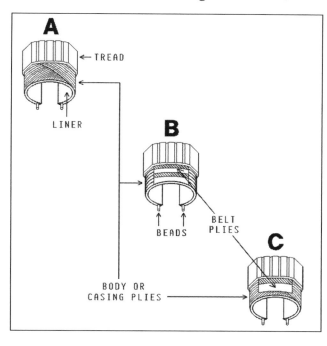

fig. 9-2
The types of tires are
(A) the bias ply
(B) the radial, and
(C) the belted bias ply.

RADIAL TIRES

The radial tire is shown in Figure 9-2(B). The **plies** on this tire **do not cross at an angle.** The ply is laid from bead to bead, across the tire. Like the belted bias ply tire, the radial also has a number of belts. The construction of the radial tire **supports the tread better** than that of either the bias ply or the belted bias ply. The radial design means the sidewalls flex with less friction. That requires less horsepower and **provides greater fuel economy.** Radial tires also:

- hold the road better
- resist skidding better
- give a smoother ride

than the bias types.

Low Profile Radial Tires

Radials are available in two standing heights: standard profile and low profile. Low profile radials lower the center of gravity which improves handling and directional stability and makes the ride more comfortable. Low profile radials also reduce the vehicle's overall height, which allows for more clearance room under bridges. They **weigh less** and offer a lower rolling resistance (the friction between the tire and road), which makes for **still greater fuel savings.**

TREAD DESIGN

Tire tread design takes two main factors into account: the job the tire must do and the conditions the tire will normally face. Tire **treads are designed to do specific jobs.** Steering tires need to roll well and provide good traction for cornering. Drive tires need to provide good traction for both braking and acceleration. Trailer tires primarily need to roll well. Tire treads are also designed to face specific road conditions. For example, drive wheel position tires need maximum traction in rain, snow, sleet, and ice.

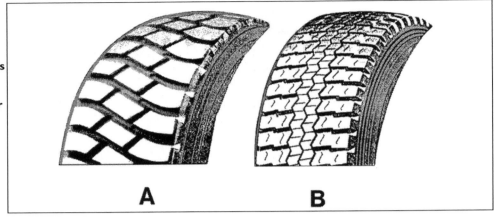

fig. 9-3
Two driving tire tread designs. "A" is designed for maximum traction in adverse conditions such as rain, snow, sleet, or ice while "B" is designed for general road and weather conditions.

TIRE SIZE AND LABELING

Tire Size

Tire size is shown by either a numerical designation or a series design designation. You find this information on the sidewall of your tires.

An example of the **numerical designation** is a 10.00 x 22 tire. The first number is the **tire's width.** This means the inflated tire measured 10 inches from the farthest outside point on one sidewall to the farthest outside point on the other sidewall. The second number in the numerical designation is the **rim size.** Our example tire will fit a 22-inch diameter rim.

The **series designation** system was developed because of the **low profile tire,** which is wide in relation to its height. Once again, let's take an example to look at this. The sidewall of our example tire reads 295/75 R 22.5. This means the section width is 295 millimeters (low profile tires are measured in millimeters rather than inches). The aspect ratio is 75, the construction type is radial, and the rim is 22.5 inches in diameter. Figure 9-4 should clear up any confusion you may have about what the series designation system tells you about the tire.

Tire Labeling

The **government requires tire manufacturers to label all tires** with the information listed below:

- the brand and manufacturer
- the maximum load
- the wheel position
- whether the tire is tube or tubeless
- the material used in the ply construction
- the load range
- the maximum pressure
- the size
- the DOT's code

Load range refers to tire strength, which is rated from A to Z, Z being the strongest. The maximum load the tire can carry in terms of weight is shown in pounds. The maximum pressure is shown in psi and is given for cold tires that have been driven for less than one mile. That should clue you in to check tire pressure before you drive. Wheel positions are listed as S for steering tire, D for driving tire, A for an all-wheel tire, and T for trailer tire. The DOT code is a series of numbers and letters that stand for most of this information. It's useful mainly in tire sales.

As you can see, the sidewall will tell you everything you need to know about the tire you're driving on.

fig. 9-4
The series designation system is used for low profile tires, which are wider than they are tall.

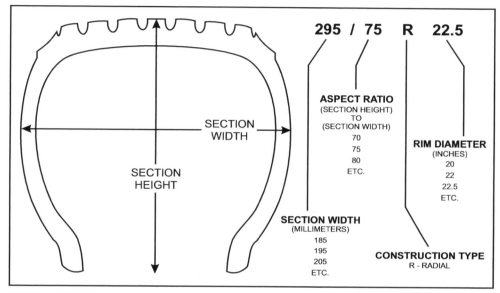

USED TIRES

Basically our discussion of tires has focused on new tires. Used tires can sometimes be restored to like-new condition. These are recapped or retreaded tires.

A retreaded, or recapped, tire has had the old tread surface removed. Then new tread is bonded to the outside layers of the belts or body plies.

Tire Wear

No tire, no matter how expensive or well-maintained, will last forever. **In normal service, some tires simply wear faster than others.** For instance, studies of radial tires show that the tires on the steering axles of tandem axle trucks wear twice as fast as those on single-axle vehicles. This is a result of the tandems pushing straight ahead and scuffing as the front wheels are turned. On tandem axles, rear axle tires wear faster than those on the forward axle. This is because when it turns, the vehicle pivots on the forward axle.

Excessive wear, on the other hand, can result from poor driving or maintenance practices. Let's look at that next.

Tire Damage

As a driver, you must know how to **prevent tire damage.** Tires are very costly so their proper maintenance is important **for economic reasons.** However, tires are even more vital **for safety reasons,** so you must be able to spot damage on tires. Chapter 8 covers some of the causes of tire damage, such as improper alignment, balance, toe-in and toe-out, and camber and caster. In this chapter, we'll take a close look at another major cause of tire damage: improper tire inflation. Then we'll give you a chart that will help you locate tire damage, its possible causes, and possible remedies.

IMPROPER TIRE INFLATION

Improper inflation is a leading cause of tire damage. **Under-inflated tires,** or tires with too little air in them, **wear rapidly at the sides of the tread.** An under-inflated tire will sag under heavy load conditions. If it's part of a dual wheel set-up, the under-inflated tire may contact the tire next to it. This will cause heat to build from the friction of the two tires. In this situation, you may be heading for a blowout. At the very least, you will **burn more precious fuel** than you would with properly inflated tires.

Even if it's not part of a dual wheel set-up, the heat build-up of running an under-inflated tire can be tremendous. This is because the sidewalls flex up and down as the tire rolls.

Overheating leads to the problems listed below:

- faster wear
- tire fires
- tread separation
- blowouts
- cord separation

Overinflated tires, or tires with too much air in them, **wear rapidly at the center of the tread** because the center of the tire is forced to carry more than its share of the load. This clearly also shortens the life of the tire. Overinflation causes extreme strain on the body plies. The extra pressure **increases the chances a blowout** will occur and that the tire will be damaged by road hazards, such as stones or potholes. An overinflated tire simply cannot withstand the normal shocks of driving. Fabric separation or tread separation or both can occur.

Your employer will probably have instructions for you regarding inflation of tires on company equipment.

How To Check Tire Pressure

You already know you should always **check the tire pressure when the tires are cold.** When you drive on a tire, it heats up and the air inside expands, increasing the air pressure. Do not hit your tires with a stick or a billy or kick them to check for proper pressure. Using a billy is a good way to quickly determine a tire is not completely flat. But it is not an accurate way to check your tire pressure. **Use a calibrated tire gauge.**

> ## OBSERVATION SKILLS TEST
> Do you recall the illustration that began this chapter? Are your observation skills improving? Go to the Observation Skills Test Grid at the back of the book and see how you're doing.

fig. 9-5
Use this chart to identify common tire problems, their possible causes, and remedies.

COMMON TIRE PROBLEMS

POSSIBLE CAUSE	POSSIBLE REMEDY
SYMPTOM: RAPID TIRE WEAR	
A. High-speed driving	A. Slow down
B. Improperly inflated tires	B. Inflate properly
C. Rapid starts and stops	C. Correct poor driving habit
D. Front end misaligned	D. Repair and realign
E. Wheels out of balance	E. Balance wheels
F. Excessive load	F. Reduce load or replace tire
SYMPTOM: UNEVEN OR SPOTTY TIRE WEAR	
A. Incorrect caster or camber	A. Adjust
B. Damaged front suspension	B. Repair and align
C. Wheels out of balance	C. Balance wheels
D. Tires under-inflated	D. Inflate properly
SYMPTOM: SAWTOOTH TREAD WEAR	
A. High-speed driving	A. Slow down, rotate wheels
B. Excessive braking	B. Correct poor driving habit
SYMPTOM: SIDE WEAR	
A. Incorrect camber	A. Adjust camber
B. Under-inflated tire	B. Inflate properly
C. Cornering too fast	C. Correct poor driving habit, rotate wheels
SYMPTOM: FEATHERED TREAD EDGES	
A. Excessive toe-in, toe-out	A. Check alignment, repair/adjust as needed
SYMPTOM: ROUNDING/ROUGHING OF TIRE EDGES	
A. Cornering too fast	A. Correct poor driving habit, rotate tires
B. Incorrect camber	B. Adjust camber

Figure 9-5 above is a tire problem chart. It lists the symptoms of some tire problems and possible causes and remedies. Most are problems you can correct or avoid. Others require the attention of a mechanic. If you see any of these symptoms while doing your routine inspections, be sure to make note of it on your report.

With tube-type tires, poor mounting can result in a torn or leaking tube. If you end up with a very low or flat tube-type tire, it could be for any of these reasons:

- rubbed, pinched, or creased tubes
- fold at edge of tube flap
- tube is sized larger than tire
- screw or nail in tire
- foreign matter caught between tube and tire casing
- stretched, used tube installed in new tire

DOT Tire Regulations

The Department of Transportation has established some very specific regulations regarding the tires you'll use on your rig (stated in Subpart G, Miscellaneous Parts and Accessories, Sec. 393.75). No vehicle that operates under DOT regulations may use tires that

- have any fabric exposed through the tread or sidewalls.
- have less than $\frac{4}{32}$ of an inch of tread measured at any point in a major tread groove on the front axle.
- have less than $\frac{2}{32}$ of an inch of tread measured at any point in a major tread groove on all other axles.

fig. 9-6
A "legal" measurement of tread depth must be taken in a major tread groove, not on a hump or in a fillet or sipe.

TREAD GROOVES

SIPES

FILLETS

HUMPS

When you measure grooves, you must not measure where tie bars, humps, or fillets are located. A hump is a pattern of tire wear that looks a little like a cupped hand. The hump is the edge or higher part of the cupping. Tie bars and fillets are not patterns of tire wear but design factors. A sipe is yet another design factor. Sipes are cut across the tread to improve traction on wet roads.

You must **take the tread depth measurement on a major tread groove** where the way is clear to the body of the tire. See Figure 9-6.

Types of Wheels

The two types of wheels used on medium and heavy duty trucks are the cast spoke wheel and the disc wheel. As you can see in Figure 9-7, not only do the wheels differ, but so do the wheel assemblies. The purpose of the wheel is to **provide a mounting device for the tire.** The purpose of the wheel assembly is to **support and connect the tire to the truck axle.**

THE SPOKE WHEEL

Although many companies now manufacture the spoke wheel, many people refer to any cast spoke wheel as a **Dayton** because the Dayton Co. originated it. Spoke wheels are also called "spokes." Most people agree that **spoke wheels, or Daytons, have more strength** than disc wheels. That's why they're used for heavy duty applications.

On a spoke wheel, the wheel consists of a **one-piece casting** which **includes the hub and spokes.** Spoke wheels are made of ductile iron, cast steel, or aluminum. A **separate rim** supports the tire. It has no center disc and is clamped onto the cast spoke wheel.

fig. 9-7
(A) Cast spoke wheel assembly; (B) disc wheel assembly.

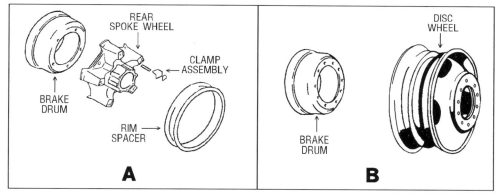

Cast spoke wheels can have five or six spokes. The **five-spoke** wheel is standard **for the steering axle** and the **six-spoke** is used **for driving wheels.** The additional spoke provides greater rim clamping.

Compared to disc wheels, spoke wheels are:

- less costly
- easier to service
- stronger

A cast spoke wheel assembly consists of the wheel, a separate rim, and a clamp assembly. When cast spoke wheels are **dual mounted,** the **rims are kept apart by a rim spacer band.** Whether the cast spoke wheel is bolted to the brake drum or the axle depends on the wheel design. As the brake drum turns, so does the wheel.

THE DISC WHEEL

The Budd Company originated the disc wheel, although many other companies now manufacture it. So, many people refer to the disc wheel as a **Budd.**

Disc wheels are made of steel or aluminum. Aluminum wheels are forged. Aluminum discs have increased in popularity because they weigh less than steel discs. The idea here is that anything you do to lighten the weight of the equipment means you can carry more cargo weight. **Aluminum wheels** are a common way to **reduce weight** and dress up the truck (make it look pretty). Like other lightweight options, aluminum wheels cost more than the standard steel wheels. So the buyer must decide if investing in aluminum wheels will pay off in the long run.

As the last section explained, spoke wheels use separate rims. They are clamped onto the wheels with wheel clamps. If the wheel clamps are not installed just right, the wheel may be out of round and wobble. Because the rim and center portion of the disc wheel are one piece, no clamp is used and so there is less chance of the wheel being out of round. When a wheel is out of round or wobbling, we say it is not true running. The main advantage of the disc wheel over the spoke wheel is that the **disc wheel is true running.** That means the **tire will wear more evenly** and **last longer** and the **ride will be smoother.**

So, on a disc wheel, the **rim is part of the wheel** and the wheel is bolted to the hub and brake drum assembly. You can see this in Figure 9-7(B). A Budd-type disc wheel assembly consists of the wheel and a stud bolt and nut assembly.

Disc wheels are **mainly used with drop center rims and tubeless tires,** although they can be used with multi-piece rims and tube-type tires.

Types of Rims

The rim's job is to **support the tire bead and the lower sidewall.** The two types of rims used on heavy trucks are the drop center rim and the multi-piece rim.

The **drop center rim** is a single piece rim and the one **most often used** on heavy trucks. It is part of the wheel. This type of rim can be used with either type tire. But it is most often used **with tubeless tires** because the center has a smaller diameter to provide room to remove the tire. These wheels are built the same as most car wheels, only larger.

There are two types of multi-piece rims: the two piece rim and the three piece rim. The **two piece rim** consists of the rim and a split side ring. Two piece rims cannot be made airtight so they're **used with tube tires only.**

The **three piece rim** consists of the rim, a continuous side ring, and a split lock ring. Three piece rims cannot be made airtight either, so they, too, **take a tube tire.** Figure 9-8 shows you what these three types of rims look like.

fig. 9-8
(A) Drop center rim;
(B) two piece rim;
(C) three piece rim.

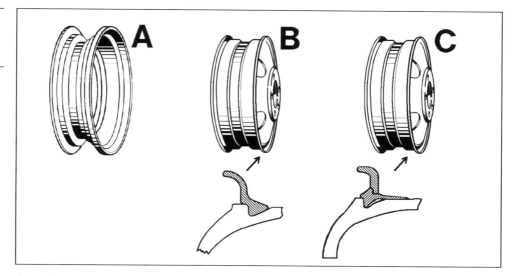

As with tires, wheels and rims share some common problems. Figure 9-9 on the next page lists the symptoms of some of these problems, along with possible causes and remedies. As with the tires, some of the problems are within your power to control or correct. The others need the attention of a mechanic to ensure the continued safe operation of your truck.

Mounting and Dismounting

For the most part, when your tires need service, you'll note it on your inspection report and the company shop or service garage will take care of it. The Federal Motor Carrier Safety Administration requires that mounting and dismounting of tires be done only by someone who has been trained for the task. So unless you receive special training, you may never perform these procedures yourself.

However, if you're a smart driver, and you are, you'll stay around whenever your tires are mounted or dismounted. You'll want to **make sure this is done properly** because you are the one who'll be riding on those tires and wheels and you are the one who is ultimately responsible for your rig. So in this section you'll learn about the things you should look out for whenever your tires are mounted or dismounted.

fig. 9-9
Use this chart to indentify common wheel problems, their possible causes, and remedies.

COMMON WHEEL PROBLEMS

POSSIBLE CAUSES	POSSIBLE REMEDIES
SYMPTOMS: CRACKED OR CORRODED RIMS	
A. Overloading	A. Reduce load, replace wheel
B. Pitting by water or chemicals	B. Clean rim or replace wheel
SYMPTOMS: DAMAGED OR SPRUNG RINGS	
A. Rings mounted improperly	A. Replace rings, remount properly
B. Rings dismounted improperly	B. Replace rings, remount properly
SYMPTOMS: CRACKED OR ERODED SIDE RINGS	
A. Mounted improperly	A. Replace side rings, remount properly
B. Collision with road hazards	B. Replace wheel
C. Excessive clamping	C. Replace side rings, remount properly
D. Overloading	D. Reduce load, replace side rings
SYMPTOMS: CRACKED, RUSTED OR WORN STUD HOLES	
A. Loose running wheel	A. Replace wheel, tighten properly
B. Overloading	B. Reduce load, repair, or replace wheel
C. Worn ball seats	C. Repair or replace
SYMPTOMS: DAMAGED WHEEL STUDS (OR BOLTS) AND NUTS	
A. Excessive tightening of studs	A. Replace studs if threads are stripped and tighten to proper specification
B. Loose or excessively tightened nuts	B. Replace all studs if one or more are broken, tighten to proper specification
C. Improperly seated wheel	C. Replace wheel, tighten to proper specification
D. Loose mounting	D. Replace damaged nuts and studs, check wheel ball seat, replace wheel if necessary

MATCH TYPES OF TIRES

If you need one of your duals replaced on the road, make sure that the replacement tire is the same type as the one already in place. In other words, your **duals should match according to ply type.** Put radials with radials, bias ply with bias ply and so forth. The same concern holds true for the steering axle—don't put a radial on one side if you have a bias on the other. On the other hand, it's acceptable to have different types of tires on the tractor than you have on the trailer.

Follow any specific rules your company may have when getting a tire replaced.

MATCH DIAMETERS OF DUAL TIRES

What will happen if you use tires with different diameters on the same side of an axle? Both tires will wear faster than they should. The larger tire will carry most of the weight, causing it to wear out very quickly. **Make sure both tires on a dual set-up are the same diameter.** "Eyeball" the newly inflated tire to compare it with the one that's in place. If the diameters don't match, you need a different tire.

SAFETY FIRST AND ALWAYS

A safety cage should always be used when a tire is being inflated. Never stand in front of a rim and tire assembly while it's being inflated or deflated. The pressure on the wheel parts is tremendous. If a ring should come loose, it can do so with enough force to go through the wall or the roof.

PRE-INFLATING THE TUBE

If your tires are tube-type tires, make sure the mechanic pre-inflates them. The mechanic should insert the tube and inflate it just enough to make it round before proceeding with the mounting process. This **helps to prevent folds and creases** in the tube. As you learned, folds and creases in a tube can tear the tube, causing it to leak.

THE PROPER BOLT TIGHTENING SEQUENCE

Figure 9-10 shows you the proper bolt tightening sequence for the three types of wheels you may use as a tractor-trailer driver. Using the proper sequence for tightening wheel bolts **helps to ensure that the wheel is square on the hub** and that each bolt is taking its share of the load. When the tire is square on the hub, it runs true. If the wheel is not square on the hub, the tire will wobble. If the tire wobbles, it will wear rapidly and unevenly.

fig. 9-10
Make sure the mechanic who mounts your wheels uses the proper bolt tightening sequence.

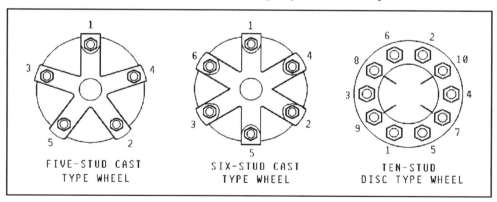

FIVE-STUD CAST TYPE WHEEL   SIX-STUD CAST TYPE WHEEL   TEN-STUD DISC TYPE WHEEL

If you have spoke wheels **make sure the mechanic** who mounts your tires **does a lateral run-out check.** This is easy to do. Just place a hammer close to the tire, spin the tire and watch the space between the tire and the hammer. If the tire is not running true, you will see it wobble in that space.

Check all the bolts and tighten any that are loose as part of your normal maintenance routine.

CLEANING THE RIM

Make sure the mechanic checks and, if necessary, cleans the rim before mounting a tire on it. This is important with both types of tires, but especially with tubeless tires. If there is corrosion and dirt on the rim, the rubber edge of the tire will not be able to seal properly against the rim. Cleaning the rim **ensures a good seal,** which **protects against leaks.**

RUNNING A LOADED TRUCK UP ON BLOCKS

At some point in your career, you will likely get a flat on an outside tire of a loaded rig. The mechanic changing that outside dual may ask you to simply run the truck up on blocks. It's easier for the mechanic and it's probably okay as long as the rig is empty.

However, if your truck is loaded, tire manufacturers recommend that it be jacked up to change that flat. Why? When you run the inside dual up on blocks to get the outside dual off the ground so you can change it, you put all the weight of that axle on one tire. Asking one tire to hold an amount of weight intended for two tires can result in serious damage to the tire plies. Your best bet in this situation is to be guided by your company policy.

Chapter 9 Quiz

1. _____ consist of separate layers of rubber cushioned nylon cord and make up the body of the tire.
   A. Beads
   B. Plies
   C. Treads
   D. Bead coils

2. Match the types of tires in the illustration to the right with the correct labels.
   A. _____
   B. _____
   C. _____

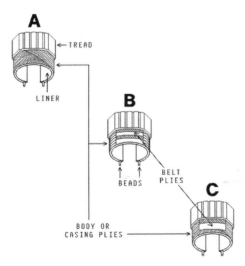

3. Radial tire construction provides less support for the tread than does bias ply type construction.
    A. True
    B. False

4. The number and letter combination 295/75 R 22.5 is an example of _____ designation labeling.
    A. series
    B. numerical

5. _____ refers to tire strength, which is rated from A to Z, Z being the strongest.
    A. Load range
    B. Maximum load
    C. Maximum pressure
    D. Series designation

6. Improper inflation is a leading cause of tire damage.
    A. True
    B. False

7. _____ tires wear rapidly at the center of the tread.
    A. Under-inflated
    B. Overinflated

8. Tread measurements must be taken in a _____.
    A. major tire groove
    B. tire hump
    C. fillet sipe
    D. tread tie bar

9. Label the types of wheels in the following illustration with the correct name.
    A. _____
    B. _____

A   **B**

10. To prevent folds and creases in a tire tube, which cause it to leak, make sure the mechanic _____ when mounting your tube-type tire.
    A. greases the rim
    B. uses the proper bolt tightening sequence
    C. pre-inflates the tube
    D. matches the diameters of your dual tires

CHAPTER 10

TRACTORS

The Power Unit

Every truck tractor has an engine, a frame, axles, a suspension, a transmission, and a cab. Beyond that, the tractor is assembled from what you could almost call a tractor kit. In fact, most truck tractors have been put together with a particular job in mind. Unlike a car, which you pretty much get as a complete piece of equipment, a truck is put together component by component to meet the challenges it will face on the job.

The average Class 8 tractor, the heavy duty type we most often think of when we think "truck," weighs upwards of 13,000 to 20,000 pounds and costs about $100,000. It's a lot to handle. Your truck will be inspected and registered, which involves some pretty hefty fees. It will get about 6 miles to the gallon, a lot less than your little subcompact, and diesel fuel costs over one dollar a gallon. Your truck will probably have two fuel tanks. Since each holds between 50 and 150 gallons, a fill up can set you back some. Like everyone else in the trucking industry, you will be trying to economize whenever possible.

Above all, you will observe the special care and handling of your tractor. Your future employer will no doubt want you to treat the tractor you drive as if you owned it. That's a reasonable request. Besides, who knows? Maybe someday you will own your own tractor-trailer rig. So, on the theory that to know your tractor is to love it, let's investigate some of its many designs and specifications.

What Is a Tractor?

First, however, let's get specific about the difference between a "truck tractor" and a plain old "truck." According to the DOT, a **truck tractor is a motor vehicle used to draw or pull other vehicles.** Except for the part of the weight it is drawing (the part resting on the fifth wheel), the truck tractor is not used for carrying a load. By itself, the tractor has no real commercial use. In other words, it **doesn't carry cargo.** The tractor is the power unit of a full rig. Its calling in life is to pull a trailer, and the trailer is what carries the cargo. For the sake of simplicity, the term "truck tractor" is usually shortened to "tractor."

To drive a commercial tractor of 26,001 pounds or more gross vehicle weight rating (GVWR) and pull a trailer of 10,000 pounds or more GVWR, you must get a Group A CDL. A Group B CDL will license you to drive an equally heavy tractor pulling a trailer weighing less than 10,000 pounds. You may have to take a special knowledge and skills test on combination vehicles.

A plain truck is a simple, self-contained piece of equipment that consists of the power unit as well as the truck body or bed. These are sometimes called "straight trucks." Although straight trucks may often be quite large and powerful, they do not articulate and there is no fifth wheel. Trailers can be towed by straight trucks by means of a tow bar.

Different sizes of **trucks are grouped into classes, based on weight.** We've already mentioned Class 8. These are the extra heavyweights, the over-the-road sleepers, dump trucks, cement trucks, and the like. The eight classes of vehicles are described in the chart below. These classes are different from the vehicle groups used in CDL licensing.

VEHICLE CLASSIFICATION		
CLASS	GROSS VEHICLE WEIGHT RATING (IN POUNDS)	EXAMPLES
CLASS 8	over 33,000	Heavy duty over-the-road tractors, construction vehicles
CLASS 7	26,001-33,000	Medium-size conventional tractors, residential fuel service vehicles, trash removal trucks
CLASS 6	19,501-26,000	Small-size cab-over-engine vans, single axle vans, furniture vans
CLASS 5	16,001-19,500	Landscaping service vehicles, beverage rack vans
CLASS 4	14,001-16,000	Large-size walk-in vans
CLASS 3	10,001-14,000	Medium-size valk-in vans, milk trucks, bakery trucks, compact vans
CLASS 2	6,001-10,000	Small walk-in vans
CLASS 1	under 6,000	Compact vans, pickup trucks, utility vans

In addition to size, trucks can be grouped into on-road and off-road types. We'll look at that next.

The On-road and Off-road Tractor

Tractors are built to go either on the road or off the road. You see on-road tractors pulling their trailers full of cargo over the highways. But of course tractors are also used in the logging, mining, and construction industries. The load could be logs, coal, equipment, or rocks. The trailers pulled may be end dumps, bottom dumps, flatbeds, lowboys, or pole trailers.

Basically, **off-road tractors** are built to **withstand more abuse** than the on-road tractor. They have a heavy duty construction to hold their own against the inevitable rough terrain and hard work. Of course, tires, axles, suspensions, transmissions, drive shafts, and engines are all heavy-duty. Power is a main consideration.

While off-road tractors spend most of their working lives on rough terrain, most of them use public roads to get to and from the job site. They therefore **must still be "street legal."** This means they have to have the safety equipment, components, and construction specified by DOT regulations.

The on-road tractor is built to **perform well on the road.** Some of its equipment **does not have to stand as much abuse as the off-road tractor.**

This means that some parts can be built lighter so the tractor will weigh less. The reduced weight can mean better fuel economy, which for the on-road vehicle may be more important than power.

Because it is often used for long hauls, the cab of the on-road tractor is designed for driver comfort. There are adjustable cushioned seats and a roomy sleeping berth. Many on-road tractors have air ride suspension which makes for a smoother ride. The wheels and tires are also made for highway use.

Part for part, let's compare features of both types of tractors.

THE ENGINE
With its larger horsepower requirements, the **off-road tractor** has a **larger engine,** radiator, and air cleaner than does the on-road tractor.

TRANSMISSION
The transmission of an **off-road tractor** is built to deliver more power in the low gear ratios since it does most of its work in that range. Often there will be **more low speed gears.** They are therefore able to pull a very heavy load up a steep, rough grade. In an **on-road vehicle,** the emphasis is on efficient operation at **highway speeds.**

SUSPENSION
The **suspension of** the **off-road tractor** must also be **heavy duty** to absorb the shock of unpaved roads. Rugged steel springs help the driver maintain control. Suspensions are rated by the amount of weight they can safely haul. Off-road tandem axles are usually rated at 44,000 pounds. An **on-road vehicle's suspension** would more likely be required to **deliver a smooth ride.** That way, the driver doesn't tire over the long haul.

TIRES AND WHEELS
Because of the tremendous loads and rough terrain the **off-road** tractor must handle, **tires and wheels** are always **heavy-duty** and designed for traction in dirt. **Tires** are generally **wider** than the on-road tire to avoid sinking in loose dirt. Most off-road **wheels** are **made of steel.** Aluminum would be no match for the rocks and uneven terrain. These tires must be strong enough to support heavy loads. On the other hand, **on-road** trucks use **tires** built to **stand up to the heat generated by rolling at higher speeds.** They have more grooves in the tread for better traction on pavement.

THE HYDRAULIC SYSTEM
Hydraulic systems are found **more often in off-road** than on-road tractors. The hydraulic system includes a tank, lines from the tractor to the trailer, and a pump. This is called a wet kit.

FUEL TANKS

Your **on-road tractor** will have at least one and most probably **two fuel tanks.** These are located under the cab or the sleeper on each side of the truck. Each tank will hold at least 50 gallons and the large ones can hold 150 gallons. When fueling you have to fill each one separately. The fuel lines from the engine usually go to the tank on the driver's side of the truck. If you have more than one tank they will be **interconnected** by a hose. This way the fuel level is pretty much the same in all the tanks even though the engine is taking fuel from only one tank.

Axles

Tractors are not only classified by their uses (on-road or off-road), but also by the number of drive axles. Tractors that you will be working with can be classified as single axle tractors or tandem axle tractors.

SINGLE AXLE TRACTORS

The **single axle tractor has one drive axle and one steering axle.** Having **a shorter wheelbase and easier to handle** than the tandem, it is used for pulling two or more trailers, or for short distances and light loads. It has a **smaller turning radius.** Turning radius depends on wheelbase. For a single axle tractor, wheelbase is the distance between the center of the steering axle to the center of the rear drive axle. (For a tandem, wheelbase is from the center of the front axle to the center of the tandem.)

fig. 10-1
The wheelbase of a single axle tractor.

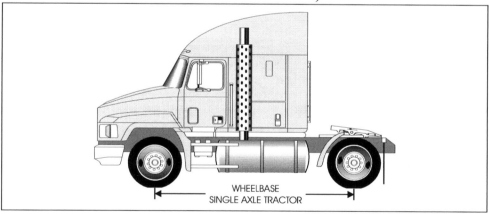

WHEELBASE
SINGLE AXLE TRACTOR

A single axle tractor is **cheaper to buy and operate.** Repair costs are lower since there are fewer parts on the single axle to repair. With their short wheelbase, however, single axles **are not comfortable over long distances.**

TANDEM AXLE TRACTORS

For heavy loads and long distances the tandem axle tractor is generally used. The **tandem axle provides four more drive tires.** That gives not only **more strength** but **more traction.**

The average wheelbase of a tandem axle tractor is 196 inches to 220 inches for a cabover and 220 inches to 260 inches for a conventional tractor. The **wide turning radius** of the long wheelbase tandem axle can make it a little **harder to maneuver** a truck within a limited space.

fig. 10-2
The wheelbase of a tandem axle tractor.

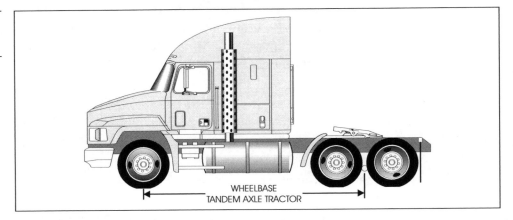

SINGLE DRIVE TANDEM AXLE TRACTORS

One other configuration is a single drive axle with an tag axle. A tag axle is a dead axle. It isn't powered by the engine, but rather freewheels. The **tag axle** has certain advantages of both the single and the tandem drive axles. Like the single, it is **not as heavy** and requires **less maintenance** than the tandem. Since it doesn't require any engine power, it **doesn't increase fuel use** the way the tandem axle does. Like the tandem it provides four more wheels and a **greater load-carrying capacity.** See Figure 10-3.

fig. 10-3
Tandem axles. (A) Single drive with tag axle and (B) two drive axles.

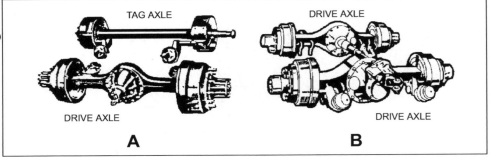

The Conventional and the Cabover

There is yet one more important system of classification. That is whether a tractor is a conventional or a cabover.

THE CONVENTIONAL

In the conventional tractor, the **cab sits behind the engine. Sleepers** are easier to get into and out of and are sometimes **larger.** The length of the hood can be classed as long, medium, or short.

Road **visibility** is **not as good** as in the cabovers, but having the engine in front can be safer if a collision occurs.

THE CAB-OVER-ENGINE

Although it was called the cab-over-engine when it was introduced just before World War II, people eventually shortened that to the "cabover," or COE. The cabover has a **shorter wheelbase** and **greater visibility** for the driver.

Cabovers are used for all types of hauling. With their shorter wheelbase and **turning ease,** they are often preferred for in-city deliveries and for pulling long trailers. Plastic, fiber glass, and aluminum are often used to reduce the weight of the cabover. That **lighter weight** means more of the allowable weight can be payload.

Its one-time advantage was that since the cabover tractor itself was shorter in length than the conventional, it could pull a longer trailer without the length of the entire rig exceeding limits set in certain states. That was a real plus for a while. Then came standardization. In 1982 the Surface Transportation Assistance Act meant states had to allow semitrailers up to 48 feet in length on all interstate and U.S. highways, including all roads within access of the pickup or delivery point. (States can set length limits beyond the 48-foot limit, however.) Having a shorter tractor was no longer of any particular advantage.

The Heavy Straight Truck

The **straight truck** is an "all-in-one" vehicle with **no articulation** (coupling device). It can be quite heavy and powerful. For example, the straight truck is paired with front end loaders in garbage collection and in construction to haul dirt and gravel. It is also used for hauling specialized items such as cranes, sheet rock, dressed stone, cinder block, and petroleum products.

Driver comforts are important in the straight truck. The truck is generally smaller in size and therefore less intimidating to the new driver. In fact, straight trucks may have fully synchronized transmission gears which might seem "too easy" for the professional driver.

OBSERVATION SKILLS TEST

Now that you can classify tractors, classify the Class 8 tractor you saw at the very beginning of this chapter. Check the Observation Skills Test grid at the back of the book to see how you did.

Specifications

Every item on the tractor has a distinct purpose. The **tractor** has been **"spec'ed out" for the job** it will be doing. A tractor that travels up, down, and across the Rocky Mountains will have different specifications than a truck that travels the flatland. Specification of the frame, axles, and springs is based on the weight of the load, type of cargo, and the sort of terrain over which the tractor will run.

Climate also plays an important role. If the tractor will be running in very cold weather, it is likely to have such add-on features as an engine block heater, fuel line heater, brake system air dryer, and battery warmer. For fragile cargo such as electronics equipment or medical supplies, air ride suspension is a must. Tractors that haul extremely heavy cargo are fitted with thicker frames and stronger rear end differentials.

AERODYNAMICS AND FUEL ECONOMY

The word **"aerodynamics"** refers to the **moving** of objects **through the air** (aero = air, dynamics = movement). When a tractor pushes against the wind it **burns up a lot of fuel.** If the tractor can be made "slicker" to glide more easily through the air, significant **fuel savings** can be realized. This **can be achieved with a few changes in the truck design.** Wherever possible, the cab will have rounded edges instead of flat surfaces. An aerodynamic design tucks in the fuel tank, exhaust stack, and all protruding parts to keep them from catching the wind and holding back the tractor. The truck on the cover of this book exhibits many aerodynamic features.

Add-on accessories include wind deflectors, automatic engine fan shut-off, formula diesel engines and even lighter-weight cabs, frames, wheels, and components. Because of the importance of fuel savings, research in the field of aerodynamics is fierce and ongoing.

ACCESSORIES

Tractor **accessories** serve many purposes. They can **make the vehicle safer,** as well as **easier to operate and maintain.** Some accessories are strictly for driver comfort, while others just make the tractor nicer looking.

Gauges, radios, cab styling, auxiliary brakes, fuel tank heaters, and power take-offs are some of the tractor accessories available. With some tractors, cab size will limit the accessories to be added.

COLD WEATHER ACCESSORIES

In cold weather, it's tempting to keep the engine running so the engine or cab will stay warm while the truck is parked. But all that idling wastes a lot of precious fuel, and can cut a year off the truck's life. An **auxiliary generator** can be added to **keep the engine or cab warm** while the truck is parked for extended periods **with the engine turned off.** Not having to idle the engine for those long periods will save fuel. A fuel heater can be added to keep the fuel from thickening up in sub-zero weather.

THE DRIVER'S SEAT

Tractor **seats** are scientifically engineered and adjustable to **provide** the best possible **support** for long hours of driving. Some of these have high backs and arms that fold up or down.

Nearly every truck you drive will have an air ride seat on the driver's side. This works just like the air ride suspension and the purpose is the same, to provide a better ride. Under your seat you will see a small air bag. You use air pressure from the air supply system to inflate the bag.

There are several different designs. There will be a knob or lever that you move one way to add air to the bag and move the other way to release air. On some seats you use this knob to adjust the seat to suit your weight. These seats have a separate lever you use to adjust the height. Other seats will use the air supply knob to adjust for weight and height. All seats will have a separate lever to move the seat forward and back.

You will be spending a lot of time in that seat, so familiarize yourself with all its controls. Be able to adjust it so it is the most comfortable to you.

GAUGES AND CONTROLS

The switches and gauges are usually located on the dash of your truck. One manufacturer's main gauges are in front of the driver with the auxiliary gauges to the driver's right. Other makers curve the dash to the right so that all gauges and switches are within easy reach.

The basic gauges are air pressure, speedometer, tachometer, oil pressure, fuel level, and water temperature. Then there are gauges to measure transmission fluid temperature, rear axle fluid temperature, manifold pressure, and temperatures of various mechanical parts. **Gauges indicate how the tractor is running.** They make it possible to take better care of your equipment. **Switches are used to control or operate the truck.** Among these are switches for lights, high beam indicators, engine stop control, auxiliary brakes, and the power take-off switch (PTO).

Chapter 2 covers gauges and controls in greater detail.

THE HEADACHE RACK

A headache rack (headerboard) is the **cab guard** that **protects the back of the cab** if the load shifts forward during a sudden stop. Obviously, this accessory could save you from getting a very bad headache! It provides not only a safer

fig. 10-4
A cab guard will stop the forward motion of cargo that's not securely loaded on the trailer.

truck but it also serves as a safe handy place to hang chains and binders. Safety regulations require that your tractor have a headache rack when pulling a flatbed trailer that does not have a front bulkhead.

THE JAKE BRAKE

"Jake Brake" is a term you'll hear used for engine retarders or engine brakes in general. It really refers to one particular manufacturer's product, and there are several different types of engine retarders. This accessory is almost a necessity for tractors that travel up and down mountains and steep grades. Using the engine's own compression to slow down the vehicle, the **engine brake controls speed on a downgrade** and can **save wear on the brakes.** A switch inside the cab will turn it on or off.

Several chapters in this book contain more information about this important accessory, such as Chapter 22.

THE POWER TAKE-OFF (PTO)

Another option is the **power take-off** for hydraulic powered equipment. The PTO **activates a hydraulic pump** that pumps fluid from the tractor to hydraulic equipment such as a dump trailer.

THE SLEEPING BERTH

The sleeping berth **("sleeper") for rest periods out on the road** has gotten pretty fancy over the years. There was a time when it was little more than a stuffy little compartment with a lumpy cot. These days, a sleeper can be plain enough for a missionary or designed to warm a lonely driver's heart. There is heat and air conditioning, often TV and stereo. Some even feature sinks, running water, microwave ovens, and queen-sized beds. Extra insulation shields against outside noise and temperature extremes.

As you will see, a lot of money can be spent on the sleeper. Larger sleepers have stand-up space, closets and drawers, writing table, carpeting. One thing a sleeper normally doesn't have is a shower, but showers are available at most truck stops.

THE FIFTH WHEEL

The **fifth wheel provides the point of rotation where the trailer fits on the tractor** and is used for load distribution. It's a very basic accessory and you'll learn much more about it in Chapters 15 and 23.

SUSPENSION SYSTEMS

There are two basic types of suspension systems: air ride or leaf spring. Of the two, air ride is the most comfortable. The air ride system uses rubber air bags rather than springs. The bags are located just inside the frame where the drive axles meet the frame. Chapter 7 covers suspension systems in more detail.

Chapter 10 Quiz

1. The truck tractor _____.
    A. is a self-contained unit
    B. has no fifth wheel
    C. consists of the power unit
    D. is sometimes called a straight truck

2. The basic difference between on-road and off-road tractors is that _____.
    A. one type must be "street legal" and the other never is
    B. off-road tractors are built to withstand more abuse
    C. off-road tractors are built for speed
    D. off-road tractors have no passenger seat

3. The single-axle tractor is ideal for _____.
    A. lightweight cargo
    B. mountain driving
    C. safety during winter storms
    D. cross-country driving

4. For hauling extremely heavy equipment, a tractor must have _____.
    A. a brake system air dryer
    B. a heavy-duty differential
    C. an automatic engine fan shut-off
    D. a mechanical suspension system

5. The device that helps cut vehicle power and slow the truck is the _____.
    A. engine retarder
    B. coupling device
    C. tag axle
    D. power take-off

6. A typical fuel-saving add-on device is _____.
   A. a shorter wheelbase
   B. an air ride suspension
   C. an air ride seat
   D. a wind deflector

7. The cab guard is required by law when the _____.
   A. road involves steep grades
   B. trailer being pulled has no auxiliary brakes
   C. flatbed being pulled has no bulkhead
   D. tractor has no power take-off

8. The distance between the rear drive axle and the center of the steering axle is the _____.
   A. first gear ratio
   B. load-carrying capacity
   C. GVWR
   D. wheelbase

9. The COE enjoyed greater popularity _____.
   A. during World War I
   B. before conventionals were introduced
   C. before 1982
   D. with those who preferred not to stand while driving

10. In a tractor, aluminum, fiber glass and plastic are used to _____.
    A. create a stylish interior
    B. reduce the tractor's weight
    C. strengthen the rear end differential
    D. provide off-road durability

```
                          DRIVING PERFORMANCE REPORT


      DRIVER:    Don Nichols        TRIP DATE:    2/22/87         TRIP NO.  201
      ID#:       2065               PAY CODE:     01


      ON DUTY DATE: 2/28/04         TIME:  7:30            TRACTOR: M-420
      OFF DUTY DATE: 2/29/04        TIME: 14:45            TRAILER: D-608


      CO-DRIVER:  Frances Sanchez                          TOTAL MILES:  638
      ID#:        2227                                     TOTAL HOURS:  31:15


                               SPEED RANGES
```

RPM RANGE	IDLE	1-25 MPH	26-35 MPH	36-43 MPH	44-50 MPH	51-55 MPH	56-59 MPH	+60 MPH
100-650	373	7	0	0	0	0	0	0
650-900	0	3	0	0	0	0	0	0
900-1100	0	1	0	0	0	0	0	0
1100-1200	0	1	0	0	0	0	0	0
1200-1300	0	1	0	0	0	0	0	0
1300-1400	0	1	0	0	0	0	0	0
1400-1500	0	0	0	0	0	0	0	0
1500-1600	0	1	0	1	1	0	0	0
1600-1700	0	4	2	4	24	0	0	0
1700-1800	0	2	4	8	35	30	0	0
1800-1900	0	4	14	43	64	221	252	15
OVER-1900	0	0	0	0	1	0	2	30

```
      TOTAL TIME:   6:13    0:25    0:20    0:56    2:05    4:11    4:14    0:45


      TOTAL TIME IN IDLE:           6:13    32%
      TOTAL TIME IN MOTION:        12:56    67%


      SPEEDING RATES ABOVE 59 MPH
      DATE          TIME      NO. MIN.       @MILE     TOTAL MILES     AV SPEED

      2/28/87       10:28       15          104,644      15.75           63
      2/29/87        6:15       30          105,604      32.50           65

      TOTALS                    45                       48.25


      PERCENTAGE OF TIME SPENT SPEEDING:                  0.03
```

Computers and Change in Trucking

Computers—they're everywhere! They're in your car, of course, and your VCR. They're in many household appliances, in the supermarket, in vending machines…As the Y2K hysteria showed at the turn of the millennium, there are few things that don't have microprocessors in them. So you won't be surprised to learn there are computing devices in your truck.

As computer systems have changed almost every aspect of our lives, so have they changed the trucking industry. The computer has changed the business management department of the carrier company. It has changed the way drivers work. Onboard computers, or **vehicle management systems,** are one way carriers **monitor and determine profits.** Over and over again, the industry learns about the positive effects of technology. Computers prove to be a good investment in terms of money management for the carrier. They relieve the driver of a lot of paperwork. They **help improve driving habits** and thus **save fuel and promote safety.** They help the carrier and the driver **provide better customer service.** And, it appears they will be able to do much more in the future.

Computers in the Trucking Industry

Running a trucking business involves a lot of work. The company manager takes charge of the business. This person makes the decisions that affect company profits. But the manager needs lots of help to run the company well. The manager needs other people to carry out the decisions and to handle the different areas of the business. This list of workers includes not only the drivers but also:

- maintenance people
- dispatchers
- salespeople
- billing clerks

With this many areas of work at one company, the paperwork can be both time consuming and expensive. This is especially true for dispatch and billing. **Computers** offer managers a much **more efficient and prompt** way to take care of business **than paper.** As it turns out, it's also a less costly way.

So, at modern trucking companies, you'll see computers everywhere. **In the maintenance department,** the computer generates inspection and other needed forms. It keeps an accurate record of inspections and maintenance performed on each piece of equipment. Computers keep track of parts and accessories. And, they do that without reams of paper and walls of file cabinets. Plus, as you'll see, a computer can help determine what needs to be maintained.

In the sales department, the computer is used for word processing to write letters and generate promotional materials and proposals. **In dispatch** it's used to keep track of where the drivers, the equipment, and the freight are at all times. **In billing** the computer generates bills and keeps track of accounts receivable.

Computers are used in all these parts of the terminal, but they're also mounted inside the cabs of the trucks. Some of these devices you'll see and touch. Some, you'll never see. All the devices gather information that you and your employer can use to do a better job. This **information enables you to drive more efficiently and safely**. You and the carrier will use the data collected to file required reports and keep the equipment in good condition. The data will help you and your employer do a better job for the customers.

When computers are mounted in trucks, they are called onboard computers.

Early Onboard Computers

Onboard computers aren't new. The tachograph was an early data collection device. It automatically recorded the number of miles driven, the number of stops made, speed, and several other factors, and printed the information on paper disks. They were impressive, except that by the end of a week, managers would have reams of records to read and analyze. They needed the information presented in a way that was easy to use.

Computers provided an answer in trucking just as they have in other industries. As large mainframe computers became small enough to sit on desktops, they also found their way into trucks. Early onboard computers monitored even more vehicle systems. Sensors and probes could monitor all the performance factors listed below.

- fuel consumption
- periods of stop-and-go driving
- departure and arrival times
- vehicle stop time
- road miles
- cruise control time
- idling time
- speed
- rpm
- driving time
- brake use
- fan clutch use
- number of stops that are longer than a set time
- number of times the exhaust goes above a certain temperature
- engine warm-up and engine cool-down times

These computers were relatively easy for the driver to use. Drivers made preprogrammed entries by pressing different keys on a panel. For example, on crossing a state line, a driver would enter a code for the state mileage report and then the code for the state. **Time and date clocks** stamped the entries with the precise time and date. The odometer kept track of the miles. Data was transmitted to a recording medium or storage device. This was usually a removable module or cartridge. Figure 11-1 pictures one of these early onboard computers.

fig. 11-1
An early onboard computer lets the driver input information by pushing buttons. Data was stored on removable cartridges.

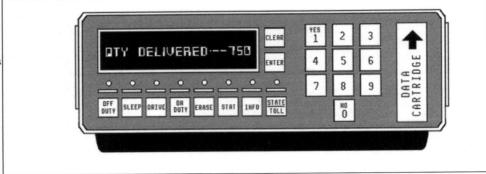

The cartridge could later be inserted into a main computer and reports generated. These reports were much easier to use than raw data.

Reports Generated by Onboard Computers

Many helpful reports can be generated from the data gathered by the onboard computer. Types of reports this information leads to include:

- driver's trip reports
- trip over/short/damage reports
- driver's expense reports
- driving performance reports
- state mileage reports

If you work for a carrier, you will not see all these reports. Some are useful mainly to the carrier or to an owner/operator. You may see driving performance reports, especially when your carrier wants to congratulate you for a good job. Or, if you need to see where you fall behind in performance, this report can pinpoint problem areas.

> OBSERVATION SKILLS TEST
> What was the subject of the report that began this chapter? What did it reveal? To check your answers, refer to the Observation Skills Grid at the back of the book.

The data for driver's trip reports and driving performance reports is gathered by sensors. The driver does not input any data for these reports. However, for the trip over/short/damage reports, the state mileage reports, and the driver's expense reports, the driver may need to give the computer some information. These last three reports all save paperwork for the driver. You'll learn how later in this chapter. The driver's trip report shows the total miles driven, the average speed, driving time, and the stopping time.

The **driving performance report** is very detailed. It includes the information listed below.

- total miles driven for this report
- total hours driven for this report
- engine idling time
- how long the engine ran and its rpm in each speed category
- how often and for how long the driver exceeded the speed limit

You can see how this report **would help** both a carrier and a driver **pinpoint performance problems** that could lead to equipment damage, loss of profits, and safety hazards.

Often the information gathered by the onboard computer can warn mechanics that a system is close to failure. It's almost always less costly to prevent a breakdown than to repair one. If the data shows that a truck system is not performing up to par, the mechanics can look into it and make adjustments. You can see how such a system would improve vehicle performance, and profits.

The **trip over/short/damage report** is helpful to your carrier. It enables your carrier to have a **detailed list of** your **overages, shortages, and any damage to the freight**. This report will help your carrier provide and maintain good customer service.

Another report that is especially helpful to your carrier is the **state mileage report**. The report that is generated is very **handy at tax time**. It shows the following information:

- number of gallons of fuel purchased in each state
- total miles driven in each state with and without a load
- total miles driven on toll roads and on regular roads

The **driver's expense report is** a report that is really helpful to the driver. It lets you keep **a detailed record of your expenses**. From the data you enter, the main computer will generate a report that tells you your total trip expenses and then breaks that total into useful categories like fuel, oil, food, and motels. Having the computer keep track of all this detail is certainly a lot **easier,** a lot **more efficient,** and a lot **less time consuming than** keeping **a written record on a piece of paper that gets lodged between the seat and the backrest of your cab.**

Replacing Your Log Book

An important report, and one that you will really appreciate, is the report on your hours of service—your log book. Taking care of the log book is a time-consuming job. Many drivers would like to eliminate it from their workload. Well, it can't be eliminated, but it can be made a whole lot easier with the use of an onboard computer.

A driver log book option has been designed to simplify keeping a log book. It's an automatic computer option which has been designed to work with the onboard computer. It lets the driver keep a log book at the push of a few buttons. Drivers are quick to learn just how simple and accurate this new option can be.

Companies who now use the electronic log book are impressed with what it can do. It does not make the same errors people often make in the course of a busy day. **Eliminating errors** can increase the company's hours of service. This is good for company profits. Computer log books greatly reduce the amount of time spent filling out logs by hand. Time is money. **Saving time** increases profits.

When duty status changes, a driver may feel that sleep is far more important than filling out a log book. And before that well deserved rest, a hot meal would relieve the tension of the day. Fatigue and hunger can tempt some drivers to put off filling out the log book.

Although this is easy to understand, it is not a wise choice. Most drivers agree that the easiest and best way to take care of the log book is to fill it out as you travel along. Drivers who let information back up almost always forget one thing or another. Experienced drivers who have onboard computers and log book programs say taking care of the logs is easier than it has ever been. Electronic logs can go even further in helping you by alerting you to potential hours of service violations before they happen.

The daily logs provided by the computer are very detailed. All vehicle and driver activity is documented. Status changes which take place are reported to the nearest minute.

Operation of this computer option could not be made easier. Simply enter the three items of information listed below:

- duty status
- identification
- location

The computer takes over from there. It reports all duty status changes until the driver logs off at the end of the trip. You can also enter other, equally important information. When you stop, you can enter your location, why you stopped, and for how long. At the end of your trip, it's possible for printed copies of your reports to be ready soon after you've finished parking your vehicle.

ELECTRONIC LOGS AND DOT REGULATIONS

The log book reports generated by onboard computers fulfill DOT requirements. However, you must still know how to fill out a log book by hand. Even if you have an electronic log book on board, you must still have paper log book supplies with you. If the computer breaks down, you must log your time by hand. Regulations do not accept a broken computer as an excuse for failing to have a current log. Also, if your company is found to have too many hours of service violations, the law can require all the drivers to return to handwritten logs.

Computers in Trucking

Today, critical information is collected and made available for use using any or all of these devices:

- onboard computers
- portable computers
- cellular phones

ONBOARD COMPUTERS

The **latest onboard computers** record much the same data as before, only with more accuracy, more detail, and often less input from the driver. Some systems **use satellites and global positioning technology** (GPS) to pinpoint the vehicle's precise location. To generate a state mileage report, for example, a driver used to have to enter a code at each state line crossing. With GPS, this information is entered automatically. All the driver has to do is to confirm the information later.

The systems can store much larger amounts of information internally. Depending on the system, instead of cartridges, data is transmitted by

- wireless communication
- direct cable connection
- handheld devices
- removable memory cards

Communication between the company and the truck **can be two-way, and almost instantaneous.** The in-truck system can advise the dispatcher if drivers are on schedule. Route and cargo information can be sent to the drivers to keep them on track or reroute them around unforeseen obstacles.

The onboard computer pictured in Figure 11-2 shows a system with an alphanumeric (letters and numbers) keyboard that the driver can use to communicate with the dispatcher. This system also has a display that transmits alerts from the dispatcher back to the driver. The onboard computer shown in Figure 11-3 on the next page pictures a touch screen which lets the driver input data. The system will prompt the driver through the process of entering information.

fig. 11-2
This onboard computer offers the driver an alphanumeric keypad for making detailed entries. The display advises the driver about messages that have been sent to or received from the dispatcher.

Onboard **computers** can do more than simply record information from the vehicle's systems. They can **relay instructions back to the vehicle.** For example, managers may study driver performance reports only to find that some drivers have a habit of speeding, or idling too long. Both practices are fuel-wasters, and speeding is unsafe. The computer can be used to program the vehicle not to exceed a preset speed as long as the truck is in gear, or to shut off the engine after a certain period of idling. (That the drivers have undesirable habits is not likely to be forgotten by the managers who read the reports!)

PORTABLE COMPUTERS

Today's truck drivers tote around the same laptop computers that desk jockeys and college students use. Well, they're not exactly the same. Trucker's **laptops** are "hardened"—able to take the bounces and jolts that come with riding in a cab. They can handle being exposed to harsh chemicals, extremes in temperature, moisture, greases, and vapors. They're also outfitted with displays that work well in less-than-optimal lighting conditions. Their operating systems are specially designed to work with the type of software that the industry uses. However, like consumer laptops, they can give you access to the Internet. You can use commonly-available software to write letters, manage your checkbook, and even entertain yourself.

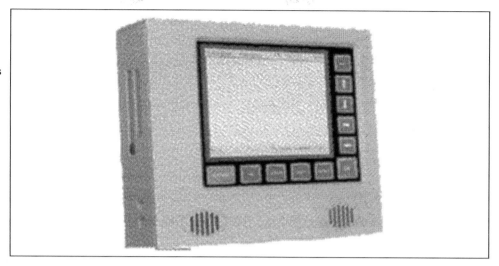

fig. 11-3
With this onboard computer, part of the Cadec Mobius TTS system, the driver makes entries using a touch screen. Messages displayed on the screen prompt the driver through the data-entry process.

You'll see laptop computers in the yard, too. Some systems will use wireless connections to transmit data from the onboard computer while you are still on the road. However, many will wait for you to reach a terminal, **connect your onboard computer to a laptop** by a cable and download—collect—the information that way.

HANDHELD DEVICES

Truckers are increasingly finding **handheld devices** in their toolkits. Equipped with memory and bar code scanners, these devices are especially **helpful at pickup and delivery** points. Data collected by the handheld can be transmitted wirelessly to the onboard computer to be used in the trip over/short/damage report, for example. This is faster, easier, and more accurate than entering the information using the onboard computer's keypad. Or, you may use a tablet computer. Instead of jotting notes on a small notepad, you'll write them on the tablet with a stylus, a special electronic pen, and the computer will store the information for later retrieval.

Personal data assistants (PDAs) are small computers that fit in the hand. Smaller than even laptops, they can still hold huge amounts of information, like your entire address book, calendar, manuals, and maps, with room to spare.

The functions of all three items—the scanner-equipped handheld, the tablet computer, and the PDA—are sometimes combined into one powerful and convenient piece of equipment.

Another common handheld device is the cellular phone. The cellular phone hasn't put the CB radio completely out of business. However, for making long distance calls, a cell phone is often more convenient and less expensive than a landline connection. As **cell phones increasingly** come equipped with cameras, and able to respond to voice commands, they **become even more useful**.

Onboard Computers and the Future

As you've seen, simple onboard computer systems were designed to read and record data from the three gauges listed below:

- tachometer
- odometer
- speedometer

More complex systems monitor these three gauges and can gather a variety of other information. To the many examples we have already listed, you can add engine water temperature and oil pressure. Going even further, sophisticated systems can control the starter, door locks, lights—even the wipers and the horn. Using GPS, it's possible to program trailer doors to open only when the cargo has reached its destination.

More and more, devices are being equipped with GPS, wireless technology, voice recognition, and video capabilities. Instead of making an entry into your electronic log by pushing a button or hitting a key, you may simply speak the words, "On Duty." A truck-mounted video camera could let you see into blind spots or keep you centered in a lane. Your truck may be equipped to exchange data wirelessly every time it passes a "hot spot" that can receive and transmit. Using such a system, mechanics could diagnose a problem with your truck while you're still on the road. Wireless and GPS **technology can** keep you in constant contact with your home terminal, **offer**ing you **greater comfort, safety, and security** while you're out on that lonely highway.

Chapter 11 Quiz

1. The computer is a more efficient way to take care of paperwork, but it's also more costly.
   A. True
   B. False

2. In _____, computers are used to write letters and generate promotional materials.
   A. Sales
   B. Maintenance
   C. Dispatch
   D. Billing

3. Two main purposes of the onboard computer are to monitor vehicle performance and _____.
   A. idling time
   B. fuel temperature
   C. driver performance
   D. engine water temperature

4. The parts of the onboard computer that monitor vehicle and driver performance are called the _____.
   A. gauges
   B. sensors
   C. cartridges
   D. trackers

5. The part of the onboard computer that stores the data is called the _____.
   A. input device
   B. download cable
   C. recorder
   D. sensor

6. Even the simplest onboard computer can read and record data from all the truck's systems.
   A. True
   B. False

7. The _____ report shows engine idling time.
   A. trip over/short/damage
   B. state mileage
   C. driver's expense
   D. driving performance

8. Although an onboard electronic log book is more efficient and more accurate, experienced drivers say it's easier to do log books by hand.
   A. True
   B. False

9. Drivers with electronic log books still need to know how to fill out a log book by hand.
   A. True
   B. False

10. An onboard computer that monitors idling time can help a
_____.
   A. motor carrier increase sales
   B. driver improve performance
   C. driver get more rest
   D. driver with log books

CHAPTER 12
TYPES OF TRAILERS

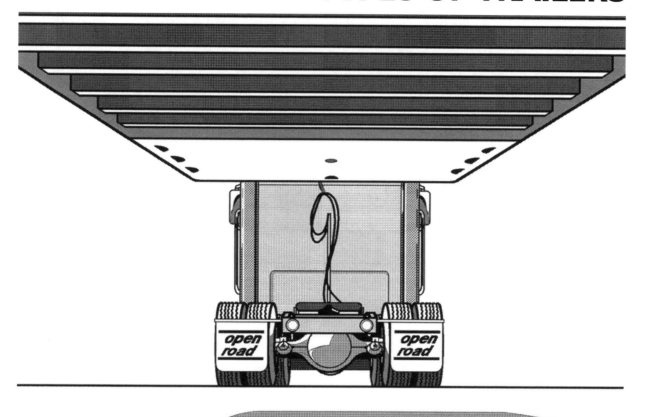

The Towed Unit

The first chapters in this book explored the power unit, the tractor. In the next three chapters we will turn our attention to the towed unit, the trailer.

As you must have noticed even before deciding to become part of the trucking industry, there are **many different types of trailers** on the road today. The simplest of these trailers is basically just a box container on wheels. You've seen these rolling boxes heading for the warehouse full of anything from shoes to television sets.

No doubt you've also noticed the refrigerated trailers that actually look like big freezers on wheels. Their job is to make sure fresh and frozen food stays that way during the trip. Another recognizable trailer type is the big tank. The tanks are filled with liquids and pressurized gases. Milk is carried in tanks, and so are flammable materials such as gasoline and other petroleum products.

Construction and Components

Transporting goods on the road calls for a **light, strong, flexible, and spacious container.** The materials used to build a trailer make a very big difference. They dictate how the equipment will operate and how long it will last. They also determine its weight, strength, and method of upkeep.

Steel, aluminum, wood, plastic, fiber glass, polyester, and stainless steel are the basic materials used in the construction of a trailer. Aluminum has replaced steel as the most common metal found in the van. A very notable **savings in weight can be achieved by using aluminum** for skin sheets, roof sheets, and frame rails.

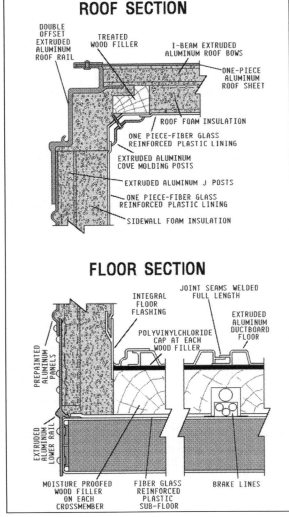

fig. 12-1
Van trailers are made of a variety of materials.

Many unseen parts may also be of aluminum—or even composite materials—including side posts, crossmembers, and roof bows. In some trailers, even the main frame rails are aluminum. However, aluminum is not the most practical metal for certain components. These parts must be as strong as possible.

Keep in mind that even though trailers come in many different shapes and sizes, they are made up of the same basic parts. They **all have running gear, a frame, and similar body construction.**

RUNNING GEAR
The **running gear includes** those parts that actually allow the trailer to be pulled down the road. To run, a trailer must have **tires,**

wheels, axles, brakes, and springs. Most trailers have **landing gear.** Some also have an optional assembly, the **sliding tandem,** which helps distribute weight.

Tires

Most commonly, trailers have dual tires on each brake drum. **Two tires are often required to support the weight** of the cargo. Also available are **extra wide tires.** One wide tire is made to carry the same load as duals.

These wide tires **are called super singles.** Super singles faded out for a while but they're coming back into popularity these days with weight savings more important than ever.

Wheels

As a general rule, **trailers use the same Daytons and Budds—spoke and disc wheels— as tractors.**

Axles

Most trailers have two axles. These axles are made very much like tractor axles. The big difference is that **trailer wheels are free-rolling rather than driven by the engine.**

Axles help support the weight of the trailer and the load. Most axles are built to carry the legal limit of 20,000 pounds each. Trailers that will be hauling very heavy loads will have two or more axles. Trailers that haul very light loads may need only one.

Brakes

Mechanically, the **trailer's brakes work the same way the tractor brakes do.** There are service brakes (air brakes) and emergency brakes (spring brakes). The trailer brakes have their own air tanks which are charged in response to a control in the tractor. The protection valve (TPV) separates the tractor air supply from the trailer air supply. Should there be a break in the trailer air lines, this valve would "protect" the tractor's air supply so at the least the tractor would still have braking power.

Suspension System

Suspension systems provide a smooth ride for driver and cargo by **absorbing bumps from the road.** These systems must be strong enough to **carry the weight of the cargo and to flex under the cargo's weight.**

A suspension system is used to **attach the axles to the trailer.** A trailer may be equipped with either a leaf spring or air ride suspension. Chapter 7 covers suspension systems in more detail.

```
OBSERVATION SKILLS TEST

Did you study the trailer you saw at the top of this chapter? What did you
observe? Check the Observation Skills Test Grid at the back of the book
to see how you did.
```

Sliding Tandems

The **slider assembly** allows the driver to slide the tandems back and forth to **adjust the wheelbase** of the trailer. This helps distribute the trailer weight correctly. In Chapter 23 we'll take a closer look at the slider assembly.

Landing Gear

Landing gear is sometimes called trailer supports or even dolly legs. The **landing gear holds up the front of the trailer when the trailer isn't hooked to the tractor.** It is usually cranked into place with a crank found on the side of the trailer. The crank has a low gear and a high gear. Use the high gear when no trailer weight rests on the landing jacks.

Aerodynamic Options

Since the early 1970s when the price of fuel flew skyward and kept going, trucking companies have been making their trailers, as well as their tractors, more **fuel efficient.** Sometimes a wind foil device is added to the top front wall of the trailer. This directs the flow of air over the top and around the sides of the trailer. That way the trailer "slides" through the air with less resistance.

Front corners of vans are often rounded or tapered to **cut down on wind drag.** A smooth exterior skin is another important design factor. The search for more fuel-efficient trailer design continues. During your career with the trucking industry, you are bound to see more interesting discoveries in the area of aerodynamics.

FRAME

The main beams and stringers of a trailer are made of steel or aluminum. It is the job of the **beams and stringers to support the load.**

Inside or Outside Rails

Inside rail trailers have supporting beams near the middle of the trailer. Most vans and reefers and some platform trailers have an inside rail. Other platform trailers have outside rails. They both provide about the same level of support. Outside rails provide perhaps a somewhat stiffer trailer. The choice often comes down to a matter of personal preference, much like the choice between cabover and conventional tractors.

fig. 12-2
Inside rails (A) and outside rails (B) provide about an equal amount of support.

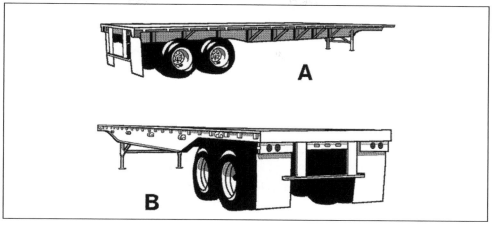

Kingpin

The kingpin is located underneath the front of the trailer in the middle of the bed plate, which is a metal plate attached to the frame. It will often be made of high strength steel or another alloy. Pure aluminum is too light and flexible.

When a tractor is backed underneath the trailer, the **kingpin slides through the slot up to the center of the fifth wheel.** At that point, the locking jaws lock into place and hold the kingpin into position so that it cannot slide forward or backward but is able to turn freely.

BULKHEAD, FLOOR, WALL, AND DOOR CONSTRUCTION

Bulkhead

The **bulkhead** is the short wall on the front edge of a platform trailer. It **keeps whatever you're hauling from sliding too far forward.** In an emergency stop, the bulkhead must hold the cargo back so that it won't slam into the tractor and possibly injure the driver.

Flooring

Depending on what the trailer is used for, the **trailer floor can be made of various materials.** A popular choice is hardwood flooring made of narrow strips of wood. Another common flooring is a ribbed aluminum, found in refrigerated trailers. Besides giving strength to the metal, the ribbing allows air to circulate around the cargo.

The Camber Design

Even though platform trailers must be very strong, they must also be very light. Use of aluminum in the construction has helped trailers meet these two requirements.

However, aluminum is one of the lightest, most flexible metals. It is so flexible that the trailer will flex as it goes down the road. Some of the lightweight platform trailers will twist, bend, and flex to an amazing degree.

To compensate for this flexing, some trailers have a **built-in arch.** This is what's known as "camber." The camber is very easy to see when the trailer is empty. When the trailer is loaded, its weight will flatten the camber.

fig. 12-3
A cambered platform trailer is not truly flat, but rather has a slight arch to it. It will flatten out under the weight of the load.

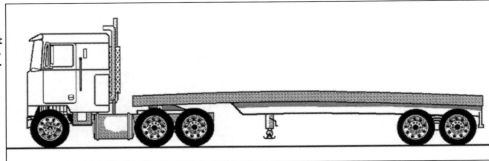

Walls
The interior of a van may be smooth or ribbed, depending on what it was meant to haul. Interior lining may be made in panels or all in one piece.

The **walls** of a trailer begin with studs that go from the floor to the ceiling. This **develops the basic frame of the trailer.** The studs are covered by plywood or heavy plastic. Plastic can take more of a beating from forklifts or cargo, but it is generally more expensive than plywood.

The inside lining of a refrigerated van is usually of pre-painted aluminum sheets which may be smooth or ribbed. The ribbed sheets are known to allow air better circulation around the cargo. Note that whatever the material used for the inside walls, it must meet health standards to qualify for hauling food products. Fiber glass is popular for just that reason. It is nonporous and very easy to keep clean.

Reefer walls are of the interior post design. As you might expect, refrigerated vans must be well insulated, with several inches of foam insulation poured into the space between the inside panels and outside sheets.

Ceiling
A trailer's **ceiling is very much like** its **walls.** That is, outside studs are covered by sheet metal or aluminum while inside studs are covered by plywood or plastic.

The basic construction of vans and refrigerated trailers is very similar. However, a van has no wall or ceiling insulation unless it is an insulated van. As mentioned earlier, the refrigerated trailer is heavily enveloped with a high-quality insulation.

Exterior Skin
The **side wall design** of the common van is **often the exterior post design.** This design has side posts with pre-painted aluminum sheets attached to the

inside of the post. This makes a simple, lightweight wall but leaves the side posts exposed to create wind drag.

Why not put the posts inside the van? Well, then they are at the mercy of forklifts and cargo. Sometimes they are left exposed but often a liner is added for protection.

Roof

The roof of most trailers is made of large aluminum sheets. Leaks are then not such a problem as with roofs that have many seams.

In some trailers the sheets are stretched across roof bows. The bows are then fastened on both sides to the trailer's upper frame rails. The roof is bonded to the roof bows with an adhesive material. A stronger type of trailer roof uses roof carlins. The sheets are riveted to the carlins, which are then riveted to the upper frame rails.

Doors

Swinging doors are the **most popular** doors for trailers. Such doors are hinged on the rear outside edges of the trailer. Refrigerated and moving vans often have a small door on the side of the trailer, which comes in handy when

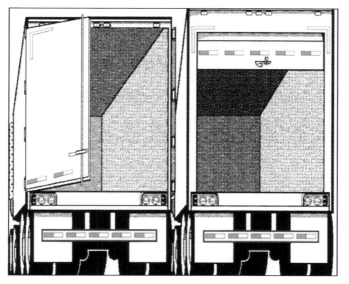

fig. 12-4
Swinging doors provide a better seal than roll-up doors, but roll-up doors don't have to be opened before you reach the dock.

unloading in narrow streets or alleyways. At any rate, a side swinging door works in the same way a rear door works. A lever holds it tight against the trailer frame. A rubber seal around the door keeps out dust, rain or snow. With insulated and refrigerated trailers, the seal also keeps the inside temperature steady.

Another popular type of door **is the roll-up.** Like a garage door, it is built with tracks on runners. You open it by pulling up on the handle and sliding it up to lie along the ceiling. When closed, a lever on the door hooks to the floor to keep it shut.

A roll-up doesn't seal as well as a swinging door, so it is rarely used on a refrigerated trailer when a steady temperature must be maintained. The roll-up is used mostly on trailers that deliver in the city.

One advantage of a roll-up door over a swinging door is that you can back up to the dock before the roll-up door is opened. That's handy for trucks that load or unload many times a day. Swinging doors must be opened before the trailer gets to the dock.

Fasteners and Hardware

For the most part, **securing cargo on platform trailers is done with ropes, chains, or nylon straps.** Tarps are used to cover the loads when required. Once again, it depends on the cargo. At any rate, the fasteners and hardware used in or on a trailer are accessory equipment. You will find all you need to know on the subject in Chapter 28, Loading, Unloading, and Securing Cargo.

Lights, Wiring, and Air System

LIGHTS AND WIRING

All of the **lights on a trailer are connected to the tractor's electrical system.** They include clearance lights, turn signals, parking lights, and brake lights. When you turn on any of these lights in the tractor, the same trailer lights will go on. The wires that control these lights are in the tractor electrical cord, commonly called the pigtail. The pigtail attaches to the trailer at an outlet in the front of the trailer.

Picture the electrical wiring system. One wire runs up from the outlet to the top of the trailer to power the front clearance lights. Several wires grouped into a cable run the length of the trailer to power the rear lights. Halfway down the trailer is a junction in the cable where two wires reach to the sides to power the side marker lamps. Finally, the cable separates at the rear of the trailer where it branches out to the various rear lights. This cable also powers the ABS system.

fig. 12-5
A typical pigtail configuration. Each circuit is color coded.

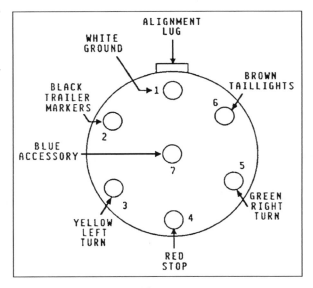

Light bulbs and wiring connections are in some ways rather delicate. As a trailer gets along in years, these will loosen and corrode. There really isn't much you can do to avoid the problem other than being aware of it and fixing whatever you have to as it occurs.

AIR SYSTEM CONNECTIONS

The **tractor also furnishes air pressure to operate the trailer brakes.** Next to the electrical outlet at the front of the trailer are two air couplings. These are commonly known as "glad hands."

One glad hand provides air to the service brakes, which use air pressure only when the brakes are being applied. The other glad hand provides air to the emergency brake, which is pressurized at all times.

Seals in the glad hands keep air from escaping when the system is pressurized. The glad hands are color coded to prevent mistakes when you connect the air lines from the tractor to the two glad hands on the trailer. The service line is colored blue and the control or emergency line is colored red.

The trailer's air lines begin in front and move underneath the floor to the rear where they are connected to all the valves and tanks that make up the trailer air brake system.

Chapter 12 Quiz

1. Of the following, _____ are NOT standard equipment on every trailer.
    A. suspensions
    B. frames
    C. axles
    D. side doors

2. Most commonly, trailers have _____ tires on each drum.
    A. studded
    B. super single
    C. dual
    D. recapped

3. The crank on the landing gear has more than one gear.
    A. True
    B. False

4. The trailer's _____ must carry the weight of the cargo and be able to flex under the weight of the load.
    A. dual tires
    B. suspension system
    C. disc or spoke wheels
    D. axles

5. In terms of support, outside rails are _____ inside rails.
   A. stronger than
   B. about the same as
   C. not as good as
   D. more flexible than

6. In the middle of the bed plate is the _____.
   A. kingpin
   B. air bag suspension system
   C. front axle
   D. leaf suspension system

7. The purpose of the bulkhead is to _____.
   A. maintain good air circulation to the cargo
   B. insulate the trailer
   C. keep the cargo from sliding into the tractor
   D. make unloading easier

8. With the exterior post design, _____.
   A. exposed side posts create wind drag
   B. the posts may be damaged by cargo and forklifts
   C. the side posts are connected to the roof bows
   D. an adhesive material seals the fiber glass rivets to the exterior skin

9. When the driver turns on the tractor's clearance lights, _____.
   A. the pigtail disconnects from the glad hands
   B. the glad hands disconnect from the pigtail
   C. the trailer's clearance lights go on
   D. the trailer's clearance lights go off

10. The service air line glad hand on the front of the trailer is colored blue.
    A. True
    B. False

CHAPTER 13

SPECIALIZED RIGS

A Trailer for Every Type of Cargo

Trailers are alike in many ways. They **all have axles, wheels, floors, and some method of attaching to tractors.** On the other hand, because each kind of trailer is **designed to haul a particular cargo,** trailers are also different in some important ways.

There are both "semitrailers" and "full trailers." Here is the difference between the two. When a semitrailer is attached to the tractor, part of its weight rests on the tractor. Not so with a full trailer. No part of a full trailer rests on the tractor. People sometimes refer to them as simply "trailers." Be aware of the official difference between the two, but for our purposes in this chapter they'll all be called trailers.

The **federal height limit for trailers is 13 feet, 6 inches** measured from the highest point on the tractor or trailer to the ground or road surface. Some western states allow heights of up to 14 feet. However, there are restricted clearances in some older cities such as New York, Chicago, and Boston so that not every trailer can go everywhere in the country.

We're now going to take a close look at the many trailer designs. Because you don't always know what sort of cargo you will find yourself hauling, it's important to become familiar with all trailer types, and to understand why they happen to be built the way they are.

Vans

Most trailers you see on the road are vans. These vans are simply **enclosed containers on wheels.** They vary according to what sort of cargo they will transport. There is a van for just about every type of cargo you can imagine.

THE DRY FREIGHT VAN

One of the most common types of van is the dry freight van. This is the **plain enclosed box** on wheels. Dry freight vans haul appliances, clothing, furniture, potato chips, and any number of other items. Whatever is hauled in a dry freight van, it won't be anything that must be maintained in a precise temperature range.

THE INSULATED VAN

However, when North Dakota potatoes need some protection from cold weather during shipment, they are hauled in an insulated van. An insulated van is simply a dry freight van with insulated walls and ceiling. The insulation **helps maintain a certain temperature range without further refrigeration.**

THE REFRIGERATED VAN

A refrigerated van is often referred to as a "reefer." A reefer has a refrigeration unit and a great deal of insulation to **maintain precise temperatures.** It is used to haul food and other perishable items. Frozen foods are hauled in nothing but reefers.

The **refrigeration unit** is built into the trailer itself. Being separate, it **requires separate maintenance.** The driver of a refrigerated van will carefully watch the reefer unit's controls and thermostat during the trip.

The unit also has its own fuel tank to be filled and its own engine to be inspected from time to time.

Reefers usually have aluminum ribbed flooring. The floor's ribbing allows the refrigerated air to circulate around the load. Otherwise, the cargo won't stay at the desired temperature, which naturally is the whole purpose of the refrigeration. The next chapter takes a very detailed look at the all-important refrigerated van.

fig. 13-1
A selection of the most common trailer designs.

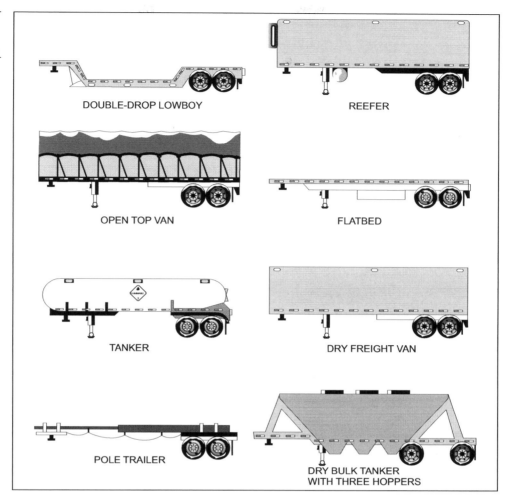

DOUBLE-DROP LOWBOY

REEFER

OPEN TOP VAN

FLATBED

TANKER

DRY FREIGHT VAN

POLE TRAILER

DRY BULK TANKER
WITH THREE HOPPERS

The Platform Trailer

After vans, platforms are the **next largest class of trailer** on the road today. Platforms are used to **haul heavy goods** such as construction equipment, lumber and pipe **that does not need to or cannot easily be loaded into vans.**

Platform trailers will sometimes be referred to as flatbeds. Whatever you decide to call them, they are very versatile and very popular. Their simplicity makes them useful for so many kinds of freight.

The standard platform trailer is a long, level deck mounted on a chassis. There are many variations on the flatbed. Some have removable sides attached to the installed stakes. The sides are usually sheets of 4-by-8 foot plywood. When not in use, they are stored on the front of or underneath the trailer. To strengthen the side walls, support bows attach to the top of each side. When a tarp is used to cover the cargo, it is held in place by the support bows.

The frame of a platform will sometimes vary. It may also be modified with certain equipment to make it more practical for hauling special goods. There is an extendable flatbed trailer that can stretch to accommodate extra long loads.

A forklift or crane is used to load and unload flatbed cargo. The cargo is secured by using some type of tie-down, either rope, strap, or chain. Other load-holding devices can be used, the type depending on the cargo. The top of the cargo is often covered by a tarp for added security and to protect it from the weather.

The floor of the platform trailer is usually made of wood like the dry freight van. However, it is built to support much heavier loads on a smaller area and is therefore a stronger floor than that of the dry freight van.

THE DROP-FRAME TRAILER, OR LOWBOY

The drop-frame, or lowboy, is simply **a flatbed with smaller diameter wheels or wheel wells to achieve a lower deck height.** It may have a single-drop deck or a double-drop deck. Besides making it possible to carry taller freight, the lowboy has a lower center of gravity than standard trailers. That adds stability for the heavier and taller loads. The lowboy is considered the heavyweight of the trailers. It is used to haul extremely heavy equipment such as cranes, bulldozers, and all sorts of machinery.

Some lowboys have built-in ramps that may be swung down to the ground for loading or unloading. The ramp is locked in place when not in use. Other lowboys use the "beaver tail" design with a rear section of the trailer sloped toward the ground as a ramp. Also, hydraulic ramps may be built into the trailer.

The Outrigger

Outriggers are something like the leaves added to the dining room table when company comes. They are used with lowboys and other kinds of drop-frame trailers to **add additional width to each side.** However, this added width will put your vehicle over the legal width limits and will require a special permit.

The Double-drop

A double-drop trailer is used to haul very tall cargo or heavy equipment. The deck of the double-drop is still lower than that of the single-drop. In fact, its deck is lower than the top of the rear wheels. Because it is so close to the ground, it usually has no landing gear. When the tractor is unhooked, the trailer sits either on blocks or the ground.

One type of double-drop trailer is extendable and can be made longer if necessary.

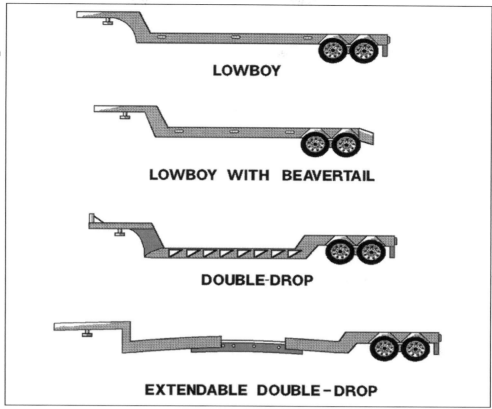

fig. 13-2
There are many different types of drop-frame trailers, each with its own special function.

Double-drop trailers are sometimes called goosenecks. One type, the **removable gooseneck,** detaches from the front of the deck. To load or unload, the gooseneck is unhooked and the tractor and gooseneck driven out of the way. Then machinery is driven on from the front of the trailer. When the trailer is loaded and ready to go, the tractor and gooseneck are backed into position. The gooseneck is hooked up and the unit is ready to roll.

Another gooseneck, the **folding gooseneck,** folds down and forms a ramp on the front of the trailer. It makes loading and unloading equipment even easier than with the removable gooseneck.

The folding part of the **folding gooseneck may be mechanical or hydraulic.** Whichever it is, the gooseneck is folded up and locked into place after the equipment is loaded. As soon as the tractor is driven back under the trailer and hooked up, you're set to hit the road.

Disadvantages of the Drop-frame Trailer

With either the single or double-drop trailers **loading and unloading can be a bit more trouble.** If you have cargo to load you can't just back to a dock and drive a forklift from front to rear. Driving equipment on and off these trailers can be tricky. Be sure you never try to load equipment until you have been trained in loading procedures and know how to drive the equipment.

Another disadvantage is the drop-frame trailer's **lower ground clearance.** For example, the frame or crossmember system could get caught on railroad tracks or anything high enough from the road to get in the way. With experience you will learn to judge whether you can clear an obstacle. The best bet is to avoid railroad crossings you're unsure about. Sometimes you'll have to park your rig, get out, and "eyeball" the clearance just to be on the safe side.

OBSERVATION SKILLS TEST

You saw two different types of drop-deck trailers in the illustration that started this chapter. Can you describe them? Turn to the Observation Skills Test Grid at the end of the book to check your answers.

Tankers

Another major type of trailer is the tanker. Tankers are used to **carry different kinds of liquids or dry bulk,** depending on the design. Note that when CDL laws mention tank vehicles, they mean only those that haul liquids and gaseous materials. You'll need a Tank Endorsement on your CDL in order to haul liquid loads in a tank trailer.

Among the liquid products hauled by tankers are petroleum products, acids, liquid chemicals, and liquified gas. They also haul many edible products such as milk, cooking oils, and even water.

Dry bulk tankers (sometimes called "bulkers") are used to haul grains, sugar, and other powdered substances. They are also used for plastics, wood chips, animal food, and dry chemicals.

Generally, tankers are filled through an opening in the top of the trailer. They are unloaded through the bottom by gravity or air pressure. Liquid gases are either "pumped off" or unloaded by "pressure" gravity feed, depending on the cargo and the particular situation.

We'll look at what sort of load each of these tankers was designed to carry, and at the special tankers used to haul hazardous materials.

THE LIQUID TANK TRAILER

Liquid tankers are available in either the **elliptical or cylindrical shape.** The elliptical is egg-shaped at the end and has the lowest center of gravity, while the cylindrical is round and considered the strongest and most versatile. There are also variations of these shapes since the liquids they haul have differing needs for drainage and weight distribution.

A liquid tanker may haul food, acids, petroleum products, or waste materials. It may be of steel, stainless steel, or aluminum. The inside of a tanker is sometimes coated with a substance to enable the tanker to withstand the harsh chemicals it will haul. It may be insulated for temperature control. Heaters are also available.

There are smooth bore tankers, compartmented liquid tankers, baffled tankers, and pressurized compartmented liquid tankers.

THE SMOOTH BORE TANKER

As the name implies, the **inside** of a smooth bore tanker **is smooth and rounded.** This tanker is sometimes referred to as a "clean bore" tanker. Its shape may be elliptical or cylindrical. It may be made of steel, stainless steel, or aluminum. Whatever it is made of, the tanker is **designed for easy cleaning.** This makes it possible to haul a load of mineral water to New Orleans, get your tanker cleaned, and haul a load of molasses back to Santa Fe.

Another great advantage of the smooth bore tanker is that with nothing to obstruct the flow out of the tanker, it **unloads very easily.**

When it's important for the cargo to stay warm during the trip, a smooth bore tanker will be insulated. Or sometimes heaters are used to keep the substance warm during the trip. A steel insulated tanker can haul materials as hot as 500 degrees F. or as cold as -350 degrees F.

The smooth bore tanker is designed to carry one particular cargo at a time. Because it is a long hollow tube with no sharp corners, it is easy to clean. Milk trucks, which by law must be kept spotlessly clean and germ-free, are almost always smooth bore tankers.

Many chemicals must be carried in lined or coated liquid tankers, while for others extra thick metal will do. However, always remember that lined tankers have no baffles. That means you must be aware of the **surge factor.** When you haul 6,000 gallons of **liquid cargo, it will surge and slosh each time you brake, shift gears, or go around a corner.** The force of that much liquid can be enough to send your rig in unexpected directions, and that could be dangerous. This force is called the surge factor. There are stories about truckers whose rigs have actually been shoved forward into intersections by the surge factor.

A partial, liquid load creates bad surge conditions. When the vehicle is 80 percent full, the surge factor is at its worst. The vehicle has less traction than it would have with a full load. The liquid load is heavy enough for weight to be a factor, and the empty space allows the load to surge. The tanker is safer at 90 percent full. There is more liquid and more weight, but less room for it to move around. At 40 percent full, the load is not heavy enough to present a great danger of surge.

THE COMPARTMENTED TANKER

Sometimes smooth bore tankers are divided into **compartments. These allow more than one type of product to be carried at the same time.** For example, a compartmented tanker would allow you to haul both diesel fuel and gasoline in one trip.

THE BAFFLED TANKER

Putting **baffles** in a liquid tanker **helps reduce liquid surge.** Baffles are partitions that simply **break up the tank area into smaller areas.** This controls forward and backward liquid surge. However side-to-side liquid surge is still possible. Make turns and take curves with caution.

There is a hole at the top of the baffle that allows air movement through the trailer. The hole on the bottom allows the liquid to flow through for unloading. The middle hole is big enough that a person can crawl inside for cleaning. A tanker may have several baffles, creating corners and joints that must be kept clean enough for the products being shipped.

When loading a compartmented liquid tanker, pay attention to weight distribution. Be careful not to put too much weight in either the front or rear compartments.

fig. 13-3
Baffles in the trailer on the left control the movement of liquid cargo. Compartments in the trailer on the right completely separate different types of liquids.

THE DRY BULK TANKER

Granular materials or powders like cement or plastic pellets **are hauled in dry bulk tankers.** A dry bulk tanker might have one to three cone-shaped compartments. At the bottom of each compartment is a hopper through which the cargo flows to unload. This is the gravity method of unloading. The compartments of this type of tanker are open at the top. Some dry bulk tankers are pressurized to force the cargo out during unloading. The top of such a tanker is closed. For unloading, the cargo is blown through the pipes.

Dry bulk tankers have a high center of gravity. Take care on curves and avoid making sharp turns.

THE PRESSURIZED TANKER

Pressurized tankers are made to haul pressurized goods. The pressure **keeps such gases as oxygen, hydrogen, and butane in their liquid form.**

Each product has its own requirements so that there are many different types of pressurized tankers. There are some substances, among them missile fuel and nuclear waste, that are shipped in nothing but special tankers that have been designed and constructed for that purpose alone.

LIQUID HAZARDOUS MATERIALS

Hazardous material must be carried in a tanker that meets codes set by the Department of Transportation. The tanker will be inspected periodically to make sure it meets the standards for the material it carries.

To haul hazardous materials, you must have a special Hazardous Materials Endorsement on your CDL. And it's likely your employer will give you more training. The training will stress all the proper handling and shipping procedures to assure your own health and safety and that of everyone around you. You'll be taught how to handle emergencies. Emergencies include not only accidents with your rig but leaks and spills of the hazardous material. Chapter 30 on hazardous materials will take a much closer look at this very important subject.

Special Trailers

As you can see, trailer design is endlessly varied even among the most typical. Let's have a quick look at some of the common "special" trailers and what they are used for.

THE AUTO TRANSPORT

One special trailer is the auto transport. This trailer is always very noticeable on the highway with its full load of shiny new cars. The auto transport design **has a double- or triple-deck hydraulic frame and ramps for loading and unloading.** These trailers are generally designed by the car companies themselves and change to suit the changing automobile styles.

THE CONTAINER

When many **small items are packed into one large container and then the container is shipped,** it is called container shipping. A number of shippers have found that container shipping is easier and that the goods are kept safer. Containers are also called containerized freight, sea/land containers, or overseas dry freight containers. The entire van body may be packed with cargo, then hauled by truck to the loading dock where the container itself is removed from the trailer and loaded on a ship for its trip overseas. So despite the fact that the cargo is going from warehouse to truck to dock to yet another dock to truck again and finally to its destination, the container is filled and emptied only once.

A container is a van body without a chassis. The trailer is a chassis without a van body. The trailer frame is I-shaped. At the ends of the frame are two crossmembers which support the ends of the container. Containers are lifted onto the frame by a crane or forklift and then locked into place by large pins on each corner.

THE DUMP TRAILER

Chances are very good that you played with a toy dump trailer as a child and are familiar with how they work. In real life, dump trailers are from 20 to 40 feet long. They are used for sand and gravel operations, and for rock hauling. The tractor that pulls a dump trailer must have a PTO and a wet kit to raise the dump bed.

THE FURNITURE (OR "WAREHOUSE") VAN

The furniture van is the popular choice of the moving industry. This van **features a drop in the floor just behind the bed plate** which gives much more space. The drop design also **makes loading and unloading easier.**

THE ELECTRONICS VAN

This van looks much like the furniture van but the floor drop is not as deep. It was designed especially **to transport delicate electronics equipment** and usually features air ride suspension.

THE LIVESTOCK TRAILER

It's easy to recognize livestock trailers, with their double- or triple-deck loads of livestock. These trailers are like vans except **they have slotted sides which let in air** as well as lend some support to the animals during the ride.

Livestock trailers are not much easier to pull when unloaded than they are when loaded. When empty, the slotted sides of the livestock trailer catch and trap the air flow, making it the opposite of aerodynamic. Also, livestock can move around in the trailer if they're not blocked in. Their movements can shift the center of gravity and make rollover more likely.

THE WEDGE VAN

The wedge van makes use of every available inch of precious cargo space. You'll recall in the beginning of this chapter we said that the maximum height for semitrailers is 13½ feet. This represents the measurement from the ground to the highest point of the load when the trailer is coupled. Due to the height of the fifth wheel, the nose of the trailer is usually slightly higher than the rear of the trailer. The wedge configuration adds a tapered extension to the top of the rear of vans. The added cargo area created by **the wedge increases the cubic capacity of wedge vans.**

fig. 13-4
A wedge-shaped trailer gives you a few more inches of cargo space at the back without exceeding height limits.

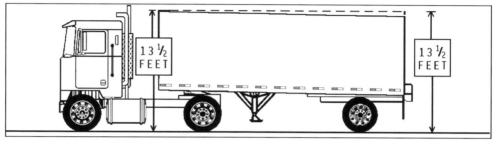

THE POLE TRAILER

This is the plainest trailer you can imagine. It is built specially **for hauling telephone poles and lengths of heavy pipe.** The front of this trailer is not much more than a rack (called a bunk) to hold cargo and a bed plate. At the rear is the running gear and wheels which have another rack attached. These two pieces are attached by a pole. This pole often will telescope. It can be lengthened or shortened to match the load.

THE SWINGING MEAT VAN

This type of van **features refrigeration, insulation, and special racks** from which sides of fresh meat are hung for shipment to market. It was once more popular than it is today. However, it is still common enough that new drivers should be aware of the special driving challenges presented by such vans. Like the surging liquid in a tanker, **swinging meat can** build up enough motion to **throw the van out of control.** To deal with the surge and high center of gravity, the driver of a swinging meat van soon learns to avoid sudden stops and fast, sharp turns.

Doubles and Triples

When a tractor pulls **two or even three trailers at the same time,** the rig is called doubles or triples. Or it might even be referred to as a "set of joints." Double and triple combination trailers are made of a semitrailer (part of its weight rests on the tractor) and one or two full trailers. The converter dolly is used to make semitrailers into full trailers. This is an assembly with a fifth wheel, at least one axle, a tongue, and safety chains.

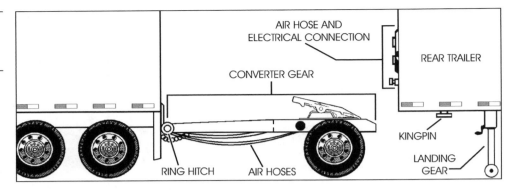

fig. 13-5
The converter dolly is sometimes called a con gear.

Pulling doubles and triples presents some driving challenges. These are covered fully in Chapter 21. If you can meet these challenges, you can pass the tests you must take for a Doubles/Triples Endorsement to your CDL. Without this endorsement, you are licensed to pull a single trailer only.

Chapter 13 Quiz

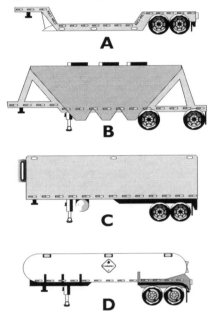

Refer to the picture at the right for Questions 1 through 5. Note that each of the trailers pictured has a letter. Put the letter of the trailer on the line next to the name that describes that trailer.

1. reefer _____

2. smooth bore tanker _____

3. double-drop trailer _____

4. dry freight van _____

5. dry bulk tanker _____

For Questions 6 though 10, match the cargo in Column B with the trailer in Column A that would likely haul that cargo.

Column A Types of Trailers
6. lowboy _____
7. reefer _____

8. compartmented tanker _____
9. livestock trailer _____
10. dry freight van _____

Column B Types of Cargo
A. a herd of Holstein cows
B. gallons of diesel fuel and gasoline
C. boxes of sweat shirts and sweat pants
D. a bulldozer
E. cartons of ice cream

CHAPTER 14

REFRIGERATED TRAILERS

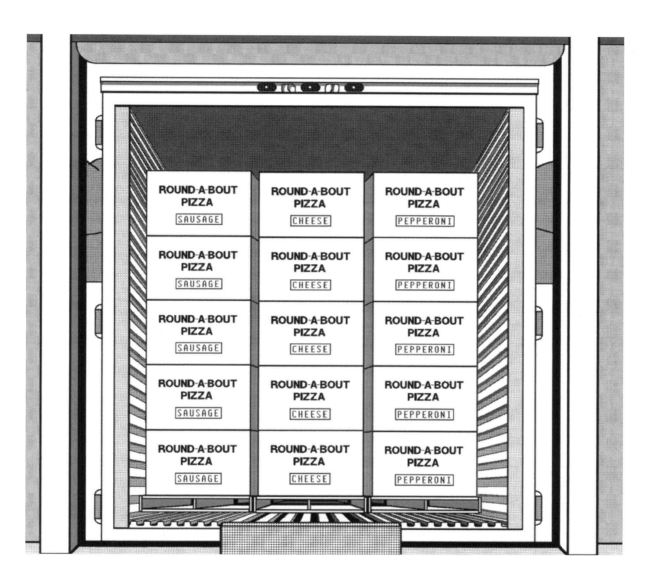

What's a Reefer?

A type of freight van is the refrigerated trailer. These trailers are many times referred to as "reefers."

Refrigerated vans are just that. The trailer has insulation in the walls, floor, and ceiling. The trailer has a refrigeration unit mounted on the trailer. The unit

maintains a steady temperature inside the trailer. This temperature can be varied **to suit the load being hauled.**

Typical Reefer Loads

A reefer is designed to haul **perishable or frozen** loads. It is also for **loads that must be kept from freezing.**

An example of a perishable load is fresh produce. Another example is milk. Milk must be kept at the proper temperature.

Frozen products are hauled in a reefer. The thermostat is set and the unit will keep the cargo at the proper freezing temperature. Examples of frozen products are frozen pizzas, ice cream, and TV dinners.

The third type of cargo for a reefer are those loads that must be kept from freezing. Some refrigeration units can heat the air in the trailer as well as cool the air. Later in this chapter, we'll give an example of when you might need to heat the cargo as well as cool it.

Construction of Trailer

Basic construction of a refrigerated van is very **similar to the dry freight van.** The framework of the walls are made up of studs. The outside wall is some type of metal sheeting. The inside wall is plastic sheeting or plywood. This is very much like a dry freight van.

The **differences** are mainly **in the insulation and flooring.**

INSULATION
To help keep a steady temperature inside the trailer, the walls, floors, and ceiling must be insulated. The insulation in a reefer is of good quality. The **floors, walls, and ceiling are insulated** as much as possible.

FLOORING
The floor in a refrigerated trailer is **ribbed aluminum.** It is **easy to clean** and wash. This is important because many times a reefer will carry food. Both the type of metal used and the ribbing play an important part in keeping the cargo at the proper temperature.

A reefer floor needs frequent cleaning, sometimes as often as after every load. Aluminum is easy to clean. A hose with good pressure will clean the floor quickly and easily. Sweeping out the ribbed aluminum floor isn't much harder

fig. 14-1
A ribbed aluminum floor in a reefer.

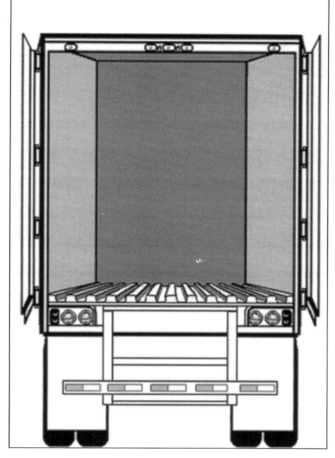

than a plywood floor. You simply have to make sure your broom has long bristles in order to get down into the ribbing.

Some types of fresh produce are packed in ice to keep them fresh longer. As the ice melts it drips on the floor. A plywood floor won't hold up if it gets wet very often. Frozen loads also may leave quite a bit of moisture on the floor. An aluminum floor can get wet with every load and not be ruined.

The ribs in the flooring help protect the cargo and pallets from this same water damage. The water collects in the bottom of the ribs and runs toward the rear of the trailer. Right inside the door jamb there are a few small holes in the floor. The water runs through these holes and outside onto the ground. This keeps the water from building up in the ribs. At the same time, the **ribs hold the pallets and cargo up out of the water.**

The ribbing has another important purpose besides protecting the load from water. It is very important that air be circulated around the load. That doesn't just mean over the top or around the sides. Air must be able to circulate underneath the load. The **ribbed floor allows air to circulate underneath the load.**

The loads hauled in this type trailer must be kept at a steady temperature. Each load will have a required temperature for the trip. The best way to keep the entire load at the proper temperature is for air to be able to circulate all the way around the load. Otherwise, the cargo on the bottom will not be at the proper temperature when the truck reaches its destination.

Proper loading procedures also help ensure an even temperature throughout the entire load. These are covered in Chapter 28.

DOORS

Reefers are most likely to have **swinging rear doors.** This type provides the best seal, helping to maintain the temperature inside. You may see an even smaller door in the rear door. This is for ventilation. Between loads, you can drive with this smaller door open, which helps air out the inside. Sometimes these trailers will also have a side door.

Refrigeration Unit Operation

A refrigerated trailer is equipped with a refrigeration unit. The term reefer, which is often used to describe the trailer, is also used when talking about the refrigeration unit itself.

PURPOSE OF THE REFRIGERATION UNIT

The refrigeration unit **cools or heats** the air that is in the trailer to keep the load at a steady temperature. There's a different temperature that's best for each type of cargo. The reefer unit is equipped with a thermostat which will start the cooling process when the temperature in the trailer gets too high. It then stops cooling when the proper temperature is reached.

It's important to remember that the purpose of the reefer is to **maintain a given temperature** inside the van. Reefers are **not** designed **to cool down the product itself** to a certain temperature. Before you load the cargo, make sure it is already at the proper temperature. Note the temperature on your shipping papers. If you assume the responsibility for cooling down a "hot" load, you may be asking for trouble.

HOW THE UNIT OPERATES

Let's take a look at the reefer unit in operation with a load of fresh produce. You're to pick up a load of fresh tomatoes, lettuce, and carrots in Pharr, Texas. The load is to be delivered to Grand Forks, North Dakota. It is the middle of January and North Dakota temperatures are 30 degrees below zero. The temperature in Pharr is 75 degrees.

The lettuce is packed with ice to cool it down quickly. The tomatoes and carrots are also packed in boxes. The trailer is loaded with the boxes of produce on pallets.

When you leave the dock, the refrigeration unit will be on to keep the load cool and as fresh as possible. Cool air circulates around the produce. All the way through Texas and Oklahoma the refrigeration unit cools the trailer.

In Kansas the outside temperature is about the same as inside the trailer. The outside temperature is about 40 degrees F. Since that is close to where the temperature inside the trailer is to be, the refrigeration unit won't be working very much.

You reach Sioux City, Iowa, where the temperature outside is ten degrees below zero. There is no danger that the outside temperature will cause the temperature inside the trailer to get too warm for the produce. The danger is that the temperature inside the trailer may go below the freezing point and ruin the produce. That is when the refrigeration unit needs to heat the trailer.

It doesn't heat the air to 70 degrees F. It keeps the air at the proper temperature. Because the air outside is so much colder, the air inside needs to be heated in order to keep the proper temperature.

All the way to Grand Forks, the unit will heat the air to keep the produce from freezing. You have been watching the temperature inside the trailer very closely all the way from Texas.

You back into the warehouse to deliver the produce. The lettuce is crisp and green. It hasn't been frozen. The tomatoes and carrots look good. You have done a good job of taking care of the cargo. You took the time to watch the refrigeration unit and check the temperature inside the trailer.

DESCRIPTION OF THE UNIT

The refrigeration unit itself is **mounted on the trailer.** It is usually mounted on the top half of the front wall of the trailer. There are many parts to the refrigeration unit. Let's discuss a few major components.

ENGINE. The refrigeration unit is run by a diesel engine. This engine is completely separate from the tractor engine. It has its own fuel tank and **requires regular maintenance** just as the tractor engine does.

COMPRESSOR. The compressor is an important part of the refrigeration system. It **pumps refrigerant to the coils in the reefer unit.** The whole system works quite a bit like the air conditioner or heat pump in your house.

FAN. The fan **circulates the cooled or heated air around the trailer.** The fan runs continuously when the engine is on.

FUEL TANK. The refrigeration unit is a separate and complete unit. As such, its diesel engine **has its own fuel tank.** It is usually mounted towards the front and underneath the trailer.

fig. 14-2
The refrigeration unit is usually mounted on the top half of the front of the trailer.

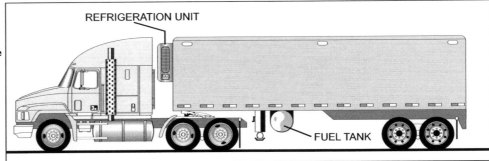
REFRIGERATION UNIT
FUEL TANK

Monitoring Unit Operation

The refrigeration unit knows how to maintain the temperature. It automatically will cool or heat the air inside the trailer to keep the proper temperature. All you have to do is **periodically check the temperature** and **make sure the unit works properly.** You can do this every time you inspect your vehicle, and every time you stop.

You can also do this while you're driving. Here's how. On the corner of the trailer is the cycle indicator. From the driver's seat, you can see it in your side mirror. Different lights will be lit for different cycles. A glance at the reflection of the indicator will tell you what cycle the unit is in.

Also, you can hear the sound of the unit's engine over the noise of the truck. Low speed simply sounds different from high speed. Over time, you'll learn simply to "hear" what cycle the unit is in.

MAINTENANCE OF THE UNIT

As we've said, the refrigeration unit's engine needs regular maintenance and periodic inspections just as the rest of the truck does. The DOT does not require you to inspect your reefer unit, but your company may have specific policies about it. A brief list of what should be inspected is as follows:

- Look for any physical damage.
- Check electrical connections and wires.
- Check fan drive belt condition and tension.
- Look for leaks of refrigerant or oil.
- Check coil and clean if needed.
- Check mounting bolts.
- Check oil level.
- Check coolant level.
- Clean defrost drains.

Controls

Each reefer unit **model has slightly different controls and starting procedures.** We'll describe one common unit. However before you start any reefer unit, be sure to **read the operator's manual** and follow the directions on the face plate of that particular unit.

The controls are found on the face of our typical refrigeration unit. There are three switches to start the unit. There is a temperature control or thermostat. The defrost switch and indicator allow you to put the unit into a defrost cycle manually. You'll see why you might want to do this later. Gauges on the face indicate how the unit operates and if anything is wrong. The cycle indicator we described earlier shows which cycle the unit is currently in.

STARTING AND STOPPING THE UNIT

There are several easy steps to start the engine and refrigeration unit. Beginning with the refrigeration unit switch in the "OFF" position, for one model of reefer the steps are:

- press and hold the pre-heater switch until it glows
- turn the refrigeration unit switch to the "ON" position
- release the pre-heater switch
- press the starter switch to start the engine
- adjust the thermostat to the proper temperature.

To stop the refrigeration unit, simply turn the refrigeration switch to "OFF."

Again, the exact steps may vary with brands of refrigeration units. Check the operator's manual for exact steps in starting the engine and unit.

THERMOSTAT

The purpose of the thermostat is to **control the temperature of the air inside the trailer.** You set the thermostat required for the load at the beginning of the trip. The thermostat then kicks in the cooling or heating cycle as the temperature inside the trailer demands it.

Some reefers will record on a calibrated chart the temperature maintained during the trip. This gives a permanent record of the air temperature inside the trailer.

Let's go back to delivering lettuce to Grand Forks from Pharr, Texas. Let's say the lettuce delivered was brown in color. You can't understand why since you had kept a close eye on the temperature. You maintain the temperature never varied from the required temperature. The permanent record of the air temperature inside the trailer would show what kind of temperature the lettuce was exposed to on the way to Grand Forks.

You were careful and checked the temperature often. The chart shows the temperature stayed steady all the way. That tells the warehouse supervisor that the lettuce probably wasn't very good from the start. You weren't at fault in this case. Next time, though, you'll check the condition of the cargo a lot more carefully before you load it.

MANUAL DEFROST SWITCH

The **coil** in the refrigeration unit **can ice up.** This keeps air from passing over the evaporator coil. When this happens the **unit should go into the defrost cycle.** Ordinarily, this will happen automatically. An air switch senses that air is not moving across the evaporator coil as it should. The air switch closes and puts the unit on defrost. But if there were a problem, or you wanted **to speed up the process,** you would use this switch to **put the unit on defrost manually.**

When the unit is free of ice, the defrost thermostat on the coil opens. This puts the unit back into the refrigeration cycle.

CUT-OUT SWITCHES

There are cut-out switches that **will turn the unit off if something goes wrong** with it.

HIGH TEMPERATURE CUT-OUT SWITCH. This switch prevents high temperatures when the unit is in the heat cycle. If the temperature gets too high, this cut-out switch will shut the unit off.

fig. 14-3
Control panel for refrigeration unit.

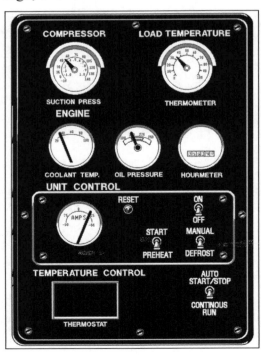

HIGH/LOW PRESSURE CUT-OUT SWITCH. The high/low pressure cut-out switch will turn the unit off in response to problems with the pressure in the compressor.

LOW OIL PRESSURE SWITCH. This switch will shut off the unit when the oil pressure falls below a safe level.

CYCLE INDICATOR

Earlier we described the cycle indicator with its row of lights. Each light represents a cycle that the unit can go through. **When the**

light is on it means the unit is in that cycle. For example, when the unit has to heat the air inside the trailer to maintain the proper temperature, the heating cycle light will be on.

Reefer Emergencies

Sometimes, despite all your best efforts, your reefer will quit while you're en route with a load. There's a number of different ways to respond, based on what you are hauling, how far you are from your destination, what the temperature is and many other factors. For instance, if you are close to your destination and the temperatures are not extreme, you just might be able to make it in without damaging the cargo. In other circumstances, you might have to get ice, or get the reefer fixed.

How do you decide? The best thing to do is **call the dispatcher.** After you explain your situation, the two of you will be able to work out the best response.

Chapter 14 Quiz

1. The basic construction of a refrigerated van is very similar to the dry freight van.
    A. True
    B. False

2. The walls of a reefer are insulated while the floor and ceiling aren't insulated.
    A. True
    B. False

3. The floor in a refrigerated trailer is a _____ floor.
    A. ribbed plywood
    B. metal sheeting
    C. ribbed aluminum
    D. plastic sheeting

4. The ribbed floor allows for air to circulate underneath the load.
    A. True
    B. False

5. The refrigeration unit heats as well as cools the air that is in the trailer.
   A. True
   B. False

6. _____ in the refrigeration unit will move the air around.
   A. Fans
   B. Compressors
   C. Engines
   D. Fuel tanks

7. A reefer is designed to haul perishables, frozen items, and loads that must be kept from freezing.
   A. True
   B. False

8. The engine of the refrigeration unit is maintenance-free.
   A. True
   B. False

9. The purpose of the _____ is to control the temperature of the air inside the trailer.
   A. engine
   B. thermostat
   C. defrost switch
   D. cycle indicator

10. The _____ will turn the unit off in case something goes wrong with it.
    A. defrost switch
    B. cycle indicator
    C. cut-out switches
    D. thermostat

COUPLING AND UNCOUPLING

Connecting the Tractor and the Trailer

It is obvious that before you can pull a trailer, the trailer must be joined to the tractor. This is the process known as coupling. How is this done? What parts of the tractor and trailer are involved in this process? How do you separate them again?

Coupling and uncoupling aren't hard procedures, but for safety's sake they must be done right. You'll have to show you have both knowledge of and skill in coupling and uncoupling to get a CDL for combination vehicles. In this chapter we'll outline a procedure that will ensure a safe couple every time.

Pre-coupling Procedures

Connecting the tractor to the trailer begins with two simple "get ready" steps. First, make sure you have picked up the right tractor and trailer. This may sound a little silly now, but wait until the first time you confront a large terminal yard packed with equipment. You'll see rows and rows of vehicles that look much the same except for their vehicle numbers. Double-check the numbers Dispatch gave you to make sure you have the equipment you are meant to have. Don't wait until you get to the right warehouse with the wrong trailer (and the wrong cargo) to find out!

Next, inspect that equipment. Chapter 25 describes pre-trip inspection procedures in detail so we won't cover those here. Before coupling, though, take a few extra minutes to check the fifth wheel and kingpin. Look for damaged or missing parts on the fifth wheel. See that the mounting to the tractor is secure. Make sure the trailer kingpin isn't bent or broken. Double-check that cargo is secure and won't shift.

Before you begin any coupling procedure, get out of the tractor and walk the area around the trailer and tractor. **Look for anything in your path that could damage the tractor or trailer.** Boards lying on the ground can fly dangerously about when popped from the ground by a tire. Nails, glass, or other objects can do severe damage to a tire. Make sure the way is clear before you begin the first stages of alignment.

Work on the most level ground you can find if you have a choice about it. Uneven ground will make your task just that much harder. Then put chocks at the rear of your trailer tires. When you **chock the trailer tires at the rear** you're making sure the trailer won't roll backward from the pressure applied by the tractor as it moves under the trailer. If your trailer has spring brakes you may not need chocks. Refer to your company policy when in doubt.

Aligning the Tractor

What's involved in coupling? To put it very simply, you're going to **back the tractor up to the trailer so the coupling assemblies connect without moving the trailer backwards.** When joining the trailer to the tractor you will be concerned mainly with just two vehicle parts: the fifth wheel on the tractor and the kingpin on the trailer. This makes it sound just a little easier than it is. A proper coupling requires you to center the kingpin in the fifth wheel within a small margin of error. So in your backing, you have to be pretty precise about how you align the tractor and trailer.

fig. 15-1

There's only about six inches leeway to the left or right of center on the fifth wheel.

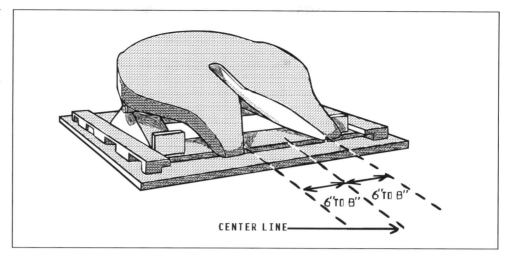

fig. 15-1

There's only about six inches leeway to the left or right of center on the fifth wheel.

The V-shaped slot in the fifth wheel allows for about six to eight inches error margin to either side of center on most models. This means that your fifth wheel must come into contact with the trailer kingpin at a point six to eight inches to either the left or right of center to complete the coupling without having to realign the tractor. It is up to you to **place the tractor so the trailer kingpin is as near to center of the fifth wheel V-slot as possible.**

Slow and steady really wins the race here. If you **follow the procedures step by step every time,** you should have few problems. This procedure involves the proper use of the rear view mirrors. As you back, watch both mirrors. If your view of the trailer is the same in both rear view mirrors, you're centered. **Know the width of the tractor as compared to the width of the trailer.** Remember that the center of the fifth wheel is always in the center of the tractor frame and the kingpin is always in the center of the front of the trailer.

OBSERVATION SKILLS TEST

Did you notice that the driver of the rig in the very first illustration skipped some steps in his coupling procedure? Name two things that will happen if he pulls out now. Check your answers against the Observation Skills Test Grid at the end of the book.

Before you attempt to align the tractor and trailer, learn about the physical characteristics of both. How wide is the tractor? If you drive the same tractor day after day you should know its width, fifth wheel height, wheelbase, and other important measurements. If the tractor is new to you, ask! It is not a sign of ignorance or inexperience to ask questions about the equipment that you will be driving. It is a sign of a conscientious, careful driver.

What about the trailer? Is it 96 inches wide or 102 inches wide? How does this compare to the width of your tractor? How does it compare to the span of the mirrors on your tractor? This is all very important for determining the approach to the trailer.

To align the units properly you must be able to locate the center of the trailer by using its sides as a gauge in your rear view mirrors. We'll discuss how in detail later.

HORIZONTAL ALIGNMENT

The first step in aligning the tractor with the trailer is approaching the trailer. To illustrate this we will imagine that there is enough room in front of the trailer to maneuver the tractor easily. Approach the front of the trailer from either side (right or left). Experienced drivers prefer to **approach the trailer from the right** side (the trailer will be at your left). This gives the driver full view of the trailer from the window at all times during the first stage of alignment. This, of course, will become a choice you will have to make as you experience the different methods of approach.

As you approach the trailer, **steer away from the front** into the area in front of the trailer (see Figure 15-2). Taking it slow and easy, watch your mirrors as

fig. 15-2
Approach the trailer, preferably from the right, and start to turn away from the trailer when the front of the tractor comes near the right corner of the trailer.

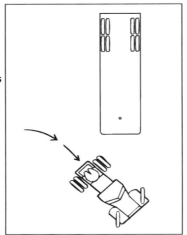

you start to straighten out in front of the trailer. Some novices assume that they should begin the turn away from the trailer after they are directly in front of it. Because each tractor has its own wheelbase and turning radius, this is a wrong assumption. Often, this would place the tractor far to the side of the trailer after the tractor is straightened out. It is wise to start the turn as the front of the tractor approaches the near corner of the trailer. This will place the fifth wheel in a closer alignment with the kingpin and less adjustment of position will be necessary.

As you pull away from the trailer, keep an eye on your mirrors. As you straighten the tractor in front of the trailer, **the corners of the trailer will appear evenly in the mirrors.** If there is an unequal amount of the trailer in one mirror, you are too far to the other side. For instance, if the right mirror shows a large portion of the trailer and the left side very little, you will have to adjust the tractor further to the right. Do this by pulling forward while steering to the right. When you think you might be positioned more evenly, straighten the tractor.

It may be in your best interest to pull the tractor far in front of the trailer when beginning alignment. That will give you more room in which to **adjust your position as you back** toward the trailer. If you back slowly you can steer the tractor in the desired direction **to align the fifth wheel with the kingpin.** It is not unusual for the novice driver, or even the experienced driver for that matter, to adjust the tractor more than once before proper alignment is achieved. Never back under the trailer at an angle. You might push the trailer sideways and break the landing gear.

When an equal amount of the front of the trailer shows in each mirror, you are aligned with the trailer kingpin. You can stop working on position and start to back slowly.

Do not back completely under the trailer at this point. **Stop when the rear of the tractor is about five feet from the front of the trailer.** To gauge the stopping distance look at your tractor drive tires in the mirror and judge their distance from the nose of the trailer. This is not to say that five feet from the trailer is the exact distance that should be left between the tractor and trailer. It should be the minimum left, though. Allow yourself enough room to walk safely and comfortably between the tractor and trailer as you inspect both. Set the tractor brakes, put the transmission in neutral, and get out of the tractor. **Inspect the area around the trailer and tractor,** making sure it is safe to back the rest of the way.

fig. 15-3
The vertical levels of the kingpin and the fifth wheel must be matched so they connect properly.

From a vantage point under the trailer, **check the alignment of the fifth wheel with the kingpin.** It is much easier to notice any extreme offset from the ground than it is from the tractor. If they are aligned properly, proceed with the inspection and coupling. If they are not, return to the tractor and make any necessary adjustments in your position.

VERTICAL ALIGNMENT

As you walk around the area compare the level of the fifth wheel with the height of the kingpin. The coupling surface of the trailer should be just about the middle of the fifth wheel skid ramps (see Figure 15-3). If the trailer is too far below the fifth wheel level, the kingpin will hit the tractor frame. If the trailer is too high, the kingpin could slide right over the top of the fifth wheel when you try to back under it. You could damage the rear of the tractor that way.

If you are either too high or two low, you will have to use the landing gear to **raise or lower the trailer to the fifth wheel level.** We'll be the first to admit that it is not at all easy to crank a loaded trailer up. It is hard on the landing gear and physically demanding of the person at the crank.

On most trailers, you turn the landing gear crank at the left side of the trailer clockwise to raise the trailer and counterclockwise to lower it. The main gear housing is under the trailer. As the crank is turned the gears spin to lower or raise the trailer landing legs. Most trailer gear boxes have two speeds. Use low gear while the landing legs are supporting most of the trailer's weight. High gear can be used when the trailer is empty or its loaded weight rests on the fifth wheel.

Although they are built of hardened steel the gears can become damaged if you aren't careful.

fig. 15-4
Note the position of the fifth wheel locking mechanism before you complete the coupling.

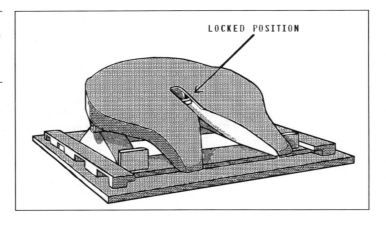

LOCKED POSITION

The landing gear crank is hinged and swings under the trailer to a latch which secures it to the frame while the trailer is in motion. If the crank handle were allowed to swing freely while the trailer is moving it could hit a nearby vehicle or passing pedestrian. Always **secure the crank handle** when you're done using it.

While you are right there at the landing gear, check the distance between the landing gear and the kingpin. Compare that with the distance from the center of the fifth wheel to the rear of the tractor's frame and mud flap brackets. A short, 28-foot pup trailer or other type of short trailer may not have the distance that could handle the rear end length of some tractors without damaging the mud flap brackets. In some cases sliding the fifth wheel rearward may provide the needed distance.

Now **inspect the fifth wheel.** Make sure that the locking mechanism (jaws) is opened. If it is closed the kingpin cannot slide into the jaws and complete the coupling. If it is even partly closed it could slam shut when the tractor comes into contact with the trailer. This would also prevent the kingpin from becoming locked in the fifth wheel. Be sure the fifth wheel is tilted down in the back, so the trailer can slide up the skid ramps when you couple.

Also check to see that the surface of the fifth wheel has been properly greased. A fifth wheel that is poorly lubricated will not let the trailer rotate freely and smoothly when turning or backing. If it's dry apply a liberal amount of grease to the surface of the fifth wheel. You should always carry a supply of grease with you since you'll probably need it the most when it's not readily available.

If you have a sliding fifth wheel, make sure it's locked. Sliding fifth wheels are covered in Chapter 23.

Now you are ready to back the tractor closer to the trailer so you can start making the connection. If the trailer is not equipped with spring brakes, back the tractor until the skid ramps of the fifth wheel just touch the apron of the upper couple of the trailer. As they touch you should feel a light bump. Stop, set the parking brakes, put the transmission in neutral, and shut the engine off. Now you are ready to start making the connections.

MAKING THE CONNECTION

The first step of actually coupling the tractor and trailer is to **connect the red supply air line.** There are two air lines, the service brake line and the emergency or supply line. These are almost always colored red for supply or emergency and blue for service. The connections at the front of the trailer will usually be painted the color of the air hose that should be connected to them, or labeled "service" and "emergency." Check the glad hand seals and secure the supply air line to the corresponding colored or labeled trailer connection.

fig. 15-5
Air control knobs. Trailer Supply (red) and Parking Brake (yellow).

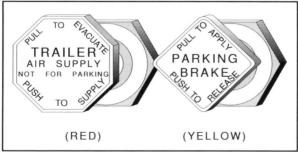

PULL TO EVACUATE
TRAILER
AIR SUPPLY
NOT FOR PARKING
PUSH TO SUPPLY

PULL TO APPLY
PARKING
BRAKE
PUSH TO RELEASE

(RED)   (YELLOW)

The supply air line should be supported so there's no chance it will be crushed or caught while the tractor is backing under the trailer.

After you return to the tractor, **charge the trailer air supply** by pushing the red trailer air supply knob. Wait until the air pressure is normal. Turn off the engine and listen for air leaks. Apply and release the trailer brakes and listen for the sound of the trailer brakes being applied and released. (If you don't hear the brakes being applied and released, you may have hooked up your air lines incorrectly.) Apply the trailer parking brakes by pulling the red trailer air supply knob back out. This activates the trailer spring brakes to keep the trailer from moving. Restart the engine and release the tractor brakes by pushing in the yellow tractor parking brake knob. Put the transmission in reverse and back slowly.

You will feel the weight of the trailer being transferred to the tractor as the apron of the upper coupler slides up the skid ramps of the fifth wheel. Continue backing slowly until progress is stopped by the kingpin locking into the jaws of the fifth wheel.

If the trailer is fairly light, you'll be able to get the tractor under it without much effort. If the trailer is heavily loaded, you will feel some resistance. If the trailer is a little too low and you can't get the tractor under it without a lot of effort, don't force it. Get out and jack the trailer up a little more. This isn't all that easy with a loaded trailer, but it's still the best solution. If your drive wheels start spinning when you meet that resistance, use the inter-axle differential lock to get more traction. For trailers equipped with spring brakes it's not necessary to connect the air lines prior to backing under the trailer. Remember, the spring brakes were set when the air pressure was released from the spring brake chamber which occurred when the trailer was parked. So, without hooking up the air lines or electrical cable, slowly back under the trailer.

To **check the connection,** try pulling forward very slowly. If the tractor will not move, the connection is complete. If it does move, stop immediately and back again.

Do not attempt to back under the trailer at high speed. This could damage the fifth wheel, the kingpin, or the rear axle differential.

Put the transmission in neutral, shut off the engine, and pocket the key. Get out of the tractor and check to **see that the fifth wheel locking jaw is closed around the shank of the kingpin.** To do this you must be under the front of the trailer and behind the fifth wheel. If the jaw is closed you will see it locked securely around the back of the kingpin and the kingpin will not be visible. There should be no space between the upper and lower fifth wheel. If the kingpin is clearly visible in the fifth wheel opening and the locking jaw is positioned to the side of the fifth wheel opening you do not have a good connection. The locking lever should be in the locked position. If the locking jaw is not secured around the kingpin, lower the landing jacks, pull the tractor forward, and start the backing procedure again.

Determine that the kingpin is secured. For a trailer equipped with spring brakes, **connect both air lines and connect the single electrical supply cable (pigtail) to the trailer.** Return to the tractor and turn on the emergency flashers and trailer lights. Walk around the trailer to **make sure the lights are working.** Check the clearance lights and side marker lights. Walk to the back of the trailer and check the turn signals (turning on the emergency flashers at the tractor will activate the turn signals).

If none are working, there is possibly a bad connection at the trailer supply plug. Disconnect, then reconnect the pigtail securely into the trailer connection. If the lights still don't work have them checked by a mechanic. Certainly if you are well versed in the electrical components of the tractor and trailer you may search for the problem yourself.

If only one light is not working its bulb may be out and need to be replaced. Always carry a supply of spare bulbs with you. This is true for the tractor and the trailer. You may have to couple to a trailer at a deserted freight yard or at an unusual hour when there is no one available to supply you with a bulb. Have at least two of every type with you at all times. When you use one, don't forget to resupply yourself.

While you're checking out the trailer tires, take the time to **gauge tire inflation** if you didn't do this in your routine inspection. Also **check for worn hoses or loose connections** on the trailer's brake system. The hiss of escaping air may be heard coming from these areas. Rusty connections should be closely inspected for cracks. Should any leaks exist, have them repaired immediately. A ruptured air hose or broken connection is sure trouble while the vehicle is moving.

The trailer can finally be considered connected and ready to roll. But you must first **remove any wheel chocks.** Never simply leave the chocks lying on the ground as you pull away, unless that is what is requested. Be courteous and place them where they belong.

Double-check the clearances between the rear of the truck frame and mud flap brackets and the landing gear. Is there enough distance to allow for turning? Also check that there is enough clearance between the top of the tractor's tires and the underside of the nose of the trailer.

Now you should crank up the landing gear as high as it will go and secure the crank handle. Optimum ground clearance is available with the gear in its uppermost position. Never drive with the landing gear part way up. This should be the last thing you do before moving the tractor-trailer.

You are now ready to return to the tractor and prepare to pull away. Do not simply disengage the parking brakes and drive off. Perform one more test to assure yourself that the trailer is secured to the tractor.

Try pulling forward slowly. If the coupling is not secure and the tractor begins to pull out from under the trailer, stop immediately and back under the trailer. Engage all brakes, get out and crank the trailer landing gear down, and begin the coupling procedure again.

If the coupling is secure, the tractor will not move. You can then release the trailer brakes and begin a safe trip. A word to the wise: When you're pulling the tractor forward to check the firmness of your connection, do it slowly! Let's say your coupling isn't secure. If you were to drive the tractor out from under the trailer while the landing gear is up the trailer nose would lose its support and land on the tractor frame or, worse, on the ground. To correct this, heavy duty wreckers would have to lift the front of the trailer so the landing gear could be lowered. The landing gear alone isn't strong enough to raise a trailer, especially a loaded one, from this position.

Coupling doubles and triples? You will find the process of coupling and uncoupling multiple trailers described in detail in Chapter 21.

Uncoupling Procedures

Once you have checked for hazards and obstacles and have parked the trailer in the desired location, set the parking brakes by pulling out both the red and yellow knobs. This evacuates the air from the spring brake chambers of the trailer and sets the brakes.

You may then **lower the landing gear.** Unhook the crank from its travel position, shift to high gear, and turn it counterclockwise. This will lower the landing gear. Turning the crank will be fairly easy until the dolly plates come into contact with the ground. Then shift to low gear and crank until some of the trailer weight is on the dollies and not on the tractor. Don't lift the trailer off the fifth wheel.

Be aware of the dolly plates as you lower the landing gear. Some landing gear assemblies have plates which sit flat on the ground in their lowered position. These plates are connected to the dolly leg by heavy duty swivels. These swivels allow the dolly to sit evenly on uneven or rough surfaces. If the plate has swung into a position which would keep it from sitting flat on the ground it could be damaged and become useless. If it is in such a position, reposition it so it will sit flat when lowered.

It is also wise to check the surface that the dollies will be sitting on when lowered. A heavily loaded trailer can sink into hot asphalt or loose dirt. On such surfaces you should always place something, a wide plank or dolly pad, under the landing gear plate. Cement is virtually the only surface which is likely to support a loaded trailer without allowing it to sink.

As you crank the gear watch and listen to the springs of the tractor. You will hear the springs relax as some of the weight is removed. When some of the weight is off the tractor, stop cranking. For an empty trailer, stop cranking when the pads or plates just barely touch the surface. After the landing gear is lowered replace the crank handle in its travel position. More than one person walking past a trailer has been injured by a free-swinging or projecting handle.

Next you should **disconnect the** air supply lines and electrical cable from the trailer. Stow each in its proper position at the rear of the tractor. Lines should be secured so they won't be damaged while driving the tractor. Hang the electrical cable with the plug down to keep water from getting in.

Now you can **disengage the fifth wheel locking mechanism.** This is done by using the release lever. The release lever may be permanently attached to the locking mechanism and can be accessed from the side of the fifth wheel. Reach under the trailer, grab the release lever and pull. This will disengage the locking mechanism. Keep your legs and feet clear of the rear tractor wheel to avoid being injured.

fig. 15-6
Some landing gear assemblies have pads for dolly plates, as shown here. Others have wheels and still others have plates that swivel.

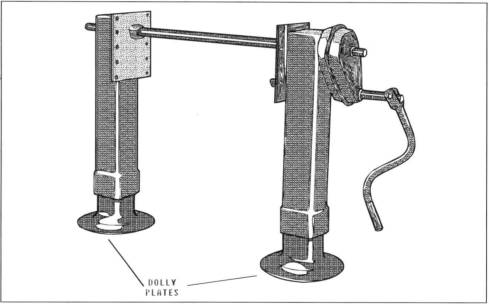

DOLLY PLATES

Other types of release levers are removable. When not in use this type should be kept in its proper place in the tractor side compartment. The removable release handle has a hook which fits into a slot on the fifth wheel jaw release. Simply place the hook in the slot and pull. If you are assigned to drive a tractor with a removable release lever handle, make doubly sure the handle is in its place before driving the vehicle. You will not be happy to find the handle missing when attempting to release the fifth wheel far from home.

Once the tractor is completely uncoupled from the trailer you can safely pull away. **Pull away from the trailer** slowly. Stop with the tractor frame under the trailer. That way, if the landing gear collapses, the tractor will keep the trailer from falling to the ground. Apply the parking brake and leave the cab. Check one last time that the ground and the landing gear support the trailer. Then get back in the tractor, release the parking brakes and drive the tractor clear.

Be considerate of the next driver to pull the trailer. Don't leave the trailer cranked to a position lower than the fifth wheel level of your own tractor. Do note any repairs that should be performed on the trailer before it is pulled next and present that to the proper people.

Safety Precautions

In the interest of safety, we'll remind you that any time you plan to back your tractor to a trailer for coupling you should **fully inspect the area for safety hazards** like boards, nails, curbs, or people. Correct any dangerous conditions before going any further.

Follow the procedures outlined, step-by-step. Don't take shortcuts, rush the job, or force anything into place. Do it the hard way, that's usually the best and safest way to proceed.

The final piece of advice is: **GO SLOWLY.**

Chapter 15 Quiz

1. Under slippery conditions, use the inter-axle differential to get more traction.
   A. True
   B. False

2. A poorly lubricated fifth wheel should be _____.
   A. salted down
   B. greased
   C. dried off
   D. sanded down

3. If a single light on the trailer is not working, the _____ should be checked.
   A. entire electrical system
   B. electrical connection to the trailer
   C. electrical connection to the tractor
   D. light bulb

Refer to this sketch of a tractor and trailer to answer Questions 4 through 9. Complete the sentence by inserting the number of the component that makes the statement true.

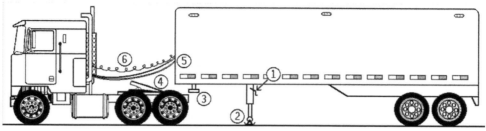

4.   The _____ should be the first connection you make from the tractor to the trailer.

5.   The jaws of the tractor fifth wheel lock onto the _____ of the trailer.

6.   The _____ must be connected to check the trailer lights.

7.   Always secure the _____ when you are done using it.

8.   When coupling, the _____ should be the last trailer component moved from its original position.

9.   The driver should check the alignment of the _____ before backing the tractor under the trailer.

10.   Only when there's ice or snow does a driver have to inspect the area around the trailer before backing.
       A. True
       B. False

PUTTING THE TRUCK IN MOTION

Get to Know Your Equipment

The first time you start a tractor engine, you might be nervous. You know there are many types of tractors and dashboards. So take the time to put yourself at ease and **get to know a new tractor before you start it.**

Look the tractor over before you climb in. A professional driver never starts the engine without first performing the **inspections** discussed in Chapter 25.

Before you climb in, look at the handhold and the steps to make sure they are free of dirt and grease. Then **use the three-point stance to enter** the cab. This means you'll be using the steps and the handhold and either both hands and one foot or both feet and one hand to enter the cab.

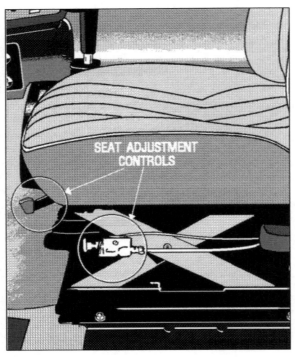

fig. 16-1
Adjust your seat for comfort, but also make sure you have clear vision and your hands and feet can reach all the controls.

SEAT ADJUSTMENT CONTROLS

Pull yourself in behind the wheel. Many driver's seats have weight and height controls and suspension systems that allow for a smooth ride even on bumpy roads. If you are too high or too low, look for the **seat adjuster**.

Find the ignition switch and put the tractor key in the switch, but don't turn it on. Look at the pedals at your feet. The pedal on the left side is the clutch pedal, the other is the air brake pedal. The accelerator pedal is to the far right.

Look at the transmission shift lever to see what type it is. Look for the shifting pattern. It will be posted in the cab. We'll show you different shift patterns later in this chapter.

Grab the gear **shift lever**, depress the clutch, and place the lever **in** the **neutral** position. Let the clutch pedal out, sit back, and locate the cab controls and gauges described in Chapter 2. See that the parking brakes are set.

OBSERVATION SKILLS TEST

Did you familiarize yourself with the truck that started this chapter? Was it a cabover or conventional? How many speeds did it have? To check your answers, turn to the Observation Skills Test Grid at the back of the book.

Starting

Now you're ready to start the engine. You know that a diesel engine burns diesel fuel instead of gasoline. Diesel engines differ from gasoline engines in other ways, too.

Do not depress the accelerator pedal when you start a diesel engine. Do not depress the pedal when the engine starts either. These procedures are unnecessary because the fuel injectors meter diesel fuel into the cylinders in exact amounts.

To start the tractor's **diesel engine, depress the clutch pedal to the floor and hold it** there. **Turn the key** if your vehicle has one, or press the starter button. This causes electricity from the batteries to flow to the starter motor. The starter motor turns the flywheel and cranks the engine. The air and fuel ignite in each cylinder in turn, driving down the pistons and turning the crankshaft. As soon as the engine fires, release the key.

The engine is now running. Before you let the clutch out smoothly and slowly, make sure the gear shift lever is in neutral position. If the tractor's transmission is in gear when you let the clutch out, the tractor could lurch forward or backwards. Many accidents are caused by drivers who think the transmission is in neutral when it isn't. This is also a good time to check the engine oil pressure gauge to make sure you have oil pressure.

Another reason you depress the clutch when you start a diesel engine is to let the starter turn as fast as it can. The transmission is filled with heavy gear oil that thickens in cold weather. If you don't depress the clutch pedal, the shaft will turn inside the transmission. This creates resistance, or drag, and slows the starter motor. If the starter motor turns the engine too slowly, the engine may not start.

The best rule is to start the engine with the clutch pedal down to the floor. Doing it every time will ensure safety and better starting.

fig. 16-2
This engine is idling at 650 rpm. The air pressure and the operating temperature show this engine is about ready to go.

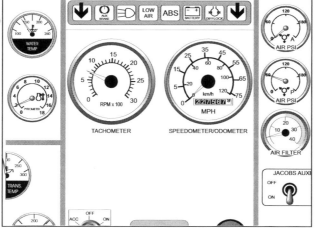

Warm Up
Engines need to warm up because they work best at operating temperatures. A diesel engine should **warm up to at least 120 degrees Fahrenheit** before you start rolling. The best operating temperature for a diesel engine is about 180 degrees Fahrenheit. See Figure 16-2.

At operating temperature, the diesel fuel and air mixture ignite best. The lubricating oil in the engine flows best. You can move the truck as soon as the air and oil pressures are up, but do not try to use full engine power until the engine has reached its operating temperature.

If a diesel engine idles at 650 rpm, leave it at that rpm while it warms. Some drivers use the hand throttle to set the rpm at 900 or 1,000. This is not to warm up the engine faster, but to build up the air pressure faster.

Shifting

When the engine is running and has reached a temperature of at least 120 degrees and all other gauges show normal readings, it's time to use the clutch and the gear shift to put the truck in motion.

Using the Clutch

You know that when the clutch pedal is up, the clutch is engaged. When the clutch is engaged, it transmits power from the engine to the transmission. When the clutch pedal is depressed, it is disengaged. The engine can be running, but no power goes to the transmission. One of the purposes of the clutch is to interrupt the power flow from the engine to the drive wheels so the transmission can be shifted. The driver **disengages the clutch to shift gears.**

Look at Figure 16-3. You see three areas the clutch moves through. When you first step on the clutch to depress it you will feel no resistance in the first inch or two of travel. This area is called the free play area. At the bottom of the free play area the working area or disengaging area begins. At the bottom end of the clutch travel is the clutch or transmission brake area. There are only certain times you will use the clutch brake which you will learn about later in this chapter. You can see from the illustration that shifting will take place while you have the clutch depressed into the working area.

fig. 16-3
The clutch interrupts the power flow from the engine so the transmission can be shifted.

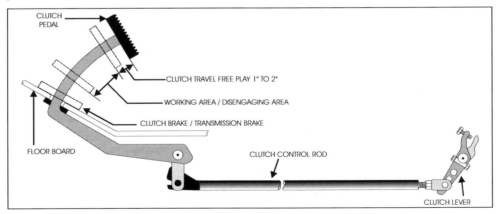

CLUTCH PEDAL
CLUTCH TRAVEL FREE PLAY 1" TO 2"
WORKING AREA / DISENGAGING AREA
CLUTCH BRAKE / TRANSMISSION BRAKE
FLOOR BOARD
CLUTCH CONTROL ROD
CLUTCH LEVER

Maybe you've seen drivers putting their tractors into motion. Some will begin rolling in a steady way, smoother than glass. Others will attract your attention as they jerk forward with engine roaring and extra smoke pouring from the stack. Next you hear a grinding noise that tells you the driver didn't shift properly. That grinding noise is gear teeth being ground together while they are trying to mesh but can't. A tractor won't stand up under this abuse for long.

How can you achieve a smooth start? When you are ready to put your truck in motion, either forward or reverse, you do not press on the accelerator as you let the clutch out. This is true whether the truck is loaded or empty. With the transmission in LO or REVERSE and the engine at idle speed, there is enough horsepower to move the truck without depressing the accelerator.

Proper use of the clutch is all important to shifting. Whether you drive an older tractor with an older model transmission or a brand new tractor with the most advanced transmission made, the clutch must be used with skill.

Chapter 7 covered the purpose of the clutch and in Chapter 3, you see why you should **shift at the proper rpm**. Operator's manuals from the manufacturer for the transmission you are about to use will tell you what "the proper rpm" is. Engine rpm is not the same thing as your road speed. Engine rpm is how fast your engine crankshaft is revolving. The tachometer tells you the engine rpm. As you know, the tachometer is labelled in hundreds of rpm. So if your tach reads 12, that means 1,200 rpm. Road speed is measured in mph. Nevertheless, when you shift at the proper rpm, that's often referred to as "matching" your engine rpm to your road speed.

As a driver, you must pay close attention to the tachometer. An engine's rpm is matched to its gears. Now, let's take a close look at how you should use your clutch.

Double-clutching

Double-clutching involves pushing the clutch in twice when shifting, instead of once. You push the clutch in the first time to move the shift lever or shifter quickly out of gear and into neutral. With the shifter in neutral, you immediately let the clutch out. The **engine speed and road speed** are now matched, or **synchronized.** You push the clutch in a second time to put the shifter in the next gear, then release the clutch pedal.

You can double-clutch when downshifting but you have to raise the engine speed by pushing the accelerator to synchronize engine and road speed. Carriers encourage their drivers not to downshift to slow their rigs. As you can see, it calls for the driver to accelerate during each downshift procedure. It's more fuel efficient to use the auxiliary brake to slow the rig. Better yet, get off the accelerator in enough time to allow the truck to slow down gradually.

TO DOUBLE-CLUTCH WHEN YOU UPSHIFT:

Depress the clutch pedal.

Move the gear shift lever into neutral.

Release the clutch pedal.

Let the engine speed slow down until engine rpm and road speed "match."

Depress the clutch pedal and quickly move the gear shift lever to the next gear position.

Release the clutch pedal, then press the accelerator.

TO DOUBLE-CLUTCH WHEN YOU DOWNSHIFT:

Depress the clutch pedal.

Move the gear shift lever into neutral.

Release the clutch pedal.

Accelerate engine speed until engine rpm and road speed "match."

Depress the clutch pedal and quickly move the gear shift lever to the next gear position.

Release the clutch pedal.

The Clutch Brake

When your truck is standing still the countershaft is stopped while the input shaft is still spinning. Then you need to **stop the input shaft to match the countershaft**. To do this, you will use the clutch brake. The clutch brake stops the input shaft from turning. It works only when you push the clutch pedal all the way to the floor.

You'll need to use the clutch brake in these circumstances. One is when you start the engine. After the engine starts, release the clutch, then let it idle to warm up. When your engine idles, the clutch pedal is out, the clutch is engaged and the input shaft turns. So, **to shift into LO gear** you have to stop the input shaft.

Then you'll use the clutch brake **at stop lights**. When you have to wait for a long red light, you'll have to keep your foot on the brake and clutch with the truck in gear.

You'll also use the clutch brake when you have been out of the truck with the engine idling. After you reenter the truck, depress the clutch into the clutch brake area. Application of the clutch brake stops the rotation of the input shaft quickly. You don't have to sit and wait for the shaft to lose momentum gradually and eventually come to a stop so you can shift into a gear without grinding gears.

SELECTING GEARS AND RANGES

The clutch is not the only device you'll use to change gears. You need to know how to use the shift lever, too. The **shift lever** is the device that **actually moves the gears or the shifter yoke** in the transmission while the clutch pedal is depressed.

On top of the shift lever you'll notice there may be additional controls, the range control, and possibly a splitter or cruise control buttons. They may look different or be in slightly different places on different transmissions but they all perform the same way.

RANGE CONTROL

The **range control** in a transmission **provides both a high and a low range of the basic gears**. A range control turns a five speed transmission into nine speeds, five low range gears and four high range gears. Most truck transmissions will have a range control. This control lets the main transmission gears do double duty. You use them once in low range and use them over again in high range.

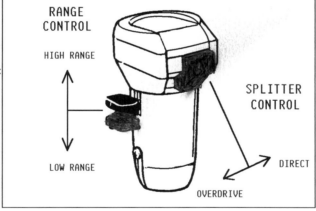

fig. 16-4
With this shift lever, you move the range control button to select low range or high range and move the splitter control to split high range gears.

This provides an economical way **to provide more gear ratio selections**. The more selections you have, the more closely you will be able to match the speed of the engine to the speed needed by the wheels to accelerate, climb grades, and cruise down the road. These selections help you to accelerate faster, hold your speed on hills better, and keep a higher average rate of speed.

SPLITTER CONTROL

As the range control button shifts the basic gears into low and high gears, the **splitter control splits** those **high gears into DIRECT and overdrive**. That means a transmission with range control and a splitter has a low range, a high range, a direct, and overdrive for each gear in high range. Figure 16-4 shows you the top of a shift lever for a transmission that uses both a range and splitter control.

Basic Shifting Instructions

What follows is basic shifting instructions for two different transmissions, the 13-speed and the nine-speed. The nine-speed has range control, and the 13-speed has both range and splitter controls. Once you're familiar with both these types of transmissions, you can use the same basic shifting theory to

fig. 16-5
A transmission has six basic gear shift positions.

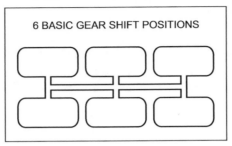

6 BASIC GEAR SHIFT POSITIONS

figure your way around any transmission you might encounter. As you look at the shifting patterns in the illustrations, you will see that LO is considered one of the speeds. Figure 16-5 shows that basically there are six positions in all transmissions. Within those six basic positions up to 18 speeds are possible.

fig. 16-6
Shift positions for a five-speed transmission.

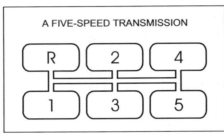

A FIVE-SPEED TRANSMISSION

R 2 4
1 3 5

Figure 16-6 shows how the six basic positions are used to give you a five speed transmission. The position on the far left and forward is the reverse gear position. Starting forward in first gear you make four gear shift changes to get into fifth gear.

UPSHIFTING

In either the nine- or 13-speed, start with the range control down, in low range. In the 13-speed, the splitter should be rearward, in the direct position. Now start the truck moving in LO gear. When you reach the shift rpm in LO gear, it is time to shift into first. Double-clutch as described and shift. Double-clutch and shift through each gear in sequence until you reach fourth (fourth position, low range).

PRESELECTING

Now, just before you want to shift into fifth (first position, high range), move the range control up, to high range. This is called "preselecting." Then double-clutch and move to fifth gear (which is the same shift position as first). The range shift does not happen when you flip the range control button up. The actual range shift occurs as you move the shift lever through neutral on the way to the next higher gear.

Preselecting when downshifting works the same way. Flip the range control button just before you depress the clutch. The range shift takes place when you move the shift lever out of gear into neutral.

Now you are in high range. If this is a nine-speed you continue to shift from fifth to eighth just as you shifted from first to fourth in low range. If you are driving a 13-speed the steps are exactly the same to fifth gear. After that you'll want to use the splitter control between each time you move the shift lever. There are two different procedures to use, depending on whether you are shifting from direct (DIR) to overdrive (OD) in the same gear or shifting from overdrive in one gear to direct in the next. Here's how that works:

Direct to Overdrive in the Same Gear Using the Splitter

This is the easiest shift to make because you only single-clutch and you don't have to move the shift lever. This is called breaking torque. Just move the splitter to overdrive, let up on the accelerator, depress and release the clutch, and you are in overdrive.

Overdrive in One Gear to Direct in the Next Using the Splitter

When you are in overdrive the next higher gear will be the direct position in the next higher gear. This is just like shifting from one gear to the next in a nine-speed with one exception. You add the step of moving the splitter to direct after you've moved the shift lever and just before you release the clutch the final time in your double-clutch.

DOWNSHIFTING

To downshift you would again take each gear in sequence. You would use the downshifting double-clutch procedure and select the next lower gear.

When you get to fifth gear (first position, high range) you have to remember to preselect the low range with the range control before moving the lever to fourth gear (fourth position, low range).

If you have a 13-speed, downshifting from overdrive to direct in the same gear uses almost the same steps as upshifting from direct to overdrive. Remember that you must raise the engine speed when you double-clutch.

Downshifting from direct in one gear to overdrive in the next lower gear is similar to upshifting from OD to DIR in the next gear. The difference is that you move the splitter to DIR before you do anything else. After that you proceed as if it were a normal downshift in a nine-speed.

10-SPEED TRANSMISSION

We have been discussing two common transmissions, the nine- and the 13-speed. Of course there are several other varieties on the road today. For instance there is a 10-speed. This is basically a nine-speed but it uses the LO gear (first position) in high range as sixth gear. There is also a Super 10 which has a selector button that does half the shifting. The selector button is similar to the splitter found on a 13-speed. With this transmission, each shift lever position has two consecutive gears which are changed with the selector button. This allows you to shift through the gears from first to tenth by moving the shift lever only four times, compared with the nine times in a standard 10-speed.

The Super 10 transmission shifts like this. With the shift lever pulled to the left and back into the first position you can let the clutch out and put your truck in motion. The first shift is with the selector button. Flip the selector, let your foot off the accelerator briefly, and the transmission shifts into second gear. Now with your foot back on the accelerator and your speed up to about five mph it's time to shift into third gear. You preselect by moving the selector button. Then with the shift lever and double-clutching you shift into the center forward position which puts you in third gear. The shift from third to fourth is with the selector button. You repeat this process until you're in 10th gear at about 35 mph. You have used four lever shifts and the rest are selector button shifts from first to 10th gear. See Figure 16-7.

fig. 16-7
The shift patterns of the nine-speed and 13-speed and the 10 and Super 10 transmissions.

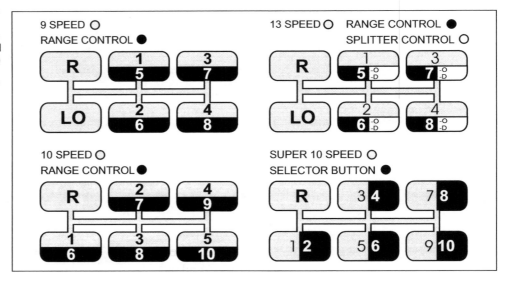

AUTOMATIC SHIFTS

There is also a Super 10 Top Two Automated transmission. It's basically the same as the Super 10 but with the top two speeds or gears automated. Linking the electronic control unit (ECU) of the engine to the transmission makes this possible.

The Super 10 Top Two transmission is shifted just like the Super 10. Let's say you are in eighth gear. With the selector button preselected back for LO you double-clutch, moving the shift lever into ninth gear when your road speed is between 35 to 40 mph. That's the last shift you make. The engine's electronics keep track of the road speed, the amount of acceleration or deceleration, and engine speed. So it's the electronics responding to your foot on the accelerator that causes the next shift automatically to 10th. Then you can bring the truck up to cruising speed.

When pulling a grade drops your rpm down again, the electronics read the drop. The electronics will cause a break in torque, you will hear a quick increase in engine rpm, and the transmission automatically shifts back to ninth gear. See Figure 16-8.

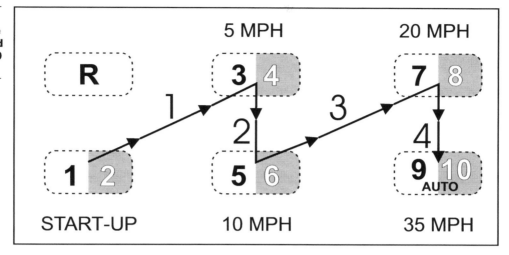

There is an 18-speed which is like the 13-speed but which lets you use the splitter in the low range as well as in the high range. There is a 15-speed which, like the 10-speed, uses the LO gear in both low and high ranges and the splitter also works in that position.

There is also a 15-speed deep reduction transmission. This is like the 10-speed but it has another control which gives a LO-LO or deep reduction range for moving very slowly on rough terrain, up steep grades, or working with construction equipment.

There are still several other different types. But as we said, if you understand the principles of the nine- and the 13-speed, you will be able to look at the shifting pattern that is posted in the truck and figure out what to do.

Just what type of transmission you will find in your truck depends on several things. When purchasing a new truck, the buyer will select the transmission based on the job the truck will probably do.

Progressive Shifting
Progressive shifting is a driving and shifting technique that allows you to take advantage of the higher horsepower, low RPM, high torque engines. When the transmission is in the lower gears it develops the most torque, or power. In the higher gears it delivers less torque but high speeds.

Progressive shifting is a way to get your truck moving in LO or first gear and make your first shift when you are up to three to five miles per hour at 1,200 rpm. When you use this technique you intentionally avoid using more rpm than necessary for the next upshift. Running the engine's rpm in the range between 1,200 and 1,600 as you upshift to the highest gear to get to cruising speed saves fuel.

Chapter 24 covers fuel economy in greater detail.

Driving Tips

The following are some very basic cautions to keep in mind for smooth, proper shifting every time.

- Loaded or empty, do not press down on the accelerator as you let the clutch out.
- Always double-clutch when moving the shift lever.
- Never force the shift lever into the next gear position.
- Never coast (drive with the shift lever in neutral or with the clutch depressed so that the power is disengaged from the driving wheels). Regulations prohibit this.
- With a nine- or 13-speed, never move the shift lever to LO when in high range.
- Never move the range control or the splitter control when the transmission is in neutral while the truck is moving.
- Never make a range shift when moving in reverse.
- Always immediately complete the shift after preselecting.
- You can save valuable fuel by operating the vehicle at less than governed rpm while cruising in the highest gear.

Chapter 16 Quiz

1. Before you start a truck for the first time, you should get to know the location of the gauges and controls.
   A. True
   B. False

2. To start the _____, depress the clutch pedal to the floor and hold it there. Turn the key or press the starter button.
   A. gasoline engine
   B. diesel engine

3. The best _____ for a diesel engine is about 180 degrees Fahrenheit.
   A. rear axle temperature
   B. transmission temperature
   C. idling temperature
   D. operating temperature

4. You know that when the clutch pedal is up, the clutch is _____.
    A. engaged
    B. disengaged

5. The Super 10 transmission is shifted from first to 10th with only six shift lever changes.
    A. True
    B. False

6. "Depress the clutch pedal.
    Move the gear shift lever into neutral.
    Release the clutch pedal.
    Let the engine speed slow down until engine rpm and road speed match.
    Depress the clutch pedal and quickly move the gear shift lever to the next gear position.
    Release the clutch pedal."
    This is a description of double-clutching when you _____.
    A. upshift
    B. downshift

7. Carriers encourage their drivers to use the downshift procedure as a way to slow their rigs.
    A. True
    B. False

8. A transmission will have a range control or a splitter control, but never both.
    A. True
    B. False

9. The shift from _____ is the easiest shift on a 13-speed to make because you only single-clutch and you don't have to move the shift lever.
    A. LO to idle
    B. fourth high to fifth low
    C. direct to overdrive in the same gear
    D. manual to automatic

10. If your transmission is being downshifted, you must raise the engine speed when you double-clutch.
    A. True
    B. False

CHAPTER 17
DRIVING TECHNIQUES

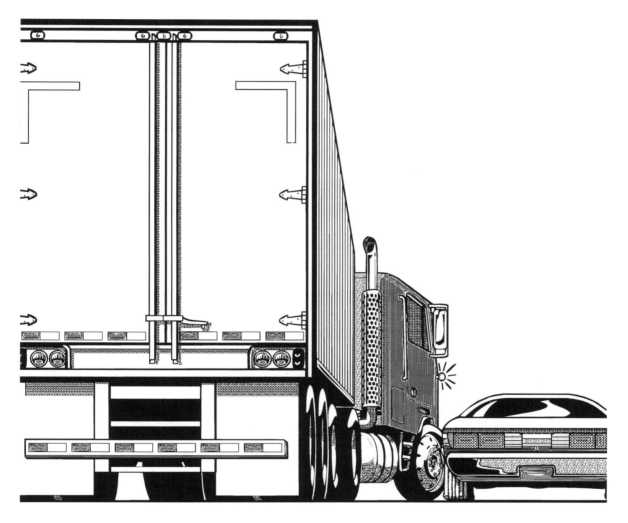

On the Road

In the last chapter, you learned how to get your truck in motion. Now that it's in motion, you're on the road where you need to know how to drive that rig. The next few chapters will focus on driving techniques. In this chapter, we'll focus on:

- steering
- serpentine maneuvers
- stopping the truck
- cornering
- bobtailing
- vehicle shutdown

Steering

Steering is more than simply directing the motion of the vehicle. You can't do a good job of steering if you:

- have poor driving posture
- have a poor grip on the steering wheel
- fight the steering wheel
- let the truck wander
- fail to stay focused on driving

Before you can steer properly, there are three things you must do: adjust your seat properly, sit properly, and grip the steering wheel properly.

ADJUST YOUR SEAT PROPERLY

Study your seat adjustment device. You may have to take out your operator's manual to find out how to use it. **Adjust the height** so your feet can rest on the floor. Adjust **the forward placement** so your left foot can push the clutch pedal to the floor without your having to stretch.

Next, set **the back** of the seat so it is straight up. Then lean back slightly and lock it in on the first comfortable setting. Look for a **lower back (lumbar)** adjustment. Set it on the first setting until you get used to it.

Your seat might also have a **weight** knob. Set it for your weight. This way you will get the right amount of shock absorption. After eight or nine hours, you will appreciate a properly adjusted seat.

Check the mirrors. Make sure you have the proper field of vision. After you adjust your seat, you may have to readjust one or both mirrors.

Last, but not least, fasten your seat belt.

MAINTAIN GOOD DRIVING POSTURE

Your **driving posture** (the way you sit when you drive) **is important** to good steering and to good driving in general. Do not slouch. Good posture:

- reduces fatigue
- helps keep you alert
- helps prevent neck and back aches
- helps you feel how the tractor and trailer respond

Adjusting your seat will help you attain good posture. Good posture is the first step to good driving techniques.

GRIP THE STEERING WHEEL PROPERLY

Now place your hands on the steering wheel. Imagine the wheel is a clock. Your left hand should be at 9 o'clock. Your right hand should be at 3 o'clock. Grip the wheel with all **fingers below and thumbs above,** resting on **the wheel.** (See Figure 17-1.)

Your grip should be firm, not too strong—just firm. When you turn or shift gears, keep one hand firmly on the wheel.

When you use this method to grip the steering wheel, your truck will not wander from side to side of your lane on a straight highway. There is no need to fight the steering wheel.

fig. 17-1
Proper steering wheel grip.

When you turn, avoid crossing your arms over the steering wheel. Instead, **reposition your hands one at a time as you turn** the wheel. Your left hand should not go past 12 o'clock when you turn right. Your right hand should not go past 12 o'clock when you turn left.

This method of turning is a safe driving technique taught to police and fire fighters, as well as commercial truck drivers. It keeps your arms from blocking your field of vision. It allows equal and maximum strength when you turn the wheel. When you use this method to turn, you will make turns more smoothly.

MANUAL AND POWER STEERING

Trucks with manual steering are harder to steer because you must provide all the power to turn the front wheels. As speed increases, steering becomes easier. It also feels easier in a cabover because you'll be sitting over the steering and that gives a more direct feel to steering.

Most drivers prefer power-assisted steering. It makes a large truck steer like the family car. There is less strain on your arms and shoulders with power steering and you have more control in side winds and on curving, twisting roads.

With both manual and power steering, **do not turn the steering wheel when the truck is stopped.** Depending on the road surface, tires or alignment can be damaged. Turn the steering wheel only when the truck is moving. It's easier on you and it's easier on the equipment.

Cornering

Steering around a corner with a 53-foot long trailer on a long nose tractor takes some extra thought. An average automobile is about 15 feet long. The rig you will drive will probably be about four times longer. It's also two or three feet wider and eight feet higher. Because of the length, the rear wheels of the trailer will not follow the same path as those of the tractor. Another way to say this is that the **trailer wheels do not track the tractor wheels (off-tracking)**. You must drive the tractor further ahead for the trailer wheels to follow around a corner.

fig. 17-2
When you take a corner with a tractor-trailer, the trailer wheels do not track the tractor wheels.

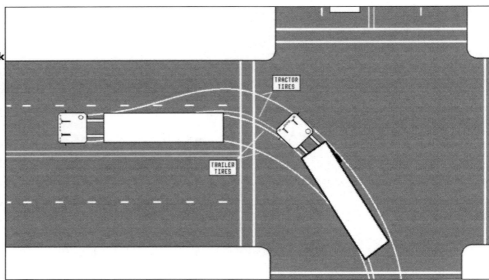

To execute the "perfect" turn, make sure you do the following things.

- Position the vehicle for turning.
- Signal well in advance.
- Check traffic conditions and turn only when the way is clear.
- Avoid swinging wide or cutting short.
- Adjust your speed so you can stop if you need to.
- Check for cross traffic regardless of traffic controls.
- Yield the right of way for safety.
- Use your mirrors to check for fixed objects and vehicle traffic.

TURNING RIGHT

Turning a right-hand corner is **more difficult than turning** a **left**-hand corner. When you turn left, you have a clear view of the corner. Turning to the right means you have a blind side at certain times.

OBSERVATION SKILLS TEST

Recall the illustration at the beginning of this chapter. A couple of problems are pictured in the situation. Did you notice them? Turn to the Observation Skills Test Grid at the back of this book and see how you're doing.

Before you turn, indicate your intention to turn by activating the right turn signal. Move only as far away from the right curb as necessary within the right hand lane. This keeps the right lane blocked so cars cannot pull in between the right side of your trailer and the curb. Check utility poles and overhead wires for clearance. Watch out for other vehicles entering the intersection. See Figure 17-3.

fig. 17-3
Once you complete a right-hand turn, straighten out your rig and pull into the right lane of the roadway you've turned onto.

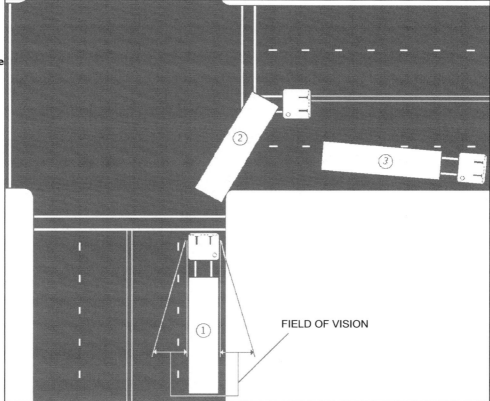

Go as far into the intersection past the right corner as you need to go for the trailer wheels to clear the curb. Be watching your trailer in your right side mirror. As soon as possible, steer the tractor into the right lane of the street you've turned onto. If you can't make the turn without swinging into another lane, **turn wide as you complete the turn.** Don't swing wide to the left at the start of the turn. Cars following you may misunderstand your intentions and try to pass you on the right. If you must cross into an oncoming lane and a vehicle comes toward you, allow it to get by you. Stop if you have to, but don't back up.

TURNING LEFT

Signal your intention well in advance when you turn left. You'll have a **clear field of vision** of the lane you're turning into. Using the left lane, drive the tractor past the center point of the intersection. Begin to turn left only after you are sure the trailer wheels will clear the centerline. Watch your trailer wheels in your side mirror for off-tracking. Steer the tractor wide of the lane. When the trailer wheels are into the lane, steer left to put the tractor in the lane and straighten up. If there are two left turning lanes, start your turn from the right-most lane.

MIRRORS

Making full use of your mirrors means you don't have to twist and turn your neck and body to see. You can

- keep good posture
- face ahead
- maintain a proper grip on the steering wheel

and still be aware of all side and rear objects.

fig. 17-4
You'll have a clear field of vision when you turn left.

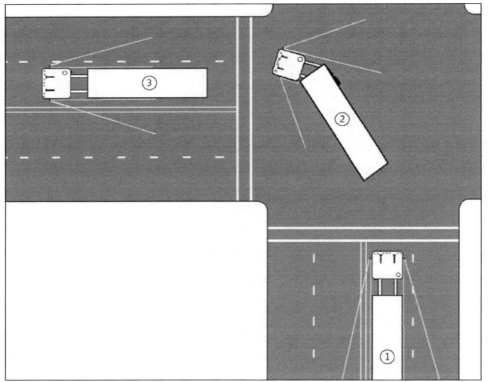

Most rigs have two mirrors on each side, one a large flat mirror and the other a convex mirror. The **large flat mirror lets you keep an eye on traffic and on your trailer.** The **smaller convex mirror lets you keep an eye on traffic and on your tractor drive wheels.** See Figure 17-5 on the next page, which illustrates the driver's view from the mirrors.

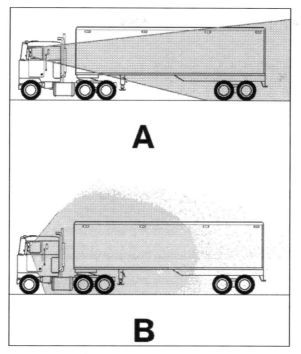

fig. 17-5
(A) What your large flat mirrors let you see and (B) what your smaller convex mirrors let you see.

When you're sitting in the driver's seat, the large flat mirrors on either side of your tractor let you see the sides of your trailer. You can see the road behind you from about the midpoint of the trailer. These two mirrors let you see the ground starting in front of the front trailer wheels, all of both lanes next to the rig, and behind the trailer.

The smaller convex mirror on each side of your tractor lets you keep an eye on traffic that's pulled up alongside of you. As Figure 17-6 shows, without this mirror you would have a very dangerous blind spot. If you were about to turn right or left and did not see a vehicle at this position, chances are you'd have an accident on your hands.

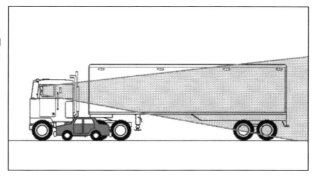

fig. 17-6
A car can hide if it comes up beside your rig behind your window and in front of your front trailer wheels. The convex mirror would let you see this blind spot.

A truck's mirrors do more than just give you a view of the surrounding traffic. They also help you keep an eye on your equipment. Make sure you adjust your large mirror so you can **see the trailer wheels in the flat mirror and the drive wheels in the convex mirror.** We hope you're never faced with the image of your tires coming apart, or on fire, or smoke coming from a cargo fire in the trailer. But if any of these were to occur, you would be able to see them in your mirrors.

Serpentine Maneuvers

Serpentine is a term used to describe the **twisting, winding movements** a driver must use now and then. For instance, suppose a sudden hailstorm has sent dozens of rigs off the highway and into a truck stop. They are parked all over the yard. You are driving in, too. You had planned to fuel up and have dinner. Just to get to the fuel pumps, you have to make a half circle across the yard. Driving between and around parked trucks, you turn left, then right, then left.

After driving around 10 parked trucks, you see your way clear to the pump islands. You have just completed serpentine maneuvers!

This kind of skill might also be called for when you drive into a customer's yard. You might be directed to proceed to a dock at the farthest corner of the plant. You have directions.

- Turn left at water tank.
- Turn right at Building N4.
- Go on to the right side of railroad tracks.
- Turn right on maintenance road.
- Turn left just before garage.

As you can see, your trip to the back dock is an obstacle course. You watch for side clearances, low overhangs, telephone wires, forklifts, and pedestrians. You slow, you stop, you check your mirrors. You use the turn signals, and if you must, you honk your horn.

Most of the time you are busy with the steering wheel turning left, then right, then left. You use the mirrors every second. As you decrease or increase speed, you use the shift lever and the clutch.

When you get to the dock, you realize that you have just wound your rig through a busy plant yard. You are pleased with yourself. You didn't drive over so much as one blade of grass!

Each maneuver means

- looking to the left and right
- checking all mirrors
- planning for off-tracking
- slowing
- looking for enough clearance

to get by on one side and then the other.

Bobtailing

Bobtailing a tractor means **driving** it **without a trailer** attached. Believe it or not, this can be **more dangerous than driving with a fully loaded trailer.** Without the weight of a trailer, the tractor tires have a smaller footprint. That is to say, they do not spread out as much and there is much less contact with the road.

The greatest danger of bobtailing is not being able to stop in time. On wet or icy road surfaces, skidding can begin with the first brake application.

A **cabover** tractor is even **more difficult to control than a conventional** tractor in such circumstances. This is mainly because of the difference in weight distribution. When you bobtail a conventional tractor, some of the engine weight is on the steering axle and some of it is on the driving axle. But on a cabover nearly all of the engine weight is on the steering axle. This means the drive wheels of the cabover will be more likely to spin when accelerating on slippery surfaces. They're more likely to lock up when braking on any surface because there is so little weight on them.

You must use extra caution when you bobtail. Drive slower and allow for more stopping time.

Pulling an empty trailer presents a similar problem. Empty trucks require greater stopping distances because they have less traction. The empty vehicle can bounce and the wheels can lock up, causing poor braking.

Anti-lock brakes (ABS), if your tractor has them, will not shorten the stopping distance of a bobtail. ABS will, however, help prevent wheel lockup and reduce the chances of skidding.

Stopping the Truck

Stopping a truck is more than just applying the brakes. Stopping smoothly means watching traffic patterns ahead of you. It means leaving enough space between vehicles in front. It means gearing down for a downgrade or slowing down well in advance of coming up on in slower traffic. A smooth stop means as little wear and tear on the equipment as possible. A smooth stop means no shifting of the cargo, and no damage. You should always:

- stop smoothly
- avoid sudden stops
- stop clear of crosswalks
- stop before leaving an alley
- stop and restart without rolling backward

Wait until the rpm is close to idle before you push the clutch in.

Vehicle Shutdown

Leaving a truck parked requires more than setting the parking brake. There are times when you'll have to park the truck for a day or two or even longer. If you are away from your terminal you must think about security. Look for a safe place for the tractor and trailer. Try to park in a lighted area in a trucking or warehouse district. These areas have private security guards as well as police patrols.

Engine parts are hot after running all day, and they **take a few minutes to cool off.** By the time you have pulled into a parking area and found a space, the engine has had a chance to cool down and may be shut off. The company you drive for may have specific instructions about engine idling and shut down.

Set the parking brakes by pulling both knobs. (Don't set the parking brakes when the brakes are very hot. Use wheel chocks until the brakes have had a chance to cool. In freezing weather, wet brakes can freeze if you don't dry them before setting the parking brake.) Never leave the vehicle unattended without first setting the parking brake.

Close all windows. Take all valuables out of the cab, or at least place them out of sight. Lock the tractor doors. Padlock the trailer doors. Lock the fuel tank caps.

Chapter 17 Quiz

1. Adjust the _____ of your driver's seat so your left foot can push the clutch pedal to the floor without your needing to stretch.
    A. height
    B. forward position
    C. back
    D. weight knob

2. You should grip the steering wheel with all _____.
    A. fingers and thumbs above, resting on the wheel
    B. fingers above and thumbs resting on the wheel
    C. fingers and thumbs below the steering wheel with a firm grip
    D. fingers below and thumbs above, resting on the wheel

3. When you turn, _____.
    A. cross your arms one at a time over the steering wheel
    B. reposition your hands one at a time as you turn the wheel
    C. lean your left arm on the driver's side door, and turn with your right hand only
    D. rest your right hand on the shift lever and turn with your left hand only

4. As speed decreases, steering becomes easier.
   A. True
   B. False

5. Whether you have manual or power steering, you should not turn the steering wheel when the truck is stopped.
   A. True
   B. False

6. When you make a turn, the trailer wheels do not track the tractor wheels.
   A. True
   B. False

7. When you turn _____, you'll have a clear field of vision.
   A. left
   B. right

8. The large flat mirror lets you keep an eye on traffic and on _____.
   A. your tractor drive wheels
   B. your trailer
   C. the area from behind your window to your front tractor tires on the driver's side
   D. the area from behind your window to your front tractor tires on both sides

9. When you are looking to the left and right, slowing, checking all mirrors, looking for enough clearance to get by on one side then the other, and turning both left and right, you are performing a _____ maneuver.
   A. backing
   B. engine shutdown
   C. serpentine
   D. bobtailing

10. When you bobtail, a cabover tractor is even more difficult to control than a conventional tractor.
    A. True
    B. False

BACKING

Backing Is Easy, Isn't It?

No, it isn't. Backing a tractor-trailer may sound like a simple task, but it isn't, not even for the experienced driver. In fact, **most accidents involving tractor-trailers happen during backing.** It takes patience and practice to develop the ability to back a tractor-trailer skillfully and safely. In this chapter, you'll learn the backing procedures used by experienced drivers. You'll learn pre-positioning, steering, and docking procedures for backing. We'll also cover another not-so-easy procedure: parallel parking. But first, let's look at where and why backing accidents occur and how you can prevent them.

Backing Accidents

A good driving record is important to you. You don't even want one minor accident on your record. So, prepare yourself well to avoid backing accidents by knowing where and why they happen and how to prevent them.

OBSERVATION SKILLS TEST

Avoid backing accidents by being aware of your surroundings. How aware were you of the illustration that began this chapter? What did you notice? Now, test your awareness by checking the Observation Skills Test Grid at the end of the book.

WHERE THEY HAPPEN

The three most frequent types of backing accidents are those that occur

- on the right side
- at the rear
- at the top

of your vehicle.

Yes, **backing into something at the top of the vehicle is** a **common** backing accident! Low hanging wires and eaves can damage the overhead area of your vehicle. This type of accident is easily avoided. In fact, it should never happen. Simply make sure the area above is clear of anything that might tear off an exhaust stack or otherwise damage the top of the cab.

Backing accidents often occur at the rear of the trailer. You may think you are backing up to something only to find out at the last minute you have backed into something. The main reason for this type of backing accident is carelessness. However, something can move behind you after you think you've made sure the area is clear. That's one reason it's good to check, and then check again.

Many backing **accidents occur on the right side** of the rig. These are the most difficult to avoid. The reason for this is many times when backing the tractor will be at an angle with the trailer and you will not be able to see the right side at all.

WHY THEY HAPPEN

Most accidents happen when the driver is in too much of a hurry. A **lack of attention** on the part of the driver **causes** many backing **accidents.** Backing takes a lot of concentration. Turn off the radio and the CB. The less noise there is to distract you, the less likely you will lose concentration and get into an accident.

However, carelessness **causes most backing accidents.** They most often happen when drivers don't take the time to:

- get out of the truck and check the area they are backing into
- use mirrors properly
- be prepared to stop immediately
- back slowly

So, right away you can see four procedures that will greatly reduce the likelihood of your having a backing accident.

HOW TO PREVENT BACKING ACCIDENTS

First, always **check the area you're backing into before you begin backing.** Get out of the truck, walk behind it, and visually check the area. Even if you're just backing up in a straight line, get out and take a good look at the area. Never make the mistake that you can catch everything with your mirrors. Look up and down and all around. And, don't forget to look under your rig to make sure a stray animal hasn't turned up out of nowhere. Always check just before you begin backing. If any time at all has passed since the last time you checked, check again just before you begin backing. In other words, you should check the area, get into your truck, and begin backing without further delay.

Whenever you can't clearly see what's next to you or behind you, you should stop, **get out, and check the area you're backing into during the procedure.** This will be the case when you back from a blind side pre-position. You'll learn about blind side backing later in this chapter. For now, you need to know that sometimes you'll need to stop, get out, and check the area after each few feet of backing.

Second, **use your mirrors properly.** Once you're sure nothing is in the way on either side of your rig, behind your rig, over your rig, or under your rig, you can begin to back using your mirrors. You may need to adjust your mirrors. Take time to do this. In some cases, it may be necessary to roll down your window and look back out of it while you back your rig. Be careful, though. If you hit something, you could slam your head into the door jamb. In any case, don't use just this or just one mirror. Watch both sides of the rig. And don't open your door and lean out of it. That makes it impossible to use the right side mirror, and increases the risk of being injured.

Third, keep your right foot off the throttle. You'll rarely need to use it to start your rig backing up anyway. Move very slowly, and **keep your right foot poised over the brake pedal.** This prepares you to stop immediately to avoid hitting anything. Also, you'll eliminate the response time it would otherwise take to move your foot from the throttle to the brake. This response time is just as crucial to stopping in time when you're going backward as it is when going forward.

So, you can go a long way toward preventing backing accidents if you take the time to:

- always check the area you're backing into just before you begin to back
- stop, get out, and check the area you're backing into during the procedure
- use both your mirrors the entire time you're backing
- keep your right foot poised over the brake

Many traffic problems and accidents result from drivers backing tractor-trailers across city and suburban streets. Big as your rig is, cross-traffic may fail to recognize it as an obstacle. Sometimes delivery areas are hard to get to other than by backing up to them. When you must back across a city street, get your co-driver to help by stopping traffic while you back. If you're alone, inquire at the consignee's business. Perhaps they can spare someone to help control traffic while you make delivery.

You can't control the actions of others. However, you can often make up for the actions of others, if you see them coming. And, you can always make sure you are not the cause of a backing accident.

How to Steer in Reverse

There are three steps to any backing maneuver: jacking, following, and straightening. **Jacking is turning the tractor so it is out of line with the trailer.** As you move backwards **this starts the trailer going back in a curve.** To do this you start by turning the top of the steering wheel opposite the direction you want the rear of the trailer to go. Or, try this: Place your hand on the bottom of the steering wheel. Then move your hand (and therefore the wheel) in the same direction you want the trailer to go first. See Figure 18-1.

After you jack the tractor, you will need to **follow the trailer** around the curve. To do this, **reverse the steering angle. As the trailer moves backwards, the tractor will follow it.** Some people refer to this procedure as chasing the trailer.

Once the trailer has curved far enough you **straighten the tractor** by bringing it back into line with the trailer. To do this you increase the steering angle and continue backing until the tractor is straight with the trailer, then straighten the steering axle.

Steering backwards should always be slow and deliberate. Use your idle speed only. If the trailer should happen to get off course, stop and move forward so you can start over once again. As you back, always pay special attention to the front of the tractor, the front of the trailer, the angle of the tractor and trailer, and the rear of the trailer.

Your ability to jack and chase the trailer is put to the greatest test by a maneuver called the backward serpentine. In this maneuver, you go through all the steps described in Chapter 17, only in reverse. You may have to do a backward serpentine as part of your CDL skills test, and you'll have to do it with few if any stops for repositioning your vehicle.

fig. 18-1
Steering in reverse.

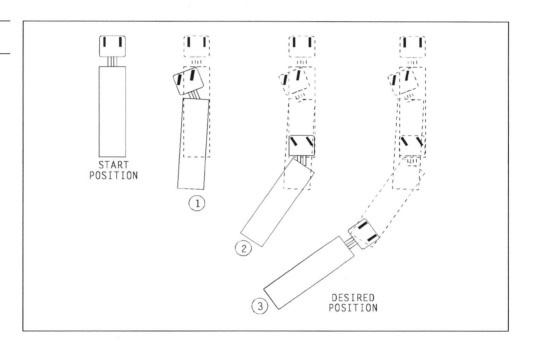

Steering in Reverse
(refer to Figure 18-1)

1. Jacking: turn the steering wheel to the right. The front of the tractor will point to the left. The rear of the tractor will point to the right, putting the tractor at an angle with the trailer.

2. Following (chasing): turn the steering wheel to the left. This maintains the angle between the tractor and the trailer. Follow the trailer around.

3. Straighten: turn even more to the left to straighten the tractor with the trailer. When the tractor is in line with the trailer, straighten the wheels.

Pre-positioning

Now that you know where and why backing accidents occur and how to prevent them, you're ready to begin learning backing procedures. The first and perhaps the most critical is **pre-positioning**. This is **the position into which you place your rig before you begin backing.** These are the three common pre-positions:

- straight back
- clear side
- blind side

As we discuss the three pre-positions, let's assume you're driving a cabover tractor pulling a 45-foot trailer. This is a popular rig on the road today and will serve as a good example of what is involved in the skill of backing. In our examples, you are backing your rig into a dock.

The distances which we will be dealing with apply to this type of rig. As you become a more experienced driver, you will learn that different sized rigs call for different distances and turning angles.

If you're pulling a trailer with swinging doors, here's an important first step to remember for all docking maneuvers. Open the trailer's swinging doors while you are still clear of the dock and other vehicles. You will not be happy to work hard getting to the dock just to find you have to pull away again to get your trailer's swinging doors open.

THE STRAIGHT BACK PRE-POSITION
Straight back backing is the **easiest and safest** to perform. So, whenever you can back straight in, you should. From this pre-position, you have a clear view in both mirrors of the space you are backing into. (You'll sometimes hear this space referred to as "the hole," as we will in the following discussion.)

Pre-positioning for a Straight Back
(refer to Figure 18-2 on the next page)

1. Stop, get out, and inspect the area.

2. Pull ahead and as tractor passes the hole, steer hard away from the hole.

3. Steer back into line with the hole.

4. Pull ahead until tractor and trailer are straight and line up with the hole. If you do this right, as soon as the tractor and trailer straighten out you'll be directly in front of the hole. You'll be able to see it in both mirrors. You can now stop going forward and start going backward.

5. Back straight into the hole, adjusting as necessary to keep centered in the hole.

fig. 18-2
Pre-positioning your rig for a straight back involves these steps.

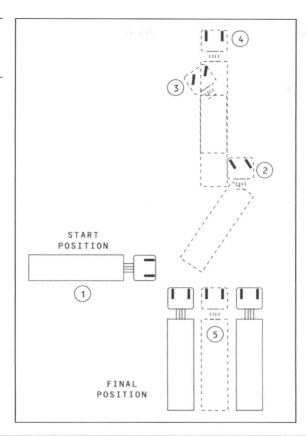

Straight backing is the basis for all other kinds of backing. Get straight backing down good before you try the more complicated maneuvers.

THE CLEAR SIDE PRE-POSITION

"Clear side" is a term used to describe **backing from a position which lets you have a clear view in your left rear view mirror of the space you back into.** This is the type of backing you'll do most often. Remember that if you can back straight in, you should. If you can't back straight in, the second best choice is to back from the clear side pre-position.

Pre-positioning for a Clear Side Back
(refer to Figure 18-3 on the next page)

1. Stop, get out, and inspect the area.

2. Pull ahead and steer away from the space.

3. When the tractor is at a 45-degree angle to the space, straighten the wheels and pull ahead until the tractor and trailer are in line and the trailer is pointing at the space. You will be able to see the space in your left mirror.

4. Start backing. Turn the steering wheel to the right to jack the tractor. Once the trailer is curving towards the space, turn the steering wheel to the left and let the tractor follow the trailer into the space.

THE BLIND SIDE PRE-POSITION

With a blind side position, it is **more difficult to see the area you're backing your rig into.** Your rear view mirrors are less useful. Your left mirror will help you when turning and pulling forward. Once you start back, you can see with the right mirror and the spot mirror, although you may have to move around in the seat to do so.

fig. 18-3
Pre-positioning on the clear side to back your rig involves these steps.

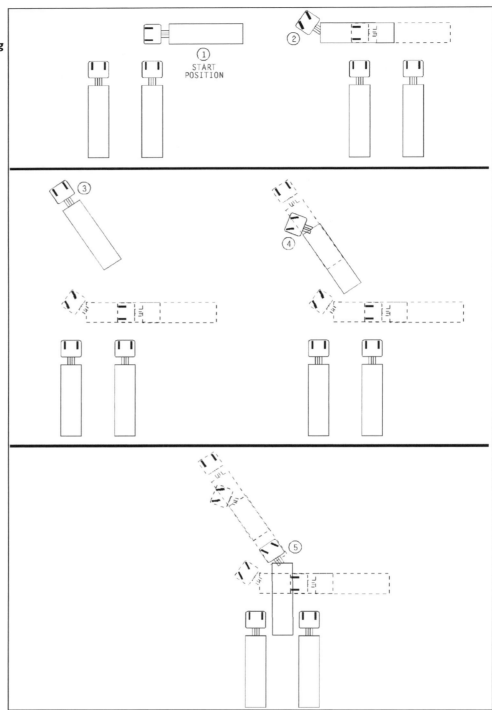

This is the **most difficult and the most dangerous** pre-position. Avoid it, if you can. Of course, you won't always be able to avoid it, so you must know how to back from this position.

Backing in from the blind side uses the same steps as clear side backing. The only difference is it's harder to see what you are doing. Your right side mirror will help you. At those times when you can't see, you should stop often and get out of your rig to check your position. It is a lot easier to stop, get out, and check where you are a few extra times than it is to explain to another driver why you backed into his brand new truck.

fig. 18-4
Pre-positioning on the blind side to back your rig involves these steps.

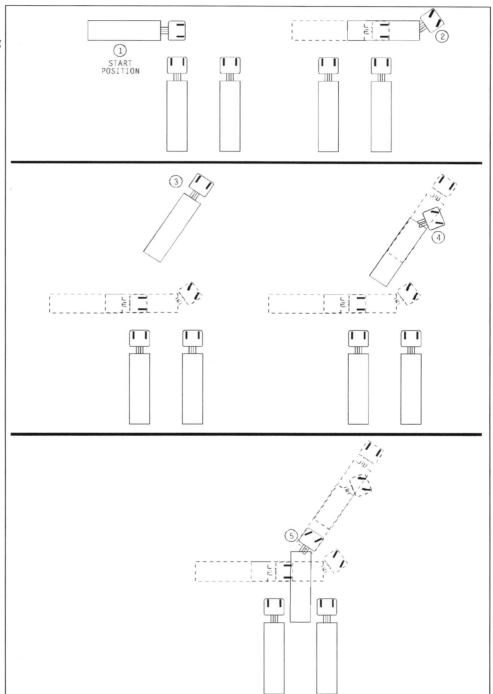

Remember, what you can see depends on your pre-position:

PRE-POSITION	WHAT YOU CAN SEE
Straight Back	You have a clear view in both mirrors of the space you are backing into.
Clear Side	You have a clear view in your left rear view mirror of the space you are backing into.
Blind Side	You are unable to see the area you are backing your rig into.

Pre-positioning for a Blind Side Back
(refer to Figure 18-4 on the previous page)

1. Stop, get out, and inspect the area.

2. Pull ahead and steer away from the space.

3. When the tractor is at a 45-degree angle to the space, straighten the wheels and pull ahead until the tractor and trailer are in line and the trailer is pointing at the space. You will be able to see the space in your right mirror.

4. Start backing. Turn the steering wheel to the left to jack the tractor. Once the trailer is curving towards the space, turn the steering wheel to the right and let the tractor follow the trailer into the space.

5. When the trailer is in line with the space, turn the steering wheel even more to the right to straighten the tractor with the trailer. Continue backing.

Docking

1. Inspect the area.

2. Pre-position the rig.

3. Open the trailer doors.

4. Operate at idle speed only.

5. Back up close to the dock.

6. Inspect the area behind the trailer and estimate the remaining distance.

7. Back easily until the trailer touches the dock.

Docking

One backing procedure that will probably be a routine part of your job is docking to load and unload. **To be able to dock, you must understand how to pre-position and how to steer backwards.** You have, however, just learned all about that. So, now you're ready for docking!

If you must dock from a blind side pre-position (or any position for that matter), **have someone help you from the ground.** If you don't have a partner in the cab, ask someone in the dock yard. All drivers know what a chore it is to back up blind. You won't find it hard to get someone to help.

Many warehouses require you to **chock your trailer tires after you have backed up to the dock.** Chocks are wood or rubber blocks placed in front of the trailer tires to keep the trailer from rolling away from the dock. This can happen because of the motion caused by loading or unloading.

"Center, straight, and easy" are the words you should keep in mind as you dock. You want to be sure that the trailer is going to be centered as it meets with the dock. You also want to make sure that the trailer and the dock contact in a straight line. And, you're supposed to ease up to the dock, not ram it.

Parallel Parking

Like backing, **parallel parking is** a **difficult** driving manuever. In terms of difficulty, it comes close to blind side backing. The exact procedure differs with each tractor-trailer. Each rig will back and turn differently. One reason for this is that different rigs have different wheelbases.

Parallel Parking
(refer to Figure 18-5 on the next page)

1. Pull forward until the trailer is halfway past Vehicle A.

2. Turn the steering wheel to the left so your tractor directs the trailer to the right and the trailer starts heading toward the space.

3. When the trailer is pointing into the space, straighten the tractor by turning the steering wheel to the right and continue backing.

4. When the middle of your tractor is at the rear of Vehicle A, your right rear trailer wheels should be about three feet from the curb. Now turn right so the tractor directs the trailer to the left. This will start the front of the trailer into the space.

5. When your tractor will clear Vehicle A turn the steering wheel to the left so the tractor aligns with the trailer.

You should avoid parallel parking whenever you can, and you usually can. However, you may find yourself somewhere, sometime with no choice but to parallel park. Some states include parallel parking in the CDL skills test. Figure 18-5 illustrates how.

This procedure should bring you within inches of the curb. The sides of your front and rear tires must be within 12 inches of the curb for you to be legally parked. Keep in mind that rigs are wide vehicles. So, 12 inches from the curb may not keep the left side of your rig out of the traffic lane. Remember you have a long rig so you will need a long space to be able to parallel park successfully. Never try to parallel park unless you're sure you have enough room.

Parallel parking is quite a tricky maneuver. You will very likely have to pull forward and adjust your position a time or two before you can back neatly into the space.

fig. 18-5
These are the steps to parallel park.

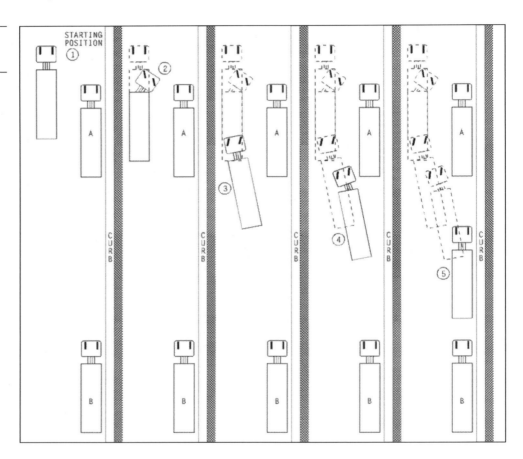

Chapter 18 Quiz

1. The three most frequent types of backing accidents are those that occur on the right side, at the rear, and _____ of your vehicle.
   A. at the fifth wheel
   B. on the left side
   C. on the top
   D. at the front

2. The most difficult backing accidents to avoid are _____ accidents.
   A. overhead
   B. right side
   C. left side
   D. rear of the trailer

3. Backing accidents most often happen when drivers fail to get out of the truck and check the area they are backing into or

   _____.
   A. use mirrors properly
   B. turn on their radios or CBs
   C. chase the trailer properly
   D. chock the wheels at the dock

4. When backing, your right foot should be _____.
   A. poised over the clutch pedal
   B. positioned between the brake and the throttle
   C. resting lightly on the throttle
   D. poised over the brake pedal

5. Straight back, clear side, and blind side are all examples of

   _____.
   A. pre-positions
   B. chasing the trailer
   C. steering procedures
   D. jacking procedures

6. When you can see your parking space in both rear view mirrors, you're in a _____ pre-position.
   A. straight back
   B. proper
   C. clear side
   D. blind side

7. When you can see your parking space in your left rear view mirror, you're in a _____ pre-position.
   A. straight back
   B. proper
   C. clear side
   D. blind side

8.   The procedure that puts the tractor out of line with the trailer is known as _____.
       A.   jacking
       B.   following
       C.   chasing
       D.   pre-positioning

9.   When you back to a dock, it's expected you'll probably ram into it.
       A.   True
       B.   False

10.   Parallel parking is a backing manuever that you _____ .
       A.   will never have to perform
       B.   should choose over straight backing
       C.   may need several tries to accomplish
       D.   should be able to perform easily

CHAPTER 19

SAFE DRIVING

The Safe Driver

Competent drivers are those who have excellent control of their vehicle. This enables them to react quickly to sudden surprises or dangerous situations.

A safe driver is something else. A safe driver is all the things we just mentioned and more. The safe driver never gets into trouble in the first place. Safe drivers are calm, cautious, and respectful. They take the time to see what is going on all around them. **Safe drivers** are so alert, so observant, and so well prepared that they don't get "surprises." They can perform evasive manuevers, but rarely have to. They **see dangerous situations developing** long before they happen and can take steps to **avoid the danger.** Safe drivers simply **don't have accidents.**

To become a good, competent driver takes a little bit of work. To become a **safe** driver takes just a little bit more. In this chapter, we'll teach you the techniques you must master to become a safe driver.

Visual Search

Perception is being able to see and **know what is going on** around the truck. You must not only see objects, vehicles, or situations, but must also **understand the situation.** For instance, you must not only see that a vehicle is approaching the intersection. You must also realize that means the vehicle will soon be in the intersection, and decide if that calls for any response from you.

A safe driver is able to see and recognize potential problems quickly. It takes time for the mind to process information the eyes and ears send to the brain. To avoid a potentially dangerous situation, this information must be processed quickly, because you'll also need time to act. That means you must keep your mind on your driving.

Watch for dangers by scanning, moving your eyes back and forth over an area. You must know what's happening—and what's likely to happen—at these areas around your vehicle.

- ahead
- to the sides
- to the rear

Visual search helps you keep from getting boxed in behind slower moving traffic. By watching ahead you will see traffic jams in time to slow down or change lanes safely. Keep your eyes moving and you will avoid unpleasant situations and surprises.

SEEING AHEAD
Distance scanning is looking ahead of the truck while driving down the road. **Scan ahead the distance the vehicle would move in about 12 to 15 seconds.** At highway speeds, that's about a quarter-mile. This gives you time to understand and react to any situation. A truck requires both space and time for safe lane changes, slowing, or stopping.

Distance scanning also helps you **position the truck properly in the lane.** You'll tend to guide the truck along whatever path you focus your eyes on. So, don't focus on the center line. That will cause you to travel too much to the left of your lane. Instead, imagine a line down the middle of your lane and focus on that.

Distance scanning is important in turns as well as straight roads. Look ahead into the turn and start planning how much space your vehicle will need to complete the turn safely.

While distance scanning, **watch the road surface** also. Pavement markings will tell you of a change in width and alert you that you may have to move over. You'll see any changes in the road surface which could affect your truck.

SEEING TO THE SIDES

Scanning ahead is important, but don't lock your eyes on the road in front of you and leave them there. Your **scanning must include the sides of the road.** There could be vehicles coming from side roads, or vehicles trying to pass you from either side. Scan the sides by moving your eyes from the front of the truck to one side of the road, then to the other.

SEEING TO THE REAR

Be aware of what's going on behind you, as well as to the front and the sides. This is where your mirrors become important.

Use of Mirrors

There are two basic types of mirrors, **plane and convex** (sometimes called the "spot mirror"). When you first get in the cab, **position both mirrors so** that while in the driver's seat you can see properly. The **plane mirrors** should **reflect the trailer body** from the inside vertical edge to a depth of about one inch. The rest of the view is the road about 15 feet out to the side of the trailer. The inside vertical edge of the **convex mirrors** should **show you part of the trailer.** The view in the top horizontal edge should overlap that of the plane mirror. You should not have to lean forward or to the side to get these views.

Note that everything you see in the spot mirrors seems smaller than it really is. Things also seem farther away than they really are. Remind yourself that what you see in the spot mirrors is closer and larger than it appears.

Use the mirrors to scan the area behind the truck. Check them every five to ten seconds. Note who's coming up behind you. When you check again, see if they're still there. If not, where did they go? Did they pull off the road, pass you, or are they tucked into your blind spot? It's like counting cards in a card game. Use your mirrors often, and **keep track of who's on the road with you.** This will help you make lane changes or merge.

This keeping inventory is especially important with regard to the vehicles that are directly behind the trailer or on the right side of the tractor. Your mirrors aren't much help here, you simply can't see these areas well. You have to have made note of who was behind you on the road. If they haven't exited or passed you, it's a pretty safe bet they're in these blind spots. Your spot mirrors will help you see these blind spots. What the spot mirrors will not show is the small vehicle that is in the right hand lane next to you. It's traveling just to the front of your right front fender.

OBSERVATION SKILLS TEST

The truck driver in the illustration at the top of this chapter will get into an accident if he isn't observant. What dangerous conditions did you notice? Turn to the Observation Skills Test Grid at the back of the book to check your answers.

Communication

All drivers, no matter the type of vehicle they are operating, must communicate with each other. This is especially important when you're driving an 18-wheeler. Other drivers may not understand how much room you need to turn, how long it takes for you to stop, and so on. It is important to **communicate clearly, early, and long** enough so other drivers are aware of what you are doing.

COMMUNICATING INTENT TO CHANGE LANES
Let other drivers know when you plan to change lanes. Remember, you have a blind spot right behind the truck and it's difficult to see any vehicles that are alongside the truck. So give other drivers on the road time to adjust their speed or lane position to make room for the truck to move safely. FMCSR 392.15 (c) requires you to **signal for not less than 100 feet in advance of any lane changes.** In bad traffic, you may want to give an even earlier warning.

COMMUNICATING INTENT TO SLOW OR STOP
You also need to **communicate your intent to slow down, turn, or stop.** For example, many automobile drivers don't realize how fast they are coming up behind a slower moving vehicle, such as your truck. When you are driving a truck slowly up a steep grade, **using the emergency flashers will alert others that you are moving slowly** (check local laws which may prohibit using the flashers for this purpose). **Signal your intent to stop by flashing your brake lights.**

Some state regulations may require you to turn on **the turn signal** at least 100 feet before the turn. This **warns other drivers that you'll be slowing down,** and gives them plenty of time to respond safely.

COMMUNICATING PRESENCE

There are times when you may need to let other drivers know that you are there. Some drivers communicate their presence with the air horn. A truck's air horn often only offends or frightens other drivers. It gets their attention, but may cause them more alarm than necessary. There are better ways to let others know you're on the road.

Communicate your truck's presence by flashing your headlights. Definitely have the headlights on in rain or snow and on cloudy days. A truck can't be seen more easily than a car just because the truck is bigger. Remember, if you are having a hard time seeing other vehicles, they are having a hard time seeing you. Lights will help others to see you. At night, have lights on from one-half hour after sunset through to one-half hour before sunrise.

MISUSE OF COMMUNICATION

Every driver, no matter what the kind of vehicle, relies on the accuracy of communication from other drivers. If you give the wrong message, the wrong message will be received.

For instance, it is just as important to turn off the turn signals after a lane change or after completing a turn as it is to turn them on in the first place. Keep in mind, the turn signal in a truck doesn't automatically snap off when a turn is completed. Make turning it off a part of the turning process. As you shift gears as the trailer straightens out after a corner, **turn off the turn signals.** Else, other drivers will think you plan to turn even though you don't. They may speed up, thinking you'll soon be out of their way, or try to pass you on the other side. Don't use turn signals to signal to other drivers that it's safe to pass.

Don't misuse the horn. Don't use it to tell another driver to speed up or get out of the way. It is dangerous to lay on the horn. A loud blast may scare other drivers and cause an accident. We suggest you use it only in an emergency. Then we'll add that if you're a good, safe driver, you shouldn't have that emergency to begin with.

The CB radio is a useful communication tool. It can be used to call for help in case of an accident, emergency stop, or to ask for directions or other needed information. But it's a misuse of this important device to treat it like a toy. Don't clutter up the airways with useless chatter, especially when another truck driver may be genuinely in need of it for help or information. Besides, while you're shooting the breeze on the CB, you are not paying attention to your driving.

COMMUNICATION FROM OTHERS

Communication is a two-way street. You communicate to others, but you must also **pay attention to the communication of others** to you. The truck may be the biggest vehicle on the road, but the road is still shared by all.

Look for and respond to the communication of other drivers, correctly and safely. Let's say the car in front of you is signaling for a turn. Notice the signal, and respond. Understand the car will likely be slowing down for the turn, so you should, too. You may even want to be prepared to stop in case the car driver runs into trouble. It would be incorrect to respond by speeding up, thinking the car will soon be out of your path. What if he changes his mind and tries to return to the road in front of you?

Speed Management

You must realize the importance of speed management. **Speed management means to know how fast to drive** according to the:

- stopping distance you'll need
- shape of the road
- traffic flow
- condition of the road surface
- visibility conditions
- speed limit

STOPPING DISTANCE

You must know **how long and how far it will take for your vehicle to stop safely** after you have decided to stop and have stepped on the brakes. Stopping distance is described in detail in Chapter 4. This distance will vary based on road conditions, the weight of the vehicle, and your traveling speed.

ROAD SURFACE

The speed at which the truck can travel safely will depend on the condition of the road surface. The following **conditions demand slower speeds of travel.**

- rough road surface
- snow
- rain
- ice

You can get the feel of the road when starting out before you work up to any great speed. Check traction (the friction between the tires and the road) by testing the steering control and the braking friction while you're still going slowly. **Friction and traction problems get worse at faster speeds,** so **maintain that slow speed on poor roads.**

Hydroplaning occurs when water or slush is on the road. Your **tires** are no longer in contact with the road but **are actually riding on the surface of the water.** This can result in your losing control of the vehicle. Several factors, such as worn or underinflated tires and the amount of water on the road, can make hydroplaning worse. Another factor is your road speed.

Wet roads can double the stopping distance. Be especially careful just after a rain begins. Rain mixes with oil on the road, resulting in a very slippery surface. **Maintain a slower speed on wet roads.** Reduce your speed by one-third.

Snow and ice can also **reduce traction.** Be aware that shaded areas, bridges, and ramps can ice up before the main road surface does. Feel the front of your outside mirror. If it is starting to ice up, so is the road.

The inter-axle differential lock can give you more traction on slippery surfaces. **Lock in the inter-axle differential** on snow- and ice-covered roads and when black ice is present. Black ice is a film of ice too thin to see but thick enough to be slippery. Melting ice is even more slippery than ice that is frozen solid.

Icy and snowy roads also demand slower speeds. Again, **travel at slower speeds** when these weather conditions dictate it.

SHAPE OF ROAD
Slow down before entering curves. Going into a curve too fast can cause skidding or cause the truck to roll over. The danger is especially great when you're hauling liquid loads. Centrifugal force will tend to push your vehicle to the outside of the curve. High speeds increase the effect of centrifugal force, so respect posted speed limits on curves. These signs guide cars to the maximum speed that is safe for the curve. This may be too fast for your truck. Because of their higher center of gravity, trucks must take curves slower than cars.

Also, slow down **enough so that you don't have to brake** while in the curve. Braking in the curve may cause a skid or jackknifing.

A truck may **lose speed while going up a hill** and may have to be downshifted. You should **get into the right lane,** or truck lane. This allows the other traffic to keep moving safely at highway speeds.

You'll tend to pick up speed **when traveling downhill.** Somehow, you'll need to brake to **control the vehicle's speed.** You should downshift before starting down, use the auxiliary brake, or the service brake. If you use the service brake, use the snub braking procedure which you will read more about in Chapter 20. **Don't fan the brakes.** That only causes them to heat up faster, and contributes to brake fade. Chapter 22 discusses the use of the auxiliary brake.

SPEED AND VISIBILITY

Your speed should be based on how far ahead you can see. Figure out your stopping distance at your current speed. Do you have a clear view of the road to where your final stopping point would be? If not, slow down.

Let's look at this problem from another angle. Say you're approaching a curve or hill or crossroads. What if a problem were to develop just around the bend, over the crest, or in the intersection? **Your speed should be based on how long it would take you to see the danger and respond.**

In all cases of reduced sight distance, slow down. You must be able to see ahead the distance it would take to make a safe response—change lanes, slow, or stop. "Don't over-drive your vision" is how this concept is sometimes phrased.

SPEED AND FLOW OF TRAFFIC

Maybe the best advice about speed management is "go with the flow." You may be on the interstate, but if traffic is moving at 35 mph, so should you. This gives you more time to avoid potential hazards.

You may think that if you drive faster you will get where you're going sooner. Perhaps you will get there just a couple minutes sooner. The extra couple minutes aren't worth the risk of injury. The faster you drive the more risks you are taking. When you are going too fast for the rest of the traffic, you have to do more passing and lane-changing. Each lane change is an opportunity for an accident which would make you very late.

Driving that fast is also tiring and causes fatigue, and that, too, leads to accidents. At this point, you probably also realize you've increased your stopping distance. That makes it harder to stop safely.

By the same token, watch your speed when traffic is moving smoothly. If the traffic is moving at a steady 50 mph, you will only create dangerous situations by moving too slowly. Again, **match your pace to the flow of the traffic within posted speed limits.**

Speed Limits

The speed limit is **the top speed anyone should ever use on that road.** It is not necessarily the safest. Speed limits take into account the design and construction of the road and the type of traffic the road is meant to bear. To a certain extent, the speed limit is an ideal. You don't have to drive as fast as the speed limit allows, and shouldn't if a slower speed would be safer.

Certainly, you should **never exceed the speed limit.** If what we've said about safety didn't convince you, a speeding ticket certainly will. You, **the driver,**

will pay that speeding ticket, not your employer. Some insurance companies will drop you if you get two moving violations in as few as three years.

Entering and Exiting Traffic

The ramp used **to enter a freeway** gives you time both to **build up to highway speed and** to **find an opening into which to merge.** In a truck, you may run out of ramp before you've reached highway speed or found an opening in traffic. All you can do is be patient and make the best of a bad situation. You'll call upon all your communication skills to alert the traffic in the right hand lane to your presence.

Slow when exiting a freeway, particularly if the exit is curved. Don't neglect to communicate to drivers behind you that you are slowing. **Flash your brakes and use the turn signal.** Allow yourself time to slow in order to exit on the ramp safely. Remember that ramp speed limits are for cars, not 18-wheelers.

Space Management

The space around the truck is one other factor you should be aware of. As a truck driver you can't control how close other vehicles are following you. But there is something that will help. **Keep free space—a space cushion—around the truck.**

As with scanning, you're concerned with three areas:

- space ahead
- space behind
- space to the side

If a dangerous situation develops, you should have enough space around the truck to respond safely.

SPACE AHEAD

You manage the space ahead by **keeping a safe following distance.** Here's how to determine your following distance.

- Identify a stationary object ahead, such as a mileage marker, or seam in the road.
- Note when the rear bumper of the vehicle in front of you passes that object.
- Begin to count the seconds aloud: "one thousand and one, one thousand and two," and so on.
- Stop counting when your vehicle's front bumper arrives at the stationary object.

This distance will vary with the speed being maintained and conditions of road surface and visibility. Basically, **for every 10 feet of vehicle length, you should allow one second if you're traveling below 40 mph.** Add another second if you're going faster than 40 mph. Add much more space for bad weather or poor visibility or road conditions. For night driving, always add much more space to the basic formula. Some states have specific requirements for safe following distance.

fig. 19-1
Use this formula and these figures to compute your following distance.

> ## BASIC FORMULA
> Count one full second for every 10 feet of vehicle length for speeds under 40 mph.
>
> ## SPEEDS ABOVE 40 MPH
> Use the basic formula, then add one second.
>
> ## ADVERSE DRIVING CONDITIONS
> Much more space is required.
>
> ## NIGHT DRIVING
> Much more space is required.

SPACE BEHIND

You must learn how to **judge distances of other vehicles behind** your truck. This is important when changing lanes. You have to determine how fast another vehicle is coming up from behind. Only then can you choose when to change lanes so you can do it safely.

Tailgaters challenge your ability to manage the space behind. Here are a few tips on how to handle tailgaters safely.

- Slow down gradually to let them pass.
- Don't slow down or turn quickly.
- Don't speed up, the tailgater will still stay with you.
- Don't turn on your tail lights or flash your brake lights to shake up the tailgater.

If you're being tailgated, leave a bigger following distance in front of you. That way, you'll be less likely to have to stop suddenly, and less likely to be rear-ended by the tailgater.

SPACE TO THE SIDES

Make sure you always have an "out" in case you have to change lanes. Keep the truck centered in the lane. Aim to **keep a space cushion on one side of your vehicle.** Keep as large a space cushion as possible.

SPACE ABOVE AND BELOW

Don't forget to **leave space above and below your vehicle to clear hazards.** Make sure you can get safely over a grade crossing or under an overpass before you attempt it. Be aware that posted clearances may not always be correct. Recent pavement improvements can raise the roadbed and decrease the clearance.

SPACE FOR TRAFFIC GAPS

A traffic gap is **the following distance between two vehicles other than your own.** These are some situations in which you need traffic gaps:

- crossing or entering traffic
- passing
- merging
- railroad crossings

The size of gap needed for safe operation of a truck is bigger than gaps needed for safe operation of a car. A **truck** is bigger in size and slower in accelerating and so **needs a bigger gap.**

You'll need to apply the principles of space management to decide if a gap is large enough for you to change lanes, merge, or complete the other maneuvers mentioned.

GIVING SPACE TO OTHERS

Road space is shared by all drivers with all types of vehicles. This is what's known as right-of-way. **There is no situation in which any driver automatically has the right-of-way.** There are times when, in the interest of safety, you will give space to another driver so the way will be clear. Yes, you may have arrived at that four-way stop sign first. But if the safest thing to do would be to let all the other vehicles proceed through the intersection first, that's what you do.

If you fail to be observant, **if you fail to receive and act on the communication of others, you risk hindering traffic.** All drivers have a responsibility to keep traffic flowing smoothly. You help by opening gaps in traffic so others can merge or make their lane changes smoothly. You can see that if you slow down a little to create a gap, you contribute to a safer situation and perhaps prevent an accident.

Night Operation

Earlier we had said that you must **automatically increase your following distance** for night driving. That's because **night driving presents special challenges to the safe driver.**

These three main factors are involved in night driving:

- driver factors
- roadway factors
- vehicle factors

DRIVER FACTORS

You start out at a disadvantage just because it's night. Drivers' **night vision** (how far or how well they can see at night) simply **isn't as good as** their vision **during the day.** Plus, night is the usual time for a person to sleep. You can more easily become tired or fatigued at night. Be well rested before beginning your trip. The following are a few hints on how to fight off fatigue.

- Avoid heavy or large amounts of food.
- Keep your eyes moving.
- Keep the cab ventilated.
- No alcohol at least eight hours before driving!
- Stop at least every two hours to rest or move around.
- Don't drive when you're fatigued, day or night.

ROADWAY FACTORS

Road conditions can affect night driving. **Street lights** don't light roads as well as sunlight does. When streets are lit, the lighting may vary from very dim to very bright lighting. Outside the city limits, some roads may not even be lit at all. This **worsens the visibility problems** we've already mentioned. Use the high beams to increase your field of vision whenever you can without blinding oncoming traffic.

Familiar roads make night driving less stressful. You'll know well ahead of time where your turns are and can get ready for them. But **trying to find your way** on a strange road at night can be tiring, and that **can add to your fatigue.** Plan your route ahead of time to present the fewest problems. This way, you'll encounter fewer "surprises" that could lead to accidents. You'll feel a little more familiar with the road, and that will be less stressful.

Other drivers on the road at night **can affect your driving.** Adjusting your eyes to oncoming lights can tire you. Sometimes other drivers don't dim their headlights for approaching traffic. It is dangerous to flash your high beams to get other drivers to dim theirs. The best thing to do is **avert your eyes from the bright light** until the car is past.

Be aware that other drivers are having the same night driving problems you are. Avoid blinding others. Dim your headlights within 500 feet of oncoming traffic and when there is traffic within 500 feet ahead of you.

At night there is a **greater possibility** of meeting **drinking drivers.** Look for drivers who are going way too fast or too slow, stopping without reason, or who are weaving across the road. Alertness and a good following distance will help you respond safely to the actions of other drivers.

VEHICLE FACTORS

Make sure your **headlights**, high and low beams, are clean and working properly. Replace burned out lights before driving. **Clearance lights need to be working** so that you can be seen by other drivers on the road.

Communication is especially important at night. Make sure your turn signals are clean and work properly. At night it's especially important that your mirrors and all lights and reflectors are clean and properly positioned.

As we've noted, vision is limited at night. Low beams let you see only about 250 feet ahead. A **dirty windshield** will impair your vision further. Then **glare** on the windshield from the dashboard or other lights in the cab can **reduce visibility** even more.

Dim the dash lights so there isn't glare on the windshield from them. Don't dim them so much that you can't read the speedometer and other gauges, though. Turn off the other lights in the cab, such as those in the sleeper, to avoid glare. If the light is being used by your partner, close the curtain of the sleeper.

The safe driver is willing to adjust speed and driving techniques to fit the situation. When vision is limited, slow down to ensure your safety and the safety of others on the road.

Emergency Maneuvers

OK, let's say you've done everything we've discussed so far and you still get into a potential accident situation. Emergency maneuvers are the **steps you take to avoid turning the possible accident into a real one.** As a safe driver, you should be able to perform these maneuvers. But your aim should be never to need them.

EVASIVE STEERING

Evasive steering is **steering to avoid an accident.** You can often turn more quickly to avoid an accident than you can stop. Start turning as soon as possible. To reduce the chance of rolling or jackknifing, turn only as much as necessary. Be careful you **do not over-steer.**

Don't use the brake during an evasive steering maneuver unless your truck is equipped with an anti-lock brake system (ABS). If possible, brake before steering. As soon as the front of the trailer is past the obstacle, you can begin counter-steering. Counter-steering is steering the truck back toward the intended path of travel.

EMERGENCY STOP

Another emergency maneuver is emergency stopping. There are two procedures. The first is **controlled braking.** This involves applying the brakes just short of them locking up, then maintaining steady pressure. It takes practice to know where that point is. Until you learn it, use the stab braking method.

Stab braking means applying the brakes fully, then releasing them slightly when the wheels lock. Releasing the brakes allows the wheels to resume turning, which helps regain traction. Repeat this stab braking and allow the brake system to recover between stabs until the vehicle slows.

For braking a vehicle equipped with ABS, the stomp and steer method is recommended. "Stomp and steer" means make a hard brake application and hold it. The electronic sensors at each wheel sense when a wheel starts to lock. The system's electronics send pulses to the ABS air relay valves which automatically apply, hold, or release air-chamber pressure up to five times per second. This eliminates wheel lockup which helps the driver control the steering. Refer to the owner's manual for the procedure recommended by the manufacturer of your ABS.

OFF-ROAD RECOVERY

If you have to go off the pavement and onto the shoulder, you still want to **maintain control of your vehicle.** Try to keep one set of wheels on the pavement. Avoid using the brakes until your speed has dropped to about 20 mph. Then brake very gently to avoid skidding on what may be a rough surface. Stay on the shoulder until you have your vehicle under control. Signal, then check your mirrors before pulling back onto the road.

To return to the road, turn assertively back onto the pavement. Don't try to edge gradually back onto the road. If you do, your tires may grab and send you out of control. When both front tires are on the pavement, counter-steer immediately. The turn onto the pavement and the straightening back out should be made as a single "steer-counter-steer" movement.

BRAKE FAILURE ON DOWNGRADES

Going slowly enough and braking properly will almost always prevent brake failure on long downgrades. If the brakes do fail however, you will have to look outside your vehicle for something to stop it. **Your best hope is an escape ramp.** If there is one, there will be signs posted telling you about it. Be alert for them. Prepare for the ramp as you approach it, then use it.

Rapid Air Loss or Blowout

A **rapid air loss or blowout on a dual tire on the drive axle** of the tractor should not cause you to lose control. The first indication of a problem will be a new and sudden vibration you will feel in the seat. Immediately **add power to the drive wheels** by accelerating. This added power helps to maintain forward force. Keep a firm grip on the steering wheel with both hands to **make any steering corrections.** Then you can decide where and when you want to slow down and pull off the road.

Don't hit the brakes when you first realize you have a loss of air from a tire or a blowout. Applying the brakes at that point would prevent you from being able to control the steering.

You have to make an extra effort to maintain control after rapid air loss or a blowout **on a tractor steering axle tire.** If you have a rapid air loss, the front or nose of your tractor will drop down noticeably and you will feel a pull toward the side on which the tire went down. When you see the nose drop and feel this side force, **add power to the drive wheels** by accelerating. In Chapter 24, Economy Driving, you will read about not running your engine up against the governor or at full throttle. You will learn it's better to run the engine under the governed speed. If you were running at full throttle up against the governor, you would not be able to add power in the event of rapid air loss from a tire. So this is just one more reason to run under the governed speed.

Again, keep a good grip on the steering wheel and **maintain control of the steering. Don't apply the brakes.** This would rob you of the ability to control the vehicle. Add power, correct the steering, keep the vehicle aimed in a straight forward direction, then decide where and when you want to slow down and pull off the road.

Skid Control and Recovery

If skidding isn't controlled, the truck could jackknife. Once a rig has completely jackknifed, it takes a wrecker to straighten it out. You can see it's crucial to **stop the jackknife before it goes too far.** So let's look at how skids happen, and how to get out of them.

SKID DYNAMICS

A **skid occurs when the tires lose their traction or grip on the road. Speeding on snow or ice can result in loss of** traction. Front wheel skids are caused by lack of tread on tires and improper cargo loading or a sudden heavy brake application. In a front wheel skid, the nose or front end of the vehicle tends to go in a straight line regardless of how much you turn the steering wheel.

Skids can be caused by wheel load. **When there is too much heavy cargo too close to the front of the trailer,** not all the wheels have a good or an equal amount of traction.

Skids can be **caused by the force of motion.** An object in motion tends to stay in motion. When a truck is moving down the road, it doesn't stop on a dime. The momentum keeps the vehicle moving even after the brakes are applied. When wheels are locked, the momentum keeps the vehicle going, resulting in a skid. Remember, when driving a truck with ABS you do not pump the brakes. Depress and hold the pedal down. Anti-lock brakes are designed to eliminate wheel lockup.

THREE BASIC TYPES OF SKIDS

There are three basic types of skids.

OVER-BRAKING. Skids are caused by braking. This happens when the brakes are applied too hard and the wheels lock up. Skids can also be caused by using the auxiliary brake while driving on slippery roads.

OVER-STEERING. Another type of skid is caused when the wheels are turned more sharply than the vehicle can safely turn.

OVER-ACCELERATING. Skids caused by sudden acceleration occur when too much power is sent to the drive wheels, making them spin.

Most skids result from driving too fast for the existing road conditions. If your speed is correct, you simply don't have to over-accelerate, over-brake, or over-steer.

ANTI-LOCK BRAKES

As the driver, you have to know whether or not your vehicle is equipped with anti-lock brakes (ABS). **Air brakes without ABS must be applied differently from air brakes with ABS.**

When a sudden stop is necessary, a heavy application of brakes without ABS will result in wheel lockup. When this happens you lose traction and control. To regain traction and control you have to release the brakes long enough to allow the wheels to resume turning. Then you apply the brakes again. This is called pumping the brakes.

When you make a sudden stop in a vehicle **with ABS** you **use a method called stomp and steer.** This means you make a heavy application of the brakes and don't let up. Even though you will feel the brake pedal pulse beneath your foot you do not pump the brake. The ABS system does that for you, electronically and automatically, while you steer clear of the reason for your panic stop.

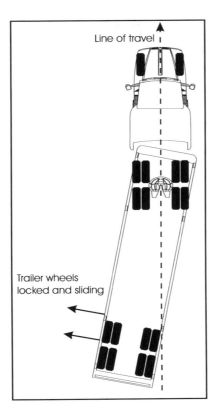

fig. 19-2
Trailer jackknife wheels locked due to braking.

Line of travel

Trailer wheels locked and sliding

Keep in mind that the ABS system will not shorten your stopping distance. What the **ABS** system **will** do is **help you stay in control of your steering.** You're more likely to **maintain vehicle stability** and **avoid a jackknife or collision.**

SKID RECOVERY

As we said, an uncontrolled skid could lead to a jackknife. But you can recover from a skid before it's too late. Recovering from jackknife skids involves four steps:

- speed control
- corrective steering
- counter-steering
- braking to a stop

TRAILER JACKKNIFE. A trailer jackknife is caused when **the wheels of the trailer lock** (see Figure 19-2). The trailer then swings around until it hits something. This is more likely to happen when the trailer is empty or has a light load. **Trailer jackknife skids can be recovered by a slight increase in speed** to pull the trailer behind the tractor. **Don't use the brakes or the trailer hand brake** to recover from this skid.

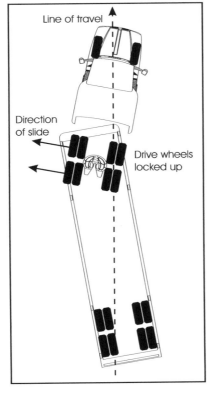

fig. 19-3
Drive wheel skid with wheels spinning due to loss of traction or locked due to braking.

Line of travel

Direction of slide

Drive wheels locked up

TRACTOR JACKKNIFE. Under sudden acceleration the drive wheels lose traction and spin out, or a heavy brake application causes the **the rear wheels of the tractor** to lock and they slide sideways (see Figure 19-3). This sends the rear of the tractor out of its line of travel. The trailer swings around until it hits the cab. **To recover from a tractor jackknife skid, first stop braking.** This allows the rear wheels to roll again. Or, **get off the accelerator** so the drive wheels can regain traction. When **the vehicle begins to slide sideways, steer in the direction you want the vehicle to go.** As the vehicle comes back on course, counter-steer quickly to regain a straight line of travel.

fig. 19-4
Front wheel skid due to loss of traction or wheel lockup.

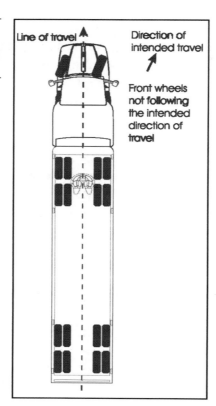

Line of travel

Direction of intended travel

Front wheels not following the intended direction of travel

FRONT WHEEL SKIDS. When the front wheels skid, **the front end tends to go in a straight line no matter which way the wheels are turned** (see Figure 19-4). When a **front wheel skid** happens, the only way to stop the skid is to **slow. If your front wheels are locked as the result of braking, reduce the amount of brake application.** Do not move the steering wheel. **If speed** excessive for road conditions **caused the skid,** again, do not move the steering wheel. Depress the clutch and **get off the accelerator** so the front wheels can regain traction. Once you have traction again, you may need to turn the wheel a little more to execute the turn you were trying to make before the skid. Be careful not to over-steer. Release the clutch and accelerate gently.

Chapter 19 Quiz

1. To be a safe driver, all you really need is to be in good control of your vehicle.
    A. True
    B. False

2. An area you cannot observe by scanning is _____.
    A. the front of the tractor
    B. the sides of the truck
    C. the rear of the truck
    D. directly behind the trailer

3. The plane and convex mirrors will help you do many things except _____.
    A. scan ahead the distance the vehicle would move in about 15 seconds
    B. keep an eye on the traffic out behind your vehicle
    C. determine if someone is alongside your trailer
    D. find opportunities to change lanes and merge

4. Failing to cancel your turn signal is about as bad as forgetting to use the turn signal in the first place.
    A. True
    B. False

5. Good speed management is _____.
    A. always doing the maximum speed legally allowed
    B. driving at the speed that's best for conditions
    C. keeping a space cushion around your vehicle
    D. scanning to the front and to the sides

6. The minimum basic following distance for a 50-foot rig traveling at 55 mph should be _____ seconds.
    A. 1
    B. 6
    C. 7
    D. 8

7. You must apply ABS brakes differently than you would brakes without the anti-lock brake system.
    A. True
    B. False

8. Evasive maneuvers are the first steps the safe driver takes to prevent accidents.
    A. True
    B. False

9. To prevent skids, _____.
    A. brake hard so the brakes lock up
    B. turn the wheels sharply
    C. hit the throttle and make the wheels spin
    D. drive at the speed proper for the conditions

10. It takes _____ to straighten out a rig that has completely jack-knifed.
    A. speed control
    B. corrective steering
    C. counter-steering
    D. a wrecker

CHAPTER 20
DRIVING CHALLENGES

Meeting the Challenge

Mountains, hilly terrain, and adverse weather conditions will challenge you as a cross-country truck driver. **Mountains and hilly terrain will challenge**

263

your shifting skills. In fact, this type of driving is so challenging that you'll need to learn how to use a runaway ramp just in case.

Sometimes **weather conditions are so bad** that there's simply **not enough traction** or not enough **visibility** to drive. Snow and ice force many drivers to sit it out in a warm, safe truck stop. Fog and dust storms can make driving even a short distance very risky. Head winds and crosswinds make driving tough, too.

In this chapter, we'll show you how you can deal with these special driving challenges.

Driving in Mountains and Rolling Terrain

A great many mountain ranges in this country create natural barriers. If you become a long distance driver, you'll probably have to cross some of them.

The Appalachians in the eastern part of the United States stretch over a thousand miles. The great Rocky Mountains run from the Canadian border south. Idaho, Utah, Colorado, and New Mexico are some of the states where giant snowcapped peaks can be seen year-round. In the Pacific Northwest, the Cascade Range crosses Oregon and Washington and the famous Sierra Nevadas of Gold Rush fame form a backbone for California.

Many smaller ranges are found in other regions of our great country. There are the Adirondacks in mid-state New York and the Alleghenies in Pennsylvania. The Great Smokies in Tennessee and the Black Hills of South Dakota pose special problems for the truck driver. And of course, much of our Midwest consists of hilly terrain.

Maybe you've heard of some of the great trucking grades in the USA. The famous Donner Pass between Sacramento, California, and Reno, Nevada, is just one of them. Heading west from Reno, you are faced with about 60 miles of a 6 percent grade, all uphill. However, Donner Pass has one extra feature the other famous grades don't have. There were so many accidents on this grade that professional truck drivers were hired to help develop signs that help truck drivers get safely to the top.

There are a number of driving skills you must master and possible problems you need to know about to meet the challenges of driving in mountains and rolling terrain successfully. We'll cover the skills needed for uphill and downhill operation first. Then we'll cover brake fade and how to use a runaway ramp.

WHAT GRADE MEANS

A small grade may be only a 4 percent grade. This means there is a 4-**foot change in altitude for every 100 feet of roadway.** In 1,000 thousand feet, there will be a 40-foot increase. A mile is 5,280 feet. That means the increase (or decrease, for a downgrade) will be about 200 feet. The grade will climb (or fall) about 200 feet per mile of roadway.

fig. 20-1
On a 4 percent grade going uphill (or down), there is a 4-foot increase (or decrease) for every 100 feet of roadway.

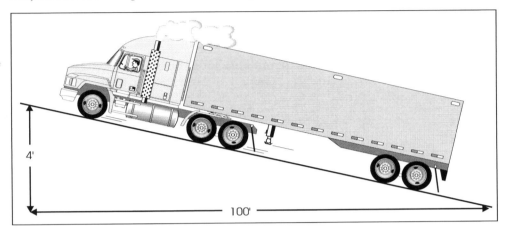

4'

100'

UPHILL OPERATION

Going uphill, your challenge will be to **maintain** as much of **your speed** as possible while fighting the natural force of **gravity** that **wants to pull you back down. Check the route** for the day by looking at a road map to see what kind of terrain you are headed for. You'll want to be prepared for uphill grades because you know a sudden uphill grade can cut your steady 50 mph down to 35 mph very quickly.

Shifting on an Upgrade

Upgrades will require you to shift into lower gears. Gravity will be slowing the wheels of your truck. If you don't downshift, you will lug the engine and eventually stall.

The problem is **downshifting on an upgrade** is different from downshifting on level ground. On level ground, when you put the clutch in to shift, the truck will slow very little. But on a grade, as soon as you take your foot off the throttle, the truck will slow down much more quickly. You will really lose speed then. So you need to **shift fast** and **your double-clutch technique must be very accurate.** You may have to downshift a few gears to reach the top of a grade. If it is a steep grade or if you haven't been paying attention and the hill surprises you, you may have to skip a gear or two when you downshift.

Until you get good at this, you may have some trouble double-clutching and shifting at all, much less while maintaining speed. You may not even be able to get back into gear because the hill is slowing the truck faster than you expect. **If you** do **"miss a gear,"** your only choice may be to **bring the truck**

to a stop, shift into first gear, and **continue up** the hill. Try to get off on the shoulder before you stop.

Now your challenge isn't downshifting, it's **upshifting on an upgrade.** Be careful when you start up again. The truck is going to want to roll backwards. You probably won't be able to upshift many gears so your trip up the hill will be a long and slow one.

Uphill Problems

You can see that maintaining uphill speed can be very difficult. Good drivers are proud when they are able to manage it. They have reasons to be proud. Traffic, poor driving habits, and the wear and tear on the rig on upgrades all present special problems.

On many upgrades, you'll find a right lane full of traffic, all kinds of cars and trucks. If one driver slows down, all the traffic in the right lane will have to slow down. That includes you, of course. A good driver always shows courtesy to other drivers.

To help reduce wear and tear on your rig, you should **watch the engine, transmission, and differential temperatures on upgrades.** Going uphill makes everything work harder, creating more heat. Your temperatures may go up a little. However, if they continue to rise above the manufacturer's recommended limits, you need to downshift and slow down so everything is not working so hard.

DOWNHILL OPERATION

The challenge in downhill operation is still **controlling your speed.** Only now gravity is forcing you to go faster, not slower. Many accidents happen on downhill grades because the driver could not control the vehicle's speed. After an accident on a downhill grade, such a driver will almost always say, "The brakes failed."

No, the brakes didn't fail. The driver failed. **Brakes can only do so much.** The rest is up to the driver. Did the driver pull off at the top of the grade and check the brake system? Did the driver know how to use the brakes? But most important of all, did the driver know how to drive downhill? Let's start with gear selection.

OBSERVATION SKILLS TEST

What did you notice about the illustration that began this chapter? Go to the Observation Skills Test Grid at the back of the book and see how your observation skills are improving.

Gear Selection

There was an old rule of thumb, used for many years in the trucking industry—"use the same gear going downhill as you used going uphill." That rule is not true anymore. Many of today's engines can pull a truck up the hill faster than it should go down the same hill. Also many hills aren't the same slope on both sides.

The new rule of thumb is to use one gear down from what you used to pull the hill. Be in the right gear before you start heading down. The best way to select a gear for a particular downgrade is to **get advice** from a driver you trust who has been down that hill. Then proceed very cautiously until you know from experience what speed and gear you can use safely.

Checking the Brakes

Heading south on I-17 from Flagstaff to Phoenix in Arizona, there is the famed 16-mile hill. From ice cold pine country over 7,000 feet up, this interstate drops to about 3,000 feet into hot cactus country.

There are plenty of warning signs at the top of this downgrade. They instruct the driver to **pull out.** This means you need to pull into the brake check area and check your brakes. Don't just step on them hard and decide they work OK. **Get out of the truck and inspect your brakes.** Check the slack adjusters on all the brakes for excessive push rod travel, and look for any other loose or broken parts. Be sure no brake has more push rod travel than your company specifies. If the brakes need adjustment follow your company's policy on brake repairs and adjustments.

Select the gear for your descent. The signs will tell you the grade (five percent) and the distance down the hill (16 miles). **Choose a gear that will set the truck's speed appropriate to the posted speed limit and driving conditions while keeping the rpm just under rated engine speed (top rpm).**

Let's go down this hill. Your mind is alert and you are ready. You drive out of the pull out area and upshift a few times until you reach the gear you have chosen. Your truck is moving at 20 mph. If the road is not slippery, you **turn on the auxiliary brake.**

You resist going any faster than your chosen speed. You have chosen the correct gear for the grade and the distance and you **do not change the gear position once the truck is going downhill.**

It is almost impossible to select another gear then, anyway. There is great pressure on the drive train. If you are foolish enough to shift out of gear into neutral, chances are that's where the shift lever will remain until you manage to stop the truck. You can imagine what a dangerous situation it would be to be halfway down a hill stuck in neutral. Do not attempt to change gears on a downhill run!

Once you have selected your gear and speed, you are free to drive safely and concentrate on how to use the brakes.

With the engine retarder on, you will probably not need the service brakes. They should be used only when either the engine rpm or the truck speed exceeds safe limits. Should that safe speed be exceeded you should then apply moderate and intermittent braking, called "snubbing." Snub the brakes moderately until the speed has been reduced five or six miles per hour. Snubbing requires a brake application of 20 to 30 psi. It should take about three seconds of brake application to reduce your speed by five or six miles per hour.

If your speed again climbs back up in excess of the safe speed, repeat the snub-and-release braking sequence until the grade flattens out and the descent isn't causing your truck to accelerate.

BRAKE FADE

Brake fade occurs when the **brake temperature gets so high** the brake drum cannot absorb it or get rid of it. Then **the brake lining surface begins to melt.** The surface of the lining is no longer solid, it's a liquid or gas. It **offers little or no friction,** and therefore no braking power. The lining will look glazed.

fig. 20-2
When brake fade occurs, the brake drum expands away from the brake lining.

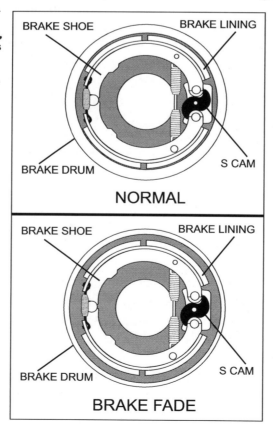

Eventually, the brake lining does no good at all. The truck is rolling with **no braking power** at all, service or emergency. Overheating the brakes can also cause one or more of the following conditions:

- the brake drums get red hot and crack
- the brake linings burn up
- the wheel grease seals get hot and leak grease
- the wheel grease heats to 900 degrees Fahrenheit and ignites

You can see that if you get stuck in neutral, you can't rely on your service brakes to stop you on a long downhill grade. If you encounter brake fade, or if you lose your brakes, look for a runaway ramp.

Runaway Ramps

Interstate highways now have runaway ramps on long downhill grades. If the driver cannot stop the truck, there is only one safety option left. The runaway ramp must be used. This is a matter of life and death to other motorists as well as to the driver. Runaway ramps stop up to 80 percent of out-of-control trucks.

Steering your truck to a runaway ramp takes strength and courage. Your truck may be traveling at high speeds, perhaps even as high as 100 mph, past other traffic. Look for runaway signs. They will show you how far away the ramp is.

As you enter the ramp, **hold the steering wheel firmly.** Runaway ramps are usually made of sand and gravel and slanted uphill to slow your truck. After about 500 feet, there is a large sand pit. Your truck will roll into it and stop very quickly in the midst of a giant sand and dust cloud. You'll strain against your seat belt, but you'll remember to turn off the ignition. Then climb out and take the fire extinguisher with you. You may need it.

ROLLING TERRAIN

Hilly country (hills with one valley after another) describes rolling terrain. You'll rarely find grade percent signs in rolling terrain because the **grades are not that severe.** The challenge in covering rolling terrain is to **maintain a steady speed despite the hills.** The problem with this kind of driving is selecting the correct gears for one hill after another. Each hill is a different height and length. You must anticipate each hill and you will be **changing gears constantly.** That means you must **always be thinking ahead** to the next hill and the next valley. Rolling terrain will demand the best of you in terms of staying alert and shifting gears, but it is rewarding driving.

Gear Selection

Picture yourself driving from San Antonio to Austin in Texas. This is rolling terrain country. Your truck begins to slow on an upgrade. You quickly shift down a gear. As you top a small hill, you see a long gentle grade, then another hill. You know what to expect because you can see for miles. You can **anticipate your gear changes.** You have time to figure out your gear changes and your speed. You upshift and increase your speed. This speed will take you almost to the top of the next hill. You will have to downshift near the top. Watching the tach closely, you can plan ahead for each gear change and maintain a steady speed.

Maintaining Speed

As you go down one hill, you'll pick up speed. You can **use** this **momentum to get up the next hill** and thus maintain a steady speed. At the same time, you **don't** want to **exceed the legal speed limit.**

Another consideration is other **traffic which will frustrate your attempts to maintain an even speed.** If you are in hilly country on a free access highway, there will be cross traffic. A driver going fast downhill is always surprised when a farmer pulls out from a field. The farmer is never surprised. The farmer has pulled out on this highway in this old green John Deere tractor a thousand times, usually at dusk and usually without lights. Sometimes the farmer wonders why the trucks come so close as they pass. Sometimes they blast their air horns. The farmer smiles and waves back.

A final consideration is **to control your speed as you top sharp hills.** Drivers trying to maintain speed will sometimes top sharp hills at 55 mph. This is like playing Russian Roulette with other people. How far can you see when your long nose conventional tractor with a 6-foot hood tops a sharp hill? For a split second, you may not be able to see the road continue at all. What is on the road? A pair of pickups parked on the pavement with two cowboys talking it over? A cow or a horse? A flock of sheep being herded across the road? A school bus letting out children? If there is an accident, some drivers will say, "I didn't see them." These drivers are as smart as the ones who say, "The brakes failed."

In rolling terrain, always be **thinking ahead to what may be over that hill where you can't see.**

fig. 20-3
Never top a sharp hill at full speed. You can't see what's on the other side.

Adverse Conditions

There are many kinds of adverse conditions. However, in the trucking industry, those words refer to weather conditions that slow you down and make driving more dangerous. The challenge here will be to **make good progress while traveling at a safe speed and maintaining control of your vehicle.**

Chapter 19, Safe Driving, takes a detailed look at some of the problems presented by adverse weather conditions and night driving. We'll review them briefly here, and present some new information.

COLD WEATHER STARTING

A diesel engine is **more difficult to start** in cold weather because of the increased drag of moving parts in cold oil. Also, the **cold air** entering the cylinders **takes longer to reach combustion temperatures.**

If temperatures are consistently below 40 degrees Fahrenheit, you may need a starting aid to get the engine going. Your tractor may be equipped with a plug-in block heater, glow plug, air pre-heater, or ether aid. All are effective during cold weather. Make sure you **know which starting aid your tractor has and how and when to use it.**

Operating a cold diesel engine can lead to excess wear of internal surfaces which have moving contact, such as bearings, bushings, the camshaft, and piston rings. **Bringing your engine up to operating temperature is important.** If you try to accelerate before the lubricant is circulating well, your truck may experience:

- camshaft lobe damage
- crankshaft and bearing damage
- turboshaft and bearing damage

After starting the engine in cold weather, don't start your trip until the needle of the water temperature gauge starts to move up.

White smoke coming from your exhaust stack during cold starts is a sign of incomplete combustion and will clear up when the engine warms up.

For easier cold weather start-ups, allow an idling period to:

- establish an oil film on the cylinder walls
- lubricate the turbocharger bearings
- allow time for the pistons to expand to fit the cylinders
- allow coolant temperature to increase

SNOW

Unless it is very cold, new snow will melt on the road and reduce traction. It may stick to the windshield and limit your vision. Slow down and be alert for other vehicles sliding out of control. Don't use the retarder. **Lock the inter-axle differential to get more traction** if you need it.

Every winter, snow is expected in many parts of the nation. Often unexpected snowstorms occur in areas that are not accustomed to snow. In your pre-trip inspection before leaving on a trip during the expected and unexpected snow season make sure you **have tire chains** in good condition. You should have one set of chains and extra cross links for at least one driving wheel on each side.

As you start into some mountain ranges, state highway signs will direct you to have tire chains mounted. If you fail to comply with the signs, you could receive a citation and a fine. Plus, you could receive the embarrassment of getting stuck and tying up traffic. If your company runs through cold country where chains are required, there will likely be policies about having and using chains.

Until you have a lot of experience with tire chains, practice mounting and removing a set. The practice will pay off when you have to install chains in freezing temperatures or in the dark.

ICE

Ice on the road **reduces traction** and your truck can slide and jackknife. On ice, trucks take ten times more distance to stop. An empty truck is worse. Black ice occurs when water seeps into the pores of the road surface and freezes. The road looks dry. In fact, except for the patches of black ice, most of it is dry.

If you must drive on ice, start gently and go slowly. Use the foot brake. If your brakes are adjusted properly, you will have better braking than trying to control braking with the trailer brakes only. Do not use the retarder. You may have to **lock the inter-axle differential** if you have stopped and poor traction makes it hard to get started again.

RAIN

When a rain starts, the first few minutes are the most dangerous. The rain mixes with a buildup of dirt and oils on your windshield and on the road. This will **reduce your visibility and reduce traction.**

Use the washer control before you turn on the wipers. Get some cleaning fluid on the glass so the wipers can do their job. **Drive as if you are on ice** until the rain washes the oil and dirt away.

NIGHT DRIVING

Night driving means **reduced visibility. Don't overdrive your vision.** That is, drive at a speed that will let you stop if an object moves into the area of your headlights. You should be well rested and have a clean windshield when you drive at night.

Twilight, or dusk, is a dangerous time to drive. The sun is below the horizon. Glare, shadows, and reduced light will play tricks with your vision. Day becomes night in 15 to 30 minutes. Your truck can cover 25 miles during this period.

Changes in light that occur at sunrise and sunset affect the vision of all drivers. Care and caution is needed.

WIND

Wind can be a friend. Driving hundreds of miles with **the wind behind** your truck can mean a good trip. It can mean **you'll change gears less often and use less fuel.** You should be sure to **check the engine temperature often,** though.

Head winds mean you and your truck have to work harder. Driving west across Nebraska into a 35 mph wind is almost the same as climbing three percent grades.

Crosswinds mean trouble. Both crosswinds and wind coming from another angle **make steering hard work.** Long high trailers have as much side surface as some highway billboards. You have seen these large signs blown over in a windstorm. Trucks get blown over in the same way. Empty trucks get blown over more easily than full ones.

With moderate crosswinds, you should **steer into the wind slightly.** When the wind is broken by trees or overpasses, you must be quick to allow straight line steering. As soon as the truck is in the open again, the wind will attempt to force the truck away. It is tricky, but a trained driver can master this type of driving.

Truckers often take refuge under overpasses when the wind is severe.

FOG

Fog, mist, fluffy snowfall, white outs, downpours, and blizzards all have one thing in common. **You'll barely be able to see** the road or the vehicles on it. You must make a decision whether to continue on at a slow speed or get off the highway. Most drivers will continue on until they spot a safe pull out such as a rest area.

If this is not possible and you are on a two-lane highway, **pull off the roadway** as far **to the right** as you can. If you can, get completely off the road. **Turn on your four-way flashers. Turn off all your other lights.** If you leave your taillights on, a driver coming from behind might try to follow them and too late realize you are stopped on the side of the road.

OTHER ADVERSE WEATHER CONDITIONS

Some parts of the country present weather condition problems that are unique to that area. For example, the Southwest has dust storms that create havoc on the highways. Very hot weather can cause tar to melt, causing very slick roads. States often have information for travelers advising them on how best to cope with local conditions. Your company may also have extra training or instructions regarding special weather conditions you might encounter on your run.

TRAFFIC JAM

A traffic jam is a sort of man-made adverse condition. The challenge here is probably to try to **keep from losing your patience.** If it's brake lights as far ahead as you can see and traffic is at a complete standstill, shift into neutral and set the parking brake. If whatever's causing the tie-up doesn't appear likely to clear up soon, look for an opportunity to pull off that road. If the traffic jam is going to take hours to unsnarl, check with your dispatcher for another route or somewhere comfortable to **wait out the problem.** It's no use burning up fuel and your patience if the traffic situation is out of your control.

CONSTRUCTION ZONES AND ACCIDENT SCENES

Roadwork zones and accident scenes are two more man-made adverse conditions. At first sight of an orange sign warning you that a construction zone is ahead, slow down. Highway Departments must close lanes and create detours to repair and improve highways. They go to great lengths to mark construction zones with warning signs. You must obey these cautions just as you must obey traffic lights.

Accident scenes cannot always be marked with large warning signs, but accident scenes are very obvious when you approach them. There is normally a lot of emergency personnel in the road trying to provide assistance. Again, as soon as you recognize an accident scene, slow down. Don't endanger the emergency crews by blasting through the area. Be watchful of other drivers who are gawking and not paying attention to their driving.

Chapter 20 Quiz

1. A five precent grade means there is a _____.
    A. five foot increase in grade for every 100 feet of roadway
    B. .05 foot increase in grade for every 100 feet of roadway
    C. 50 foot increase in grade for every 100 feet of roadway
    D. five degree angle to the road

2. If you miss a gear on an upgrade, you should _____.
    A. downshift quickly
    B. stop off the roadway and start again in low gear
    C. coast to the bottom of the hill
    D. stop on the roadway and start again in low gear

3. At first sight of a construction site warning sign, _____.
    A. advance as far into the zone as possible, as fast as you can
    B. immediately slow down
    C. get out and check your brakes, then proceed through the zone
    D. use the air horn to encourage traffic in front of your truck to speed up

4. To help reduce _____ on upgrades, you should watch the engine, transmission, and differential temperatures.
   A. wear and tear on your rig
   B. traffic problems
   C. shifting
   D. poor driving habits

5. Many of today's engines can pull a truck up the hill faster than it should go down the same hill.
   A. True
   B. False

6. Do not change the gear position once the truck is _____.
   A. parked
   B. going downhill
   C. going uphill
   D. in a head wind

7. If you must use the service brakes when you're going downhill, you should _____.
   A. stub them forcefully
   B. snub them moderately
   C. use a slight pressure on the brake pedal and keep it the same
   D. use heavy pressure on the brake pedal and let it up from time to time

8. When you drive in rolling terrain, you should _____.
   A. use the service brakes rather than the brake retarder
   B. always be thinking ahead
   C. try to maintain your speed so you are at top speed at the top of hills
   D. lose speed as you go down hills

9. When the road looks dry but is in fact slippery, you may have run into _____.
   A. snow
   B. rain
   C. sleet
   D. black ice

10. Match the adverse weather condition in Column A with the remedy in Column B.

Column A Condition

A. traffic jam _____

B. rain _____

C. severe winds _____

D. night driving _____

Column B Remedy

1. Take refuge under an overpass.

2. Shift into neutral and keep your right foot poised over the brake.

3. Use the washer control to remove any buildup of dirt and oils so you have better visibility.

4. Drive at a speed that will let you stop if an object moves into the area of your headlights.

HANDLING DOUBLES AND TRIPLES

Long Combination Vehicles

A three-axle tractor pulling a two-axle semitrailer, the "18-wheeler," is the most popular heavy duty over-the-road vehicle in the trucking industry. Nearly all of the nation's highway freight is hauled in this type of rig.

The other popular combinations are doubles and triples. A **double** consists of a **tractor and two trailers.** The first and second trailers are **coupled with a converter, or dolly.** A **triple** consists of a **tractor and three trailers.** The first and second and the second and third trailers are coupled with dollies. A few states and Canadian provinces allow triples. You'll need a special Endorsement on your CDL to pull doubles and triples.

There are some special terms you'll run into with combination trailers. For instance, a set of joints is industry slang for any double or triple combination. A **turnpike double** consists of a **three-axle tractor, two full-length tandem trailers, and a tandem-axle dolly.** A **Rocky Mountain double** consists of a **three-axle tractor, a full-length tandem trailer, a single-axle dolly, and a short (28½ foot) single-axle trailer, or pup.** A **western double** is a **single axle tractor, two pups, and a single-axle dolly.**

Pup trailers make good combination units for LTLs, or less than full load shipments. They can also be used for shippers who ship lighter than average freight. Because of their length, city tractor drivers can handle them easily. Using one pup at a time, the city driver can pick up LTL shipments. This saves the time and labor of picking up LTLs in city trucks and then reloading the freight onto line haul trailers.

One line tractor and one driver can pull two or three pups or two full-length trailers or a combination. The trailers can be dropped off en route. And, trailers can be ready to be picked up in the same way.

fig. 21-1
Types of combination trailers:
(A) Tractor semitrailer;
(B) western double;
(C) Rocky Mountain double;
(D) turnpike double and
(E) triple.

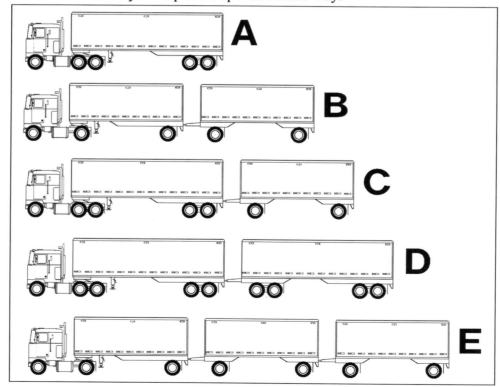

Loading Doubles and Triples

Whether you're pulling a single trailer or a double or triple combination, you must make sure the weight is distributed properly and within the legal limits. Even if you don't load the trailer, you are still responsible for how it is loaded. Make sure each trailer is loaded so that the cargo weight is even on each axle. Uneven load distribution can easily lead to rollovers.

We'll use a triple combination, all pups with single axles, as our example. The freight for each trailer is listed below.

- cartons of toys
- mattresses
- LTL freight

The LTL trailer will be loaded with freight going to a number of different receivers, or consignees. It's being loaded at your terminal dock. The foreman is told to load 24,000 pounds.

While the trailer is being loaded, you'll watch to **make sure the load is secured properly.** If freight is damaged, you'll be held responsible. You'll also weigh the trailer when the loading is finished to **make sure the total weight and the axle weights are within legal limits.** You're the one who's responsible for that, too.

The mattresses were loaded on their trailer at a local mattress factory to 100 percent capacity. In other words, it's holding all the mattresses that will fit in it. The cargo weight is 14,000 pounds. Because each mattress weighs about the same amount, the weight is evenly distributed. So, this trailer is ready to go.

You direct the loading of the children's toys onto the third trailer. Some cartons are heavy and some are light. Looking at the shipping papers, you see that the total shipment weighs 20,000 pounds. You must load so that half the weight is in the front of the trailer and half in the back. This would be an even distribution of weight.

You load heavy cartons to about four feet high at the front of the trailer. Then you stop and check your weight. You've loaded 200 cartons that weigh 40 pounds each. That's 8,000 pounds in front.

Then you load 2,000 pounds of light cartons on top. The front half of the trailer will have 10,000 pounds of cargo or half of the shipment. You load the back half the same way. There will be 10,000 pounds in the back half of the trailer.

The total shipment weight of 20,000 pounds will be evenly distributed. Weighing the trailer shows the weight on each axle to be less than 20,000 pounds. The foreman seals the trailer for you and gives the loading copies to the line dispatcher.

All three of your trailers are properly and securely loaded. They've been weighed and all three are legal. The line dispatcher now has all three trailers in the yard. The line dispatcher studies each trailer load. The heavy trailer (24,000 pounds of cargo weight) must be first behind the tractor so that the most weight will be on the tractor. That will give the tractor better road traction.

Trailer 2, at 20,000 pounds of cargo weight, is the load of toys. The third is the mattress load at 14,000 pounds of cargo. With the heavier trailers first and second, the three trailers will be safer to pull. If there are severe crosswinds or if the driver has to make an emergency stop, the triple combination will handle better and stay in line.

With a double combination, you'd also **couple the heavier trailer behind the tractor.**

Once the trailers are coupled to your tractor, you'll weigh the entire rig. Then, you'll be ready to go!

Coupling and Uncoupling

Chapter 15 covers how to couple and uncouple a tractor-trailer. You should have a good command of that chapter before you begin this one. This chapter will focus on coupling the double combination and the triple combination, and on uncoupling them, too. You'll have to show you know how to do this to get your CDL Doubles/Triples Endorsement, which you'll need if you want to pull double or triple trailers.

DOUBLES AND TRIPLES

A double rig consists of a tractor, two trailers, and a converter gear. A triple rig consists of a tractor, three trailers, and two converter gears. The converter gear is needed to couple semitrailers. It's also called a con gear or a dolly. We'll call it a dolly.

Basically, a **dolly** is a **fifth wheel on an axle.** Except for the use of the dolly, coupling and uncoupling doubles and triples is basically the same as coupling and uncoupling the tractor and the first semitrailer. When you couple a tractor and one semitrailer, it helps to be on level ground. With doubles and triples, this is a must.

As we outline the steps for coupling doubles, we'll refer to the trailer closest to the tractor as Trailer 1. We'll call the trailer at the end of the combination Trailer 2.

fig. 21-2
A converter dolly.

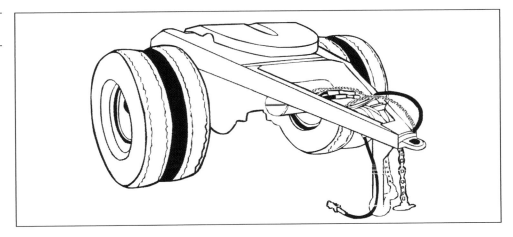

Coupling Doubles

Before you begin this procedure make a visual inspection of the area, the tractor, a dolly, and the two trailers. If all is in good order, proceed.

The spring brakes will be set on Trailer 2 so it won't move during the coupling process. If Trailer 2 doesn't have spring brakes, drive your tractor to Trailer 2, connect the emergency line, and charge the trailer air tank. Then disconnect the emergency line. This will set the trailer emergency brakes. Chock the wheels according to your company's policy.

Next, couple your tractor to Trailer 1 as described in Chapter 15. Make sure that the valves on the back of the trailer are closed.

Once you've coupled the tractor to Trailer 1, you'll couple the dolly to Trailer 2. Follow the steps listed below:

- Inspect the dolly thoroughly. Check the brakes, tires and wheels, eye hook, and air and electrical lines. Make sure the fifth wheel is greased properly. Release the dolly brakes by opening the air tank petcock or depressing the air release valve which is located under the fifth wheel.
- With a helper, put the dolly in front of Trailer 2. Place the dolly so its fifth wheel touches the front of Trailer 2 and its fifth wheel jaws are in line with the Trailer 2's kingpin. (Don't have a helper? Use the tractor and Trailer 1 to pick up the dolly, drive it to and position it near the front of Trailer 2.)
- Back Trailer 1 into position in front of the dolly. Lock the tractor-only brake if you have one, put the trailer air supply valve in the emergency position, and get out of the cab.

- Lift the tongue of the dolly by hand and hook the dolly eye hook onto the pintle hook of Trailer 1. Close the pintle hook safety latch and hook the safety chain from the dolly onto the "O" ring of Trailer 1.
- Raise the dolly landing gear and connect the dolly air lines and electrical cord to the back of Trailer 1. Make sure the petcock drain valve on the dolly and the shut-off valves on Trailer 2 are closed. The dolly fifth wheel jaws should be open.
- Make sure Trailer 2's height is correct. It should be slightly lower than the fifth wheel of the dolly.
- If Trailer 2 is equipped with spring brakes, the parking brakes will be "on" or "set," so you don't have to hook up air lines at this point. You are ready to return to the tractor and back the dolly under Trailer 2.
- If Trailer 2 does not have spring brakes, connect the air lines and the electrical cable from the dolly to Trailer 2. Open the shut off valves on the back of Trailer 1.
- Make sure nothing and no one is behind Trailer 2 or between or under any of the units.
- Return to the cab, put on the four-way flashers, put the trailer air supply valve in the normal position, and test the brake lines. Now turn off the engine so that you can hear air during the rest of the test. You learned how to do this in Chapter 15. After you have restarted the engine and the compressor has cut out, pull the trailer air supply valve back out. This will set the trailer brakes.
- Release the tractor-only brake and slowly back the dolly under Trailer 2 until you hear and feel the fifth wheel jaws lock around the kingpin. Raise Trailer 2's landing gear just slightly to prevent damage if the trailer moves. Shift into low and gently try to move the tractor forward to make sure you have coupled.
- Get out of the cab, visually check the coupling. There should be no space between the trailer upper coupler plate and fifth wheel. Secure the fifth wheel locking lever. Then crank up the trailer landing gear and secure the landing gear handle.
- Test the air brakes. Go to the back of the last trailer. Open and close the emergency air valve. No air there means you did something wrong. While there, check the four-way flashers to make sure they are working. If you found emergency air at the rear of Trailer 2, return to the cab and apply 20 to 30 pounds of brake application with the trailer hand valve. Return to the rear and open and close the service air valve. No air means something is wrong. If you have air, remove the chocks.
- Recheck everything. Then move the truck forward at about two to five mph and test the trailer brakes with the hand valve. If everything is in order, you're ready to go.

Coupling Triples

To couple a third trailer, couple the last trailer, Trailer 3, to Trailer 2 first. Simply repeat the procedure for coupling Trailer 1 and 2. Couple the tractor to Trailer 1 as described in Chapter 15. Then couple Trailer 1 to Trailer 2.

Uncoupling Doubles

The general procedure for uncoupling outlined below assumes you are going to leave all the trailers at the terminal. If you are not going to leave all the trailers at the terminal, you should remain coupled to the last trailer you dock. In the procedures outlined below, we refer to the rearmost trailer as Trailer 2, and the trailer nearest to the tractor as Trailer 1. The steps to uncouple Trailer 2 are as follows:

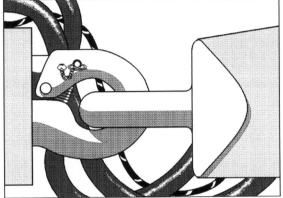

fig. 21-3
The drawbar or tongue of the dolly locked into the pintle hook of a trailer.

- Set the parking brakes.
- Chock Trailer 2's wheels if your company requires it.
- Crank down the landing gear on Trailer 2 slightly to remove some weight from the dolly.
- Disconnect the air lines and pigtail between the dolly and Trailer 2 and secure them.
- Close the valves on the rear of Trailer 1; drain the dolly air tank.
- Release the fifth wheel locking mechanism on the dolly.
- Pull ahead. At this point, you're taking the dolly with you.
- Drive off to park the dolly out of your way.
- Set the brakes and put down the dolly jack stand.
- Disconnect the safety chains of the dolly. Chock the wheels.
- Disconnect the air and electrical lines.
- Disconnect the dolly from Trailer 1.
- Slowly pull clear of the dolly.
- Back Trailer 1 into the dock.
- Uncouple the tractor from Trailer 1.
- Return to Trailer 2 and couple the tractor to it.
- Dock Trailer 2.

Uncoupling Triples

Uncoupling triples is more or less the same as with doubles, but there are some extra steps. This time you'll leave Trailer 2 and Trailer 3 coupled to each other and dock Trailer 1. Then you'll return to Trailers 2 and 3, unhook them, and pull Trailer 2, with the dolly, away. Get rid of the dolly and dock Trailer 2. Then go back for Trailer 3.

If you're lucky, you'll be at a terminal that has a **yard hostler** who **does all this coupling, uncoupling, and driving around.** A yard hostler's job is to uncouple all incoming trailers, fuel the tractors, make sure the tractors and trailers get any needed maintenance, and couple all outgoing trailers. Large terminals may have more than one hostler.

Handling Characteristics

Now you know how to load doubles and triples and how to couple and uncouple them. You're ready to learn about some of the handling characteristics of these long combination vehicles. In general, combination trailers are heavier, longer, and more complex, so it takes a little longer to do things. It takes longer to:

- load
- change lanes
- couple

- inspect
- park
- uncouple

and get there. You must drive more slowly when you pull doubles and triples because it takes longer to be safe. The most effective thing you can do **for safety** when you pull doubles and triples is **slow down and take your time.**

If you pull doubles or triples, please take that extra time. There are more dead axles to pull with your drive axles, and more chances of skids and loss of traction.

For these reasons, drivers of double and triple rigs should be well-trained. You should have experience with tractor-trailers and then with doubles before you pull triples.

STEERING CHARACTERISTICS

Drivers find that pulling doubles or triples can bring some surprises. A crosswind or uneven road will make steering more difficult. The trailers are harder to keep in a straight line under such conditions and will tend to sway. To compensate for this, you'll need to **slow down and make your maneuvers with care.**

The fact that there are **more pivot points** in double and triple rigs **makes slippery road surfaces even more dangerous.** There is a pivot point at each fifth wheel and at each pintle hook. If you're pulling a triple, you have five pivot points. On a slippery road surface, you must be even more careful not to jackknife.

fig. 21-4
This 110-foot long
combination has five
pivot points.

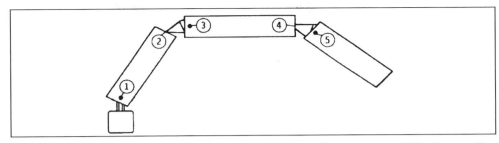

You need to be even more careful on swerves and curves, too. The last trailer will tend to sway or lean more and can roll over when you take a curve. This can be explained by the old game of "crack the whip." The last person will break away at a certain point because there is more force exerted or applied to the last unit when it goes out of line. The same is true when you pull double and triple trailers. This is known as rearward amplification. **Go slowly**.

Also watch out for dips, speed bumps, tight turns, or any road characteristic that causes the vehicle to bounce.

CORNERING CHARACTERISTICS

Most terminals are built near freeways, but you'll probably have to drive on city streets to get to the freeway. That means you probably can't avoid cornering. One thing to remember is that **double pups will turn tighter than most tractor semitrailers.**

If you're not pulling double pups, you'll need more space on the right side to make a right turn. Longer combinations offtrack more than shorter ones. This means taking up part of another lane on the left to make a right turn. Make sure you signal the turn well in advance. If another vehicle pulls up on your right side, stop and let it proceed. Left turns are easier because you have a wider field of vision on the left.

STOPPING CAPABILITIES

Previous chapters emphasize the fact that it takes a lot longer to stop a tractor-trailer than it does to stop a car. At 60 mph most cars can stop in 140 to 150 feet. At 60 mph, a loaded tractor-trailer usually takes about 300 feet to stop. Depending on the type, a **double or triple rig will take even longer to stop,** even more when empty.

You also learned that the faster you go, the longer it takes to stop.

What does this mean for the driver of a double and triple rig? The two major things it means are:

- Make sure your brakes, all of them, are properly inspected.
- Allow more following distance.
- Go slowly.

PARKING

Chances are you'll never park doubles or triples anywhere but at a rest stop, a truck stop, or in a truck yard of some type. Never attempt to back doubles or triples into a parking space. In fact, you should **avoid backing doubles and triples** at all. If you must back a double, make sure the rig is in a straight line before you start. Backing doubles is hard. Backing triples is nearly impossible. The company you drive for will have rules about backing.

All this about no backing means you should always park in a straight line where there is enough room to get out again driving forward. So, when you pull into a rest stop or a truck stop, pull straight in and **park where you can pull straight out again.**

OBSERVATION SKILLS TEST

We've discussed a problem that our beginning figure illustrated. Did you notice it? Also, who has the signal to cross the street, the woman or the two men? Go to the Observation Skills Test Grid at the back of the book and record your progress.

Using the Freeway

When you're on the freeway, **avoid emergency stops,** especially while changing lanes or turning. An emergency stop during either of these procedures is apt to result in a jackknife. **Doubles jackknife more often than singles,** and often Trailer 2 will break free as a result of the crash! How do you avoid this? Slow down. Stay alert. Plan ahead. **Take your time.**

FREEWAY RAMPS

One of the most common mistakes drivers of double and triple rigs make is entering or exiting a freeway ramp at too high of a speed. Remember that posted speed limits are the maximum for cars. Trucks must take ramps much slower. If the ramp is curved, too much speed can cause the last trailer to tip over. For all maneuvers, driving a double and triple rig requires more thinking ahead, more planning the next move.

Jackknives and **overturns are common** on freeway exit ramps. The driver will realize too late the **truck is going too fast for the curve.** The brakes are applied too hard and too late. The tractor and trailers are "out of line" on a curve. Force from the onward motion makes the trailers want to pass the tractor. The driver turns the wheel harder. The tractor is now being pushed by the trailers into a sideways motion. The trailers go straight, the tractor is at a 45-degree angle. It crashes into a guard rail or goes over the edge.

When you use a freeway ramp, use even more caution and leave even more space between you and the vehicle ahead of you than you would pulling a single trailer. If the ramp is curved, turn off your Jake brake or retarder. Using them results in the tractor drive wheels providing the braking force. On a curve, the trailers could then push the tractor into a jackknife.

And, most of all, when you drive doubles and triples, go slowly.

Chapter 21 Quiz

1. When you couple double and triple trailers, the trailer with the most weight should be coupled _____.
    A. first
    B. last

2. Except for the use of the _____, coupling and uncoupling doubles and triples is basically the same as coupling and uncoupling the tractor and the first semitrailer.
    A. tow hook
    B. tow pin
    C. dolly
    D. landing gear

3. You should learn how to couple and uncouple double and triple trailers because you'll always have to do it yourself.
    A. True
    B. False

4. The most effective thing you can do for safety when you pull doubles and triples is _____.
    A. couple the heaviest trailer first
    B. perform a pre-trip inspection
    C. couple the heaviest trailer last
    D. go slowly

5. One of the most common mistakes drivers of double and triple rigs make is entering or exiting a freeway ramp _____.
    A. at too low of a speed
    B. at too high of a speed
    C. too closely behind other traffic
    D. without fanning the brakes

Refer to the figure below to answer Questions 6 through 10. Match the doubles and triples in the figure with their correct names.

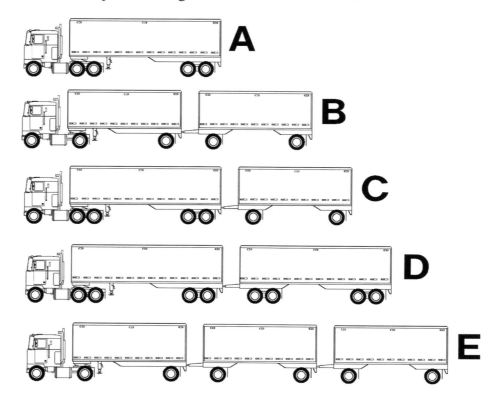

6. Example _____ is a triple.

7. Example _____ is a Rocky Mountain double.

8. Example _____ is a tractor-semitrailer.

9. Example _____ is a western double.

10. Example _____ is a turnpike double.

CHAPTER 22
AUXILIARY BRAKES

What They Are

If you've just heard the term "auxiliary brakes," you might think they must be devices that attach to the service brake system. Actually, auxiliary brakes are **separate from the service brake system.** It is true, though, that auxiliary brakes **help the service brake system,** at least in the sense that they assist in:

- slowing the vehicle
- controlling the vehicle when slowing or descending a grade
- saving wear and tear on the service brakes

It's important to remember that **auxiliary brakes are not used to stop a vehicle, only to slow it.** They can provide almost all the slowing power needed in any ordinary driving situation that calls for reduced speed. They are **often called vehicle retarders.**

THE ADVANTAGES

Auxiliary brakes provide increased savings and increased safety to today's truck driver.

Increased Savings

Studies from the Highway Research Institute show that auxiliary brakes save thousands of dollars a year per truck. These savings are found mainly in **reduced service brake maintenance** costs and in **reduced trip time.**

Not only is maintenance on the service brakes decreased, but the life of the service brakes is increased. In fact, one manufacturer claims that if you use an auxiliary brake, your **service brakes will last** up to three times **longer.** How does an auxiliary brake accomplish this? If you use the auxiliary brake to slow, rather than or in addition to the service brakes, you cut down on your use of the service brakes.

Auxiliary brakes also **reduce tire wear.** Nothing wears tires out faster than pounding down on the brakes. With a retarder helping to slow you down, flat spots and other types of tire wear are reduced.

Increased Safety

A report from the Insurance Institute of Highway Safety shows that a Class 8, heavy duty over-the-road vehicle without an auxiliary brake is almost three times more likely to get into a runaway situation on a downhill grade than a Class 8 vehicle with an auxiliary brake.

An auxiliary brake:

- gives you better control of the vehicle
- reduces service brake overheating and brake fade
- reduces brake lining and drum wear by providing another means of slowing
- slows the vehicle more smoothly
- reduces driver fatigue
- provides better control on downgrades

To sum up, auxiliary brakes share the job of slowing the vehicle with the service brakes. The use of an auxiliary brake makes the truck easier to control, safer to drive, and more economical to operate.

OBSERVATION SKILLS TEST

What did you notice about the illustration that began this chapter? Go to the back of the book to check your answer and record your progress on the Observation Skills Test Grid.

WHY THEY'RE NEEDED

Auxiliary brakes are becoming more popular and more necessary due to many factors, such as:

- aerodynamic designs of modern rigs
- the trend toward heavier payloads
- increased popularity of pulling double and triple trailers

Aerodynamic designs increase fuel savings, but also **make a vehicle harder to stop.** Because the air drag that holds the truck back is reduced, the brakes have to work harder to slow or stop the truck. This increases the chance of brake fade and wears the brakes out faster. Heavier payloads and pulling more than one trailer all add to the weight the brakes must stop.

Types of Auxiliary Brakes

Some auxiliary brakes work by slowing the engine. So, they are also called engine retarders or engine brakes. Other auxiliary brakes work differently. No matter how they work, though, the purpose is still the same. They assist the service brakes in slowing your truck. That's why they're also called retarders.

THE ENGINE RETARDER

Engine retarders **work by changing the timing** in the valves. As usual, the engine compresses air on the compression stroke. Then when the piston is near top dead center, fuel is injected. It ignites and the piston is pushed back down in the power stroke. However, when the engine retarder is switched on, just before the piston reaches top dead center, the exhaust valve opens and releases the compressed air before fuel is injected. The energy used to compress the air goes up the exhaust stack and out into the atmosphere. No energy is transmitted to the drive train. Thus, the engine is slowed, and so is the rig.

As you can see, an engine retarder **changes the power-producing diesel engine into a power-absorbing air compressor.** There are many types of engine retarder, but the most popular is the Jacobs, or Jake, Brake.

The Jake Brake

The **four major components** of any Jake Brake are **the solenoid valve, the control valve, the master piston, and the slave piston.**

The solenoid valve activates the movement of pressurized engine oil to the brake housing and the control valve regulates it. The master piston senses engine timing and transmits it to the slave piston. At the proper time the slave piston moves and opens the engine exhaust valves.

Let's step back now and see how the Jake Brake retards the engine. When the truck is in operation, simply the force of its moving makes the engine turn. It takes energy to make the pistons rise during the compression stroke. Under normal operation, the engine creates more energy than it uses when the fuel is injected and burned. But the Jake Brake opens the exhaust valve and releases the compressed air before the fuel is injected. This means the engine can't produce any power. In fact, as the pistons rise, they absorb power from the force of the moving truck and thus slow it down.

The Jake Brake is **activated by controls located in the cab.** Once the system has been turned on, the operation is usually automatic. It comes into play whenever you take your foot off the throttle. The switch that turns the Jake Brake on and off is located on the dash. On many engines the Jake Brake can be progressively applied. This means **you can control how many cylinders are affected** and used to provide braking. **The more cylinders you use, the more braking force** is provided.

Progressive application can be controlled in several different ways. One way is that the on-off switch will have three positions: off, low, and high. Another way is to have two switches, one to turn the system on and off and the other to control the application.

The Mack Dynatard system operates on the same principle as the Jake Brake system.

THE EXHAUST BRAKE

The exhaust brake slows the rig by **partly closing the engine's exhaust system** and putting back pressure on it. This makes the pistons work against the pressure that builds up in the exhaust manifold. **Instead of sending energy to the driveline, the engine works hard to force the exhaust buildup out of the stack.** This is how the exhaust brake retards the engine. Exhaust brakes are also referred to as **"compression brakes" or "butterfly type"** exhaust brakes.

The Williams Blue Ox Exhaust Brake

The Williams Blue Ox is one example of an exhaust brake. The **main components** of this brake system are **the brake housing, the air cylinder, and the baffle plate.** When you activate this retarder, the air cylinder moves the baffle plate. The baffle plate nearly closes off the exhaust pipe. This creates back pressure in the exhaust system. Instead of the exhaust flowing freely out the exhaust pipe, the piston has to work hard to force it out. As the pressure builds up, the engine has to work harder to try to push more exhaust out of the stack.

fig. 22-1
(A) A piston and cylinder operating with the Jake Brake not activated.
(B) What happens when you turn the Jake Brake on.

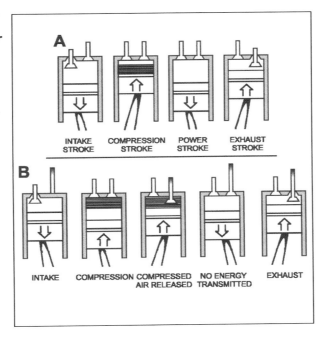

In other words, on the exhaust stroke, the exhaust valve is open. With the exhaust brake on, that exhaust air is partly prevented from escaping into the exhaust manifold. With the exhaust buildup, it will take more effort to turn the engine. Because **the engine has to use more energy to fight** this **back pressure,** its energy output is reduced. This causes the truck to slow.

When you turn the retarder off, the baffle plate returns to the "open" position and the engine returns to normal operation.

THE HYDRAULIC RETARDER

The hydraulic retarder is either built into the transmission or added to its side. It works by **causing the engine to work against the pressure of a fluid,** usually transmission or engine oil.

Hydraulic retarders use the same principles as an automatic transmission. In the transmission there is a rotor that is attached to the crankshaft of the engine and a stator that is attached to the input shaft of the transmission. These are mounted close together and oil fills the space between. As the engine spins, the vanes on the rotor cause the oil to spin with it. The spinning oil makes the stator turn the transmission. See Figure 22-3(A).

The hydraulic retarder **has a** similar **rotor and stator.** But the stator is not attached to the transmission input shaft and cannot turn.

Once the hydraulic retarder unit is activated, engine oil is pumped into the unit through a valve. The vanes of the turning rotor pick up the oil and force it against the stator. Since **the oil cannot turn the stator it acts as a drag on the engine, thus slowing the truck.** See Figure 22-3(B).

fig. 22-2
The principle of (A) automatic transmissions and (B) hydraulic retarders.

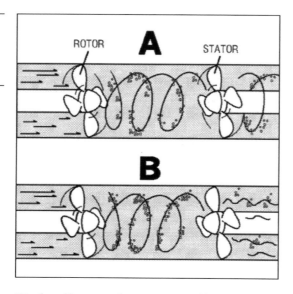

You can control the amount of oil allowed to enter the unit. In this way, **you control the retarding effect.** To get a greater retarding effect, you allow more oil to be pumped into the unit.

When the hydraulic retarder is turned off, the hydraulic retarder control valve shuts off the oil supply. The rotor pushes out the remaining oil from the hydraulic retarder unit. This permits the engine to run freely again.

Hydraulic retarders use an oil cooler because the friction built up inside the unit is extremely high, causing high heat. Hot oil flows through the cooler which is usually mounted on the side of the engine.

This retarder **can be set to work automatically** whenever you take your foot off the throttle, just like a Jake Brake. Or it **can be operated manually.**

Let's look at some examples of the hydraulic retarder.

The Cat BrakeSaver

The Caterpillar, or Cat, BrakeSaver is usually mounted between the engine and the flywheel. Its major components are the brake housing, stator, and rotor. This manufacturer uses engine oil.

Allison Retarders

Detroit Allison has two types of hydraulic retarder, one an add-on, the other a built-in part of the transmission. This manufacturer uses transmission oil.

The Allison MTB is an add-on retarder mounted on the back of the transmission. An **add-on hydraulic retarder is also called an output retarder.** In addition to hydraulic fluid, this retarder also uses a friction clutch that continues retarding at low speeds, making this retarder **more versatile.**

The Allison Brake Preserver is a part of the transmission. **A built-in hydraulic retarder is also called an input retarder.** Its operation is very similar to that of the Cat BrakeSaver, but it's located between the automatic lockup clutch and the gears.

Allison retarders are air-activated and have the following controls:

- throttle apply interlock
- system control valve
- service brake protection
- retarder on light

The throttle apply interlock prevents you from activating the retarder while the accelerator is depressed.

The service brake protection system protects against a leak in the retarder apply system. Both the retarder and the air brakes are fed by the same system. A leak in the retarder apply system would bleed the air out of the service brake system. If this happened you'd be left without the primary brake system—the service brakes—and without your retarder. The protection system senses a leak in the retarder and shuts off the air supply to the retarder. This protects the air supply for the brakes.

The system control valve allows you to turn off the retarder apply system. The retarder on light alerts you when the retarder apply system is on.

The Hale Retarder
This hydraulic auxiliary brake is mounted on the power take-off part of the transmission. It can be mounted on almost any type of vehicle. It works at low rpm and you can control the amount of retardation.

THE ELECTRIC RETARDER
Electric retarders are driveline devices, actually large alternators that are usually installed between the transmission and the axle. They'll be attached to the vehicle's frame or to the transmission itself. They work by creating **powerful electromagnetic fields** that **pull on the driveline or on the trailer axle** and thus **slow the vehicle.**

The Jacobs ER
This electric retarder is mounted on the drive shaft. It has four retarding positions and works off a hand control and/or a foot control. Its powerful alternator can put enough drag on the driveline to stop the vehicle. Its greatest advantage is that it can be used on any type of heavy duty vehicle.

The Ilasa
This electric retarder is similar to the Jacobs ER. It can be mounted on a tractor axle, but it's intended to be mounted on a trailer axle. It consists of two

rotors, one on each side of a very powerful electromagnet. It's more powerful than the Jacobs ER, but it's also a lot heavier.

When to Use Your Auxiliary Brakes

How you will use your auxiliary brakes depends in part on the type of system that is installed in your truck. However, no matter what type of vehicle retarder your truck uses, you'll activate it in the following situations.

BOBTAILING
Do not use the retarder when you bobtail. Do not use it when you're pulling an empty trailer, either. If the retarder is on and the service brakes are applied in these circumstances, **the wheels may lock up.**

CITY DRIVING
Although **most auxiliary brakes will stall the engine at low rpm,** some still function very well. For instance, the following retarders all continue to operate very efficiently at low rpm. If you have one of these retarders, leave it on in the city as long as the road surface is flat and dry:

- Jake ER
- Allison MTB
- Ilasa
- Hale

The other retarders work best at high rpm and should be turned off during periods of low rpm driving. Also **the Jake Brake should rarely be used in town.** This is because **it makes a lot of noise.** It is not a good idea to drive through a residential area and have your Jake Brake on every time you approach a stop light. Some communities have noise ordinances so you can be ticketed for doing this.

When a hydraulic retarder is used with an automatic transmission, the transmission fluid can overheat. You may have to reduce the retarder power or turn it off.

HIGHWAY DRIVING
In normal weather conditions when the road surface is flat, leave your **auxiliary brakes on all the time**. They will help you maintain good control on the highway. Whenever you take your foot off the accelerator, the retarder will come into play and immediately begin to slow your vehicle. The company you work for may have a policy about when to use the auxiliary brakes.

DRIVING IN ADVERSE WEATHER CONDITIONS
If the road surface is wet or **slippery from rain,** snow, or ice, the driving conditions are considered "adverse." If you leave your auxiliary brakes on in these conditions, you can increase the risk of a skid or a jackknife. The reason

for this is that all the braking force from the retarder is transmitted to the drive axles. Then, if you also apply the air brakes, even more braking force is on the driving axles. If the road surface is slippery this can cause the drive axles to slide. When that happens you are headed for an accident.

If the road is covered with ice or snow, **turn the retarder off.**

If the road is clear, but the weather is generally wet and the temperature is below freezing, turn the retarder off whenever you approach a bridge or a freeway ramp.

If it begins to rain, turn the retarder off for the first few minutes. These are the most dangerous minutes of a rainstorm because as the water mixes with the oil buildup on the road, the surface becomes very slippery.

If it's raining or **the road is wet, reduce retarder power.** If your retarder doesn't have more than one setting, turn it off.

DRIVING IN ROLLING TERRAIN

Service brakes don't cool much between downgrades in rolling terrain. This is one time when you'll appreciate your auxiliary brakes. Instead of relying on your service brakes, **turn on your retarder** and select a gear that lets you go down those hills at a safe and controlled speed. **Gear down, keep the engine speed near its rated rpm,** and let the retarder do the work.

DRIVING DOWN HILLS

This is when your retarder will come in most handy. In fact, it could save your life. If you use it well, it will save your service brakes, a lot of money and a lot of fatigue.

As always, before you start down a hill, **choose a gear that will let you descend at a constant, controlled speed with almost no use of the service brakes.**

The old rule was that to descend a hill you should use whatever gear you used, or would use, to climb the hill. With the new trucks and engines though, you can ascend a grade much faster than you should descend it. With some retarders, however, the old rule of thumb applies.

What follows is a list of general rules that may help you choose the gear **depending on the type of auxiliary brake installed** in your truck, the type of engine installed in your truck, your load, and the hill.

ENGINE RETARDERS. Use the same gear you used, or would use, to climb the hill.

EXHAUST RETARDERS. Use one gear lower than the gear you used, or would use, to climb the hill.

HYDRAULIC RETARDERS. If the retarder is a built-in part of the transmission, use the same gear you used, or would use, to climb the hill. If the retarder is an add-on, use one gear higher than the one you used, or would use to climb the hill.

ELECTRIC RETARDERS. Use one gear higher than the one you used, or would use to climb the hill.

As you descend a grade, **use the service   brakes only if the rpm or vehicle speed gets too high.** Retarders can make you over-confident about your ability to stop the truck quickly. Drivers have been known to drive too fast, depending on the retarders and service brakes to stop the truck quickly. This is a dangerous practice. It also puts more strain on both the retarder and the service brakes. As a driver, **don't rely on the retarder to do all the work of stopping** the truck. Always **drive** the truck **at a safe speed.**

Chapter 22 Quiz

1. Auxiliary brakes _____.
    A. attach to the service brake system and are used to stop the vehicle
    B. are separate from the service brake system and are used to stop the vehicle
    C. attach to the service brake system and are used to help slow the vehicle
    D. are separate from the service brake system and are used to help slow the vehicle

2. Using auxiliary brakes increases the life of _____.
    A. the engine
    B. the transmission
    C. the service brakes
    D. the drive train

For Questions 3, 4, 5, and 6, match the description in Column A with the type of retarder in Column B.

Column A Description   Column B Retarder Type

3. The _____ changes the timing in the valves.   A. electric retarder

4. The _____ partly closes the engine's exhaust system.   B. engine retarder

5. The _____ causes the engine to work against the pressure of a fluid.   C. exhaust brake

6. The _____ slows the vehicle with a magnet.   D. hydraulic retarder

For Question 7, refer to the figure at right.

7. The illustration shows the Jake Brake in operation.
   A. True
   B. False

8. An input retarder is an add-on device, while an output retarder is built-in.
   A. True
   B. False

9. When you bobtail, you should put your retarder on the lowest setting possible.
   A. True
   B. False

10. If the road is covered with ice or snow, turn off the retarder.
   A. True
   B. False

CHAPTER 23

SLIDERS

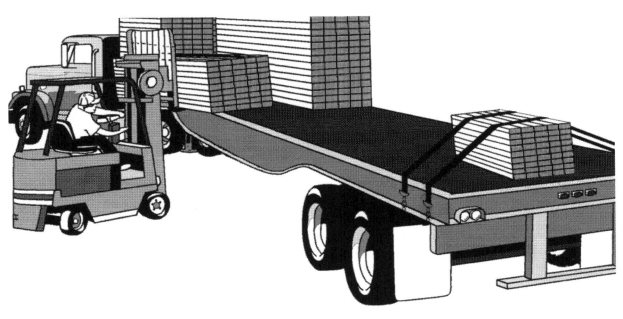

The Purpose of Sliders

The name of the game in the trucking industry is to **haul as much as you legally can, as cheaply as you can.** Because of this, driving with full and usually very heavy loads is a way of life with most truckers.

When loads increase in weight, that **weight must be distributed** to all of the rig's axles. Federal law limits total weight on each set of tandems to 34,000 pounds or 20,000 pounds on a single axle.

To compensate for these weight restrictions, some tractors have a fifth wheel that can slide forward or backward on the tractor frame. This sliding motion shifts and balances the trailer's kingpin weight put on each tractor axle without moving cargo around. This adjustable fifth wheel is called a **sliding fifth wheel or a "slider."**

Some trailers also are built to help distribute weight more evenly. They have a **sliding tandem axle,** also called a slider, that **moves forward and backward.** A sliding tandem helps balance the weight held up by the sliding tandem and the trailer's kingpin.

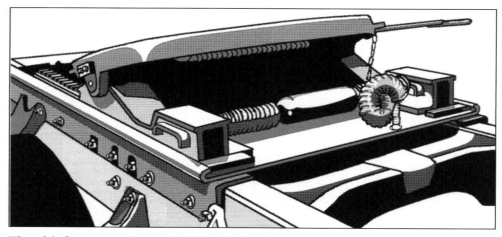

fig. 23-1
A sliding fifth wheel.

The chief purpose, then, of sliders is simple. Sliding fifth wheels and tandems, when used correctly, help distribute the weight from a heavily loaded trailer more evenly to all of the tractor-trailer's axles. **Sliders let you adjust the wheelbase** in order to be in compliance with the bridge law. You will learn about the bridge law in Chapter 28.

Another purpose the sliding fifth wheel serves is to **make it possible for a tractor to pull trailers with various kingpin settings.** Not all trailers have the same kingpin settings. A trailer with more than a 36-inch kingpin setting might put the trailer's landing gear too close to the tractor's rear wheels. To keep the wheels and the landing gear from coming into contact with each other, slide the fifth wheel backward.

A sliding fifth wheel can also improve mobility. When you move a sliding fifth wheel forward, you will have a shorter vehicle for tighter spaces.

Driver comfort is **greater when** the **fifth wheel** is located **closer to the center line of the rear axle.** When the rear axles are not overloaded, you can move the fifth wheel rearward for maximum comfort.

fig. 23-2
A sliding tandem axle.

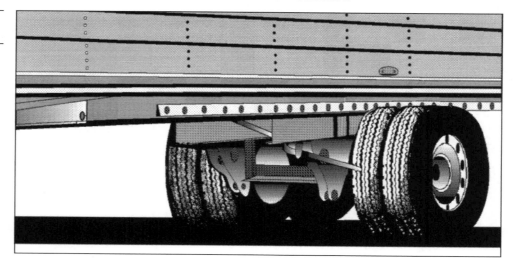

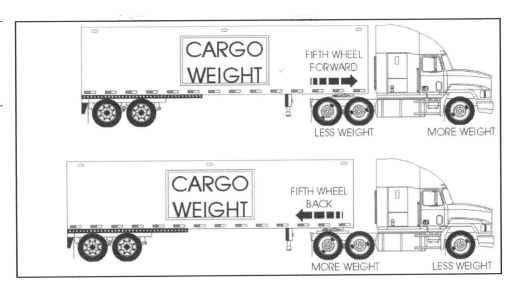

fig. 23-3
Sliding the fifth wheel forward or backward affects the tractor's steering axle and drive axle weight.

What You Should Know About Sliders

The most important thing for you to know is **how sliding** the tractor's fifth wheel or changing the location of the trailer's axles **will affect weight distribution** to all of the axles.

HOW SLIDERS WORK
When you **slide the fifth wheel forward or toward the tractor's cab,** more **weight is shifted to the tractor's steering axle.** When you **slide the fifth wheel back or away from the cab** toward the trailer's nose, the **tractor's rear axles will carry more** of the load.

The same principle applies to sliding the trailer's tandem axles. If the trailer's **tandem** is slid forward, **closer to the tractor, the tractor's axles will carry less** of the trailer's weight. The further to the rear you slide the trailer's tandem, the more trailer weight the tractor's axles will carry (see Figure 23-4).

fig. 23-4
Sliding the trailer's tandem forward or backward affects the trailer's kingpin and tandem axle weight.

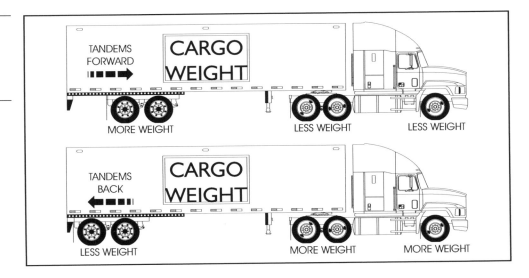

The idea is simple. But different types of tractors, trailers, and trailer loads make operating sliders more challenging. To operate sliders efficiently and accurately, you will need to do a little pre-trip thinking and rely on a lot of experience.

COMPONENTS

A sliding fifth wheel has three main components. They are:

- the slide baseplate
- the bracket
- the lock pins

The **slide baseplate** is **attached to** the **tractor's** frame. Then the **bracket fits over** the slide **baseplate.** The **fifth wheel is** then **mounted on** top of the **bracket.** Lock pins on the mechanism keep the fifth wheel from sliding. Most tractors have an **"air powered" switch** on the tractor's dash that **locks and unlocks** the lock pins. When the **lock pins and locking mechanism** are **disengaged,** you can **slide the fifth wheel forward or back.** (Usually notches are about two to three inches apart.)

The trailer's sliding tandem's main components are:

- the subframe (the sliding axle)
- the slide rails
- the lock pins
- the stop bar (on some sliding tandems)

The **subframe** of the sliding tandem **slides on** the **slide rails.** This shortens or lengthens the wheelbase. Sliding tandems also have **lock pins** but you will usually **unlock** these **manually with** a lever called **a locking bar.** Some trailers have "stop bars," a safety feature that fits at both ends of the rails on which the tandems slide.

SWING RADIUS

Before you adjust a sliding fifth wheel you need to **make sure the tractor has plenty of room to pivot** and move. The tractor's ability to pivot on the fifth wheel without striking the trailer is called **its swing radius.** Generally, **a tractor should have room to make a 90-degree turn** without touching the trailer.

If the trailer's nose is too close to the rear of the tractor's cab, a sharp turn might be a sharp turn into disaster. Be aware of other tractor and trailer equipment that might interfere when you are turning sharply. This equipment might include sleeper boxes, exhausts, refrigeration units, and aerodynamic devices. On the other hand, some trailers have **rounded front corners.** This **allows you to adjust the trailer closer** to the tractor.

You also should make sure there is enough **room between** the **tractor's rearmost tires and the trailer's landing gear** for the tractor **to make a 90-degree turn.**

Be careful to take exact measurements. Do not just guess or take a visual estimate. Owners manuals should include formulas to help you figure how far back or forward the fifth wheel should be placed. If you prefer, get some help from someone experienced in working with sliding fifth wheels.

To Slide or Not to Slide

Now that you've taken care of your swing radius, you know how far forward you can slide the fifth wheel. Now you come to the reason sliders were invented: to help shift trailer weight among all the axles.

The weight of your tractor, trailer, and cargo follows a natural course downward and outward through your axles and wheels and finally to the road.

A trailer's cargo, when possible, should be distributed evenly throughout the trailer. This isn't always possible, however. **When a load must be unevenly distributed or concentrated, the concentrated loads affect weight distribution.**

To figure out mathematically how to distribute weight evenly using sliders, here are a few things you will need to know:

- how much your tractor weighs
- how much your "empty" trailer weighs
- how much your cargo (or payload) weighs
- how much your loaded trailer weighs

You should also know the distance from the trailer's tandem center point to the kingpin. This is the trailer's wheelbase. Last, know the distance from the trailer's tandem centerpoint to the center of the trailer. This is known as the trailer's "A" dimension.

fig. 23-5
Find the tractor, trailer, and cargo weight, as well as the trailer and tractor's wheelbases and "A" dimensions.

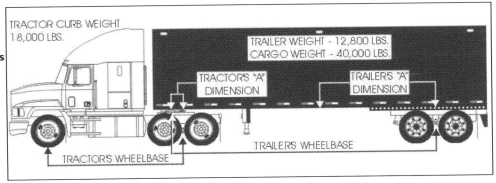

As you slide the trailer's tandem forward or backward, the wheelbase and "A" dimension of the trailer will change. (See Figure 23-5 on the previous page, for these dimensions.)

From the example trailer weights below, you will be able to find out the following:

- how much weight is resting on the kingpin. (The kingpin weight is the weight of the trailer the tractor's axles must support.)
- how much weight is resting on the trailer's tandem

To find out your kingpin weight, multiply the cargo (or payload) by the trailer's "A" dimension. Let's say the cargo is 40,000 pounds and the trailer's "A" dimension is 216 inches. 40,000 pounds of cargo multiplied by 216 inches (the trailer's "A" dimension) equals 8,640,000.

$$
\begin{array}{r}
40,000 \ \textit{pounds of cargo} \\
\times \quad 216 \ \textit{inches (the trailer's "A" dimension)} \\
\hline
= \ 8,640,000
\end{array}
$$

Now divide that number by the trailer's wheelbase. Let's say the trailer's wheelbase is 468 inches.

$$
\begin{array}{r}
8,640,000 \\
\div \quad 468 \\
\hline
= \ 18,462 \ \textit{pounds}
\end{array}
$$

18,462 pounds is how much of the load is resting on the kingpin. To figure out the cargo weight resting on the trailer's tandem, subtract the kingpin weight from the total cargo weight.

$$
\begin{array}{r}
40,000 \ \textit{pounds of cargo weight} \\
- \ 18,462 \ \textit{pounds of the cargo weight resting on the kingpin} \\
\hline
= 21,538 \ \textit{pounds of cargo weight resting on the trailer's tandem}
\end{array}
$$

21,538 pounds is the amount of cargo weight resting on the trailer's tandem. You now know that 18,462 pounds of the cargo weight is resting on the trailer's kingpin and 21,538 pounds of the cargo is resting on the trailer's tandem. But the cargo weight does not include the weight of the trailer itself.

The weight of just the trailer when it is empty is the trailer tare weight. Most trailers will have information in the owners manual about how much of the trailer's tare weight is supported by the kingpin and how much is supported by the trailer's tandem. Let's say that the trailer's tare weight is 12,800 pounds. Of the total, 2,815 pounds go to the kingpin (to be supported by the tractor's axles) and 9,985 pounds go to the trailer's tandem. To find the total kingpin weight, add the empty trailer's kingpin weight (2,815 pounds) to the cargo weight resting on the kingpin (18,462). See Figure 23-6.

18,462 *pounds (the cargo weight resting on the kingpin)*
+   2,815 *pounds (the front portion of the trailer's tare weight)*
= 21,277 *pounds of total kingpin weight*

21,277 pounds is the total kingpin weight (see Figure 23-6).

To find the total weight resting on the trailer's tandem, add the cargo weight on the trailer tandem (21,538 pounds) to the rear portion of the trailer's tare weight (9,985 pounds).

21,538 *pounds of cargo weight*
+   9,985 *pounds of the trailer's rear tare weight*
= 31,523 *pounds*

31,523 pounds of weight are resting on the trailer's tandem.

Phewww! Is your head spinning? That was a lot of math. But wait… we're not done yet. We now know a lot about the trailer but we don't know anything about the combination tractor-trailer. Here are a few things you need to know about the tractor to find out the effects of weight on each of its three axles:

- the distance the fifth wheel is set ahead of the tractor's tandem center point. This is the tractor's "A" dimension. (As you slide the fifth wheel forward or backward, the tractor's "A" dimension will increase or decrease.)
- the distance between the tractor's steering axle and the centerpoint of the tractor's tandem. This is the tractor's wheelbase.

See Figure 23-5 for these dimensions.

Take the kingpin weight (21,277) and multiply it by the tractor's "A" dimension. Let's say the tractor's "A" dimension is 24 inches.

21,277 *pounds (total kingpin weight)*
×   24 *inches (the tractor's "A" dimension)*
= 510,648

Then divide that number by the tractor's wheelbase. Let's say the tractor's wheelbase is 200 inches.

510,648 *(kingpin weight × "A" dimension)*
÷   200 *(the tractor's wheelbase)*
= 2,553

2,553 pounds is the total amount of kingpin weight resting on the tractor's front axles. So of the 21,277 pounds of kingpin weight, the tractor's front axle takes 2,553 of those pounds. That means the rest of the kingpin weight, 18,724 pounds (21,277 pounds of total kingpin weight minus 2,553 pounds of kingpin weight on the front axles) must be supported by the tractor's rear tandem. **18,724 pounds is the total amount of kingpin weight resting on the tractor's rear tandem.**

Now, all we need to do is find out how much the tractor weighs and add that weight to the tractor's three axles (see Figure 23-6). **Tractors, like trailers, usually have vehicle "tare" weight** listed in an owner's manual. Remember, tare weight is empty weight. Let's say your tractor's tare weight is 16,000 pounds. **When its fuel tanks are full of diesel,** the tractor weight has increased. **This weight added to the tractor's tare weight is known as curb weight.**

For this example, let's say your tractor's curb weight is 18,000 pounds. Let's say the front of the tractor weighs 10,000 pounds and the back of the tractor weighs 8,000 pounds. **This means the total weight on the tractor's front axle is 12,553 pounds** (10,000 + 2,553) and **the total weight supported by the tractor's rear tandem is 26,724 pounds** (8,000 + 18,724). See Figure 23-6.

fig. 23-6
Total combination weight and weight distribution per axle on the vehicle pictured in Figure 23-3.

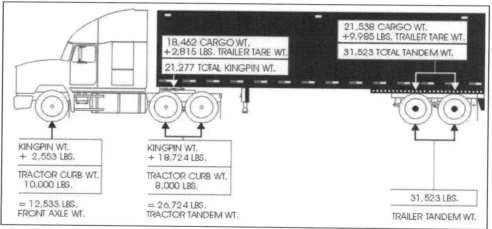

Okay, let's see if we're legal. The trailer's tandem weight is 31,523 pounds. The legal limit is 34,000 pounds. Just under the legal limits.

The total weight on the tractor's tandem is 26,724 pounds. The tractor's rear tandem is legal with room to spare.

The total weight on the tractor's steering axle is 12,553 pounds. The steering axle is only built to carry 12,000. We need to lose 533 pounds.

Our best bet would be to shift some of the tractor's steering axle load to the tractor's tandem. To lose 533 pounds from the steering axle slide the fifth wheel back a few notches, to 18 inches. The weight on the steering axle is reduced by 638 pounds to 11,915 pounds. The tractor's tandem picks up the 638 pounds of kingpin weight raising its total weight to 27,362, still under 34,000 pounds. We're safe. Relax and take a load off!

OBSERVATION SKILLS TEST

There was a problem pictured in the illustration that began this chapter. Do you recall what it was? How would you correct it? Go to the Observation Skills Test Grid at the back of the book and see how your observation skills are improving.

An Easier Way to Slide

Of course you do not have to be a rocket scientist to figure out when and how to use your sliders. You will learn to make good sliding decisions through experience. Many drivers wait for the scales to tell them they have an overweight axle. This is fine as long as you can make pretty good judgments about which slider (fifth wheel or tandem) to move and how far to move it. Otherwise you will be spending a lot of time (and money) on the scales.

So why did we bother you with the high math in the first place? Because if you will try it just once, you will be able to visualize the weight distribution of every load you haul and you will be able to make the correct sliding adjustments easily.

Adjusting Overweight Axles

Let's say that you've done your pre-trip homework and you find that one or more of your axles is beyond the legal limit. What do you do? You might be able to lighten your load by removing some of the payload. Sometimes this is the only option. A better solution would be to adjust the sliding fifth wheel and or the sliding tandem.

Manufacturers' designs allow for 12,000 pounds of weight on the tractor's front axle (or steering axle). **If your tractor's steering axle is too heavy, slide the fifth wheel back.** This will move some of the tractor's front axle weight to the tractor's rear axles. Generally, **sliding the fifth wheel two inches represents from 150 to 300 pounds of weight being shifted.**

If your **tractor's tandem** is **too heavy,** you have two choices. You can **slide the fifth wheel forward.** This will take away some of the weight on the tractor's rear axles and move it to the steering axle. Or you can slide the trailer's tandem forward toward the tractor. This changes the kingpin weight because you changed the "A" dimension of the trailer along with its wheelbase. This will take some of the tractor's rear axle weight away and shift it to the trailer's axles.

On the other hand, if your **trailer's tandem** is **too heavy,** you can **slide the trailer's tandem back** toward the rear of the trailer. This will put more weight on the trailer's kingpin which will be taken by the tractor's axles. **Sliding the trailer's tandem one notch could represent between 400 and 600 pounds.**

How to Adjust a Sliding Fifth Wheel

Some drivers are content to leave sliders unmoved from load to load in "standard" positions. This is fine when the same type of tractor and trailer is used and the load distribution and weight remain the same. But when the tractor, trailer, or load change, you had better make sure your axles are still within the legal limits. Otherwise you might find yourself on the road paying for a fine for being overweight. When you are required to **adjust a sliding fifth wheel,** do the following:

- Stop your rig in a straight line on level ground. Be absolutely sure your tractor and trailer are straight. The slightest pivot of the fifth wheel will cause the sliders to bind.
- Engage the differential lock.
- Set the trailer brakes only.
- Chock the trailer's tires.
- Lower the trailer's landing gear.
- Release the lock pins. For vehicles with a power air slide release, flip the air slide release valve on the dash to the "unlock" position. (On vehicles with a manual release, pull the operating lever located by the fifth wheel.)
- Check to see that both lock pins have released. If lock pins are not released, try to lower the trailer landing gear a few more inches. This will release pressure on the lock pins and will allow the fifth wheel to slide more freely. Mark the notch the fifth wheel is currently using.
- The tractor's fifth wheel should now be able to slide. Very slowly, move the tractor forward or backward to the desired fifth wheel position.
- Engage or set the slide lock pins. With the air slide release, put the control valve in "locked" position. With a manual slide release, trip the operating lever to allow the lock pins to engage.

- Check both lock pins. Make sure they are fully engaged. If they are not, keep the trailer brakes locked and drive the tractor forward slightly. This will engage the lock pins in the lock pockets.
- Raise the landing gear, remove the chocks, unlock the differential lock and release the trailer brakes.

Do not try to **slide** the fifth wheel **while** your **vehicle is in motion.** Doing so puts your tractor and trailer in danger of breakaway or rollover.

How to Adjust a Sliding Tandem Axle

When you are required **to adjust a sliding tandem,** do the following:

- Stop your vehicle in a straight line on level ground.
- Engage the differential lock.
- Set the brakes on the tractor and the trailer.
- Chock the trailer's tires.
- Remove the stop bar from behind the slider.
- Pull the operating handle all the way out, place it in its unlocking position. This will release the lock pins. Mark the notch the tandem is in now, or place the stop bar in the desired location.
- Release the tractor brakes only and slowly drive forward or backward until the tandem is in the desired location.
- Release the operating handle and visually check to make sure the lock pins have locked. (You should see each lock pin extending through the holes in the track rails.) Make sure the axles are not out of line. Misaligned axles will cause their tires to "scrub" or scrape the road rather than roll with it.
- Remove the chocks.
- Lock the stop bar in both body rails immediately behind the slider.
- With the trailer brakes applied, gently rock the trailer backward and forward to make sure the sliding tandem is locked. (You should check the lock pins at every stop to make sure each is locked.)
- Unlock the differential lock.

Do not try to **slide** the trailer's tandem **while** your **vehicle is in motion.** Doing so puts your tractor and trailer in danger of breaking away.

When Sliders Bind

Sometimes, sliders will stick or "bind" and will not slide easily. When this happens, do not keep trying to release the bind with tractor power. One slow steady tug forward and backward is all the stress you should put on your tractor's driveline and rear end. If your sliders are still bound, restraighten your tractor-trailer. Most binding, particularly in sliding tandems, is caused when the trailer sits on uneven ground. A little water on the trailer's sliding tandem rails can often loosen stubborn binds. Never use oil or grease. Sometimes, on the air-powered sliding fifth wheel, the lock pins will lock up or get stuck. When this happens, try tapping on the lock pins with a hammer.

Chapter 23 Quiz

1. Usually, when the trailer's sliding tandem binds, _____.
    A. your load is too heavy
    B. your tractor-trailer combination is not parked level and straight
    C. the slide rails need greasing
    D. your tractor needs to be serviced

2. Most five axle tractor trailer combinations are limited to _____.
    A. 12,000 pounds of weight on the steering axle and 34,000 pounds of weight per tandem axle
    B. half the kingpin weight on the steering axle and 34,000 pounds of weight per tandem axle
    C. equal amounts of weight up to 34,000 pounds, on every axle
    D. 80,000 pounds of kingpin weight

3. Sliding the fifth wheel forward _____.
    A. increases the tractor's "A" dimension number
    B. reduces the tractor's "A" dimension number
    C. increases the trailer's "A" dimension number
    D. reduces the trailer's "A" dimension number

4. A sliding fifth wheel adjusts the weight placed on the trailer's tandem.
    A. True
    B. False

5. The position of the _____ can affect the swing radius of the tractor.
    A. sliding tandem
    B. sliding fifth wheel
    C. steering axle
    D. payload

6. Each two-inch notch on a fifth wheel represents roughly 150 to 300 pounds of kingpin weight.
    A. True
    B. False

7. Before sliding the fifth wheel you should _____.
   A. set the landing gear
   B. unplug the electrical connection to the trailer
   C. chock the tractor's wheels
   D. make sure your differential lock is not engaged

8. To lose weight from the steering axle, slide the fifth wheel backward.
   A. True
   B. False

9. To lose weight from the tractor's tandem, slide the fifth wheel backward or the trailer's tandem backward.
   A. True
   B. False

10. To increase the trailer's kingpin weight_____.
    A. slide the tandem forward
    B. slide the tandem backward
    C. slide the fifth wheel backward
    D. slide the fifth wheel forward

CHAPTER 24

ECONOMY OPERATING

What is Economy Operating?

Professional truck drivers have to do more than just move the truck down the road. They have to do this safely, quickly, and in today's economy, efficiently. In trucking, the end does not justify the means. It is not enough to get where you're going, at any price. With the cost of diesel fuel well over a dollar a gallon, you have to get where you are going and **use as little fuel as possible** doing it. Economy operating is also the practice of using and caring for the vehicle in a way that keeps it out of the repair shop, and on the road, longer. You also want to operate your equipment in a way that squeezes every possible mile out of the vehicle and its components before they have to be repaired or replaced.

New, ever more **aerodynamic designs** for tractors and trailers **help** trucks to be more fuel-efficient. Still, it's the **driver** who **makes the biggest difference.** The fact that so many carriers offer bonuses to their fuel-saving drivers proves it's important to master economy operating techniques. Fortunately, that's not hard to do. All you have to do is know and maintain your equipment, understand the natural forces that act on your vehicle, and learn a few driving tricks.

OBSERVATION SKILLS TEST

Think back to the title page illustration. The driver of the truck pictured was driving economically. Were you able to see that, and can you explain how you were able to tell? Check your answers with the Observation Skills Test Grid at the back of the book.

Natural Forces and Fuel Use

To understand how to save fuel, you need to have an idea of how your vehicle uses fuel. You have to burn some fuel just to get your truck moving, keep it moving, and pull a load. What makes it use more or less?

Friction, gravity, and inertia are the three main natural forces acting on your moving vehicle which **affect how much power you get from a given amount of fuel.** Economy operating is about compensating for these forces so you don't waste fuel.

FRICTION

Simply put, friction is the rubbing of one surface against the other. This rubbing restricts the motion of one surface against the other to a greater or lesser degree. You're probably aware that there is friction between your truck tires and the road. This is known as **"rolling resistance"** or traction. You need some friction with the road to start and stop. If there were no friction between the tires and the road, you could never get your truck moving. Your tires would just spin on the surface. If you did get it moving, you wouldn't be able to stop. You need friction in the brake assembly, and friction between the tire and the road. But if the rolling resistance is too great, you use extra fuel in building up the power to overcome it.

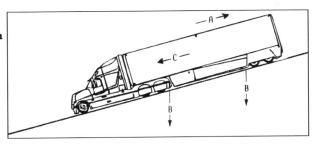

fig. 24-1
Natural forces acting on a moving vehicle.
A = friction,
B = gravity,
C = inertia.

Just as there is friction between your tires and the road, there is friction between your vehicle and the air. This is true of every surface of your vehicle that is in contact with the air. This friction is what is meant by the term **"air resistance."** When your vehicle is in motion and the air resistance is great, you can actually feel your truck pushing against it. This effect is called "aerodynamic **drag**" and it takes power (and therefore fuel) to overcome it.

GRAVITY

Almost everyone is familiar with the concept of gravity. But let's give a formal definition. Gravity has to do with the natural attraction between two masses. Like friction, gravity helps to hold your vehicle on the road. But again, too much gravity will keep your vehicle from moving.

Gross vehicle weight is an important factor that **affects the influence of gravity on a truck,** particularly when going up or down a hill. A heavier vehicle will have to work harder against the pull of gravity when climbing a hill. Then, it will require more braking power to slow and stop it against the pull of gravity on the downhill side.

INERTIA

Inertia is the tendency of an object that is in motion to stay in motion (and to stay still if it is already still). If your truck is moving, it will want to continue to move. If it is standing still, you will have to **overcome inertia to get the truck to move.** This takes power and power requires fuel. The more inertia there is to overcome, the more fuel you will use.

Many of the factors that affect friction and gravity also affect inertia. For instance, if your vehicle is very big or very heavy, there's just that much more mass to move.

Economy Driving Techniques

There's much that can be done with the design of the truck to lessen the effects of natural forces. But there's so much more that the driver can do towards saving fuel. So let's look at just what those economy operating techniques are.

KEEP YOUR SPEED DOWN

Driving at a speed appropriate for conditions is an important economy operating technique. This is especially true since speed management is totally within the driver's control. You might say **speed management is economy operating.** Using the truck's cruise control as much as possible helps maintain constant speeds and that increases fuel economy.

When the truck is first put in motion, the air resistance is very slight. At 35 mph, though, air resistance is definitely noticeable. At speeds greater than 35 mph, air resistance is a force to be reckoned with. After 60 mph, the impact of air resistance takes another big jump. As we said, the faster you go, the more air resistance. The more air resistance, the more fuel is burned, just to overcome friction. So one of the very best ways to save fuel is simply to drive at lower rpm, say, 70 percent of top governed speed. So **go slowly, don't increase your speed to buck the wind.**

What can the driver do about gravity? Again, **go slowly.** Don't up your speed when you approach a grade thinking you'll get a running start on it. This will help only to a very limited extent. You will still have to go through a certain range of gears on the way up. When you get to the top, you will be in the same gear as you would be if you hadn't gotten the running start. But you will have burned more fuel. So **approach a hill going no faster than the posted speed limit.** Climb the hill using just enough power to reach the top without lugging the engine. Try to stay at the lowest rpm you can.

It takes more power and more fuel to get your truck moving from a complete stop (overcome inertia) than to do just about anything else with it. So you want to **keep the number of stops you make to a minimum.** Does that mean you run yellow lights and kind of coast past stop signs? No, it doesn't. Instead, anticipate yellow and red lights. Go slowly. If you travel slowly enough, the red light may go green again by the time you get there and you won't have had to come to a complete stop.

Cut out all those extra panic stops you have to make because you're driving too fast. Again, slow down. Keep a safe following distance between your vehicle and the vehicle ahead. Decrease your speed for adverse driving conditions such as dusk, dark, rain, or snow.

DRIVING WITH AN ECONOMY ENGINE

Most engines and transmissions are now designed to be used with progressive shifting. These are often referred to as "formula engines." They **run at lower rpm,** perform better at low speeds than other engines and have higher torque ratings at lower engine speeds. So they perform as well as older engines, but use less fuel to do it. They also require a slightly different driving technique.

Since there is increased torque (power) at lower rpm, you do not need to accelerate to top governed speed before shifting. A higher rpm would mean more speed, but it would also use more fuel. On the other hand, low gears also mean more power. At very low speed, the gears are doing the work of the engine at higher speeds in higher gears.

Progressive Shifting

There's a specific driving technique that will help you do this. It's called **progressive shifting.** With this shifting method, the truck is brought up to highway speed using the least rpm between shifts. The engine is **not brought to maximum rpm with every shift.** Rather, you shift at about three-quarters top governed speed.

When first putting the truck in motion, use the least number of rpm it takes to get moving. Then shift into the next gear. Continue to shift just when you have obtained enough power to increase your speed without lugging the engine (making it work too hard at too low an rpm). The point is to reach the speed you want with the lowest rpm in each gear. The shift pattern goes something like this:

FIRST GEAR. 0 to 3 mph. You may only need 1,200 rpm.

SECOND GEAR. 3 to 6 mph. You may only need 1,300 rpm.

THIRD GEAR. 6 to 9 mph. You may only need 1,400 rpm.

FOURTH GEAR. 9 to 15 mph. You may only need 1,500 rpm.

FIFTH GEAR. 15 to 20 mph. You may only need 1,600 rpm.

fig. 24-2
Progressive shifting is a little bit different from regular shifting.

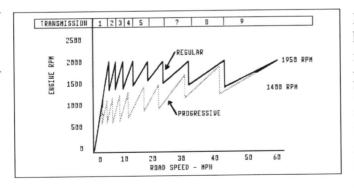

Looking at a graph will help you to see what's involved. In Figure 24-2, you see the older regular and newer progressive shifting patterns for a Roadranger nine-speed transmission. Notice the differences.

Economy Operating Techniques

There are some other things you can do to save fuel that involve how and where you drive.

TRIP PLANNING

A **well-planned, well-driven run** will get you where you want to go in the **most economical** way. You should aim to get the most done in the least amount of time, and with the least amount of effort. If you plan your route, it's within your power to pick the most direct path, with the least amount of stops and obstacles.

For example, on a long trip you might have two possible routes. One way goes through a lot of mountains and the other goes around them. Unless it is a lot further, choose the flatter route. You won't have to shift as often and will be able to hold a more even speed.

Another way to save fuel is to stay out of heavy traffic. Again, if you have a choice about it, drive around rather than through a city, unless that makes for a much longer trip. Schedule your day so you stay out of rush hour traffic. In many cities you can cruise right through if you are driving before 6:00 A.M. But if you wait until 8:00 A.M. you'll be in stop-and-go traffic. If you get caught in a traffic jam, think about pulling off and parking in a safe area. Wouldn't it be better to take a nap for an hour, then drive through the city in a hour, than spending two hours fighting traffic? You'd not only save fuel but you won't go bald from pulling your hair out!

Even if you don't plan your own route, you can plan your time so you make as few stops as possible. Then, when you do stop, try to combine several activities in that one stop. If you've stopped for fuel, a phone call, or a meal, take advantage of the time to bring your log up to date or inspect your vehicle. That will save your having to stop another time for these activities. Since stopping your vehicle is a fuel waster, **every stop saved is fuel saved.**

ROAD MANAGEMENT

Road management means **watching the traffic and planning ahead.** If you see a line of brake lights a half mile in front of you, you know you, too, will have to slow down when you get to whatever's stopping traffic. So why not back off the accelerator now and let the engine slow down gradually instead of rocketing at top speed until you are close and then using the brakes? If you are in town and the stop light three blocks ahead turns yellow, you know you are going to have to stop. So, again, why not get off the accelerator now? You'll save fuel and if you can gauge it right, the light might turn green before you get there.

These situations illustrate how to apply some of the safe driving techniques discussed in Chapter 19. The same things that make you a safe driver will help your fuel economy. **Drive at a steady speed.** Every time you speed up, slow down, then speed up again, you waste fuel. Try to set a pace, then stick with it.

Your best chance to do this is, again, to be driving at a conservative speed so you don't have to make lots of sudden adjustments.

Vehicle Management Systems

If your truck is equipped with a vehicle management system, you'll find it a great **help in maintaining a slow, steady driving speed.** Such a system can be as simple as a tachograph, or as complex and sophisticated as an onboard computer. Both make a record of the speeds and rpm at which the truck has been driven during a given period. The onboard computer will reveal even more information, such as how often the truck was stopped and for how long. What's important to the professional driver is the fuel use information. Let your vehicle management system be your guide to economy operating. Vehicle management systems are covered in more depth in Chapter 11.

IDLING AND SHUTTING DOWN THE ENGINE

Another fuel saving driving technique is to **idle your engine as little as possible.** Idling wastes fuel and wears out the engine. You are burning fuel and wearing out the engine, all to go nowhere.

There will be times when you'll be tempted to let it idle because it's more convenient than shutting down the engine. Remember, though, you will pay a high price in fuel costs for this convenience.

Then there are times when you simply have no choice. One example is in very cold weather. If it is below zero and you are going to shut down for more than an hour or two, you may not be able to start the engine again. In that case, you will have to idle the whole time. If you must do this in cold weather, set the throttle so it idles at around 1,000 rpm. That way the oil pressure will stay high enough to provide lubrication.

The company that you drive for may have a policy about idling. Know what that policy is and follow it.

ECONOMY OPERATING AND WEIGHT DISTRIBUTION

Overloading cargo affects the steering axles, tires, and brakes. Overloaded trucks require more fuel to get rolling and gain too much speed going downhill. Then you have to stand on the brakes to keep the vehicle under control. That can lead to early brake wear if not immediate brake failure. Too much weight on the steering axle can damage the steering axle and tires. Proper weight distribution extends the life of these parts.

Other Fuel Savers

There are other fuel savers that bear mention. A device you should know about is the fan drive equipped with a fan clutch. A fan that runs all the time, whether it's needed or not, is a fuel waster. **A fan clutch turns the fan on only when the engine heat climbs to a certain level.** At low temperatures, the clutch turns the fan off. Studies have shown that the fan is needed only about five percent of the time that the engine is running. You can see how the fan clutch would be a big fuel saver. For best results, run the fan clutch on automatic.

MAINTENANCE

A good program of preventive maintenance is a very important fuel-saving technique. **A well-tuned vehicle simply runs better,** giving you more power for fuel used. For instance, a leaky braking system will cause the compressor to run more often. Axles that are out of alignment increase rolling resistance, so this should be corrected. Dirty oil filters require a higher oil pressure. This forces the pump to work harder than it has to, which uses more fuel. A clogged air filter reduces the engine's oxygen supply. The right amount of oxygen is needed for good combustion. If the engine doesn't get the right amount of oxygen, you get quite literally "less bang for your buck." Proper tire inflation improves rolling resistance and eliminates premature wear and tear on each tire.

As the driver, you are in the best position to keep the vehicle in good running condition. You'll be the first to notice poor performance, worn out parts, and leaks. In your vehicle inspections, you can check for flaws and repair them (or see that they get repaired). Your reward will be fuel-efficient equipment.

Just the way in which you handle the vehicle can make it either break down faster, or last longer. If you drive too fast, you have to use the brakes more often. The more you brake, the harder the air compressor has to work. This not only uses extra fuel, it puts a greater strain on the braking system and shortens its life.

A driving style that calls for a lot of braking also wears out the tires faster. Those short stops scrape the rubber right off the tires (so do jackrabbit starts). Driving at an excessive speed means you have to take corners more sharply. This puts stress on the sidewall of the outside tires, which weakens them.

These factors all strengthen the case for driving at a slow, steady speed.

Aerodynamic Design

More and more, trucks and tires are designed to **combat rolling and air resistance.** The science of aerodynamics studies how air interacts with solid objects. The findings are applied to vehicle designs that move more easily through the air. You'll see vehicles rated as to how aerodynamic they are. This rating is given as a **"coefficient of drag"** or "Cd." A low Cd means little air resistance.

Radial tires make a great deal of difference when it comes to fuel saving. **Radial tires roll better** than the older bias type. They also flex better, to mold around rough road surfaces instead of fighting them.

Air resistance impacts two main areas on the truck, the front and the sides. Most of the aerodynamic drag is caused by pressure on the front of the truck. So this is an important target area for aerodynamic design. The idea is to direct the flow of air up, over, and around the truck.

In modern, aerodynamic trucks, **square or sharp edges** are **rounded off** so as not to break the flow of air. Wide bumpers are placed low on the vehicle. This prevents air from being trapped under the truck by directing it around the sides. **Wind deflectors** are put on top of the tractor to **direct the air up and over,** rather than pushing against the face of the trailer. Fairings on the sides prevent air from being trapped between the tractor and the trailer. Many of these features are included in the sketch on this book's cover.

The smoother the sides of the truck, the less skin friction there will be (skin friction is the result of air dragging along the sides of the truck). In aerodynamically-designed tractors, parts that protrude, such as lights, mirrors, and steps, are inlaid when possible to produce a smoother, slicker surface. A van sided with smooth, polished aluminum will produce less drag than one with ribbed sides. A box van with smooth sides will produce less drag than one with support posts that stick out.

Lightweight materials are used whenever possible. That **keeps** the truck portion of the **gross vehicle weight low** compared with the cargo weight. That way, when you're climbing a hill, fuel is being used to pull cargo, not truck.

Chapter 24 Quiz

1. The best way to save fuel is to drive at maximum speed so you complete your trip in the least amount of time possible.
   A. True
   B. False

2. _____ makes the biggest difference in fuel economy.
   A. Aerodynamic design
   B. The driver

3. Air resistance is a type of _____.
   A. friction
   B. gravity
   C. inertia
   D. truck design

4. _____ tires are most effective at reducing rolling resistance.
   A. Radial
   B. Bias

5. Which of the following components is not a fuel saving device?
   A. side fairing
   B. bias tire
   C. fan clutch
   D. wind deflector

6. It takes more power and more fuel to _____ than to do just about anything else with it.
   A. bring the vehicle to a stop
   B. get the vehicle moving from a complete standstill
   C. slow down the vehicle
   D. turn the vehicle

7. Progressive shifting is _____.
   A. driving at top governed speed
   B. lugging the engine
   C. driving at about three-quarters top governed speed
   D. skipping some gears

In Questions 8, 9, and 10, match the components in Column A with their fuel-saving function in Column B.

Column A Component

8. formula engine

9. tachograph

10. fan clutch

Column B Fuel Saving Function

A. helps the driver maintain a steady speed

B. turns the fan off at low engine temperatures

C. requires less fuel to perform well

CHAPTER 25
VEHICLE INSPECTION

DRIVER VEHICLE INSPECTION REPORT

(TO BE COMPLETED DAILY IN ACCORDANCE WITH RULE 396.11
OF SAFETY REGULATIONS AS PRESCRIBED BY THE D.O.T.)

OWNER'S NAME _Beck Trucking Co._   VEHICLE NUMBER M·420 D-608

DRIVER _Frances Sanchez_   DATE 2-22

ITEMS TO CHECK	DRIVER'S REPORT	MECHANIC'S REPORT	ITEMS TO CHECK	DRIVER'S REPORT	MECHANIC'S REPORT
BEFORE STARTING ENGINE			**AFTER STARTING ENGINE**		
OIL – IF ADDED INSERT # GALS.	✓		FUEL SYSTEM	✓	
FUEL – IF ADDED INSERT # GALS.	✓		COOLING SYSTEM	✓	
COOLANT	✓		ENGINE	✓	
BRAKE LINES TO TRAILER	X		LEAKS	✓	
ELECTRICAL LINES TO TRAILER	✓		HEADLIGHTS	✓	
DRIVE LINE	✓		TAILLIGHTS	✓	
COUPLING DEVICES	✓		STOP & TURN LIGHTS	✓	
TIRES & WHEELS	✓		CLEARANCE & MARKER LIGHTS	✓	
SPRINGS	✓		REFLECTORS	✓	
BODY	✓		**AFTER STARTING ENGINE**		
GLASS	✓		AIR PRESSURE WARNING DEVICE	✓	
EMERGENCY EQUIPMENT			OIL PRESSURE	✓	
TORCHES, LANTERNS OR REFLECTORS	✓		AMMETER	✓	
FUSEES	✓		HORN	✓	
FLAGS	✓		WINDSHIELD WIPERS	✓	
SPARE BULBS	✓		PARKING BRAKES	✓	
FUSES	✓		CLUTCH	✓	
FIRE EXTINGUISHER	✓		TRANSMISSION	✓	
TIRE CHAINS N/A			REAR VISION MIRRORS	✓	
AFTER STARTING ENGINE (OUT OF CAB)			STEERING	✓	
FUEL SYSTEM	✓		SERVICE BRAKES	✓	
			SPEEDOMETER	✓	
			OTHER ITEMS NONE		

DAILY MILEAGE RECORD

SPEEDOMETER READING END OF DAY 49,185

SPEEDOMETER READING START OF DAY 48,980

TOTAL MILES DRIVEN TODAY 205

DATE OF TRAILER LUBRICATION IF ON THIS TRIP _____

I MADE INSPECTION AS REQUIRED ON LISTED ITEMS
DRIVER'S SIGNATURE: _Frances Sanchez_

I CERTIFY THAT REPAIRS CHECKED WERE MADE TODAY:
MECHANIC'S SIGNATURE:

REPAIR ORDER NO:

DRIVER: USE ✓ IF ITEM IS SATISFACTORY
USE X IF ITEM IS NOT SATISFACTORY

MECHANIC: USE ✓ WHEN ITEM IS CORRECTED
AND SIGN YOUR INITIALS.

REMARKS: _____

Need for Inspections

Part 396 of the Federal Motor Carrier Safety Regulations covers the vehicle inspections required by the Department of Transportation. You may wonder why the government makes such an issue of inspections. When you take a truck out, you have a responsibility to uphold. You are sharing the road with others, in vehicles large and small. You want to be sure that the truck will respond to your control so you can drive it safely.

Your truck must be in top running order for this to take place. And the only way for you to be sure your vehicle is in good condition before you get behind the wheel is to make a personal inspection of all parts and accessories.

Don't you think it makes sense to make sure everything is in order before taking off down the road with a large and very expensive piece of equipment? Certainly you would check your car before taking off on a cross-country trip. You would want to **make sure everything is in good running order** so you can avoid any unnecessary trouble on your trip.

Personal Safety

No one is more important to you than yourself. Therefore, **to ensure your personal safety on the road** should be your first concern. When you comply with the laws and regulations set down by the Federal Motor Carrier Safety Regulations, you ensure your safety as a driver.

After you inspect your vehicle, you gain a **feeling of confidence.** You are free from worry that something might break down and lead to further complications. This feeling alone can make a difference in your driving habits. If you're not worrying about whether your brakes will hold or your lights will work, your mind is free to focus on the traffic. This simply **allows you to be a better, safer driver.**

Required by Law

Why are there laws requiring the inspection of vehicles you plan to operate? Laws are **guidelines** which have been set up **to protect everyone:** the carrier, the client, the public, and you. They set standards and provide some assurance that these standards will be met. If there were no regulations, what would stop a less professional driver from jumping in an unsafe truck and heading down the road? The fact that you completed a full inspection on your own vehicle would be small comfort if he plowed into you because his brakes failed.

Regulations also serve as a constant reminder of the steps which should be taken for the safe operation of the vehicle. Without a set of guidelines, it is too easy to forget all the steps that must be taken each and every time you head out on your trip.

CARRIER'S REQUIRED RECORDS

According to the regulations, it's actually **the carrier** who **is charged with seeing that vehicles are inspected and that records are kept** of these inspections. In practice, though, it's **the driver** who usually **does the actual inspection** and **fills out the reports.** In doing so, you're acting as the carrier's agent. And, if the vehicle you're driving is found to be unsafe, it's you, the driver, who is most likely to be fined. That's why you have to know what is required.

Regulations call for carriers to **maintain a regular system of inspection** covering all their vehicles. Also, they must **keep a maintenance record** on each of the vehicles.

DRIVER'S RESPONSIBILITIES

As a driver, you will **inspect your vehicle before and after your run.** Specifically, the regulations require you inspect your vehicle at the end of your run and report any repairs that should be made. Then, in your pre-trip inspection, you verify those repairs have been made.

But here's where practice differs slightly from policy. What usually happens is that the pre-trip inspection is more thorough than the post-trip. In the pre-trip, you not only check that repairs were made, but also make sure that various systems and components are in good working order. This makes sense when you consider that you may not always have the same truck today that you had yesterday. You want to be confident the truck you are about to drive is safe. We'll look at how these two inspections work together later in this chapter.

> OBSERVATION SKILLS TEST
>
> Did you notice the pre-trip inspection form at the start of this chapter that Frances Sanchez filled out on the truck she plans to drive for Beck Trucking Co.? Based on the results of her inspection, will Frances drive her truck out of the yard or turn it in for maintenance? Explain your answer. Then check your response with the Observation Skills Test Grid at the back of the book.

Types of Inspections

There are several types of inspections. They each have a slightly different purpose.

PRE-TRIP INSPECTION

Your **pre-trip inspection involves a complete circle check** of the vehicle you will be driving. You'll check a number of sites along the **inside and outside of the tractor and trailer,** and your inspection will take you full circle around your vehicle. By following the same steps every time you will not overlook any part of your inspection duties.

You'll have to show you can perform a pre-trip inspection to get your CDL.

IN-TRANSIT INSPECTION

Your responsibility to make inspections doesn't stop once you move out on the road. In-transit checks are something you should include as part of proper road operations. Being aware of the condition of your vehicle while you drive can prevent a major problem from taking place.

The law does not require that you **inspect your vehicle while you are in transit.** However, it is good practice to do so. Your vehicle may have passed your pre-trip inspection, but **problems can develop while you are out on the road.** It is suggested you make a quick check at every meal stop.

There are circumstances which even warrant a stop alongside the road to make a check of certain conditions. A load of hazardous materials demands a tire check at the beginning and end of your trip and each time you park. Driving a reefer means you will want to stop and check the temperature periodically. This is the time to make an in-transit inspection just to remain on the safe side.

POST-TRIP INSPECTION

According to Section 396.11, a **report of the vehicle's condition must be made at the end of each day's work.** Section 396.3 and Part 393 detail the parts and accessories which must be checked. Any defects must be reported and repaired. Whoever makes the repairs, be it you, someone in Maintenance, or an outside garage, must **sign the report to certify repairs have been made.**

This driver's vehicle inspection report (DVIR) then forms the basis of the next pre-trip inspection. You'll verify that needed repairs were made and that nothing else is wrong with the vehicle.

OFFICIAL ROADSIDE INSPECTIONS

Section 396.9 of the DOT safety regulations authorizes **a special agent of the Federal Motor Carrier Safety Administration (FMCSA) to stop and** inspect your vehicle. This agent could be a federal or state DOT representative, highway patrol officer, weigh master, or Commercial Vehicle Safety Alliance (CVSA) official. This inspection could take place alongside the road, or at a port of entry station.

fig. 25-1
The post-trip inspection form requires you to identify any needed repairs. On this detail of a Driver Vehicle Inspection Report, the driver has indicated a problem with the brake lines.

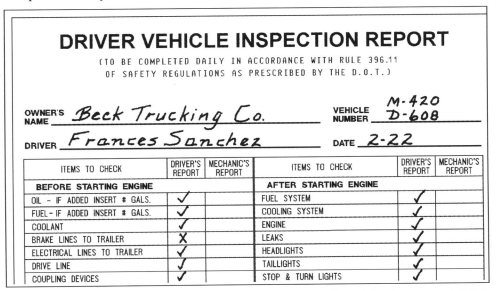

DRIVER VEHICLE INSPECTION REPORT
(TO BE COMPLETED DAILY IN ACCORDANCE WITH RULE 396.11 OF SAFETY REGULATIONS AS PRESCRIBED BY THE D.O.T.)

OWNER'S NAME _Beck Trucking Co._   VEHICLE NUMBER _M-420 D-608_

DRIVER _Frances Sanchez_   DATE _2-22_

ITEMS TO CHECK	DRIVER'S REPORT	MECHANIC'S REPORT	ITEMS TO CHECK	DRIVER'S REPORT	MECHANIC'S REPORT
BEFORE STARTING ENGINE			**AFTER STARTING ENGINE**		
OIL - IF ADDED INSERT # GALS.	✓		FUEL SYSTEM	✓	
FUEL - IF ADDED INSERT # GALS.	✓		COOLING SYSTEM	✓	
COOLANT	✓		ENGINE	✓	
BRAKE LINES TO TRAILER	X		LEAKS	✓	
ELECTRICAL LINES TO TRAILER	✓		HEADLIGHTS	✓	
DRIVE LINE	✓		TAILLIGHTS	✓	
COUPLING DEVICES	✓		STOP & TURN LIGHTS	✓	

This is an inspection you definitely want to pass. If you don't, **your vehicle can be declared "out of service"** by the special agent. The inspection takes only about 15 or 20 minutes. If there are no problems found with your vehicle, you can be on your way once again knowing that you are behind the wheel of a safe vehicle. If your vehicle is declared out of service by the inspector, you cannot drive the vehicle until the repair has been made and the vehicle has been reinspected. If the vehicle cannot be repaired right where it is, it will have to be towed to a repair shop.

The roadside inspection is concerned with the most common violations that can take place as a result of the driver's failure to make the pre-trip inspection. **The driver is also subject to inspection.** The agent will check **to see if you are keeping your logs up to date.** Your condition is also observed to make sure you are truly able to operate the vehicle safely.

If your vehicle does not pass the roadside inspection, you must deliver the report to your carrier within 24 hours. Once the motor carrier has received the inspection report, the carrier has 15 days to take care of the problems stated on the report.

To make the business of official roadside inspections more efficient, 48 states, Canada, and Mexico have joined an organization called the **Commercial Vehicle Safety Alliance.** The CVSA **developed a standard inspection** that can be conducted quickly by a mobile unit. That's the **Critical Item Inspection,** which involves checking the brakes and steering, tires and wheels, the fifth wheels, drawbars, and suspension.

Once you pass the inspection, you will receive a sticker for your vehicle. The sticker is good for three months. It shows concerned officials that your vehicle has been inspected recently and passed. In CVSA member states, **if you pass the Critical Item Inspection, you're not likely to be subject to another roadside inspection for 90 days** unless the official notices something clearly wrong.

Making Inspections

When making inspections, it helps to **follow a routine.** That way you don't forget anything. One routine you might use has seven steps:

- Note the vehicle's condition in general as you approach it. Review the most recent vehicle inspection report looking for problems that require special attention.
- Check the engine compartment.
- Start the engine and inspect inside the cab.
- Turn off the engine and check all the lights.
- Walk all around the vehicle checking critical parts.
- Check the signal lights.
- Start the engine and check the brakes.

Here are some specific things to look for.

OVERVIEW

Make sure the vehicle is level, **not leaning to one side** or the other. Check the ground under your truck for puddles or **wet spots,** which **mean something is leaking.** Search until you find out where they are coming from. Are there any black streaks of oil on the inside sidewall of a tire? That likely means a wheel seal is leaking. Review the most recent DVIR.

IN THE ENGINE COMPARTMENT

Make sure the parking brakes are set or chock the wheels. **Check fluid levels.** You should be able to see the radiator water level just below the neck of the filler cap. Use the dipstick to check the oil. **Check** the tension and condition of **belts** by pressing down on them. There should be no more than $\frac{3}{4}$ of an inch of slack. **Look for** small **oil leaks. Check the battery connections, the battery box,** and holddowns. Look for corrosion around the battery posts. Unless you have a maintenance-free battery, you should **check the battery fluid level.** Make sure all the **vent caps** are **in place.** Look for cracked or **worn wiring insulation and broken** or disconnected **wires. Check the compressor oil supply** and the supply of alcohol in the alcohol evaporator, if you have one.

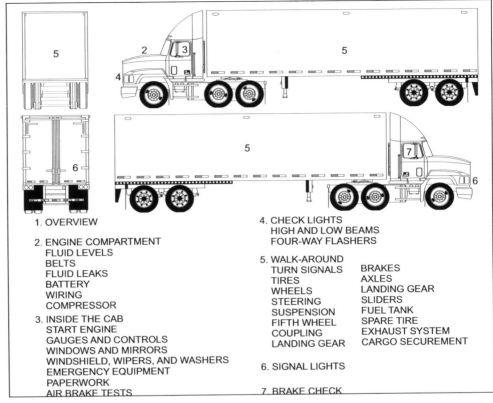

fig. 25-2
This is one procedure to use when inspecting your truck. Your company may want you to use something slightly different.

1. OVERVIEW

2. ENGINE COMPARTMENT
   FLUID LEVELS
   BELTS
   FLUID LEAKS
   BATTERY
   WIRING
   COMPRESSOR

3. INSIDE THE CAB
   START ENGINE
   GAUGES AND CONTROLS
   WINDOWS AND MIRRORS
   WINDSHIELD, WIPERS, AND WASHERS
   EMERGENCY EQUIPMENT
   PAPERWORK
   AIR BRAKE TESTS

4. CHECK LIGHTS
   HIGH AND LOW BEAMS
   FOUR-WAY FLASHERS

5. WALK-AROUND
   TURN SIGNALS   BRAKES
   TIRES   AXLES
   WHEELS   LANDING GEAR
   STEERING   SLIDERS
   SUSPENSION   FUEL TANK
   FIFTH WHEEL   SPARE TIRE
   COUPLING   EXHAUST SYSTEM
   LANDING GEAR   CARGO SECUREMENT

6. SIGNAL LIGHTS

7. BRAKE CHECK

INSIDE THE CAB

Put the gearshift in neutral ("park" if you have an automatic). **Start the engine** and listen for strange noises. **Check all the gauges.** Make sure they work and give normal readings. (Chapter 2 has details on what normal readings to expect.) **Test all switches and controls** to make sure they work.

Check the air brake system. The air brake system checks are described in Chapter 4. Unless you want an air brake restriction on your CDL, you'll have to show the examiner you can perform these tests. Do them during the engine start part of the pre-trip inspection.

Clean and **adjust your mirrors. Check** your windows **for cracks.** If the glass is dirty clean it. **Check the supply of windshield washer fluid.** Make sure your wiper blades are in good condition, and that the wipers work. If there is anything (stickers, signs) that will obstruct your view remove it. **Only stickers and decals required by law** are permitted.

Make sure you **have a properly charged and rated fire extingusher.** It must be rated at least 5 B:C. If you are hauling haz mat, it must be rated at least 10 B:C. You must also **have three reflective triangles.** Unless the truck has circuit breakers, you must also **have spare fuses.**

Make sure you have cargo manifests and any special permits you might need to haul your load, and supplies for doing your log.

CHECK THE LIGHTS

Turn off the engine. Turn on the headlights and the four-way flashers. Leave the cab (take the key with you) and **make sure the headlights and four-ways are working.** Make sure **both high and low beams** work. Turn these lights off. **Turn on** the **parking, clearance, side marker and identification lights, and right turn signal** before starting the walk-around inspection.

WALK-AROUND INSPECTION

Start at the **left front side.** Walk toward the **front** of the truck, inspecting as you go. Inspect the front of the truck. See that all the lights there are clean and working. They should be amber in color.

Walk down the **right side,** inspecting critical areas there. Note that the right turn signal is working. It should be amber or white in color. If your tractor is a cabover, see that the cab lock is engaged.

Go on to inspect the **back** of the truck. Check all the lights and reflectors there. They should be red. If you have mud flaps, make sure they're not torn, dragging, or rubbing on the tires. Make sure the license plate is securely in place and clean.

Work your way back to the cab, inspecting the **left side** of the truck. Check that all the lights and reflectors are clean and free of damage, amber color in front, red at the rear. If your battery is here instead of the engine compartment, inspect it now.

During the walk-around, closely inspect the following parts and systems:

TIRES. **Check the tread depth.** Remember, $\frac{4}{32}$ of an inch of tread are needed on the steering axle and $\frac{2}{32}$ of an inch on the rest of the tires. Are there any cuts in the rubber? Do any of the plies show? Are duals touching? Are tire sizes, or radials and bias types mixed on the same axle? Check for cut or cracked valve stems. **Check the pressure** with a gauge.

WHEELS. **Check the lug nuts** for tightness. Look for any cracks starting to form around the lug nuts. Rust or bright metal are signs the nuts are loose and the wheel is not mounted tightly. Look for damaged rims and missing parts. Check for welding repairs, which are prohibited. **Check** the **hub oil level.**

SUSPENSION. **Check for cracked or broken leaves.** Check for deflated or hissing air bags. Note spring hangers that allow the axle to move out of position. Look for damaged or missing torque rods or arms, U-bolts, or spring hangers. Check the condition of the shock absorber.

BRAKES. Check for loose or missing parts and **check the push rod travel.** Refer to Chapter 4 for more details on adjusting the slack adjusters. See that brake linings have not worn thinner than $\frac{1}{4}$ inch. Brake shoes and linings should not have oil, grease, or brake fluid on them.

AXLES. Powered axles should not leak oil. Check the condition of the lift mechanism on retractable axles. If they're air-powered, **check for leaks.**

SLIDERS. Make sure **lock pins** are firmly in their holes **and locking devices** are **in place.**

AIR SYSTEM. Look for hoses that are kinked, rubbing, or worn. Listen carefully for hissing noises. **Search for the source of the leak.** Drain water from the air tanks.

COUPLING. **Make sure** the trailer air and electrical **connections are made properly** and that lines are not dragging. Be sure to check all air and electrical connections throughout a double or triple combination.

FUEL TANKS. **Double-check the fuel level** in all tanks. See that the tanks are mounted securely, and that fuel crossover lines aren't hanging dangerously low.

FIFTH WHEEL. **See that the coupling is secure.** Make sure the fifth wheel release lever is locked. There should be no space between the upper and lower fifth wheel. Don't forget to **check** the fifth wheel, locking lever, and safety chains on **the dolly** in a double or triple rig.

LANDING GEAR. If the trailer is coupled to the tractor, the **landing gear should be up and the handle stowed away.**

SPARE TIRE. If you have a spare tire, **make sure** that **it's in good condition and** that it's **mounted securely** in the rack.

EXHAUST SYSTEM. Look for loose, broken, or missing pipes, mufflers, or stacks. See that **exhaust system parts aren't rubbing against** fuel system parts, tires, or **other** moving vehicle **parts. Check for** exhaust system **leaks.**

STEERING SYSTEM. Look for bent, broken, or missing parts. If you have power steering, make sure you **check** the hoses, pumps, and the **level of power steering fluid. Check for leaks. Steering wheel free play should be no more than two inches** to either side of a 20-inch steering wheel. **Shake the steering arm, tie rod, and drag link at each wheel to see they are not loose.**

CARGO SECUREMENT. Make sure you have the **minimum number of tiedowns** according to FMCSR Part 393.110, and that **all bindings and chains are in good condition** and secure. **Check blocking and bracing** to assure yourself that the load won't shift once the truck is in motion. **Check the seals** on sealed cargo. Check locks and latches on trailer doors. Check the tailboard or endgate, if you have one. Any canvas or **tarp must be tied down** so it won't flap or billow out. If you're hauling an oversized load, make sure you have the signs, lights, and flags you need. If you have side boards or stakes, make sure they are free of damage and securely in place. Check the headerboard, if you have one. Make sure that it's in good condition.

CHECK THE SIGNAL LIGHTS

When you've been all around the vehicle, get back in the cab. Turn off the lights. Pull down the trailer brake hand valve. Next, turn on the turn signal. Go out and **make sure the stop lights** are on and that **front and rear signals are working.** The front signal should be amber or white, the rear signal red, amber, or yellow.

CHECK THE BRAKES

Checking the brakes means checking the service and parking brakes, as well as the air brake system. Put on the trailer brakes, then try to move forward in the lowest gear. **If the trailer brakes are working and the coupling is secure, they should hold you back.** Use a similar method to check the service brake. Release the parking and trailer brakes. Then **test the service brake's power to stop the truck while moving forward in low gear. Test the parking brake** by applying it while stopped. Then **see if it holds as you try to move forward.**

Daily Vehicle Inspection Report Form

Just as you make your inspection each day before you go out on the road, so too will you need to fill out your daily vehicle inspection report form. This is a checklist of all the items which must be inspected and which must be in safe operating condition before the vehicle may be driven.

You saw one example of a vehicle inspection report form in the Observation Skills Test. There's another type you might see. With this form, you check off only those items that need attention. The vehicle inspection report form is often combined with the driver's daily log in the same book.

Actually, the inspection report form serves two functions. It helps to remind you of all the things which must undergo your keen examination each day. And it is written proof that the inspection did take place. The law requires that this report be filled out, and it must be turned in at the end of each day's completed work assignment.

FILLING OUT THE REPORT

Make sure that you do not overlook any part of your checklist. Don't rush through it. Your report must list any and all problems that could hamper the safe operation of the vehicle in question. If your inspection fails to turn up any defects, this too should be stated in your report.

fig. 25-3
On this driver's inspection report, you would check off only those items that need attention. If there are no defects, you would mark the "NO DEFECTS" box.

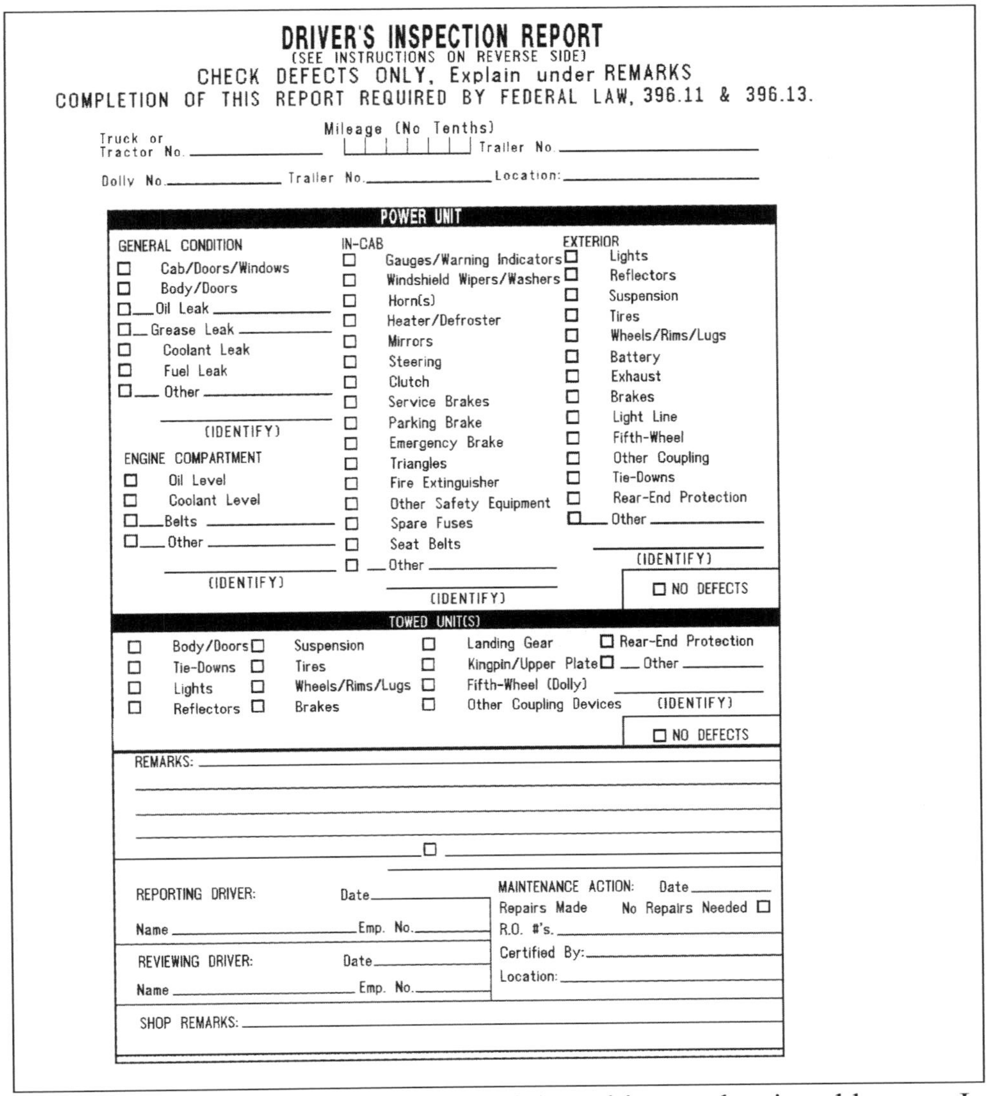

DRIVER'S INSPECTION REPORT
(SEE INSTRUCTIONS ON REVERSE SIDE)
CHECK DEFECTS ONLY, Explain under REMARKS
COMPLETION OF THIS REPORT REQUIRED BY FEDERAL LAW, 396.11 & 396.13.

Mileage (No Tenths)
Truck or Tractor No. _____ Trailer No. _____
Dolly No. _____ Trailer No. _____ Location: _____

POWER UNIT

GENERAL CONDITION
- ☐ Cab/Doors/Windows
- ☐ Body/Doors
- ☐ Oil Leak _____
- ☐ Grease Leak _____
- ☐ Coolant Leak
- ☐ Fuel Leak
- ☐ Other _____
(IDENTIFY)

ENGINE COMPARTMENT
- ☐ Oil Level
- ☐ Coolant Level
- ☐ Belts _____
- ☐ Other _____
(IDENTIFY)

IN-CAB
- ☐ Gauges/Warning Indicators
- ☐ Windshield Wipers/Washers
- ☐ Horn(s)
- ☐ Heater/Defroster
- ☐ Mirrors
- ☐ Steering
- ☐ Clutch
- ☐ Service Brakes
- ☐ Parking Brake
- ☐ Emergency Brake
- ☐ Triangles
- ☐ Fire Extinguisher
- ☐ Other Safety Equipment
- ☐ Spare Fuses
- ☐ Seat Belts
- ☐ Other _____
(IDENTIFY)

EXTERIOR
- ☐ Lights
- ☐ Reflectors
- ☐ Suspension
- ☐ Tires
- ☐ Wheels/Rims/Lugs
- ☐ Battery
- ☐ Exhaust
- ☐ Brakes
- ☐ Light Line
- ☐ Fifth-Wheel
- ☐ Other Coupling
- ☐ Tie-Downs
- ☐ Rear-End Protection
- ☐ Other _____
(IDENTIFY)
☐ NO DEFECTS

TOWED UNIT(S)

- ☐ Body/Doors ☐ Suspension ☐ Landing Gear ☐ Rear-End Protection
- ☐ Tie-Downs ☐ Tires ☐ Kingpin/Upper Plate ☐ Other _____
- ☐ Lights ☐ Wheels/Rims/Lugs ☐ Fifth-Wheel (Dolly)
- ☐ Reflectors ☐ Brakes ☐ Other Coupling Devices
(IDENTIFY)
☐ NO DEFECTS

REMARKS: _____
_____
_____
_____ ☐

REPORTING DRIVER: Date _____
Name _____ Emp. No. _____

REVIEWING DRIVER: Date _____
Name _____ Emp. No. _____

MAINTENANCE ACTION: Date _____
Repairs Made   No Repairs Needed ☐
R.O. #'s. _____
Certified By: _____
Location: _____

SHOP REMARKS: _____

The report must identify the motor vehicle and it must be signed by you. In the case of team operations, only one driver need sign the report. If you operate more than one vehicle in one day, it is your responsibility to fill out a vehicle inspection report on each vehicle.

REPAIR DEFECTS PROMPTLY

A defect can affect the safe operation of your vehicle. No matter what it is, the problem should be taken care of promptly.

In fact, the regulations require the **carrier to see to it that any defect is taken care of** to return the vehicle to a safe condition of operation.

If repairs are not made to correct the defect, it is against the law to take the vehicle out onto the road. Don't forget, the safety of the public is threatened by the presence of an unsafe truck on the public roadway.

Attitude

The attitude toward inspections is one of the differences between a truck jockey and a professional driver. It is very easy to get into a habit of walking around your truck and saying you "inspected" it. You look without seeing. You start saying to yourself "It was fine yesterday. I don't need to check it again." You start filling out the inspection report from the cab of your truck.

Because your truck is designed to be a reliable piece of equipment you might get away with a slipshod attitude toward inspections for a good long while. But the mark of a true professional is taking pride in the little everyday things that no one sees you doing. You don't inspect your truck just because it's required, or you're afraid of being put out of service. You do it because **it's part of doing your job right.**

Also, inspection is something you should be doing all day long, not just once a day. You should **always be listening to, watching, and paying attention to your truck.** For example, every time you walk back to open your trailer doors, inspect that side of the truck. Then take the long way back to the cab and inspect the other side.

Listen to the truck when you are driving. Get used to its normal noises. Then when you hear something new, figure out what caused it. Watch your tires in the mirrors. Be sensitive to the feel of the truck.

Just paying close attention to the truck will go a long way toward making it a safe vehicle. Make inspecting the truck a habit that you do whenever you are around it.

Chapter 25 Quiz

In Questions 1 through 3, match the section or part of the FMCSR in Column A with the area of inspections it regulates in Column B.

Column A
1. Section 396.11
2. Section 396.3 and Part 393
3. Section 396.9

Column B
A. vehicle inspection
B. official roadside inspections
C. the driver vehicle inspection report

4. There is only one official vehicle inspection report form.
    A. True
    B. False

5. If your vehicle bears a CVSA inspection sticker, you don't have to do your pre-trip inspection.
    A. True
    B. False

6. You must fill out a vehicle inspection report form _____.
    A. only on the first vehicle you take out each day
    B. only if the vehicle you take out is different than the one you had the day before
    C. only if you're an owner-operator
    D. on each vehicle you operate during the day

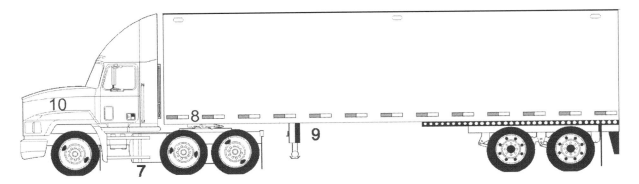

Refer to the illustration above to answer questions 7 through 10. The numbers in this illustration indicate some of the sites you would check in your required inspection. Match the inspection activities listed in Column B with the numbered sites in Column A.

Column A Inspection Sites

7. _____

8. _____

9. _____

10. _____

Column B Inspection Activities

A. Landing gear is up and the handle is stowed away.

B. Coupling is secure and the release lever is locked.

C. Turn signals and emergency flashers work properly.

D. Fuel level is correct.

CHAPTER 26

THE LOG BOOK

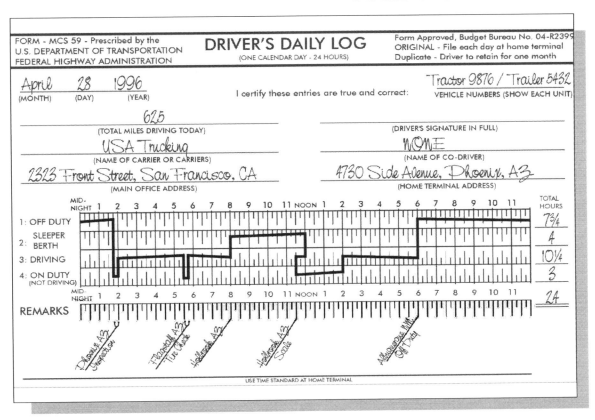

| FORM - MCS 59 - Prescribed by the U.S. DEPARTMENT OF TRANSPORTATION FEDERAL HIGHWAY ADMINISTRATION | DRIVER'S DAILY LOG (ONE CALENDAR DAY - 24 HOURS) | Form Approved, Budget Bureau No. 04-R2399 ORIGINAL - File each day at home terminal Duplicate - Driver to retain for one month |

April 28 1996
(MONTH) (DAY) (YEAR)

I certify these entries are true and correct:

Tractor 9876 / Trailer 5432
VEHICLE NUMBERS (SHOW EACH UNIT)

625
(TOTAL MILES DRIVING TODAY)

USA Trucking
(NAME OF CARRIER OR CARRIERS)

(DRIVER'S SIGNATURE IN FULL)

NONE
(NAME OF CO-DRIVER)

2323 Front Street, San Francisco, CA
(MAIN OFFICE ADDRESS)

4730 Side Avenue, Phoenix, AZ
(HOME TERMINAL ADDRESS)

	TOTAL HOURS
1: OFF DUTY	7¾
2: SLEEPER BERTH	4
3: DRIVING	10¼
4: ON DUTY (NOT DRIVING)	3
	24

REMARKS

USE TIME STANDARD AT HOME TERMINAL

Goodbye, Nine-to-Five

If you don't know this by now, you'll soon find out that being a truck driver is different from almost every other profession. In any other kind of job you probably know that you will work certain hours, the same hours, the same days every week. Then when quitting time comes you can punch out and go home. It's not that way at all with truck driving.

As a driver, you are concerned with three kinds of time. Your job—the run—could take from a few hours to several days to complete. You don't stop driving just because the clock says it's 5:00 p.m.. That's one kind of time.

Second, your job (the run) could start, and end, at any point in the day: morning, midday, or night. Again, you don't stop driving just because Monday is about to turn into Tuesday.

The third kind is your "legal" day. **Regulations state that you can work just so many hours at a time.** So your legal day is the number of hours you can work before you have to stop to rest according to these hours of service regulations.

There's one other factor that's unusual about the truck driver's "day." **The number of hours you can work today and the kind of work you can do is determined by the hours you worked yesterday, the day before, and up to seven days in the past.**

A log book helps keep track of all these different kinds of "days."

Keeping Track

A log book shows how you spent your time and where you were on the road. On the monthly summary sheet, you record your hours for the month. Both **the daily log and the monthly summary** help you stay within the regulations. In fact, the log book is to **make sure you comply with regulations** regarding your hours of service.

You **record each 24-hour period on a separate log sheet.** Log books can seem awkward at first because you **start** recording your activities **at midnight** and **end** that page **at midnight the same calendar day.** Within that 24-hour period, any number of things can happen. You could finish one run and start another. You could "run out of hours" and have to stop to rest before regulations let you start again. And of course at midnight, one calendar day will end and another will begin. But with a little practice, keeping a log will be no problem at all.

Department of Transportation **regulations require you to complete your log book every day.** They are very specific about how you complete your log book. It is a task that takes time and skill. You must keep an accurate and updated account of your activities. If you fail to do this, you may be penalized.

The Hours of Service Regulations

Department of Transportation regulations are very specific about how you may spend your time on the road. You can find the rules about hours of service and log books in **Part 395, Hours of Service of Drivers,** of the Federal Motor Carrier Safety Regulations **(FMCSR).**

If you don't keep track of your time properly or don't obey the rules about how much time you spend working, you can be declared "out of service." Any agent of the Federal Motor Carrier Safety Administration can inspect your log book and declare you out of service. These agents include highway patrol officers, DOT inspectors, and weigh masters.

Once you have been declared **out of service,** you must spend **the next 10 hours off duty** before you can return to the wheel. The 10 hours may be spent as sleeper berth time. You must also mail or deliver to your carrier a copy of the out of service form within 24 hours. Your carrier cannot require or permit you to drive during this 10-hour period.

DUTY STATUS

As a driver you are required by FMCSR 395.8 to keep track of your time 24 hours a day every day. On a log sheet you'll have to **break your time up into four different categories,** called duty statuses:

- off duty or "OFF"
- sleeper berth or "SB"
- driving or "D"
- on duty (not driving) or "ON"

Off-duty Time

This is the **time that you are not responsible for your truck or your job** in any way. Roughly speaking this is all the time you spend after you leave work and before you come back the next day. You can be doing anything you want as long as you aren't being paid for it by anyone. **If you are doing paid work it counts as on-duty time, even if you work for someone else, and even if you don't work as a driver.**

Sleeper Berth Time

This is similar to off-duty time. The main difference is that you are spending this **time resting in the sleeper berth.** You must be in the sleeper. You can't be in the passenger seat or inspecting the truck.

Driving Time

This is the **time you spend at the wheel of a motor vehicle while it is in operation.**

On-duty (Not Driving) Time

From the moment you begin your work day **until** the time **you are relieved of your duties,** you are on duty. If you are required to be ready for work, then you are on duty. Even if all you are doing is sitting at the terminal waiting for your truck to be loaded, you are on duty. **All of the time you spend working** but not driving is called on-duty (not driving) time.

Here are some examples of on-duty (not driving) time:

- waiting to be dispatched
- inspecting or servicing your vehicle
- time spent as a co-driver (unless you are in the sleeper berth)
- loading and unloading, including supervising and taking care of paperwork
- participating in a random drug testing program
- performing duties related to accidents
- repairing, obtaining assistance for, or attending a disabled vehicle
- providing a service for the carrier
- performing any other work that you are paid for by the trucking company or another job

DRIVING AND ON-DUTY LIMITS

You are allowed to be driving only so many hours at a time. Here's where that last unusual factor we mentioned at the start of this chapter comes into play. You will see that the number of hours you may work today will depend on how many you worked yesterday, and up to seven days before that.

There are **four basic time rules** you must understand and obey. After many years in force, some of these long-standing rules were changed to give drivers a better chance to get sleep and to reduce fatigue-related accidents.

11 HOUR RULE. If you have had 10 straight hours of off-duty time you cannot drive for more than 11 hours.

14 HOUR RULE. You cannot drive beyond the 14th consecutive hour after coming on-duty, following 10 straight hours off duty.

60 HOURS/7 DAY RULE. If your company does not work every day of the week you must not drive after being on duty for 60 hours in seven straight days.

70 HOURS/8 DAY RULE. If your company does work every day of the week you must not drive after being on duty for 70 hours in a period of eight straight days.

The monthly log summary sheet is the part of the log book that will help you comply with the 60/7 and 70/8 rules. You'll learn about the monthly log summary sheet later in this chapter.

EXCEPTIONS TO THE RULES

Certain types of drivers are exempt from the rules we just outlined.

Some of these exemptions involve local drivers and special situations. **Exceptions to the hours of service regulations are made under certain conditions**. These exemptions and exceptions are found in Section 395.1 of the FMCSR. You should read them carefully to see if they apply to the type of work you are doing and what you must do to comply with them.

Under a rule effective January 2004, any period of seven or eight days will end after any off duty period of 34 or more consecutive hours.

OBSERVATION SKILLS TEST

You need good observation skills to fill out a log book correctly. These skills will let you see errors right away. Did you notice the errors on the illustration that began this chapter? Check the Observation Skills Test Grid at the back of the book to see what your observation skills showed you.

The Log Book

You will have to **fill out an original and one copy** of each log. The original must reach the carrier within 13 days after you complete the form. You must **keep the copies of your logs for the past seven straight days with you.**

You can't use just any form for a log sheet. The DOT has approved only certain ones. They can be obtained from your carrier or a truck stop. They are:

- The Daily Log, Form MCS-59
- The Multi-day Log
- MCS-139 and MCS-139A

Also, you must fill out your own forms and only your own forms. No one may fill out a form for you. There are a couple of exceptions to this. One is that the company name and address may be pre-printed if you work for one carrier. And, as we pointed out in Chapter 11, many carriers now use computer-generated logs. If your company uses computer-generated logs, you'll be instructed in their use. But whenever you use log books, the **entries must be in your own handwriting, and** they must be **legible.** Neatness and accuracy are important! If a DOT inspector can't read your writing, you can be put out of service even if your log is correct.

The log book is made up of daily log sheets. In addition to filling out the grid which the FMCSR requires, each log sheet you complete **must include the following** information.

- the date—the month, day, and year of the beginning of the 24-hour period
- the carrier's vehicle numbers
- the number of miles you drove that day
- your legal signature
- the name and main office address of your motor carrier
- the name of the co-driver, if any
- the number of hours in each duty status
- the total hours, which must add up to 24
- any shipping document numbers or names of shippers and commodities

Starting at the top of the form shown in Figure 26-1 here are some things to remember when filling out the log.

fig. 26-1
A sample log form.

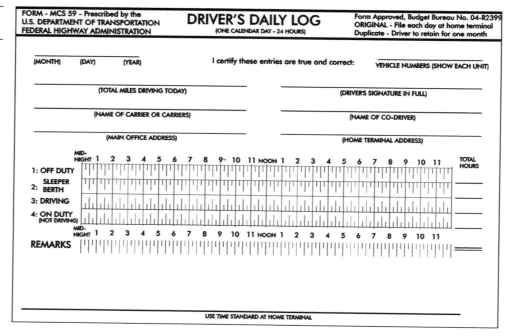

When you fill out the date, you may **spell out the name of the month.** This would avoid any confusion as to whether 1/6/88 means January 6 or June 1. (Some companies require that you enter the date with numbers only, because the logs will be scanned by computer. As always, you should follow your company's policy in these matters.)

To fill out the **vehicle identification numbers,** you look for tractor numbers on the front of the cab or on the door. You can find trailer numbers on the front panel or the rear doors. If you cannot find the vehicle identification numbers, use the license plate number.

If you are working with a co-driver be sure to write down **only the miles you drove** on the Miles Driven Today line. Don't put the total miles the truck moved.

When you sign the log you are saying everything is true and correct and that you are legally liable for everything you wrote. You must **use your legal signature,** not your nickname or initials.

FILLING OUT THE GRID

To keep the log current you **must update it every time you change your duty status.** In practice this will be just about every time you stop the truck and every time you start moving again. A good habit to get into is to keep your log handy and update it right after you stop and right before you start moving.

The horizontal lines in the grid show the length of time spent in each duty status and the vertical lines show the actual time when the duty status was changed. Each block in the grid is one hour. Each long line in the middle of each block is the half hour (30 minutes). The short lines are quarter hours (15 minutes). The first one is one-fourth (15 minutes after the hour) and the second is three-fourths (45 minutes after the hour). In other words, each hour is broken into fourths and each line within each box is one-fourth hour. The reason for this is you are required to **keep track of your time to the closest quarter hour.**

To record the length of time spent in each duty status, start at the vertical line that represents the correct time. Put your pencil on that vertical line in the horizontal area that represents the duty status you are about to begin. Draw a horizontal line that continues until you switch duty status. Draw a vertical line up or down along the line that represents the time you switch status until you get to the right horizontal area. Then start a new horizontal line in the new duty status. (We guarantee you this is easier to do than to describe!)

Whenever you **change duty status,** you must **record the name of the city, town, or village, with the state abbreviated,** where the change took place. This is done in the Remarks section. If you were not in a city, town, or village when the duty status change took place, the FMCSR gives you three other ways to record your location. You can record the:

- highway number and the nearest milepost
- highway number and the name of the service plaza or truck stop
- highway numbers of the nearest two intersecting highways

followed by the name of the nearest city, town, or village with the state abbreviated, in that order.

Always use the local time at your home terminal. This is very important for long haul drivers. If your home terminal is in Los Angeles and you drive to New York City, you will cross three time zones. But the time in Los Angeles is the time that will apply as you fill out your log.

Total hours is all the time you record, off-duty time plus sleeping berth time plus driving time plus on-duty (not driving) time. It **must add up to 24.**

In the Remarks section you must **identify the load you are hauling.** This could be a manifest number, bill of lading number, the name of the shipper and the commodity hauled, or a "pro" number, which is a number assigned to that load.

EXAMPLE

As an example, let's look at the log for one day of a trip from Phoenix, Arizona, to Corpus Christi, Texas. The date is January 8, 2004, and the carrier you are working for is called USA Trucking. The main office address is 2323 Front Street, San Francisco, CA. Your tractor identification number is 9876 and the trailer's is 5432. Be sure to put the bill of lading number (10020031) in the lower left corner of the Remarks section.

Following is a summary of what happened on the first day of the trip. As you read it, check the log in Figure 26-2 on the next page to see how each activity was recorded.

MIDNIGHT TO 1:45 a.m. You were off duty the night before and came into work at 1:45 a.m.

1:45 to 2 a.m. You were on-duty but not driving because the first thing you did was a pre-trip inspection. You did that until 2 a.m. Since Section 395.8 of the FMCSR requires a location be shown for every change of duty status, you make a loop in the Remarks section from 1:45 a.m. to 2 a.m. to span this time period. Figure 26-2 shows how to make this loop. Then make a diagonal line below the loop. Above the line, write "Phoenix, AZ." Below the line, write "safety inspection."

2 to 4:30 a.m. Driving. You were driving toward Corpus Christi, Texas.

4:30 to 4:45 a.m. On-duty (not driving). You stopped in Tucson to inspect your load, tires, and vehicle. In the remarks section, draw a loop, then a diagonal line. On the top of the line write "Tucson, AZ."

4:45 to 7:15 a.m. Driving. You were driving toward Corpus Christi, Texas.

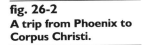

fig. 26-2
A trip from Phoenix to Corpus Christi.

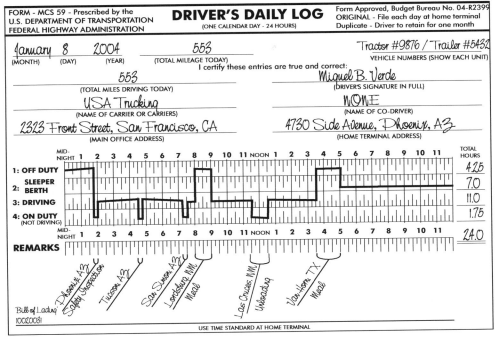

7:15 to 7:30 a.m. On-duty (not driving). You stopped at the weigh station near San Simon. They checked your paperwork and you checked your load and vehicle again. In the Remarks section, draw a loop and a diagonal line. On top of the line write "San Simon, AZ."

7:30 to 8 a.m. Driving. You were driving toward Corpus Christi, Texas.

8 to 9 a.m. Off-duty. You stopped in Lordsburg, New Mexico, for a meal. Because you have written authorization from your company, you log this meal as off duty. Without that written authorization to take meal breaks off duty, you would have had to show this time as on-duty (not driving). In either case, the time spent eating counts the same under the 14-hour rule. The advantage of taking meal breaks off-duty is that it does not count as on-duty time under the 70-hour rule.

9 to 11:30 a.m. Driving. You were driving toward Corpus Christi, Texas.

11:30 a.m. to 12:30 p.m. On-duty (not driving). You arrived in Las Cruces, New Mexico. Here your trailer was partly unloaded. You were on-duty (not driving) while you watched the unloading and completed the necessary paperwork. You inspected your rig, brought your log book up to date, and then headed out for Corpus Christi to deliver the rest of the load.

12:30 to 3:30 p.m. Driving. You were driving toward Corpus Christi, Texas.

3:30 to 5 p.m. Off-duty. You stopped at a truck stop in Van Horn, Texas, for some rest. You got something to eat, took a shower, and then went into the sleeper berth.

5 to 12 a.m. (midnight) Sleeper berth. At midnight, a 24-hour period has ended. You will stay in the sleeper until 2 a.m. the next day. After breakfast, you will have had at least 10 straight hours off duty and will be ready to begin your day.

When you get up, you complete this log sheet. Fill out the totals. Here you need to measure the length of time you spent in each of the rows on the grid.

The first row is easy. You were off-duty from midnight to 1:45 a.m. That's one and three-quarters blocks or one and three-quarters hours. You were also off duty from 8 a.m. to 9 a.m. which is one hour. That makes the total so far two and three-quarter hours. Finally, you were off duty for one and one-half hours from 3:30 p.m. to 5 p.m.

That brings the total time off duty to four and one-fourth hours. Put that down in the first line of the Total Hours column (If you use decimals, that would be 4.25 hours.)

Figuring sleeper time is even easier. You were in the sleeper berth from 5 p.m. to midnight for a total of seven hours.

Figuring the driving time and on-duty (not driving) time is a little harder but do it the same way you figured off-duty time. Figure the length of each line and add those lengths together. It might help to think of it in terms of dollars and cents. Each whole block is one dollar. Each quarter block is a 25 cent piece (a quarter).

Now add the numbers in the Total Hours column. They must equal 24. If they don't, go back and check each row to find your mistake.

The last thing you must do is fill in the **Total Miles Driving Today.** Since you don't have a co-driver the number of miles you drove is the same as the number of miles the truck moved.

After you update the monthly summary, which we'll look at next, you start a new log for a new 24-hour period. Note that you finished a log in the middle of your run. Your "log day" ended but your "job day" didn't. You're still headed for Corpus Christi, and will keep driving (except for the necessary rest periods and stops) until you get there.

The Monthly Summary Sheet

The monthly summary sheet is just that: a summary. At a glance, it tells you:

- how many hours you worked each day
- the days you did not work at all
- how many hours you can work tomorrow

Look at Figure 26-3. The monthly summary sheet has a space at the top for the month and is **divided** down the middle. The column on the left is for the **70 hour/8 day** driver. The right column is for the **60 hour/7 day** driver. We will talk about the 70 hour/8 day column. This is the one used most often by drivers since most carriers work seven days a week.

**fig. 26-3
The monthly log
summary sheet.**

The monthly summary sheet records the number of on-duty hours each day of the month. It also shows the hours available to work tomorrow. To keep a clear account of your hours, **update your monthly summary sheet every day.**

The monthly summary sheet is divided into five columns. The first column is already filled in with the days of the month. It is your job to fill in the rest.

HOURS WORKED TODAY. This column is the total of your on-duty hours for the day. Remember on-duty means both your driving (Line 3 on the grid) and on-duty not driving (Line 4) time.

COLUMN A. This will tell you your total hours on-duty the last seven days. You find that by adding the last seven figures you entered in the Hours Worked Today Column. This column is tricky. To do it right use just the last seven entries in the Hours Worked Today column. Don't start at the top and add the whole column. Don't take yesterday's total and add the hours worked today to it. See Figure 26-4 .

fig. 26-4
This is the proper way to figure out Column A.

MONTHLY LOG SUMMARY SHEET

MONTH _____

If you operate on the period of 70 hours in 8 days, use the summary sheet on the left. If you operate on the period of 60 hours in 7 days, use the summary sheet on the right. The figures 1 to 31 represent calendar days, and entries should be made for each day even when driver does not work. If no work is performed, enter zero (0) in the first column and compute other columns as explained below.

70 HR/8 DAY DRIVERS ONLY

DAY OF MO.	HOURS WORKED TODAY (TOTAL LINES) 3-4 DAILY LOG	A TOTAL HOURS ON-DUTY LAST 7 DAYS	B TOTAL HOURS AVAILABLE TOMORROW (70 HOURS MINUS COL. A)	C TOTAL HOURS ON-DUTY LAST 8 DAYS
LAST 7 DAYS OF PRECEDING MONTH	8			
	10.5			
	7.25			
	9.5			
	6.5			
	8.25			
	12.5	62.5	7.5	
1	4.25	58.75	11.25	66.75
2	8.5	56.75	13.25	67.25
3	8.5	58	12	65.25
4	8	56.5	13.5	66
5	9.5	59.5	10.5	66
6	5	56.25	13.75	64.5
7	4	47.75	22.25	60.25
8	12.75	56.25	13.75	60.5
9				
10				
11				
12				

60 HR/7 DAY DRIVERS ONLY

DAY OF MO.	HOURS WORKED TODAY (TOTAL LINES) 3-4 DAILY LOG	A TOTAL HOURS ON-DUTY LAST 6 DAYS	B TOTAL HOURS AVAILABLE TOMORROW (60 HOURS MINUS COL. A)	C TOTAL HOURS ON-DUTY LAST 7 DAYS
LAST 7 DAYS OF PRECEDING MONTH				
1				
2				
3				
4				
5				
6				
7				
8				
9				
10				
11				
12				

COLUMN B. This will tell you how many hours you can work tomorrow. You arrive at that by subtracting the number of hours in Column A from 70. **Always remember to enter today's hours before you figure out how many hours you can work tomorrow.**

COLUMN C. This tells you how many hours you've worked in the last eight days. Regulations say you can't drive after being on duty more than 70 hours in eight days. This column helps you obey that regulation. You figure this column the same way you figured Column A except here you add the last eight days instead of seven.

If you follow the procedures you've learned in this chapter every day, you'll always know exactly where you are with respect to how many hours you have been on duty and how many hours you can work tomorrow.

Chapter 26 Quiz

Chapter 26 Quiz

For our quiz in this chapter, let's continue our trip to Corpus Christi, Texas, fill out a daily log, and continue your monthly summary sheet.

The January 9, 2004 daily log picks up where our example left off. You are in Van Horn, Texas, in the sleeper berth as the new day begins at midnight. You wake up at 2 a.m. and eat breakfast until 2:45 a.m. (Remember, you have written authorization from your company to take meal breaks off duty). At 2:45 a.m. you begin doing a safety inspection on your vehicle and bring your log book up to date. This takes 15 minutes and then you begin driving. After driving for 121 miles, you stop in Fort Stockton, Texas, at 5:30 a.m. and spend 15 minutes making sure everything is still OK with your rig. You drive for 141 miles and at 8:30 a.m. you stop for 30 minutes to eat in Sonora, Texas. After lunch, you drive for 150 miles to San Antonio, Texas, where you stop at noon to do a safety inspection on your rig. This takes 15 minutes and then you drive the remaining 144 miles to Corpus Christi. You arrive in Corpus Christi, Texas, at 3 p.m. You spend 30 minutes checking in, doing paperwork, and dropping your trailer at the dock. At 3:30 p.m. you grab a bite to eat and take a shower. You climb into the sleeper for a well-deserved rest at 5 p.m. and remain there for the rest of the day.

On the basis of the information we just gave you, fill in the daily log below, and the monthly summary on the next page. For the monthly summary, the

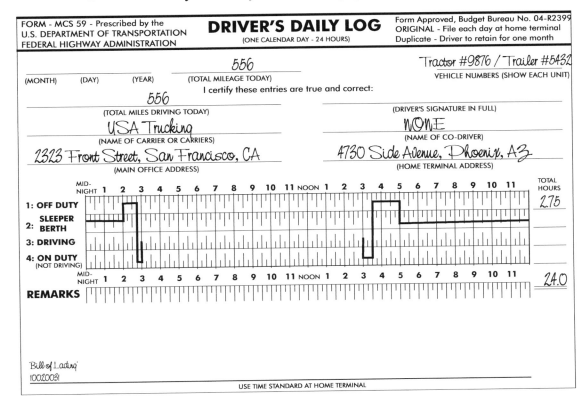

hours are filled in for the days leading up to the day that you just logged. After making the entries for January 9, 2004, how many hours will you have available for the next day?

MONTHLY LOG SUMMARY SHEET

MONTH _____

If you operate on the period of 70 hours in 8 days, use the summary sheet on the left. If you operate on the period of 60 hours in 7 days, use the summary sheet on the right. The figures 1 to 31 represent calendar days, and entries should be made for each day even when driver does not work. If no work is performed, enter zero (0) in the first column and compute other columns as explained below.

DAY OF MO.	HOURS WORKED TODAY (TOTAL LINES) 3-4 DAILY LOG	70 HR/8 DAY DRIVERS ONLY A — TOTAL HOURS ON-DUTY LAST 7 DAYS	B — TOTAL HOURS AVAILABLE TOMORROW (70 HOURS MINUS COL. A)	C — TOTAL HOURS ON-DUTY LAST 8 DAYS	DAY OF MO.	HOURS WORKED TODAY (TOTAL LINES) 3-4 DAILY LOG	60 HR/7 DAY DRIVERS ONLY A — TOTAL HOURS ON-DUTY LAST 6 DAYS	B — TOTAL HOURS AVAILABLE TOMORROW (60 HOURS MINUS COL. A)	C — TOTAL HOURS ON-DUTY LAST 7 DAYS
LAST 7 DAYS OF PRECEDING MONTH	8				LAST 7 DAYS OF PRECEDING MONTH				
	10.5								
	7.25								
	9.5								
	6.5								
	8.25								
	12.5	62.5	7.5						
1	4.25	58.75	11.25	66.75	1				
2	8.5	56.75	13.25	67.25	2				
3	8.5	58	12	65.25	3				
4	8	56.5	13.5	66	4				
5	9.5	59.5	10.5	66	5				
6	5	56.25	13.75	64.5	6				
7	4	47.75	22.25	60.25	7				
8	12.75	56.25	13.75	60.5	8				
9	12.25	60	10	68.5	9				
10					10				
11					11				
12					12				
13					13				
14					14				
15					15				
16					16				
17					17				
18					18				
19					19				
20					20				
21					21				
22					22				
23					23				
24					24				
25					25				
26					26				
27					27				
28					28				
29					29				
30					30				
31					31				

60 hours - 7 days

Follow the same instructions provided for completing the summary sheet for 8 days 70 hours, except substitute last six days for last seven days and 60 hours for 70 hours.

70 hours - 8 days

Enter the number of working hours (on duty & driving) for each of the last seven days of the preceding month in the first seven spaces under the column headed "Hours Worked Today." Enter in the first space under column A the total of the number of hours worked during the last seven days. Subtract the figure entered in column A from 70 hours and enter this figure--hours available for tomorrow--in column B.

At the end of each day, complete the first three columns adjacent to the day of the month in the same manner as explained above. Total the number of hours worked during the last 8 days and enter in column C. Any number in column C which exceeds 70 indicates a violation and should be circled for easy identification.

CARGO DOCUMENTATION

		STRAIGHT BILL OF LADING-ORIGINAL-NOT NEGOTIABLE			PAGE 1 OF 2	

B/L #

DATE

TERMS

CARRIER

APPLY
PRO LABEL
HERE

SHIPPER	CONSIGNEE (On Collect on delivery, the letters "C.O.D." must appear before consignee's name or as otherwise provided In Item 430, Sec. 1)
DISCOUNT SUPPLY SECOND STREET WEST PHOENIX, AZ	DISCOUNT STORE 1234 WEST ST. DENVER, CO
BILL TO	**GENERAL COMMENTS**
DISCOUNT SUPPLY SECOND STREET WEST PHOENIX, AZ	ROUTING	DELIVERING CARRIER

PIECES	HM	DESCRIPTION	WEIGHT (pounds only) (subject to correction)	RATE	CHARGES	CLASS
22 PALLETS OF 800 CARTONS		CANNED SOUP *Exceptions: 30 Cartons Open,* *Contents Appear Okay*	32000			
50 CARTONS		TVs *10 Cartons damaged*	3750			
50 CARTONS		TV STANDS *5 Cartons short*	500			

This is to certify that the above named materials are properly classified, described, packaged, marked and labeled and are in proper condition for transportation according to the applicable regulations of the Department of Transportation.

SHIPPER DISCOUNT SUPPLY	CARRIER CFG TRUCKING SERVICES, INC.				
PER	DRIVER *Canson W. Biggs* SEE BACK ☐	PCS	DATE	SINGLE SHPT. (✓)	

From Delivery Receipts to Expense Reports

Cargo documentation is simply the paperwork needed for every shipment of freight. Not many people like doing paperwork, but there is a saying that is as true as it is old: "The job is not finished until the paperwork is done." Today's professional truck drivers must do their paperwork, and they must do it precisely and accurately. From log books to bills of lading to trip reports, you must learn them all. And, it's really not as bad as it might sound. In this chapter, you'll learn what's involved.

There are four different kinds of bills you will work with as a driver:

- the bill of lading
- the waybill
- the freight bill
- the manifest

The Bill of Lading

This is basically a contract between the trucking company and the shipper. The shipper says what the load is, what it weighs, and where it is going. The trucking company promises to deliver it in good condition to its destination.

Every interstate shipment of freight by a common carrier is covered by a bill of lading and its conditions. A common carrier of goods must comply with the conditions. The shipper and the consignee must obey them as well.

When it's filled out and signed, the bill of lading is a **legal and binding contract.** It's a contract between the owner of the shipment and the carrier. Its legal name is the Uniform Domestic Straight Bill of Lading. Created by an act of the U. S. Congress a long time ago, it **covers interstate shipments** by railroads and barge lines as well as trucks. There is also an Order Bill of Lading and an Export Import Bill of Lading, but most truck drivers see only the most used Straight Bill of Lading. For short, it's called a bill of lading. Its abbreviation is B/L.

When you arrive at a shipper's dock, you'll be shown a bill of lading. It may be the long form with all the conditions and rules printed on the back, but most likely it will be the **short form.**

The B/L shows to whom the shipment is going (the consignee), the destination (the city or town), and the delivery address. The shipper fills out the date, the shipping number, and the company name and complete address. The shipper also fills in the spaces to show if the freight charges are collect or prepaid. In most cases, the carrier bills the shipper for the freight charges.

If the space or box "Collect On Delivery $...." is filled in by the shipper, then the carrier must collect the amount of money shown. This is also called a cash on delivery or **COD,** and the money must be paid to the carrier upon delivery of the shipment. In other words, **you must collect the money when the shipment is unloaded.** If you must deliver a COD shipment, talk to your dispatcher first to find out what to do when you collect the money.

The B/L shows the number of pieces being shipped. The shipper fills in the first column under number of packages. For instance, this column might show 22 pallets of 880 cartons or 880 cartons on 22 pallets.

Next is the description of the contents of the cartons, special marks, and exceptions.

Then comes the weight column. It reads: "Weight, Subject to Correction." This means the carrier can weigh the load and change the shipper's weight.

fig. 27-1
A sample Bill of Lading.

STRAIGHT BILL OF LADING — SHORT FORM — Original — Not Negotiable

RECEIVED, subject to the classifications and tariffs in effect on the date of issue of this Original Bill of Lading

Shipper's _____

(Name of Carrier) _____ SCAC. _____ Carrier's _____

At _____ 19 _____ From _____

The property described below, in apparent good order, except as noted (contents and condition of contents of packages unknown), marked, consigned, and destined as indicated below, which said carrier (the word carrier being understood throughout this contract as meaning any person or corporation in possession of the property under the contract) agrees to carry to its usual place of delivery at said destination, if on its route, otherwise to deliver to another carrier on the route to said destination. It is mutually agreed, as to each carrier of all or any of said property over all or any portion of said route to destination, and as to each party at any time interested in any or all of said property, that every service to be performed hereunder shall be subject to all the terms and conditions of the Uniform Domestic Straight Bill of Lading set forth (1) in Uniform Freight Classification in effect on the date hereof, if this is a rail or rail-water shipment, or (2) in the applicable motor carrier classification or tariff if this is a motor carrier shipment.
Shipper hereby certifies that he is familiar with all the terms and conditions of the said bill of lading, including those on the back thereof, set forth in the classification or tariff which governs the transportation of this shipment, and the said conditions are hereby answered to by the shipper and accepted for himself and his assigns.

(Mail or street address of consignee -- for notification purposes only)

Consigned to _____

Destination _____ State _____ County _____ **Delivery Address*** _____
(*To be filled in only when shipper desires and governing tariffs provide for delivery address.)

Route _____

Delivering Carrier _____ **Car or Vehicle Initials** _____ **No.** _____

Number of Packages	KIND OF PACKAGE, DESCRIPTION OF ARTICLES, SPECIAL MARKS, AND EXCEPTIONS	*Weight (Subject to Correction)	Class or Rate	Check Column	
					Subject to section 7 of conditions of applicable bill of lading, if this shipment is to be delivered to the consignee without recourse on the consignor, the consignor shall sign the following statement: The carrier shall not make delivery of this shipment without payment of freight and all other lawful charges.
					(Signature of Consignor)
					If charges are to be prepaid, write or stamp here "To be Prepaid"
					Received $ to apply in prepayment of the charges on the property described hereon.
					Agent or Cashier Per (The Signature here acknowledges only the amount prepaid.)
Collect On Delivery and remit to $		C.O.D. Charge Shipper to be paid by Consignee $			Charges Advanced

*If the shipment moves between two ports by a carrier by water, the law requires that the bill of lading shall state whether it is carrier's or shipper's weight.

NOTE: Where the rate is dependent on value, shippers are required to state specifically in writing the agreed or declared value of the property.

The agreed or declared value of the property is hereby specifically stated by the shipper to be not exceeding _____ per _____

"This is to certify that the above named materials are properly classified, described, packaged, marked and labeled and are in proper condition for transportation according to the applicable regulations of the Department of Transportation." per _____

Shipper, Per _____ **1** _____ Agent, Per _____

Permanent post-office address of shipper.

The carrier needs a scale ticket and a weight correction certificate to prove a different weight.

The back of the B/L contract has all the conditions and rules.

When the truck is loaded **you will** affix a pro number to the B/L. You will also be asked to **sign the B/L.** Once it has been signed, the shipper keeps the original and you take two other copies with you. One copy, called the shipping order, is for your carrier's records. The memorandum copy is for the consignee. No freight charges show on the bill of lading.

The **B/L cannot be changed once it is signed.** A **Corrected Bill of Lading must be issued** if there is an error. This is federal law. Signing a B/L is like signing any other contract. You cannot state at a later time that you did not read it or understand what it said. The B/L becomes a binding contract between the owner of the goods, the carrier, and you, because you are acting as the carrier's agent. Smart drivers **treat the B/L with the same care as a large personal check.**

It is very important to be sure the B/L is accurate when you sign it, because when you do, you are saying, "I accept the count and description on the B/L as given to me." In other words, you **sign for the exact count.** If for some reason you are unable to count the load, you must write alongside your signature that the load is the shipper's count.

Making sure of the count is very important. And, it's your responsibility. If the difference in a count is just a couple of cans of soup, it wouldn't cost you much. However, if the difference is half a dozen TVs, you'll be in the soup!

Also, a smart driver will **always weigh the load** before starting a trip. The B/L may say 48,000 pounds and you know you can haul that legally. But a five percent error on a 48,000 pound load may be a 2,400 pound overload for the truck driver. That can mean a fine of $250 or more. The shipper will not pay the fine. **The overload ticket will be written against the driver.** Who do you think pays the fine?

The Freight Bill

The freight bill is more **like an invoice.** Information on the bill of lading is used to prepare the freight bill. So, the freight bill has much the same information that the bill of lading has but it also includes the freight charges. These freight charges are the price the shipper must pay to have cargo shipped by the trucking company.

When you turn in the B/L copy to your office, it is sent to the Rate Department. The Rate Department assigns the correct rate to the shipment from a tariff, or rate, book. All the charges are figured from the B/L. These charges may be for extra deliveries, collection, or special services and can include cooling or heating the load. After a rate auditor checks for errors, the B/L is sent to the Billing Department where a freight bill is typed, or generated by a computer.

The **freight bill has all the information contained on the B/L and more.** It shows:

- all charges
- the trailer number
- the origin and destination terminals
- any additional information the driver needs

such as special instructions for handling or delivering the load.

The freight bill may have as many as fifteen copies. Copies will go to Sales, Traffic, Customer Service, Operations, Accounting, and many other departments at the carrier's main office.

If you must collect freight charges or a COD amount, you'll have the original freight bill and two more copies. These copies show that the consignee paid the COD. Write on the copies whether the charges were paid by cash or check. Once you're paid, date the copies and sign them. Then give the original freight bill to the consignee.

After unloading the shipment, the consignee signs the delivery receipt in a space that states the shipment was received in good order. You sign it too, noting the number of pieces delivered and the date. The consignee gets **the consignee copy** and you keep **the delivery receipt. Both copies should have exactly the same information** on them.

fig. 27-2
An example Freight Bill.

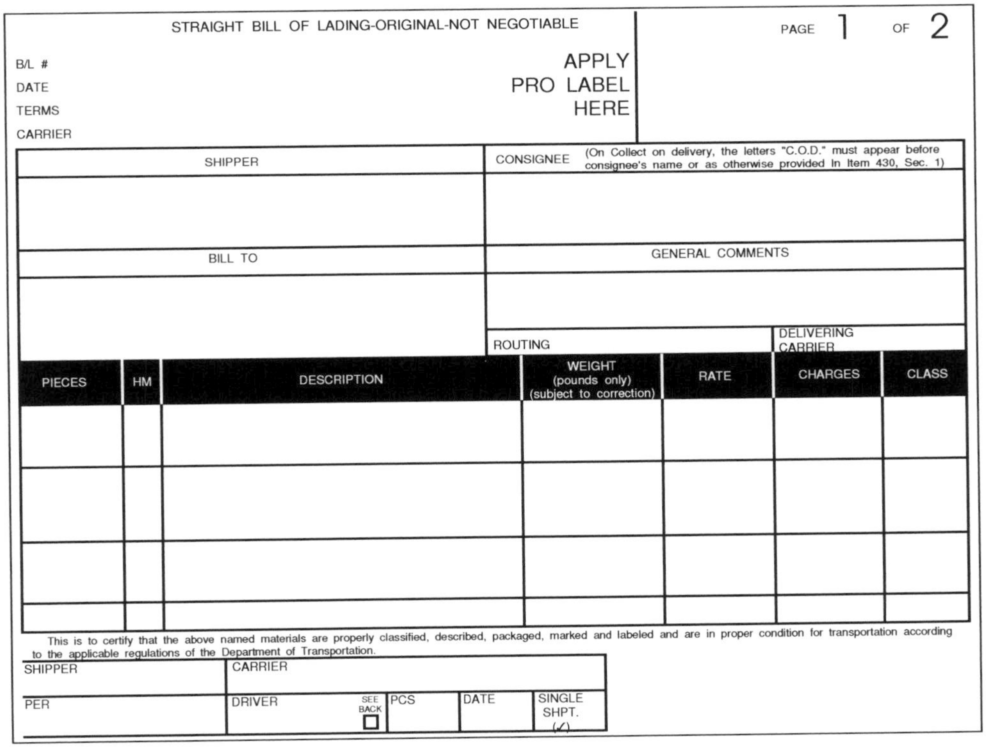
STRAIGHT BILL OF LADING-ORIGINAL-NOT NEGOTIABLE

PAGE 1 OF 2

B/L #
DATE
TERMS
CARRIER

APPLY PRO LABEL HERE

SHIPPER

CONSIGNEE (On Collect on delivery, the letters "C.O.D." must appear before consignee's name or as otherwise provided in Item 430, Sec. 1)

BILL TO

GENERAL COMMENTS

ROUTING

DELIVERING CARRIER

PIECES	HM	DESCRIPTION	WEIGHT (pounds only) (subject to correction)	RATE	CHARGES	CLASS

This is to certify that the above named materials are properly classified, described, packaged, marked and labeled and are in proper condition for transportation according to the applicable regulations of the Department of Transportation.

SHIPPER | CARRIER

PER | DRIVER | SEE BACK ☐ | PCS | DATE | SINGLE SHPT. (✓)

The Waybill

A waybill is used **to deliver split shipments or** to deliver **a shipment before the charges have been applied.**

A shipper has 5,000 cartons going to one customer. Each carton weighs 45 pounds. This is enough to make five loads, each 45,000 pounds. So, the shipper splits the shipment, but makes one bill of lading to earn a lower shipping rate. As a rule, the larger a shipment is, the lower the rate.

The carrier types five waybills and one freight bill. **Each waybill shows the number of cartons, the weight, and the trailer number or the trip number.** The freight bill shows all the information from the bill of lading and all the freight charges. **Each load is delivered on a waybill.** A waybill set consists of a delivery receipt, consignee copy, and a memo or extra copy. **No freight charges show** on the waybill.

The delivery receipt and consignee copy are signed and dated the same way freight bills are. Bring the delivery receipt and any extra copies back to your dispatcher.

The Manifest

A manifest is used **when there is cargo from more than one shipper in your trailer.** It **lists all the cargo in the load.** It shows the number of pieces and the weight for each shipment. If there is a pro number or a shipper's number, they are listed as well. (A pro number is a special number used to identify the load.) A brief description of the freight and packaging is included.

The manifest heading shows the carrier's name and the owner-operator or the driver's name. There is space for the date and the truck equipment numbers. Figure 27-3 shows a brief example.

Just about every carrier uses a different format for the manifest. Some show the freight charges. Some show the origin city and the destination city. But, simply put, a manifest is a document that lists the cargo that is being carried.

fig. 27-3
An example manifest.

XYZ CARRIER MANIFEST						
Jan. 1, 2004					Equipt. #s 38/44	
					O/OP DRIVER Joe Smith	
PRO#	**SHIPPER**	**S/N**	**PCS**	**PKG**	**DESC**	**WEIGHT**
D445321	Cont. Foods	4455	100	ctns	canned food	4500
D778662	American Supply	778	50	pails	peanut oil	3000
S999777	Texas Mills	none	350	bags	flour	35000

Pro Numbers

Pro numbers are the numbers assigned to freight bills and waybills. The name is taken from Progressive Freight Bill Numbering System. This means an advancing set of numbers given to freight or waybills. Just like the pages in a book, the numbers go from 1 to 2 to 3, and so forth. A carrier's Atlanta, Georgia, terminal might start the new year, 2004, by numbering the first freight bill cut like this: ATL4-0000001.

- ATL is for Atlanta
- 4 is the last digit of the year, 2004
- 0000001 is the first bill cut in 2004

The next freight bill is numbered ATL4-0000002. In a few months, the numbers might be ATL4-3357749. The next year they would start with ATL5-0000001. This makes it **easy to keep track** of shipments and paperwork. Delivery receipts can be filed in numerical order, keeping each year separate.

Carriers refer to their freight bills often. Shippers and consignees send in freight claims for loss and damage months after a delivery. Disputes about freight charges can result in overcharge claims a year or two later. Pro numbers allow the freight bills to be filed in order, day after day. They can easily be pulled from the file to settle claims and disputes.

OBSERVATION SKILLS TEST

What did you notice about the illustration that began this chapter? Did you read it carefully? Can you recall the three items of cargo described on the form? Was anything damaged? Turn to the Observation Skills Test Grid at the back of the book and see how your skills are improving.

The Delivery Receipt

The delivery receipt copy of the freight or waybill set **has a lot of value to the carrier.** It is so valuable that it's usually filed in a room that can be entered only by employees. This document **can be used to prove that a shipment was delivered to the correct consignee.** It shows:

- the name of the person who received the shipment
- the name of the truck driver who delivered it
- if the charges were paid at the time of delivery
- if there were any exceptions at time of delivery
- the date and the time of the delivery
- the truck or trailer number
- the shipper's number

Sales people use delivery receipts to prove good service in their efforts to secure more business from shippers. The delivery receipts document on-time delivery and good service.

Both the Traffic and Cargo Claims and the Maintenance and Safety departments also use the delivery receipt. They may have to find out what happened to a trailer or a tractor on a certain day. For instance, they may need to find out how it was damaged. The delivery receipt will give them this information and tell who the driver was, too.

If there is any **damage or shortage,** it **must be noted and signed by the driver and the consignee** on the delivery receipt and the consignee copy. Be very careful that you **describe the damage or shortage exactly.** Do not simply write that 10 cartons are damaged. State exactly how they are damaged.

Shortages must show what is short. "Five cartons short" is not enough to protect the carrier. Suppose the load consists of large color TV sets and wood stands or carts for the sets. What is short, the TV sets or the wood stands?

Carriers also do not want drivers to deliver **overages.** An overage is when there **are more pieces to deliver than what the freight bill or B/L calls for.** Usually an overage is part of someone else's shipment that got loaded in error.

Most carriers have a rule stating the driver must **call the dispatcher before accepting an exception to a clear delivery** (without loss or damage).

Once a delivery receipt is signed by both parties, you should treat it like gold. It might have more value than gold someday.

The Trip Report

Although "trip report" is the most common name for this document, it's also sometimes called a trip record, trip register, or mileage report. The document may have different names, but the data that is noted is pretty much the same. The trip report **shows all the important facts about a trip,** including:

- date and place the trip began
- the driver's name
- truck equipment numbers
- beginning and ending odometer reading
- each state entered or crossed
- odometer readings each time a state is entered
- amount of money advanced to the driver for expenses
- fuel purchases, where the fuel was purchased, the amount, and the cost

Figure 27-4 shows a sample trip report. Trip reports can also be generated automatically by on-board computers. This is covered in greater detail in Chapter 11.

fig. 27-4
Example of a trip report.

TRIP REPORT

TRIP NO. _____

PRO NO. _____   CARRIER _____
DATE _____ TIME _____
FROM _____
TO _____
TRAILER NO. _____
TRAILER WT. _____

CASH CONTROL

BEGINNING CASH ON HAND _____
ADVANCE CHECKS   _____

TOTAL   _____
TOTAL EXPENSES   _____
CASH LEFT   _____

BEGINNING ODOMETER READING [   ]
ENDING ODOMETER READING [   ]
TOTAL MILES [   ]

EXPENSES

PAID TO	FOR WHAT	AMT	COST
	TOTAL EXPENSES		

STATE	ODOMETER

STATE	ODOMETER

Cost control is a big factor in the trucking industry. Your carrier strives to keep track of the number of miles its trucks travel, both loaded and empty miles. By **using trip reports, carriers can figure** the **cost per mile** and the **cost per shipment.** They can also figure **which tractors cost less to operate** and **which break down more often. A trip report shows all the money paid out for a trip.** It also shows **money advanced to the driver.** This is money given to you before you leave on a trip or sent to you while you're on the road. Advances are routinely wired to truck stops where they can be received by drivers who run out of cash. By listing all money received and all money paid out, the expense report helps the carrier keep track of the costs for each trip.

To figure their costs accurately, carriers need a complete expense report. They must know if they are making a profit or taking a loss. By reading expense reports for many trips, they can see where the money is going. Is the tractor using too much fuel? Are there too many repair bills, with resulting down time? Are meal and motel expenses higher than necessary? Expense reports show repairs, long distance phone calls, protective clothing purchases, and more.

The carrier also wants to know how many miles were driven in each state. That is why **you enter the odometer reading each time you enter a state.** Each state has a fuel tax that must be paid. All states demand that a fuel tax be paid even if fuel is not purchased in their state. The **number of miles driven in a state determines the amount of fuel tax that state must be paid.**

You may hear the term **"IFTA,"** which means **International Fuel Tax Agreement,** or the term **"RFTA,"** which stands for **Regional Fuel Tax Agreement.** Your carrier's trucks may be registered in one of the states that participate in those agreements. These agreements were established to simplify the way carriers pay taxes.

Carriers can figure pay from the trip report, too. You should keep a copy of every trip report. By doing this, you can be sure you're getting paid the correct amount.

Chapter 27 Quiz

1. A _____ is a legal and binding contract.
    A. freight bill
    B. waybill
    C. bill of lading
    D. trip report

2. If a shipment is prepaid, you must collect the money before the shipment is unloaded.
    A. True
    B. False

3. If there is a fine for an overload of freight, the _____ must pay it.
    A. shipper
    B. consignee
    C. dock foreman who weighed the freight
    D. driver

4. The freight bill includes all the charges which are figured from the
   _____.
   A. bill of lading
   B. pro numbers
   C. expense report
   D. waybill

5. The _____ is used to deliver split shipments or to deliver a ship-
   ment before the charges have been applied.
   A. freight bill
   B. delivery receipt
   C. waybill
   D. bill of lading

6. _____ make it easy to keep track of shipments and paperwork.
   A. Pro numbers
   B. Trip reports
   C. Delivery receipts
   D. Bills of lading

7. The _____ is so valuable that it's usually filed in a room that
   can be entered only by employees.
   A. bill of lading
   B. pro number
   C. delivery receipt
   D. waybill

8. If there is any damage or shortage, it must be noted and signed by the
   driver and consignee on the delivery receipt and the consignee
   copy, but you don't need to worry about overage.
   A. True
   B. False

9. Just about every carrier uses a different format for their manifest.
   A. True
   B. False

10. Two documents that help drivers and carriers keep track of costs are
    the _____.
    A. trip report and the waybill
    B. trip report and the freight bill
    C. the waybill and the manifest
    D. the expense report and the trip report

LOADING, SECURING, AND UNLOADING CARGO

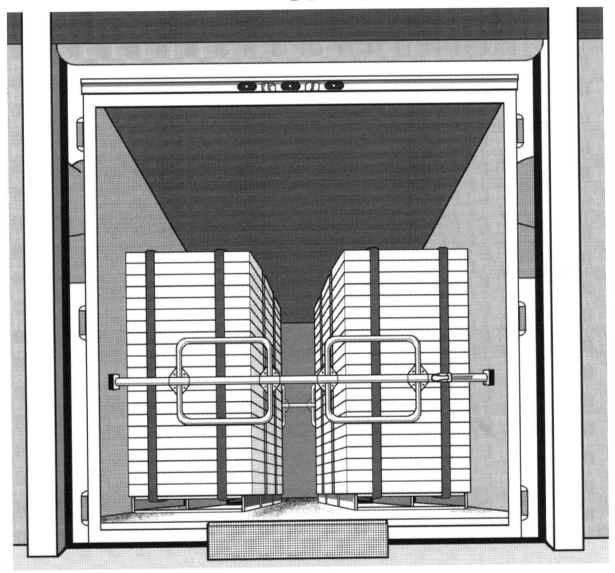

The Responsibilities of the Drivers

Like the captain of a ship or the pilot of an airplane, you will be responsible for the truck you drive. **No matter who loads a trailer, the driver is responsible for the condition of the cargo.** Not only must you make inspections to ensure your truck is safe and road ready, you must also periodically check the cargo to be sure it is secure, within legal weight limits, and properly balanced. The only exception to this is when the trailer is sealed.

Here is what the Department of Transportation says about those responsibilities in Federal Motor Carrier Safety Regulations Part 392.9: No person shall drive a motor vehicle and a motor carrier shall not require or permit a person to drive a motor vehicle unless:

- the vehicle's cargo is properly distributed and adequately secured.
- the vehicle's tailgate, tailboard, doors, tarps, spare tire, and other equipment used in its operation and the means of fastening the vehicle's cargo are secured; and
- the vehicle's cargo or any other object doesn't obscure the driver's view ahead or to the right or left sides, interfere with the free movement of his arms or legs, prevent his free and ready access to accessories required for emergencies, or prevent the free and ready exit of any person from the vehicle's cab or driver's compartment.

Avoiding accidents that result from improper loading and securing is a big responsibility placed upon the driver. It will affect you daily so study FMCSR Parts 392.9 and 393.100 through 393.136 until you know all the details about your responsibilities, for example:

- 393.100 Protection Against Shifting or Falling Cargo
- 393.102 Securement Systems
- 393.104 Blocking and Bracing
- 393.106 Front End Structure
- 393.110 Minimum Number of Tiedowns

You'll have to answer questions about cargo safety to get your CDL.

The other major reason for proper load securement is the prevention of damage claims against the carrier. Every item the driver allows to be damaged by improper handling or tieing down will be noted as it's unloaded, inspected, and received at the destination point. A claim for the damage is then made against the carrier. Thought and effort on the part of the **driver** as loads are being secured **can prevent** such **claims.** In this chapter we'll look at the proper ways to load, secure, and unload cargo so as to prevent damage.

Loading Platform Trailers

The term "platform trailer" may refer to either a flatbed trailer or a low boy. There is no end to the kinds or types of loads you may encounter if you are pulling either type of platform trailer. Some loads may be light, bulky loads. Others may be very compact heavy loads. Normally the loads that are destined to be hauled on platform trailers are loads that simply cannot be loaded into a box van through its back doors, due to size or weight.

Loads going onto platform trailers are those that are lifted and placed on the trailers by forklifts or cranes. Some loads may be driven onto the beds of the platform trailers.

HEIGHT LIMITS

Loads can only be stacked so high on flatbeds. First, there are **height limits for travel on the interstate.** This limit is **usually 13½ feet** measured from the surface the vehicle stands on. Some states will allow taller loads, and may or may not require you get a permit, usually in advance, for such loads. A good trucker's map book would have details on specific state height limits. Second, for stability, you must keep the center of gravity low or you are more likely to tip. Load the heaviest pieces on the bottom.

Low boy trailers are perfect for high loads. Since the trailer itself is built so low, more of the height can be taken up by cargo. Also, the low slung construction keeps the trailer and load stable.

The regulations can get pretty specific about how certain loads, such as coils, pipes, and lengths of metal, are tied down. FMCSR Part 393.100 has the details and sketches of the requirements. The fact that metal loads are covered in such detail is not to say that all other type loads are not important. They are, and we'll discuss some of the more common ones in this chapter. Your carrier may also give you specific tiedown instructions for flatbed loads.

SECURING PLATFORM LOADS

The most common methods used to secure loads on platform trailers are:

- cables and winches
- webbing straps and winches
- chains and load binders

All are easy to use. However, as you tighten them, they can crush, bend, or cut the load. So you must take steps to **protect the cargo from being damaged by these securement devices.** Place "V boards" or wooden blocks between the cable, strap, or chain to protect the edge of the load.

Regulations require that the working load limit of all tiedowns must be at least one half times the weight of what's being tied down. Follow the guidelines in FMCSR Part 393.110 to determine the minimum number of tiedowns needed.

Chains and Binders

Some types of steel pipe, heavy steel beams, heavy machinery, rubber tired vehicles, and construction equipment are best secured by chains and load binders (boomers). The whole purpose of **chaining** is to **hold the load down and prevent its movement sideways or forward or backward.** As you can see from Figure 28-1, proper placement and the direction of the chains will prevent such movement.

The steel hooks on the chain are hooked to a steel rail on the sides of the trailer or to hook rings in the floor. The chain is placed over or around the cargo and stretched tight by hand.

However, no matter how hard you try, when you stretch chain by hand, it will not be tight enough to keep the cargo from shifting. The chain must be tightened even more. That's what the binder is for. You attach the binder end hooks to the chain with the binder lever open. Then you **pull the binder lever** to the closed position to **tighten up the chain.**

fig. 28-1
(A) Chains pulling away.
(B) Chains pulling to.
(C) Cross chained.

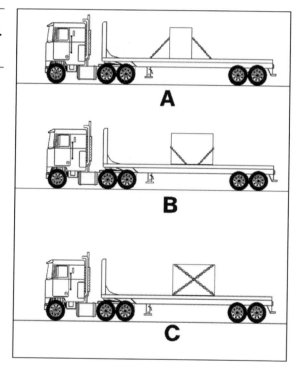

Lots of broken fingers and arms have resulted from tightening load binders. Aim to keep your fingers clear when using this device. The proper way to install the load binder is with its legs open. Hook the load binder to the chain so you can operate it while standing on the ground. Make sure your footing is secure. Use both hands to pull the handle down or toward you as you attempt to snap it over center.

The use of a handle extender or cheater pipe (a piece of pipe slipped over the handle) is not recommended. It's not safe. If you can't get enough leverage using the handle of the lever-type binder by itself, use a ratchet-type binder.

When you release a binder, remember there is a great deal of energy in the stretched chain. This will cause the handle of the binder to fly up very quickly and with great force when it is unlatched. Keep your body away from the handle's path of travel.

Never use a cheater pipe to release the handle of a binder. It's best to use a steel pry bar under the handle to pry it open. Again, keep your body out of the path of the handle as it releases.

If you release the handle by hand, use an open hand under the handle and push upward. Do not close your hand around or grip the handle. Even when you release the handle by hand, it will fly up with tremendous force. Keep all parts of yourself out of the path of the moving handle.

Blocks and Braces

In addition to chains and binders, you may need to use blocks of wood to **keep machinery mounted on wheels from moving.** The federal rules specify four-by-four inch wood as a minimum size. The **four-by-fours** must be **nailed to the wood floor.** If the trailer floor is metal, you can use chains to hold the timbers in place against the wheels.

fig. 28-2
A lever type chain binder in the open position (A) and the closed position (B).

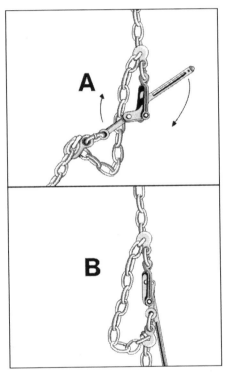

Many kinds of equipment demand a brace or support. The shipper often knows what kind of bracing to make and use. So it's the shipper's employees who usually make it. And although you may not be the one who makes the brace, you are the one charged with seeing the cargo is secure. If the brace or support does not hold, the results will be your responsibility.

Make sure the **lumber** used **for the brace** is **without knots or cracks.** Many a good looking brace or crate has failed because one board had a knot or a crack. Make sure the **nails** which are used are at least **twice as long as the thickness of the board** they are being driven through. They should be nailed straight down or at an angle against the movement of the cargo. Bracing should go from the upper part of the cargo to the floor.

If the brace or support does not look like it will do the job, call it to the attention of the person in charge. Ask to speak in private and be diplomatic. Tell the person of your concerns, and your reasons. Explain that once you are on the road it might be too late to make corrections. Be polite, but be firm.

If you cannot correct the problem, ask to use the phone. Call your dispatcher and explain the problem. The dispatcher might want to speak to the shipper's employee. Don't leave until the situation is corrected. Remember, once the cargo leaves the shipper, **you are completely responsible** for any damage to the cargo and for any damage to roads, property, or persons caused by the cargo. Don't take chances with cargo securement.

PROTECTING PLATFORM LOADS

Tarps

A tarpaulin, commonly known as a tarp, is **a protective cover.** In the trucking industry, tarps are used to cover cargo on platform trailers. You may need to tarp a load not only to protect the load, but also because state or local ordinances require it to protect people from spilled cargo.

Tarps are tied down with rope, fabric webbing, or elastic cords with hooks. To tarp a trailer, you'll lift the rolled up tarp to the top of the front racks and unroll it across the bars to the back of the trailer. Then you pull it tight and tie it to cross bars on the racks. If the tarp is even and tight, it will not flap at normal highway speed.

It's a lot tougher to tarp an uneven load of machinery or equipment. Place the tarp directly on the cargo after the tiedown assemblies are tight. Then tie down the tarp so wind and weather don't get inside. An overlap in the front will help. Fold the tarp so there are no open spaces to catch the wind. You may need extra lengths of rope when you tarp uneven cargo.

Some examples of cargo that must be tarped when hauled on a platform trailer are listed below.

- plywood and lumber for indoor use
- cement and plaster in paper sacks
- restaurant kitchen equipment
- laundry and dry cleaning equipment
- military hardware
- iron, steel, and aluminum
- nails in paper boxes
- pipe used for drinking water

Water can damage any of these loads, so inspect the bed of your trailer for holes. If your trailer floor is not waterproof you should cover the floor with plastic. Shippers often cover the top and sides of loads with plastic, but this plastic usually does not go around the bottom of the load. Placing plastic on the trailer bed and tarping over the plastic used by the shipper will keep the load dry.

You may be required to **"smoke tarp"** a load. This means **using a tarp** to cover the front part of the load. The tarp prevents the cargo from being discolored by smoke coming from the exhaust stack. If you fail **to protect a load from smoke discoloration,** a claim will be made against your carrier for the damage.

Prepare the trailer bed to accept a large heavy load that will be set in place by forklift or crane by putting **dunnage** (usually lumber) in place for the load to rest on. This **will enable a forklift or sling to get under the load** at the receiving destination. Placing a solid heavy load directly on the surface of the trailer would cause major unloading problems.

INSPECTING PLATFORM LOADS

All cargo, including tarped loads, **must be inspected** for security by the driver in transit according to FMCSR, part 392.9. The only exception is sealed cargo. Once you're on the road, you must check the load often. Look closely at all wood bracing and supports. Make sure none of the nails are pulling away. Pull at each chain. If there is any slack, open the binder and adjust it. Make your **first inspection within the first 50 miles.** Often, if anything is going to move slightly and loosen the chains, it will happen early on, as soon as the truck vibrates and bounces down the road a short distance. **Reexamine the load**:

- **after three hours or**
- **after driving 150 miles or**
- **at a change of duty status**

whichever comes first. Some unusual loads should be checked more often.

You should carry a hammer, nails, chains, binders, and a good supply of rope, especially when you pull a platform trailer. With these supplies, you can make repairs to bracing or place another chain on a piece of machinery that appears loose.

When you perform your three-hour checks, you'll walk around the truck to check tires and lights as well as the cargo. At night, you should have a flashlight in one hand and a tire hammer in the other. Lightly tapping the chains with the hammer will tell you if they are tight or loose. A tight chain will cause the hammer to bounce back.

Some types of cargo are more prone to shifting than others. If you pull a load that requires tiedown assemblies of any kind, you should **adjust your driving techniques to reduce the chance of shifting.** Make no sudden moves, no swerving, and no fast stops. Do not pull off the roadway onto an uneven surface. Drive more slowly than usual when you enter and exit expressways. Avoid parking areas that have sharp inclines.

Loading Van Trailers

Most cargo for van trailers will either be **stacked by hand on the floor (floor load)** or come **on pallets (palletized).** Sometimes the **shipper will do all the loading.** You will only supervise it. Maybe we should not say "only." Remember you are responsible for everything that happens to the load after you sign the paperwork. **Be sure the loading is done properly.**

Examine each pallet as it comes into the trailer. Look for any boxes that are damaged. If you find any, don't accept them. Also be sure the forklift driver doesn't damage any boxes when loading them. You should be careful to do this because when you get to the delivery point the receiving clerk will look at each box. If any are damaged you will pay. It doesn't matter that the box was damaged before it ever got on your truck. The receiver will assume it was your fault.

Make sure each pallet is stacked so it does not lean. Make sure each pallet is placed so it is tight against the one in front of it and that it is square with the trailer. If you don't do this the pallets will take up too much room and they may not all fit in the trailer. In most cases there will be two rows of pallets down the length of the trailer. Position each one so there is the same amount of space between the pallets and between the pallets and the walls.

OBSERVATION SKILLS TEST

Did you notice the loaded trailer in the illustration that began this chapter? Did the load look secure to you? Why or why not? Check your answer with the Observation Skills Test Grid at the back of the book.

Tiered Stacking

Not all freight is loaded on pallets. Now and then, you will hand-stack a load of cartons or sacks. To load boxes securely, use the **tiered stacking** method shown in Figure 28-3 on the next page. This **will distribute the weight** of a tier of freight **equally.** By overlapping rows so the freight in the tier ties together, there's **less chance the cargo will shift.**

Start on either side on the floor in the nose of the trailer. Load the first carton in the corner against the front wall. Load all the way across the floor, completing one row of cartons in the tier.

Start the next row of the tier on the side of the trailer opposite the start of the first row. If the cartons in the first row do not exactly fit across the unit, leave the space. As long as the carton being loaded to start the next row does not overhang more that half its width, do not worry. This overlap is good and it starts an overlap all the way across the row. Wedge this first carton tight against the trailer wall and each carton in the row against the loaded cartons.

Continue loading rows across the trailer as outlined above. Always start the next row on the side on which the previous row was finished, thus building a tier of freight from the floor to the roof.

The different sizes and shapes of the freight being loaded will dictate how closely you can follow the tier technique of loading. You will have to make some adjustments for different sizes of cartons. For instance, you could load the length of the freight the long way in the trailer, not across the trailer. This reduces the possibility of the tier shifting backward or forward in stop-and-go travel. The overlapping rows reduce shifting from side to side.

fig. 28-3
(A) Tiered stacking method. (B) A full trailer with tiered stacks. This method for securely loading dry freight cartons can be used for sacks as well.

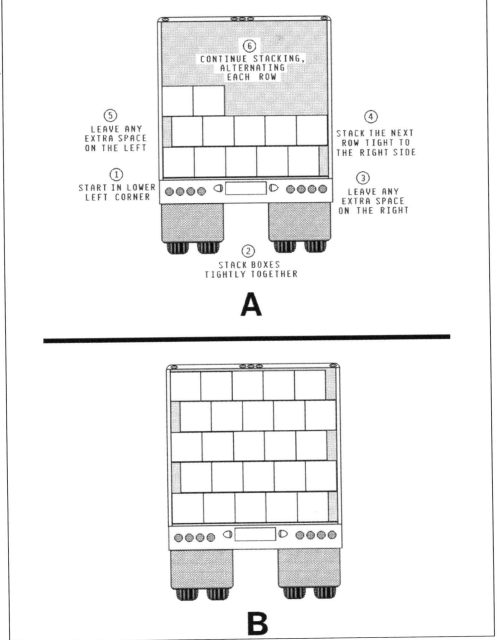

⑥ CONTINUE STACKING, ALTERNATING EACH ROW

⑤ LEAVE ANY EXTRA SPACE ON THE LEFT

④ STACK THE NEXT ROW TIGHT TO THE RIGHT SIDE

① START IN LOWER LEFT CORNER

③ LEAVE ANY EXTRA SPACE ON THE RIGHT

② STACK BOXES TIGHTLY TOGETHER

A

B

Aim to build your tiers so the side facing the loader is as straight as possible and the top row is as level as possible. Put the heavier, stable freight in the bottom tiers, the lighter freight on top of the tiers. Always place cartons right-side up as indicated on the cartons.

Loading Reefers

It's particularly important that reefer cargo be loaded properly. **Air must be permitted to circulate all around the load.** This helps to maintain an even temperature and keeps sections of the cargo from drying out. With both floor and palletized loads, be especially careful to leave spaces around and between the rows. Keep the load away from the rear door, especially when extreme outdoor temperatures could affect the cargo.

SECURING VAN LOADS
Securing van loads doesn't present the same challenge that securing platforms loads does. The **van body** itself **provides stability** to the load. There is however one device, the load lock, that provides extra stability to the van load.

Load locks are long poles that stretch across the width of the trailer. Once in place they are pushed against the sides of the trailer with a jack-like mechanism. These should always be used in the rear of the load to **prevent** any **boxes from falling.** Place one near the top of the load and another about halfway down. Be sure they are firmly in place.

PROTECTING VAN LOADS
In a similar fashion, the **van body** itself **protects the cargo,** so you don't need tarps or plastic. Before you load, though, make sure the inside of the trailer is clean and dry. Check for nails, splinters, or other protrusions that could damage the cargo.

INSPECTING VAN LOADS
Inspecting a van load is also a fairly simple procedure, consisting of just a simple **check to make sure nothing has shifted** out of place. If you have done a good job of loading and securing the cargo, nothing should.

Loading Liquid Tankers

The person in charge of loading and unloading a cargo tank must be sure someone is always watching. The person watching the loading or unloading must:

- have a clear view of the cargo tank
- be within 25 feet of the tank
- be aware of the hazards
- know the procedures to follow in an emergency
- be authorized to move the cargo tank and able to do so

Turn off your engine before loading or unloading any flammable liquid. Only run the engine if needed to operate a pump. Ground a cargo tank correctly before filling it through an open filling hole. Ground the tank before opening the filling hole, and maintain the ground until after closing the filling hole.

Keep liquid discharge valves on a compressed gas tank closed except when loading and unloading. Unless your engine runs a pump for product transfer, turn it off when loading or unloading. If you use the engine, turn it off after product transfer, before unhooking the hose. Unhook all loading and unloading connections before coupling, uncoupling, or moving a chlorine cargo tank. Always chock trailers and semitrailers to keep them from moving when uncoupled from the power unit.

Never load a liquid tanker completely full. Liquids need **outage**—room to expand when they warm. Your dispatcher will tell you the outage needed by the liquid you'll be loading.

Some liquids are very dense, and even a small amount is quite heavy. You will **fill a liquid tanker only partially full of such heavy liquids.** A liquid level sensing device and controller will help you load liquids to the proper level.

As you know, some tankers are compartmented. This means you must be careful not to overload any one compartment. You could put too much weight on an axle if you do.

SECURING AND PROTECTING LIQUID LOADS

As with van loads, the tanker body keeps the load secure. Tankers are often insulated, cooled, or heated to keep the load at a specific temperature. They are also often pressurized to keep certain substances stable enough for transport. The dispatcher and the shipper will tell you at what temperature and pressure the load should be kept.

INSPECTING LIQUID LOADS

Inspect the tank trailer's hoses and valves often to make sure there are no leaks. Check temperature and pressure gauges to see that proper levels are being maintained.

Picking up a Shipment

The procedure for picking up a shipment will vary somewhat from place to place, but they'll all be pretty much the same. It will likely go something like this:

When you arrive at the shipper's yard you stop at the front gate. The guard looks at your I.D., logs you in, and calls the shipping office to report your arrival. You're told where to park your truck and where to go for the shipping papers. After you park the truck, you walk to the dock shipping office. A sign over a window says "Drivers Report Here."

An office clerk asks for your company name and your name. You are handed a copy of a bill of lading and a blank tally sheet. The clerk has written "Door

23" at the top left. You are told to back the trailer to that door and wait for the foreman.

After you back to the dock, use the stairs and go to the trailer. Inspect the roof and sides for any holes. Check the floor for dirt or nails. Return to the loading dock and stand at your door. Wait for the foreman. Do not walk into the warehouse or into any of the offices.

When the foreman arrives, your trailer will be checked again. The foreman will send a loader to your door. Make sure you **check your loading papers against the loader's papers** because there have been times when the wrong freight was loaded on the wrong trailer.

Many warehouses stage the loads in the shipping area at a place called the ready line. The 1,056 cartons you're to take have been brought out earlier to the shipping floor. They have been checked for damage and counted.

You should **check your load at the ready line before it is placed in the trailer.** Count the pallets and cartons. As the pallets are placed in the trailer, use the tally sheet to check off the number of cartons. If the pallets all have the same number of cartons, in this case 48 each, you will check off each pallet as it is loaded. Then show that each pallet contained 48 cartons and 22 pallets X 48 cartons = 1,056 total cartons. Write down the trailer number, the bill of lading number, the date, and your name.

The foreman will bring the **bill of lading. Check** that **it** has not been changed. If it is in order, print your company name, then sign it. Show the number of cartons you received and the date and trailer number. Circle the total number of pieces, then affix a pro number. Accept your copy of the bill of lading. Ask to use the phone. Call your dispatcher, state your name and number, and report that the trailer has been loaded.

When you leave, pull the trailer out very slowly. Because you signed for a complete load in good order, any damage will be your responsibility. Continue to pull out slowly until you are clear of the dock and any other trucks. Then check the load again before you close the doors.

Proper Weight Distribution

Your main concerns when your trailer is being loaded are:

- gross weight
- axle weight
- loading to bulk capacity
- weight rating

Gross vehicle weight (GVW) is the **total weight of the tractor or trailer plus its load. Gross combination weight (GCW)** is the **total weight of the power unit and the trailer or trailers plus the cargo.** The **GVW or GCW** of your vehicle **cannot exceed the limit set by each state** you drive through. If your truck is found overweight at a port of entry or inspection station, there may be a stiff fine which you, the driver, must pay. In addition, you may have to unload the extra weight at the weigh station before you can proceed. Then you'll have to come back for it, or pay someone else to take it for you.

The allowed GCW for an 18-wheeler on National Interstate and Defense Highways is 80,000 pounds. In addition, the axle weights must not be exceeded. **Axle weight is the weight any axle or combination of axles transmits to the ground.** Examples of common state axle weight limits are:

- steering axle—12,000 pounds
- single axle—20,000 pounds
- tandem axle—34,000 pounds

If the weight on your rear tandem is 37,000 pounds, you can still be fined even if the GCW of your rig is less than the allowed total.

Further, you must comply with **bridge laws.** These state laws set **maximum axle weight for axles that are close together.** This prevents overloading bridges and roadways. A bridge law may permit even less weight on an axle than would be allowed otherwise.

Some states even limit the amount of weight you can put on each wheel. You'll have to know about these laws in states you'll travel through so you can distribute your load properly.

Loading to bulk capacity is the attempt to **fill all space in a trailer and still stay within weight limits.** The real problem is to get all the freight inside a trailer without overloading a set of axles.

After you load you should always check your weight on a public scale. If there is no scale where you load, ask someone there where the nearest one is. Most larger truck stops will have one.

If your truck has sliders, this is where they can be a big help in weight distribution. Chapter 23 shows how to use sliders in order to be legal on all axles.

When you scale your truck be sure to **weigh each axle or pair of axles separately.** It is not enough to know only your GVW or GCW weight. You must know the weight on each axle and each group of axles to be sure you are legal.

One final consideration is the **weight rating.** Manufacturers assign a **gross vehicle weight rating (GVWR)** to a single vehicle plus the cargo, and a **gross combination weight rating (GCWR)** to a tractor with its trailer or trailers and the load. These ratings state **how much weight the vehicle can support safely.** Tires, suspensions, and coupling devices also have weight rating. Exceeding the **weight rating** is illegal and it abuses the vehicle and its parts. This leads to early breakdown. It **can** also **be dangerous.** An overloaded vehicle is harder to steer and stop. A badly overloaded truck could break down in traffic.

Loading for Proper Weight Distribution

Loading your truck within weight limits isn't your only concern. You also want the weight to be properly distributed. When cargo is piled too high, the vehicle becomes top-heavy. It's more likely to rollover in curves and on banked roads. Overloading the steering axle can make it hard to steer. You'll also have steering problems if the front axles don't have enough weight on them. Too little weight on the drive axles can reduce traction and lead to skidding. When cargo is unevenly distributed, it's more likely to shift and become damaged in transit.

Before the first box goes into your trailer, you should have **planned** out exactly **how you are going to load the whole trailer.** A little planning will make your life a lot easier. If you do this you won't have as many problems with too much weight on an axle. This might be a little difficult at first, but after a while you will get to know your trailers and the kinds of loads you usually haul.

If your whole load is one kind of product, let's say boxes of nails, then you have a fairly simple task. As a general rule, most vans can be loaded evenly from front to back. So, first **figure out how many boxes or pallets you can put in the trailer without going over your gross weight.** Then be **sure they are spaced evenly from the front to the back.**

If you have a very bulky load that takes up a lot of room but doesn't weigh very much, you have a different problem. Your challenge is to get as many boxes as possible into your trailer. Be sure to use all the available space in the trailer. Even though you are loading something you think is light, you would be wise to watch the weight. It is not impossible to overload a trailer with little, light boxes.

The most difficult load to load is one that has several different kinds of cargo, some heavy, some light, some bulky, and some dense. In this case you have to plan very carefully. Your weight is the most important consideration but you may want to plan for unloading too. If you have several stops, **the last cargo**

loaded should be destined for your first stop. If you have any questions about how to load, ask your dispatcher or a fellow driver.

Sealing and Locking the Trailer

Once a trailer is loaded, it must be locked and perhaps sealed. Any trailer with doors must have a padlock for each door. The better quality the padlock, the better the load is protected.

In addition, many shippers and trucking companies have their own seals. A seal is a band of metal or plastic with a company name and a serial number. Once the seal is applied, it must be cut to remove it. Seal numbers are recorded on bills of lading and other shipping documents. A sealed load means **the driver should not remove the seal until the consignee looks at it or removes it just before unloading.** A sealed trailer is the only exception to the rule which says the driver must periodically check the load for security.

Delivering a Shipment

When you unload, use the same tally sheet or a new one. **Keep track of** the number of **pallets and cartons as they are taken off** the trailer. **Watch the forklift driver** carefully. Some operators are careless. If the forklift tines are not low enough, they will puncture the cartons and cause damage. If you see this happen, stop the operator and call for the foreman. If they have caused damage, it should not be marked on your delivery receipt. It is their responsibility.

When unloading is complete, **have your delivery receipt signed.** Make sure the number of pieces is circled, show the date and trailer number. Do not allow them to sign with notations such as "Subject To Recount Or Damage."

Never leave the trailer when the doors are open. Do your own checking and counting. Never accept someone else's count. You are responsible.

Chapter 28 Quiz

1. No matter who loads a trailer, the _____ is responsible for its security.
   A. shipper
   B. driver
   C. consignee
   D. manufacturer

2.   Cables or webbing straps with winches, or chains and load binders are commonly used to secure loads because although they are hard to use, they're easy on the cargo.
     A.   True
     B.   False

3.   The whole purpose of chaining is to hold the load down and prevent its movement sideways or forward or backward.
     A.   True
     B.   False

4.   Slipping a piece of pipe over the handle of a load binder is a safe way to get added leverage.
     A.   True
     B.   False

5.   When a brace, crate, or support is built for cargo securement, the nails used should be at least_____ as the thickness of the board they are being driven through.
     A.   as long
     B.   twice as long
     C.   half as long
     D.   three-quarters as long

6.   If your trailer floor is not waterproof you should_____.
     A.   refuse the load
     B.   spread sawdust over the floor
     C.   cover the floor with plastic
     D.   borrow any other trailer sitting in the lot

7.   You should make your first cargo inspection within the first _____ of driving.
     A.   two hours
     B.   50 miles
     C.   30 minutes
     D.   two miles

8.   Three main concerns you must pay attention to when your trailer is being loaded are gross weight, axle weight, and _____.
     A.   the air pressure in the trailer tires
     B.   the route you will use to your next destination
     C.   loading to bulk capacity
     D.   dunnage weight

9.   The allowed gross weight for an 18-wheeler is 80,000 pounds per axle.
      A.   True
      B.   False

10. The only exception to the regulation that says you must inspect your cargo is the _____ trailer.
      A.   tarped
      B.   reefer
      C.   dry freight
      D.   sealed

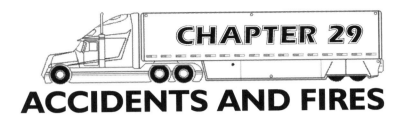

CHAPTER 29
ACCIDENTS AND FIRES

Accidents Do Happen

In spite of all our best efforts, accidents do happen. If you have an accident, you must know exactly what to do. The first minutes after an accident are crucial. Stopping, warning other traffic, giving first aid, protecting property, and taking notes are all things you'll need to know how to do. You must know whom to notify. You must know what forms to fill out and how. You may have to secure the area. You may have to deal with a vehicle fire.

If an accident happens, there are things you must do and things you must not do. Legally, **"must"** does not mean "may;" it does not mean "should." It **means you have no choice.** If you do not do what the law says you must do, the penalty can be a fine, jail, or the loss of your license—perhaps all three.

Company Policy

The company you drive for will have very specific policies you will have to follow if you are involved in an accident. The company policy tells you how and when and to whom you must report an accident. From the notification and reports you give your company, your company in turn files a report with authorities and insurance companies.

The accident reporting kit provided to you may list these instructions: IN CASE OF AN ACCIDENT

- STOP. Failure to stop is a serious violation. Do not move vehicle until police arrive.
- PROTECT THE SCENE. Turn on four-way flashers. Set out warning devices.
- NOTIFY POLICE. Request help for the injured. *DO NOT MOVE* injured persons unless they are in immediate danger.
- NOTIFY THE COMPANY. If necessary, complete *ACCIDENT NOTIFICATION CARD*. Ask someone to call the company collect for you.

plus others.

These instructions will be printed on the outer cover of the accident kit.

Some of the forms in the accident reporting kit are:

- an accident report to record information required for state and insurance reports
- witness cards to record witness information
- accident notification card to be given to a bystander so the bystander can notify your company while you stay on the scene
- an exoneration card should the other driver admit fault

The kit may even include a camera. Figure 29-1, on the next page, shows an example of an accident report form.

If the company you go to work with hauls hazardous materials, the policy on accidents and reporting will be more extensive. There are many more requirements placed on the driver hauling hazardous loads than non-hazardous loads.

fig. 29-1
Fill this form out carefully. It asks for some of the information your carrier will need to report the accident to the proper authorities and to the insurance company.

VEHICLE ACCIDENT REPORT

ACCIDENT DATA

Driver	Drv. Code:
Terminal	Driver Manager
On Date	Time	am/pm
City	State
Location	
Describe road	
Describe weather	

INJURY

Was anyone hurt or did anyone complain of pain/ injury?

If so, who?

If yes, describe injury/pain

Person(s) taken from scene for medical help?

Who and where taken?

Persons killed? ¨ Yes ¨ No

Driver(s) 1 ¨ 2 ¨ 3 ¨ Passengers(s)1 ¨ 2 ¨ 3 ¨

VEHICLE #1

Tractor	List damaged areas
Trailer #1	List damaged areas
Trailer #2	List damaged areas
Other	List damaged areas

Cargo damaged? ¨ Yes ¨ No

Trip number Driver wearing seat belt?

Shipper to consignee

VEHICLE #2

Driver	
Address	Phone
City	State
Owner	
Address	Phone
City	State
Insurance Co.	
Phone	
Policy No.	
Year Make	Model
Damaged area(s)	

PROPERTY OR VEHICLE #3

Owner	
Address	Phone
City	State
Property & Damage	

ACCIDENT DESCRIPTION

Describe what happened in your own words:

The Regulations

The Department of Transportation regulations tell you what your company and you must and must not do. You'll find those regulations in the Federal Motor Carrier Safety Regulations (FMCSR) handbook. **You must know these regulations.** There's no maybes about that. Section 390.5 of the FMCSR gives you the definition of an accident.

STOPPED VEHICLES

Sections 392.22 and 392.25 of the FMCSR tell you what you must do if you stop on the traveled portion or shoulder of a highway (for other than traffic stops). Make sure the parking brake has been set. Use chocks if you must to be certain the truck won't move while you're gone. Park to the side of the road, not in traffic. Make sure other traffic can get around your truck, and that oncoming and following vehicles can clearly see your parked truck.

When you're involved in an accident that results in either or both injury or death to anyone or property damage of any kind, no matter how small, you must **stop immediately.** This does not mean at the next rest area or at the next port of entry, but immediately, and in a safe place at the scene of the accident.

You must do everything you can to prevent the accident that's just happened from causing another accident. Another way to say this is that you must **secure the accident scene.** You'll learn how to do that later in this section.

You must **give assistance** to injured persons. Your company's policy may warn you not to move people if moving them is likely to cause further injury. There are many cases where the trained truck driver is the only one who knows what to do at the scene of an accident. Many professional drivers have taken a course in first aid or life-saving techniques. It is a good idea to get yourself Red Cross certified.

If your truck is equipped with a CB radio, call the local police or highway patrol promptly. The sooner an ambulance or other emergency vehicle arrives, the better are the chances to minimize any injuries. Keep any accident victim warm until help arrives. Stop heavy bleeding by applying direct pressure to the wound.

You must show your driver's license and give anyone who asks:

- your name and address
- the name and address of your carrier
- your vehicle's state tag registration number

Finally, you must **report all the details** of the accident to your carrier as soon as you can. You'll learn more about that later in this section, too.

There are **two important things you should not do.** One is **leave the accident scene.** Section 391.15 contains the regulation about leaving the scene of an accident. The other concerns the use of alcohol or drugs. Section 382.303 provides for the testing of a driver for alcohol and drugs following an accident. Section 382.209 states a driver shall not **use alcohol** for eight hours following the accident or until tested in accordance with Section 382.303.

SECURING THE SCENE OF AN ACCIDENT

When you secure the scene of an accident, you must **follow the same rules you follow when you stop your vehicle on the road.** The rules covered here about emergency devices and those about how to set out warning signals apply any time you stop your vehicle on the road, whether there is an accident or not.

There are two parts to securing the scene of an accident.

- Put on your four-way emergency flashers.
- Set out warning devices.

Section 392.22 and 392.25 of the FMCSR requires you to **put on your emergency flashers** whenever you stop on the traveled portion of a highway or on the shoulder of a highway. You must put them on and leave them on until you set out warning devices and while you pick up warning devices. You may leave them on while the warning devices are out. You must not use the emergency flashers instead of warning devices.

The emergency flasher switch will most probably be found on your dashboard. Turn the flashers on immediately. Until you set out your warning devices, they may be the only warning to other drivers that an emergency has occurred.

Section 393.95 of the FMCSR tells you what emergency equipment you must carry and Section 393.22 tells you how you must set warning devices around your rig.

You must carry a fire extinguisher. You'll learn about that later in the chapter.

If your truck was made on or after January 1, 1974, you must carry **three emergency triangles** that reflect from both sides. The regulations give exact specifications for these reflectors. See Section 393.95(i)(1-7) of the FMCSR to make sure your triangles conform to those regulations. There are other devices you may carry to supplement the triangles, but you must carry the triangles.

fig. 29-2
The general rule for how to place emergency warning devices in case you must stop, or if you have an accident, on the road or on the road's shoulder.

The general rule in Section 392.22 says you must **set out warning devices** as soon as possible, but for sure **within 10 minutes of stopping.** It says you must set out the three triangles as follows:

- Place one triangle at the traffic side and within 10 feet of the front or the rear of your rig.
- Place one triangle about 100 feet from your rig in the center of the traffic lane or the shoulder on which you've stopped facing the traffic that's approaching in that lane.
- Place one triangle about 100 feet from your rig in the center of the traffic lane or the shoulder on which you've stopped, in the direction opposite the second triangle just described.

Since this is the general rule, you should suspect there are some specific rules for specific circumstances.

If the accident occurs (or you stop for any reason) within 500 feet of a curve, crest of a hill, or other object that would keep drivers from seeing you, you must place one triangle at a distance of 100 to 500 feet from your rig in the direction of approaching traffic. This is to make sure that approaching traffic has ample time to slow down.

If the accident occurs on a divided or one-way road, you must:

- Place one triangle at a distance of 200 feet from your rig in the direction of approaching traffic.
- Place one triangle at a distance of 100 feet from your rig in the direction of approaching traffic.
- Place one triangle at the traffic side and within 10 feet of the rear of your rig.

Once you have placed your emergency triangles properly, you can turn your emergency flashers off.

Now that you've secured the scene to prevent further accidents from occurring, it's time to **take care of** any **accident victims** as we discussed earlier. Once you call the authorities, you'll need to gather information for your accident report.

fig. 29-3
Secure the scene of an accident that takes place on a divided or one-way road like this.

NOTIFICATION

When you called the police, highway patrol, fire fighters, or other local authorities, you began the notification process. Now you must call your company dispatcher and begin the process of the accident report.

There are a number of forms you must **fill out** if you have an accident. The highway patrol or local police will give you a **local or state accident report**, or perhaps just an information card, to fill out. You should be sure to get the officer's name and the address of the police agency. The dispatcher or company accident investigator will ask you for this.

That is just the beginning of the information your carrier will need to make the reports it must make. Your carrier must fill out an accident report for its insurance company. The forms used by the insurance companies are very similar. They all need pretty much the same information to process a claim.

Of course, if you decide to become an **owner/operator** you'll be the carrier, too, in the sense that you'll be **responsible for filling out forms and filing them with the proper agency. You'll also be responsible for reporting to your insurance company.**

The **driver accident report form** helps you collect the information you or your carrier will need to fill out the forms required by the DOT and by the insurance company. You saw an example of this form in Figure 29-1. Make sure you fill it out neatly. Accidents, even minor ones, are at the very least upsetting. Your handwriting might not be legible at such a time. If you print, that will slow you down and give you more time to think about the questions and answers you'll need to deal with. Plus it will be easier to read later.

The **accident description form** is very helpful. It's a card with lines at the top and a blank space at the bottom. At the top, it asks you to **explain in your own words what happened.** Make sure you print this description clearly. At the bottom, it asks you to **draw a diagram of the accident.** Now don't worry about drawing a truck that looks like a truck. The important thing is to show how the vehicles involved in the accident approached the scene and where they were following the accident.

Next, **hand out witness cards to anyone at the scene who may have witnessed the accident.** These cards ask witnesses to answer the questions listed below:

- Did you see the accident?
- Were you or anyone else hurt?
- Were you a passenger in our vehicle?
- Was our driver at fault?

The card then asks for a short explanation and for the witness's name, address, and telephone number. Be sure to collect these cards. Be very polite when you hand them out and when you collect them. Always remember that you represent your carrier. People will remember if you are efficient, competent, and polite at an accident scene. It will reflect well on you and on your carrier.

Make sure your accident kit is complete and accurate. It is crucial to your carrier.

HAZARDOUS MATERIALS

If you haul hazardous materials and have an accident, you must **notify your carrier immediately.** The carrier must notify the DOT immediately. This is so crucial that the DOT has provided a toll-free number for carriers to use in cases of hazardous materials accidents. A call to this number will bring out members of the First Response Team, who are specially trained to respond to this type of accident. Chapter 30 covers this in more detail.

With hazardous materials, a leak can constitute an accident. Depending on the cargo, a leak could mean disaster to anyone in the area. That's one reason drivers hauling hazardous materials are specially trained and have a special endorsement on their CDL.

Some of the rules regarding accidents with hazardous materials are printed in Section 397.19 of the FMCSR. Make sure you know these rules if you haul hazardous materials. Your carrier will also provide you with special training if you are to haul hazardous materials.

Vehicle Fires

Vehicle fires are accidents. Sometimes vehicle fires cause accidents and sometimes accidents cause vehicle fires. As a professional driver, you must know what causes vehicle fires. You must know how to prevent them. And, you must know what to do when a fire starts.

To start and burn, **a fire needs fuel, air, and heat.** Fuel is anything that will burn. Most things will burn, given enough air and heat. Air, or oxygen, is essential. A fire cannot burn without air. (That's why one way to put out a fire is to "smother" it.) Heat is needed until the fuel reaches its ignition point. That's the point at which it will burn. Then it creates its own heat. As you'll see, **friction is a main source of heat in vehicle fires.**

As a professional driver, you have major responsibilities in the case of a vehicle fire. First of all, you must seek to **protect your life and the lives of others.** Then you must **try to save your vehicle and its cargo.**

TYPES OF VEHICLE FIRES

One way to group vehicle fires is to look at where they can start:

- the tires
- the trailer
- at a fuel island
- the electrical system
- the cab
- as the result of an accident

Tire Fires

Tires catch on fire because they become overheated. The major cause of over-heating in tires is under-inflation. An **under-inflated tire overheats** because the tire flexes too much. As it flexes, its parts rub against each other and create friction. Friction creates heat. It can get hot **enough to produce a flame,** and rubber burns very well.

You can see that the best way to prevent tire fires is to make sure your tires are properly inflated. Chapter 9 tells you how to do that. Section 393.75 of the FMCSR requires it.

An overheated tire should be removed and placed at a safe distance from the vehicle. Follow your company's policy for handling overheated tires. If a tire is actually burning, use your fire extinguisher. We'll discuss how to do that later in this section.

fig. 29-4
Under-inflation causes tire fires. This chart lists some other causes as well, and some preventive measures.

TIRE FIRES

CAUSES	PREVENTION
A. Under-inflated tires	A. Inflate tires properly
B. Running on a flat tire	B. Change or repair flat tire
C. Accumulated grease or oil around brake drum	C. Clean, find leak, and repair
D. Overloaded rig	D. Reduce load or change tires
E. High-speed driving	E. Slow down

Electrical Fires

Problems with wiring and with the battery can cause fires. Electrical fires can also be caused by faulty wiring, worn wiring, loose connections, and overloaded circuits. Sections 393.27 through 393.33 of the FMCSR contain regulations regarding your electrical system. These regulations seek to promote safety by preventing electrical fires.

The way to prevent electrical fires is to make sure your truck conforms to the FMCSR. That will require some **preventive maintenance** on your part. Check the wiring under the hood every time you raise the hood. Make sure there are no loose or bare wires. It also means keep the engine clean. That way if the battery should go bad and spark, there won't be any oil or fuel to burn. Also be sure to replace worn or frayed battery cables.

If you do have an electrical fire, follow the steps listed on the next page:

- Shut the engine down.
- Don't open the hood if you can avoid it.
- Break the circuit by pulling one of the battery cables loose.
- Use your fire extinguisher, shooting through louvers, the radiator, or from beneath the vehicle.

When you turn off the truck, you stop the flow of electric current in the truck. When you jerk the battery cable loose, you stop the flow of electricity from the battery. Never use water to fight an electrical fire. Use the fire extinguisher. We'll tell you how in a later section.

Trailer Fires

Cargo fires in the trailer are often caused by **poor loading.** A load that is not properly secured **can create more than normal friction,** which creates heat and can cause fire, especially if the cargo is flammable.

If you smell smoke or see smoke or fire coming from the doors of your trailer, you may have a cargo fire. **Immediately pull off the roadway** to an area away from people and other vehicles. Make sure nothing is overhead, such as telephone or electrical wires, a building, or an overpass. Make sure the area is clear in case the fire cannot be contained.

In some cases, the best thing to do is **call for help** on your CB. Give your exact location. Mileposts or intersections are good points of reference. If possible, **uncouple the tractor and drive it away from the trailer.**

If you open the trailer doors, you'll introduce a large amount of oxygen into the fire. That will only make the fire burn faster and hotter. Drivers have lost their lives by opening the doors of a trailer that contains burning cargo. **Do not open the trailer doors.** There can be a fireball type of explosion. Wait for the fire fighters. Have your shipping papers ready to show the fire fighters. How they will fight the fire depends on the cargo.

A hazardous material fire can be very dangerous. If you haul a hazardous material, you'll be trained in exactly what to do if a fire should start.

Cab Fires

Cab fires are almost always **the result of** cab **litter and carelessness.** They could be called "trash fires" because the main cause of these fires is cab trash. Cab trash includes snack wrappers and sacks, fast food bags and cups, and oily rags used for maintenance. If you're a smoker, the danger of a cab fire is increased.

It's obvious how to prevent these fires. Keep your cab clean and be careful what you do with cigarettes, cigars, pipes, and matches.

Fuel Island Fires

This type of fire is also **caused** almost exclusively **by carelessness.** There have been serious fuel fires at truck stops, even though the rules covering fueling are common sense rules. Some of them are listed in Section 397 of the FMCSR. To prevent a fuel island fire, follow these rules:

- Turn off the engine.
- Put the fuel nozzle all the way into the fuel tank and leave it there until you have finished fueling.
- Do not smoke or allow any lighted smoking material within 25 feet of the fuel island.

Another important rule is: Do not leave the truck until you have finished the fueling process. Don't prop open the fuel nozzle with a screwdriver or pliers and leave it unattended while it's filling. Fuel can overflow and run onto the pavement. A fire could easily start. Even if it doesn't, the spill must be cleaned up. Fuel spills end up costing a lot of money, for the high cost of the diesel as well as for the cleanup. There are specific rules for cleaning up spills and for disposal after cleanup. All of this makes a fuel spill time consuming, dangerous, and expensive. Your carrier may be charged for your carelessness. That will not earn you a raise.

If a fuel fire does start, never use water on it. Water will only spread the fuel—and the fire. Use a fire extinguisher.

```
OBSERVATION SKILLS TEST

Recall the illustration that began this chapter. A dangerous situation is
about to happen. How are the driver and her co-driver contributing to an
accident in the making? Turn to the Observation Skills Test Grid at the
back of the book to check the accuracy of your observation skills.
```

THE FIRE EXTINGUISHER

Section 393.95(a) of the FMCSR tells you that your truck must carry a fire extinguisher. This regulation also specifies exactly what types of fire extinguishers are acceptable. Make sure the extinguisher in your truck conforms to the regulations.

Fires have been grouped according to class. When the fuel for the fire is **wood, paper, cloth, trash, and other ordinary material,** the fire is a **Class A** fire. When the fuel is **gasoline, grease, oil, paint, and other flammable liquids,** the fire is a **Class B** fire. **Electrical** fires are **Class C** fires.

Most trucks use a 10 B:C type fire extinguisher with a rating of "A," "B," and "C." This type of extinguisher can be used for all classes of fires. It's filled with a **dry chemical** and weighs about four pounds when charged. When you squeeze the handle, an air pressure cartridge inside the tank is punctured. The released air pressure forces the powder out of the tank, through the hose, through the nozzle, and onto the fire. The dry chemical **puts the fire out by smothering it.** In other words, the chemical coats the burning material and prevents air from fueling the fire.

Your fire extinguisher will come with a manual that shows in detail how to use it. Read this manual. Become familiar with the fire extinguisher before you need to use it. What follows here are the instructions which are printed on a fire extinguisher:

- Keep the wind to your back.
- Hold the extinguisher upright.
- Pull out the ring pin.
- Stand back six feet.
- Aim the nozzle at the base of the fire.
- Squeeze the handles.
- Use a side to side motion.

Continue until the fire is completely cooled. Simply the absence of smoke or flame does not mean the fire is out.

The extinguisher should be inspected monthly. Check the nozzle to make sure it's clear. Check the ring pin to make sure the tip is intact. Check the pressure gauge. The needle should be in the green area.

Take good care of your fire extinguisher. It's your fire fighting tool. Of course, **the best fire fighting tool is prevention.**

fig. 29-5
The fire extinguisher in your truck should be able to put out all three classes of fires.

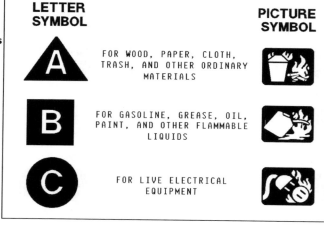

LETTER SYMBOL		PICTURE SYMBOL
A	FOR WOOD, PAPER, CLOTH, TRASH, AND OTHER ORDINARY MATERIALS	
B	FOR GASOLINE, GREASE, OIL, PAINT, AND OTHER FLAMMABLE LIQUIDS	
C	FOR LIVE ELECTRICAL EQUIPMENT	

Chapter 29 Quiz

1. There are DOT regulations in the FMCSR that tell you what you must and must not do in case of an accident. You _____ know these regulations.
    A. should
    B. may
    C. must
    D. ought to

2. The DOT rules covering emergency devices and how to set out warning signals apply any time you stop your vehicle on the road whether there is an accident or not.
    A. True
    B. False

3. In case of an accident, you'll find reminder instructions such as stop, protect the scene, set out warning devices, and notify police on the _____.
    A. front page of the FMCSR
    B. back cover of your Drivers Manual
    C. back of the witness card
    D. outer cover of your accident kit

4. The _____ helps you collect the information you or your carrier will need to fill out the forms required by the DOT and by the insurance company.
    A. hazardous materials bill of lading
    B. driver accident report form
    C. state or local accident report form
    D. police information card

5. To start and burn, a fire needs fuel, heat, and _____.
    A. water
    B. dry chemicals
    C. air
    D. cargo

6. Many cargo fires are caused by _____.
    A. poor loading
    B. hazardous cargo
    C. opening the trailer doors
    D. driving too fast

7. Most trucks use a 10 B:C type size fire extinguisher that will put out fires with a class rating of _____.
    A. "A"
    B. "B"
    C. "A" and "B"
    D. "A," "B," and "C"

8. Refer to the illustration below, which shows the placement of emergency triangles according to the general rule for stopping on the shoulder of a road. How far should the triangles be placed from the vehicle? Write the correct number of feet in the blank next to the letter that corresponds with the triangle.

A. _____

B. _____

C. _____

9. Refer to the illustration below, which shows the placement of emergency triangles according to the general rule for securing the scene of an accident that takes place on a divided or one-way road. How far should the triangles be placed from the vehicle? Write the correct number of feet in the blank next to the letter that corresponds with the triangle.

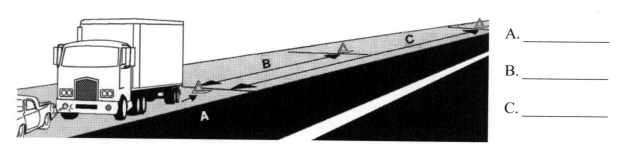

A. _____

B. _____

C. _____

10. The best way to prevent tire fires is to make sure your tires are properly _____.
    A. demounted
    B. inflated
    C. sized
    D. retreaded

HAZARDOUS MATERIALS

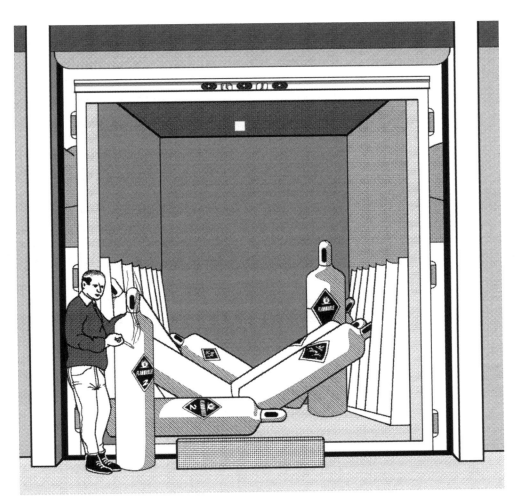

Safe and Secure Transportation

Transporting hazardous materials sounds like a dangerous assignment. It isn't for those who know the rules involved and follow them carefully. But it is a challenge. Drivers who haul hazardous materials must have a **special endorsement** on their CDL. They must pass background checks that include their criminal, immigration, and Federal Bureau of Investigation records and fingerprints. An additional tank vehicle endorsement is required to haul hazardous materials in a cargo tank. **To haul hazardous materials or operate a cargo tanker** without these special endorsements is a crime for which you can be cited, fined, and put out of service immediately.

The Department of Transportation regulates hazardous materials:

- packaging
- loading
- labeling
- transporting

This includes everyone who is involved with the operation, the upkeep, and repair of the tractor-trailers, as well as the dispatcher and the drivers. The Federal Hazardous Materials Regulations, Parts 171-215, also cover this issue. We'll cite both HMR and FMCSR regulations in the chapter.

As a driver, your responsibility is to **be able to recognize, load safely, placard correctly, and transport safely hazardous materials** shipments. You refuse leaking packages and keep papers in the proper place. Section 177.816 requires your carrier to provide you with training on how to recognize and handle hazardous materials.

KNOW YOUR SHIPMENT

Generally speaking, a **hazardous material** (or "haz mat" as you may hear it called) is something that by its nature **could pose a health or safety risk to human, animal, or plant life.** Anything that **could damage property** is also considered a hazardous material. Section 171.8 of the HMR defines hazardous materials as those products determined by the Secretary of Transportation to pose "a risk to health, safety, and property when transported in commerce." This also includes radioactive materials and hazardous wastes, the dangerous by-products of many chemical processes.

A hazardous material could be in solid, gas, or liquid form. It might be flammable, combustible, poisonous, corrosive, even infectious. A few common examples are gasoline, fuel oil, acetone, rubber cement, and various types of acids and chemicals.

There are nine classes of hazardous materials. Those nine classes and their divisions include every substance that is known to be flammable, combustible, poisonous, or otherwise harmful. The class tells you what type of danger the material presents. The Hazardous Materials Table, Section 172.101 of the HMR, lists all classes and their divisions.

Hazardous materials are not the only dangerous product you might transport. You may also handle hazardous substances and hazardous waste. A hazardous substance is a product that is listed on the List of Hazardous Substances and Reportable Quantities. Appendix A to HMR 172.101 contains Table 1 and Table 2 which list hazardous substances and reportable quantities. Both the DOT and the Environmental Protection Agency (EPA) want to know about RQ spills. The EPA is also concerned about the transport of hazardous wastes. Hazardous substance and hazardous wastes are regulated just as hazardous materials are, but identified differently, as you'll learn later in this chapter. Appendix B to HMR 172.101 lists marine pollutants.

It is most important for you to understand and be able to use the Hazardous Materials Table, Section 172.101 of the regulations. Once you can use this table, you will be able to:

- determine if a material is regulated or forbidden for transportation by truck
- determine the proper shipping name in order to match shipping papers and package marking
- identify the hazard class for the material
- verify the proper identification number
- identify the packing group
- verify the label is correct
- verify the shipper used the proper package
- determine what placards are required

Figure 30-1 shows you a sample of the Table. Your carrier will provide a complete Table and extensive training on how to use it.

fig. 30-1
A sample of the Hazardous Material Table 171.101.

HAZARDOUS MATERIALS TABLE

COL 1 Shipping Mode	COL 2 Proper Name and Description	COL 3 Hazard Class or Division	COL 4 ID Number	COL 5 Packing Group	COL 6 Required Label(s)	COL 7 Special Provisions	COL 8 Regulation(s) on Packaging Requirements			COL 9 Applies to Non-Highway Transport		COL 10 Applies to Non-Highway Transport	
Symbols	Hazardous materials descriptions and proper shipping names	Hazard class or Division	Identification Numbers	Packing group	Label(s) required (if not excepted)	Special provisions	Packaging (8) Section 173 ***			(9) Quantity Limitations		(10) Vessel Stowage	
							Exceptions (8A)	Non-bulk (8B)	Bulk (8C)	Passenger aircraft/ rail (9A)	Cargo aircraft only (9B)	Location (10A)	Other (10B)
(1)	(2)	(3)	(4)	(5)	(6)	(7)							
	Batteries, dry, containing potassium hydroxide solid, *electric, storage*	8	UN3028	III	8		None	213	None	25kg gross	230kg gross	A	11
	Batteries, wet, filled with acid, *electric storage*	8	UN2794	III	8		159	159	159	30kg gross	No limit	A	11

Five different symbols may appear in COL 1:
+ Shows the proper shipping name, hazard class, and packing group to use, even if the material does not meet the hazard class definition.
A Means the hazardous material described in COL 2 is subject to HMR only when offered or intended for transport by air unless it is a hazardous substance or hazardous waste.
W Means the hazardous material described in COL 2 is subject to the HMR only when offered or intended for transport by water unless it is a hazardous substance, hazardous waste, or marine pollutant.
D Means the proper shipping name is appropriate for describing materials for domestic transportation, but may not be proper for international transportation.
I Identifies a proper shipping name that is used to describe materials in international transportation. A different shipping name may be used when only domestic transportation is involved.

Being able to recognize a hazardous materials shipment is the first step in handling it correctly and safely. You might suspect the load contains haz mat by the shipper's business. The packaging might give you a clue. Haz mat is often shipped in cylinders or drums. Package labels and markings will tell you the cargo is hazardous material. In any case, always check the shipping paper and manifest. Non-hazardous materials may not be described with haz mat classes or ID numbers.

SHIPPING PAPERS AND MANIFESTS

When offering a load of hazardous materials, it is the shipper's duty to make up a proper shipping order. Forms vary from shipper to shipper. As the driver of that load, you must **confirm that the shipping papers include the right information.**

fig. 30-2
This shipping paper shows hazardous materials three ways: they're listed first, there's an X in the HM column, and a different color has been used to identify them. Note that the shipping names are spelled out, not abbreviated, the hazard class, total quantity, and U.N. number are listed.

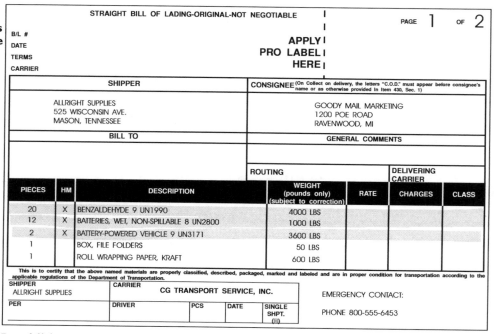

In addition to an emergency contact number, three items must be included:

- page numbers if the shipping paper has more than one page
- a proper description of the hazardous product
- a shipper's certification signed by the shipper

The shipper's certification states that the materials named on the shipping paper were prepared for transport according to regulations. This certification isn't required when the shipper is a private carrier.

Hazardous materials should be clearly identified on the shipping paper. They may be the first entries, they may be marked with a different color than the rest of the entries, or there may be an X in a special HM column on the form.

The basic description of a hazardous material includes the proper shipping name (names in italics are not proper shipping names), hazard class, the identification number, and the packing group, if any, shown in Roman numerals and possibly the letters "PG"—in that order.

Abbreviations of the shipping name may be used only when regulations permit it. The identification number is a four digit United Nations (UN) number used for U.S. and international shipments, or North American (NA) number, used for U.S. and Canadian shipments only. The description also includes the total quantity and the unit of measure used.

If a shipment includes a reportable quantity of a hazardous substance, you'll see the letters RQ on the shipping paper. The word WASTE on the shipping paper shows the product is hazardous waste. For generic descriptions, the haz mat's technical name will be shown.

HMR 172.205 requires the shipper of hazardous waste to prepare, date, and sign a **Uniform Hazardous Waste Manifest** which serves as the shipping paper. Check for each item on the manifest, date it, and sign your name. When you make delivery, get the signature of the person who received the shipment. You keep a copy of the manifest. The manifest sets up a paper trail that tracks all the movements of the hazardous waste.

The manifest will include this information:

- document number
- total number of pages
- generator's name, mailing address, emergency contact number, and Environmental Protection Agency (EPA) identification number
- shipper's name, mailing address, phone number, and EPA ID number
- name and EPA identification number of each carrier
- name, address, and EPA ID number of the designated facility (plus an alternate facility, if given)
- description of the material including hazard class
- quantity (by units of weight or volume)
- type and number of containers loaded on the vehicle
- emergency response information

You must receive three copies of the manifest.

Once you have approved the shipping papers and manifest, there are regulations about where to put them in the cab. These two documents must be readily available in case you are stopped. Tab the shipping papers related to haz mat, or keep them on top of any other shipping papers. Most drivers keep them in the holder mounted on the inside of the driver's door. They must be within your easy reach even when you are wearing your seat belt. Don't take them along when you leave your tractor. Instead, leave them on the driver's seat in plain view. You do this so that in case anything happens in your absence, emergency crews can find out exactly what kind of haz mat is involved.

LABELS

You may find the shipper's or consignee's name and address on the package. Package labels are required by the regulations. **Any package or container of hazardous materials must be marked** in such a way that people know what is inside. Standard labels are diamond-shaped and 3.9 inches in size. They are attached near the shipping name which must be on the package. The name of the hazardous material on the label must be the same as the one on the manifest and the shipping name on the package. They all must match. Some packages may require more than one label.

The **Hazard Class Number** is shown in the lower corner of the diamond. The number will correspond to the number in column (3) of the Hazardous Materials Table, HM 172.101. The hazard class number will be one of the following:

- Class 1—Explosives and Fire Hazards
- Class 2—Gases
- Class 3—Flammable Liquids
- Class 4—Flammable Solids
- Class 5—Oxidizing Substances
- Class 6—Poisons
- Class 7—Radioactive Materials
- Class 8—Corrosive Materials
- Class 9—Miscellaneous Materials

When the shipping container is shaped so that regular labels cannot be attached, hang tags are used. The hang tags are attached to the container with wire. Containers of compressed gas are labeled with hang tags.

If rules require it, the shipper will put RQ or Inhalation Hazard on the package. You may also see directions for how to keep the package positioned.

The shipper should prepare the packages with the labels in place, but you should make sure they are there and know what you're carrying.

Loading Hazardous Materials

Before loading your trailer, check the inside for anything that could damage the containers. Make sure each package is properly labeled with its warning. **Do not accept any container that is damaged** in any way. If you are at all unsure about any container, check with your dispatcher. It's much better to be safe than to let it go and worry for the whole trip. Don't use hooks or tools that could damage the packages.

LOAD PACKAGES PROPERLY

When you have a mixed load, carefully inspect the shipment to be sure that no laws are being broken. **Certain hazardous materials may NOT be transported with other hazardous materials.** For example, a poisonous gas (Class 2) may not be shipped with a blasting agent (Class 1). Poison (Class 6) cannot be loaded with any form of foodstuff (intended for human or animal consumption) unless it is specially packed in an approved container and securely bound for the trip. The rules about mixed loads are detailed in the Separation and Segregation Chart in the HMR 177.848.

There are **special procedures for loading certain specific hazardous materials.** Do your loading away from any sources of heat. Don't use a cargo heater when you're loading explosives, flammable liquids, and flammable gas. Do not smoke when loading these, or oxidizers and flammable solids.

Make sure the parking brake is set on your vehicle. The wheels of trailers and semitrailers should be chocked and the engine turned off, whether loading or unloading. See that the containers are not dropped, bumped, or slid across the floor of the trailer. Most hazardous materials should be loaded to the rear of the trailer whenever it is practical. This is done so that the containers will be easy to get to in case of emergency. Load them so they don't bounce or shift in transit. Don't load any packages that are damaged or leaking. You can't have overhang or tailgate loads of explosives, flammable solids, or oxidizers. These must be loaded into a closed cargo space.

If you are loading by hand, load breakable containers of corrosive liquid one by one. Keep them right side up. Do not drop or roll the containers. Load them onto an even floor surface. Be careful around packages with valves or fittings. You may stack carboys (glass jugs) only if the lower tiers can bear the weight of the upper tiers safely. Never load corrosive materials (Class 8) next to or above Division 1.4 (Explosives C), Class 4 (Flammable Solids, Class 5 (Oxidizers), or Division 2.3, Zone B (Poisonous Gases). Don't load corrosives liquids with Division 1.1 or 1.2 (Explosives A), Division 1.3 (Explosives B), Division 1.5 (Blasting Agents), Division 2.3, Zone A (Poisonous Gases), Division 4.2 (Spontaneously Combustible Materials), or Division 6.1, PG1, Zone A (Poison Liquids).

Do not load nitric acid above any other product, or stack it more than two high.

Load charged storage batteries so their liquid won't spill. Keep them right side up. Make sure other cargo won't fall against or short circuit them. You can load them only one tier high and they must rest level.

Compressed gas cylinders must be loaded either securely upright or braced lying flat. Then they must be supported in racks or in boxes so they stay that way.

There's a limit to how many packages of radioactive materials (Class 7) you may carry at one time. Radioactive materials have a **transport index.** The shipper should label packages of radioactive material with this number. The total transport index of your load should not be more than 50. Also, radioactive materials have to be loaded a certain distance away from any people, animals, or unexposed film that may also be with the vehicle. A table in HMR 177.842 lists the distances for each transport index.

Never load a package labeled POISON or POISON GAS in the driver's cab or sleeper or with food material for human or animal consumption. Flatbeds that will carry poisons must have racks that keep the packages from falling off or sliding out. You will almost definitely have to tarp a load like this to protect it from the weather. You will also have to fix placards to a tarped load.

Before you load or unload explosives, turn off your engine. Disable cargo heaters. Disconnect heater power sources and drain heater fuel tanks. Use a floor liner with Class 1 Division 1.1, 1.2, and 1.3 (Class A or B Explosives). The floor liner must not contain steel or iron. Be especially careful not to damage packages of explosives. Do not transport Division 1.1 or 1.2 (Class A Explosives) in triples or in vehicle combinations if there is a marked or placarded cargo tank in the combination or if the other vehicle in the combination contains

- Division 1.1 A (Initiating Explosives)
- Packages of Class 7 (Radioactive materials labeled "Yellow III")
- Division 2.3 (Poisonous Gas) or Division 6.1 (Poisonous) materials
- hazardous materials in a portable tank, on a DOT Specification 106A or 110A tank

A person loading or unloading a cargo tank must make sure a qualified person is always watching. This person must be alert, have a clear view of the cargo tank, be within 25 feet of the tank, know the hazards presented, know emergency procedures, and be authorized and able to move the tank.

To prevent leaks, close all manholes and valves before moving a tank of hazardous materials. Turn off the engine before loading or unloading any flammable liquids. Run the engine only to operate a pump. Ground a cargo tank before opening a filling hole and maintain the ground until the hole is closed. Keep liquid discharge valves on a compressed gas tank closed except when loading or unloading. Except to run a pump for product transfer, the engine should be off when loading or unloading. If you do run the engine, turn it off after the product transfer, before you unhook the hose. Unhook all loading and unloading connections before coupling, uncoupling, or moving a chlorine cargo tank.

Before you leave the warehouse, make sure you completely understand what procedures you would take in case of an accident, fire, or spills. Make sure you have the proper emergency equipment.

PLACARDS

Placards are required by regulations. A placard is similar to a label. However, **a placard is attached to the outside of the vehicle** to show clearly that it contains a load of hazardous materials. They may be displayed even if not required as long as the placards identify the transported material. Placards are diamond-shaped, about 10¾ inches in size, and usually made of plastic or metal. The placard for a certain material will be of the same color and wording as its label. Look at Figure 30-3.

Legally, it is the shipper's responsibility to provide placards, although sometimes the carrier will supply them. The class and quantity of the material listed on the shipping papers will determine the placard needed. Next, check the Class on the Hazardous Materials Table. Placards for that Class will be found in Column 8.

Tables 1 and 2 in HMR 172.504 tell you what placards to use. Placards are re-

fig. 30-3
The label and placard for this shipment show that the driver is hauling explosives (Class I). The hazard class or division number is in the lower corner. No hazard class or division number is allowed for secondary hazards.

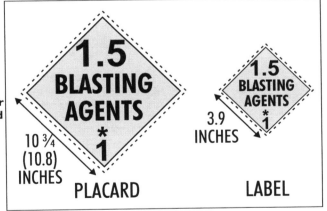

quired for any amount of haz mat listed in Table 1. Note that if you are carrying more than one type of haz mat, you'll need more than one type of placard. Some hazard classes need placards only if the amount transported is 1,001 pounds or more including the package. These are listed in Placard Table 2 in the HMR. Add the amounts from all shipping papers for all the Table 2 products you have on board. You may use DANGEROUS placards instead of separate placards for each Table 2 hazard class when:

- you have a total of 1,001 pounds or more of two or more Table 2 hazard classes requiring different placards, and
- you have not loaded 5,000 pounds or more of any Table 2 hazard class material at any one place. (You must use the specific placard for this material.)

Use POISON or POISON GAS placards along with the other required placards when INHALATION HAZARD appears on the shipping paper. Any placards you use must be in good shape, and of their original color. Your placards must be securely attached to all four sides of the vehicle. They must be placed so the lettering is level, readable from left to right, and at least three inches from all other markings, and away from ladders or pipes. Of course they must be kept clean and easy to read from all directions at all times. Make sure they're properly in place before you drive. You may move an improperly placarded vehicle only during an emergency to protect life or property.

fig. 30-4

Tables 1 and 2

PLACARD TABLE 1 — ANY AMOUNT	
If your vehicle contains any amount of...	Placard as...
1.1	EXPLOSIVE 1.1
1.2	EXPLOSIVE 1.2
1.3	EXPLOSIVE 1.3
2.3	POISON GAS
4.3	DANGEROUS WHEN WET
6.1 (PG1, Inhalation hazard only)	POISON
7 (Radioactive Yellow III label only	RADIOACTIVE

PLACARDING TABLE 2 — 1,001 POUNDS OR MORE	
Category of Material (hazard class or division number and additional description, as appropriate)	Placard Name
1.4	EXPLOSIVES 1.4
1.5	EXPLOSIVES 1.5
1.6	EXPLOSIVES 1.5
2.1	FLAMMABLE GAS
2.2	FLAMMABLE
3	COMBUSTIBLE*
Combustible liquid	FLAMMABLE SOLID
4.1	SPONTANEOUSLY COMBUSTIBLE
4.2	OXIDIZER
5.1	ORGANIC PEROXIDE
5.2	POISON
6.1 (PG1 or II, other than PG 1 Inhalation Hazard	POISON
6.1 (PGIII)	KEEP AWAY FROM FOOD
6.2	(NONE)
8	CORROSIVE
9	CLASS 9**
ORM D	(NONE)

*FLAMMABLE placard may be used in place of a COMBUSTIBLE placard on a cargo tank or portable tank
**Class 9 Placard is not required for domestic transportation

Bulk Packaging

Refer to Column 4 on the Hazardous Materials Table for the identification number that you must display on bulk packaging—cargo tanks and portable tanks. The rules require black, 3.9-inch numbers on orange panels, placards, or a white, diamond-shaped background if placards aren't required. Cargo tanks required to meet DOT specifications must display their retest markings. Portable tanks must display the lessee or owner's name and the shipping name of the contents. On tanks with capacities of more than 1,000 gallons the letters must be at least two inches high and the ID number must appear on opposing sides and each end of a portable tank. On smaller tanks with smaller capacities, the letters must be one-inch high and on opposing sides.

Safe Transport on the Road

Now that everything is in order with your load of hazardous materials, you're ready to start on your trip. But you're not off the hook yet. There are more special laws and regulations to be followed.

TIRE INSPECTION

Do a **tire inspection at the beginning and end of your trip, and each time you park** your vehicle, and use a tire gauge.

If you have a low or leaking tire, do not drive except to get to the nearest truck stop or gas station and have it fixed. A hot, overheated tire, on the other hand, must be replaced then and there. Once it has been taken off the truck, it must be moved a safe distance from the vehicle. That way, if it does burst into flame, it won't touch off anything else. Continue on your trip only after the problem with the tire is fixed.

PARKING

Parking is even trickier than usual when your cargo is potentially dangerous. The regulations on parking and attending your rig are set forth in Section 397.5 and 397.7 of the FMCSR. If you are carrying Class 1 Division 1.1, 1.2, or 1.3 Explosives, it's against the law to park your rig within five feet of a roadway. You may not park on private property, including fueling and eating facilities, without the consent of the owner. Neither are you allowed to park within 300 feet of a bridge, tunnel, dwelling, building, or any place where people work or gather.

Someone must **attend your vehicle** at all times when it is located on a public street, highway, or shoulder of the road. In other words, this person is required to be **awake and inside your vehicle (not in the sleeper), or no more than 100 feet away, with a clear view** of the entire rig. This person must be aware of the hazards, know what to do in an emergency, and be able to move the truck if it becomes necessary.

Exceptions to this rule exist when the vehicle is parked in an assigned area on the property of the motor carrier, shipper, or consignee. Another exception would be if the vehicle is in a "safe haven," a lot approved by the Department of Transportation especially for parking vehicles carrying hazardous materials. A safe haven will be marked by a sign and surrounded by barrels. In a safe haven, you may park your vehicle and leave it unattended.

You may park a placarded vehicle not carrying explosives within five feet of the traveled part of a roadway if your work requires it, but someone must still watch the vehicle. Do not uncouple a haz mat trailer and leave it on a public street.

ROUTING

When routing hazardous cargo, your purpose is not to take the easiest and fastest highways. Convenience does not determine which route you may take. Instead, you must **avoid roads that take you through heavily populated areas.** The only exception to this is when there is no other possible way to get to your destination. Avoid potential traps such as tunnels and narrow streets. The dispatcher can answer any questions you might have about your route. Routing is covered in Section 397 of the FMCSR .

For Class 1 Division 1.1, 1.2, and 1.3 explosives, the carrier must give you a written route plan. This written plan must include curfews and permits from those cities that require them. The permit must be applied for prior to the trip. Attach the permit to the written plan. That plan will remain in the truck with you.

Depending on the area through which you are driving, your written plan may list certain hours of the day during which you may travel through a city. Some cities have ordinances as to what time of day hazardous materials are allowed to pass through. Other cities require permits which, as mentioned earlier, must be applied for in advance. More and more cities and states are passing laws that deal with hazardous materials. These laws change often. If you run into a situation that would require you to change your route, call your dispatcher. Don't just take off in some new direction.

Whenever there are two or more sets of regulations, you should follow the strictest set. This is known as the **higher standard of care rule, as set forth in Section 397.3 in the FMCSR.** The thinking behind it is that if you **follow the strictest regulations,** you will automatically meet the requirements of those that are less strict.

RAILROAD CROSSINGS

The following vehicles must stop at railroad crossings:

- all vehicles that are placarded
- those that are hauling any amount of chlorine
- tankers used to haul hazardous materials, whether loaded or empty

Turn on your four-way flashers and move to the right lane if it is safe to do so. The vehicle must stop between 15 and 50 feet from the tracks. Once you have come to a complete stop, look both ways down the track and listen for the sound of an oncoming train. Provided no train is on its way, continue across the tracks. **Do not shift gears while crossing.** Don't forget to turn off your four-way flashers when you're again underway.

AVOID FIRE

A truck hauling hazardous materials may not be driven past an open fire unless it is completely safe to do so. You may have to get out and investigate the situation. Also, you should know that you **do not park your truck within 300 feet of an open fire.** This is according to Section 397.11 of the Federal Motor Carrier Safety Regulations.

As for smoking, Section 397.13 states that you do **not smoke within 25 feet of the vehicle** when carrying any explosives, flammables, or oxidizing materials, or when your vehicle is a cargo tank placarded for Class 3 (flammable liquids) or Class 2 (gases). This rule applies even after the tank has been emptied. Nor are you allowed to smoke in the cab with your windows closed. If you're a smoker and plan to do any hazardous materials hauling, this is yet another reason to consider giving up the habit entirely.

You must have a fire extinguisher rated 10 B:C or more. But use it only to control small truck fires. Don't try to fight haz mat fires yourself. Leave that to fire fighters who have been specially trained for this type of emergency.

Section 397.15 covers fueling. It states that you must add fuel to your vehicle only when the engine is turned off. The fuel tank must not go unattended while fueling. Either you or a station attendant must be right there during the entire fueling process.

In Case of an Accident

If you are involved **in an accident, stop immediately.** Never continue driving, not even to get help. Send someone else for help. Do what you can to warn other drivers and those in the area of the danger. Your plan will be to follow the same procedures as for any other accident, plus your special haz mat emergency procedures. You will have been instructed on emergency procedures for the specific cargo you are hauling.

This is especially true if you are transporting Class 1 Division 1.1, 1.2, or 1.3 explosives. Your carrier will give you a copy of FMCSR Part 397. The carrier must also give you written instructions on what to do if delayed or in an accident. The written instructions must include:

- the names and telephone numbers of people to contact (including carrier agents or shippers),
- the nature of the explosives transported,
- the precautions to take in emergencies such as fires, accidents, or leaks

You must be familiar with, and have in your possession while driving:

- shipping papers
- written emergency instructions
- a written route plan
- a copy of FMCSR Part 397

While every accident has its own circumstances, there are some basic steps that you must always follow.

KEEP SHIPPING PAPERS WITH YOU. Provide emergency responders with information from those documents.

DON'T USE FLARES. Don't you use or let anyone else use liquid burning flares or fusees. Use reflective triangles instead.

KEEP PEOPLE AWAY. Warn them of the extreme dangers. Don't let them breathe the material, walk on it, or handle it. If it is flammable and subject to explosion, clear the area immediately. If possible, approach the accident site from an upwind direction. Do not assume that gases or vapors are harmless just because you can't smell them. Don't allow bystanders to smoke.

NOTIFY THE AUTHORITIES. Notify the police and the fire department. Explain that it is a hazardous materials emergency and give them the name of the material and its classification, including the UN or NA number. That way they can send out members of the First Response Team. These are people who are specially trained to deal with emergencies of this nature. Both the police and the fire department have Emergency Response Guidebooks to guide them. Notify the shipper if compressed gas is involved in an accident.

CONTAIN THE SPILL. If the shipment has spilled out onto the ground, it must be contained. Plain dirt is good for soaking up and containing liquids. Later, this dirt and the liquid it absorbed can be properly disposed of. Take care to prevent any poison from contaminating streams or sewers. If the poison is in powder form, try to keep it from being scattered by the wind. Avoid touching the leaking material. Don't try to repack leaking containers. Don't eat, drink, or smoke around the spill.

DON'T MOVE THE VEHICLE. Don't move the vehicle unless it's dangerous to leave it where it is and then move only as far as safety requires. Moving could cause the spill to spread. Don't try to pull apart vehicles involved in a collision until any explosive cargo is removed. Move explosives at least 200 feet from vehicles and occupied buildings.

DON'T TRANSFER MATERIALS. Don't transfer haz mat from one package to another, or flammable liquid or flammable compressed gas from one vehicle to another on a public roadway except in an emergency, or if you are fueling road construction or maintenance machinery. Don't open smoldering packages of flammable solids or oxidizers, but remove them and any unbroken packages from the vehicle if it is safe to do so, to prevent a fire.

NOTIFY YOUR CARRIER. Contact your supervisor if packages of Division 6.2 (Infectious Substance) have been damaged in transport. **Call your dispatcher** and report the accident. Get the name, address, and insurance company of anyone else involved. You will need such information for your

Hazardous Materials Incident Report. Also, get the name and address of each witness.

CHEMTREC

People involved with any aspect of haz mat transportation are very familiar with an agency called CHEMTREC, a public service of the chemical business that **provides immediate advice for those at the scene of emergencies.** Based in Washington, D.C., it operates 24 hours a day, every day of the year, to receive toll-free calls from anywhere in the country. That toll-free number is (800) 424-9300. It's a number you will see very often should you become involved in the shipment of hazardous materials. In order to help you, CHEMTREC will need the name of the product or its identification number, as well as the nature of your problem.

THE NATIONAL RESPONSE CENTER

The National Response Center helps coordinate emergency response to chemical hazards. They are a resource to the local police and fire fighters. You may have to phone the National Response Center (their toll-free number is 800-424-8802). This call will be in addition to any made to police or fire fighters. You or your employer must phone when any of the following occur as a direct result of a hazardous materials incident:

- a person is killed
- a person receives injuries requiring hospitalization
- the general public is evacuated for one or more hours
- one or more major transportation arteries or facilities are closed or shut down for one hour or more
- fire, breakage, spillage, or suspected radioactive contamination occurs or if a shipment of etiologic agents (bacteria or toxins) is involved
- estimated carrier or other property damage exceeds $50,000
- a situation exists, such as continuing danger to life at the accident site, that the carrier thinks should be reported

You (or whoever makes the call) should be ready to give:

- his or her name
- the name and address of the carrier he or she works for
- the phone number where he or she can be reached
- the date, time, and location of the incident
- the extent of injuries, if any
- the classification, name, and quantity of hazardous materials involved, if such information is available
- the type of incident and nature of hazardous material involvement and whether a continuing danger to life exists at the scene

If a reportable quantity of hazardous substance was involved, the caller should give the name of the shipper and the quantity of the hazardous substance discharged.

Be prepared to give your employer the required information. The carrier will need to file a report within 30 days or the incident.

THE HAZARDOUS MATERIALS INCIDENTS REPORT

An accident involving haz mat will be reported both as regular accidents are reported and as a "hazardous materials incident." An accident involving hazardous materials can happen not only on the road but also during loading, unloading, or temporary storage. That is, if a driver is loading a drum of chemical waste product into a van and the drum falls and begins to leak, that incident must be reported. Everything from a damp spot on a haz mat package to a major accident must be reported. The pertinent information will be sent by your carrier to the DOT on a Hazardous Materials Incidents Report form.

Radioactive Materials

If you should ever be called upon **to handle radioactive materials you must have had special training** within the past two years **and routing** information. At the end of the training period you'll receive a certificate. More than an award, the certificate is actually a document. It must be kept with your other papers during the trip.

Under normal shipping conditions, radioactive materials will pose no danger to the driver or to anyone else along the way. Still, you will want to observe the following cautions.

- Limit your contact with radioactive materials. Do what you have to do and then remove yourself from that vicinity.
- Always use a cart or other such equipment to move containers of radioactive materials. Never touch them with your bare hands.

In case of an accident, don't touch or inhale the material. Don't use the vehicle until it's been checked with a survey meter.

At Your Destination

When you have reached your destination, call the dispatcher to announce that you have arrived. Tell the dispatcher what kind of condition your shipment is in. **There is to be no delay when delivering a shipment of hazardous materials.** This includes the time when loading began to the time unloading is finished. Once your cargo has been unloaded, be sure to remove your placards.

Deliver Division 1.1, 1.2, or 1.3 (Class A or B) explosive only to authorized persons or leave the cargo in specially designed locked storage. If the hazardous material shipment is refused or you are unable to unload for 48 hours, you may be told to do any of the following:

- Return it to the shipper.
- Store it in a proper storage area.

Give a hazardous waste shipment only to another registered carrier, or to a treatment facility. Make sure you get the receiver's signature on the manifest, and keep a copy for yourself.

Often the trailer used to transport a haz mat will be contaminated. It must not be returned to service until it has been completely decontaminated at an EPA facility just for this purpose. If you drive such a rig, make sure you find out "where" to decontaminate the trailer once it is unloaded. After a spill of corrosives, vehicles must be washed out before reloading. Vehicles that had a load of Division 2.3 or 6.1 Poison must be cleaned and checked before reuse.

A good rule of thumb when hauling haz mat is this: **if you are** involved in hauling any sort of toxic or poisonous material and **are not sure of something,** stop right there and **call your dispatcher.** Never, ever guess about how to handle potentially dangerous cargo. Never trust in your good luck. You may regret that for the rest of your life.

Chapter 30 Quiz

1. Of the following, _____ is NOT one of the 9 hazardous materials classes.
   A. poisonous gas
   B. pharmaceutical
   C. radioactive waste
   D. flammable liquid

2. Shipping papers must be kept _____.
   A. within reach of the haz mat containers
   B. in the shipper's possession
   C. with the responsible emergency authorities
   D. within the reach of a driver even when wearing a seat belt

3. Labels may be omitted when haz mat shipping containers are shaped in such a way that the labels can't be put on.
   A. True
   B. False

4. The label and placard for an oxidizing material must _____.
    A. have contrasting colors
    B. be the same size
    C. be placed securely on the outside of the trailer
    D. have the same color, number, and wording

5. One standard placard is used for all hazardous materials classes.
    A. True
    B. False

6. After notifying the police and fire department of a haz mat emergency, you can expect members of the _____ to arrive at the scene.
    A. First Response Team
    B. CVSA
    C. National Guard
    D. National Transportation Safety Board

7. At a "safe haven," drivers hauling haz mat cargo can _____.
    A. park their rigs and leave them unattended
    B. enjoy a well-balanced meal
    C. safely transfer the materials to lead-lined packages
    D. forget about the safe handling of their cargo

8. When your vehicle is a cargo tank placarded for Class 3 (flammable liquids) or Class 2 (gases), smoking is allowed only _____.
    A. inside the cab with the windows rolled up
    B. 25 feet away from the rig
    C. after the tank has been emptied
    D. in the vicinity of a safe haven

9. Tire inspection must be done _____.
    A. every 150 miles
    B. by a licensed government inspector
    C. at the beginning of each trip and whenever you park
    D. only at refueling stops and safe havens

10. Containers of radioactive materials _____.
    A. do not leak and are therefore rarely hazardous
    B. require special handling, and often special routes
    C. must be delivered to your dispatcher
    D. may be carefully unloaded at certain safe havens

MAP READING

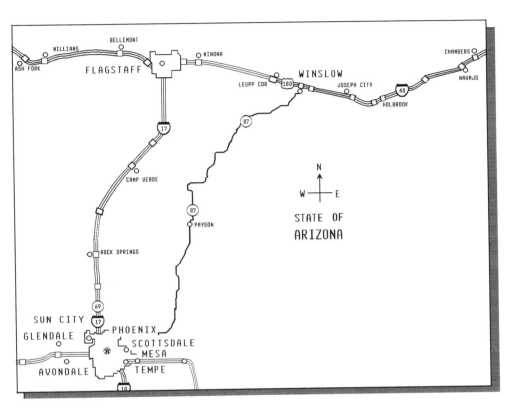

Plan to Have a Good Trip

For the truck driver, a **good trip first means getting to a certain place safely.** After that, it means getting there **in the shortest possible time with the best possible mileage.** To do so means less driving time and less wear and tear on the rig. It also means savings on fuel and on road expenses.

Obviously, a good trip doesn't just happen. It **requires** some clever **planning** with the aid of a good, up-to-date map or road atlas. In fact, learning how to use a map will be one of your basic skills. It's interesting, too. There's no end to the information to be gleaned from a map.

Every driver must know how to read a map. Even if a dispatcher gives you a route to take, you must be able to follow a map. What if construction delays or other problems you run into along the way force you to change your route? If you can't read a map and chart another course, you're stuck.

Map Reading

There's really nothing to reading a map. A map is just a big symbol for some area: the world, a country, state, or city. Other **symbols**—shapes, lines, and pictures—stand in for the real features, the borders, roads, and bridges that unfold before your eyes as you drive.

There are many different maps put out by many different map makers. Most professional drivers, though, will settle on one or two favorites from the several made especially for truckers. These often contain more than the usual types of information you'd expect to find on a map, like the locations of cities and the routes of highways. Truckers' maps also tell you about the locations of weigh scales, size and weight limits, and other facts that are useful mainly to commercial drivers.

The Interstate

Highways are shown by various **lines** in different colors. The lines will grow thinner, ending with a straight black line which indicates a secondary road, country road, or connecting road. A highway may be an ordinary, public sort of road with stop signals and crossroads. Or it may be one of the following:

- limited access (on and off at interchanges only)
- toll (private road, you pay a small fee to pass)
- multi-lane (four lanes or more)

Highway route symbols begin with the interstate symbol, then U.S. highways, then state and local. Some maps will show county and Indian roads. Some will add Canadian and Mexican highway symbols. Each sort of highway is given a distinct shape or design.

If you're used to reading maps, you're already familiar with the red, white, and blue **symbol for** the **interstate highway.** This is a **shield-shaped** form with the name of the state and the highway number inside. The shield shape is just one of many symbols road maps use to show or identify places and things. To read a road map properly, you will have to understand map symbols.

Fortunately, you don't have to memorize them. This is a good thing, since different maps use different symbols. But **every map will have a key, an explanation of the symbols used.** Usually you'll find that near the title or on the first page. The heading will read "Explanation of Map Symbols" or "Roads and Related Symbols" or simply "Highway Route Symbols." There you will find examples of all the symbols used and what each one stands for.

fig. 31-2
Map highway symbols let you know whether to expect a high-speed non-stop through route or a slow, scenic, stop-and-go one.

Explanation of Map Symbols
Roads and Related Symbols

============	Free Limited-Access Highways
======	Under Construction
============	Toll Limited-Access Highways
▬ ▬ ▬ ▬ ▬	Under Construction
============	Other Four-Lane Divided Highways
▬▬▬▬▬▬▬	Principal Highways
───────	Other Through Highways
───────	Other Roads (conditions vary – local inquiry suggested)
───────	Unpaved Roads (conditions vary – local inquiry suggested)
----------	Scenic Routes
90 190 80/90	Interstate Highways
AL17 183 18	U.S. Highways
8 18 14/83	State and Provincial and Country Highways
4 43 147	Secondary State, Provincial and County Highways
N WW	County Trunk Highways
1 20	Trans-Canada Highway, Canadian Autoroutes
5	Mexican and Central American Highways

Interstate highways have a very simple numbering system. Primary routes are given one or two numbers only. The longest routes end in 0 or 5. **Odd-numbered routes run north and south with the lowest numbers in the West. Even-numbered routes run east and west with the lowest numbers in the South.** The four directions will always be indicated by a compass symbol on the map. See Figure 31-2, on the next page, which shows some of the interstates we've just described.

OBSERVATION SKILLS TEST

Can you name the state pictured in the map that began this chapter? How many principal north-south routes were shown? Check your answers with the Observation Skills Test Grid at the end of the book.

Most major cities have loops to the interstate system that allow you to travel around the outskirts of the city rather than through the busy heart of it. Following the loop around a city will allow you to escape heavy downtown traffic. Loops are identified with the same signs as the interstate except the loops will have a three-digit number. For example, look at a map of St. Louis.

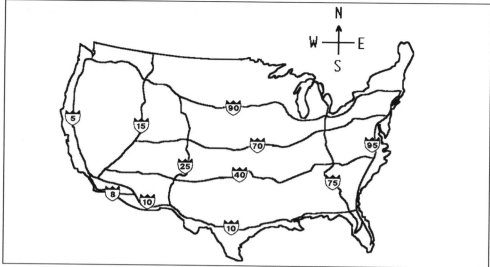

If you were eastbound on I70 you would take loop 270 which skirts the city to the north. Then east of the river a short distance, 270 runs right back into I70 East.

HIGHWAY MILEAGE

Most maps will have several different ways to **estimate mileage between points.** The system your map uses will be explained in the map key, but it usually works like this:

- Distances between intersections and small towns will be shown by a small black number.
- At major intersections and large towns there will be a dart or a dot. Between the darts there will be a larger number (usually printed in red) that shows the distance between the darts.

Some maps show a different way to figure distances on interstates. There will be a number at each interchange (usually a small white box). Each of these numbers indicate how far the interchange is from the state border. You can figure the distance between any two interchanges by subtracting the smaller number from the larger.

HIGHWAY FEATURES

Rest Areas

Something that will become important to you as you begin your driving career is the rest area. Rest areas have parking spaces for large trucks, rest rooms, drinking water, and telephones. Some have special lighted maps and information for the driver. Rest area symbols are often shown as a larger square with a different color from the highway. Truck drivers must **make safety checks** en route. A trained driver will plan ahead to stop **at rest areas** to do this.

Wayside rest stops and roadside parks will often have a picnic table as their symbol. This may mean no rest rooms and some may not have parking space for large trucks.

A service area will have two small triangles or some other marker on each side of the highway to show its location.

Tolls

Toll booths for toll highways or toll bridges will be shown as **TOLL** or indicated by color. This **means you will have to pay a toll charge to use the highway or bridge.** If you'll want to use these, you will also want to have the price of the toll in hand. Some of these highways and bridges do not allow large trucks. You'll want to know about these well in advance.

Tourist Attractions

There are many symbols used for national and state parks, national forests, historical sites, Indian reservations, and so on. These are mostly for the vacation-minded motorists that flock to these areas during the summer months. If it's vacation time, keep in mind these areas will be full of slow moving vehicles. You'll want to change your route to **avoid winter sport areas as well as summer vacation spots.** No trucker wants to be stalled in heavy ski traffic on a snowy day.

Airports and Ferries

Other symbols that are helpful to planning a trip are those used for ferries and airports. Most truckers will use a ferry at least once in their career. Ferries are common in states and provinces that have many lakes, wide rivers, or ocean bays and inlets. Again, there's **often a fee to take a ferry,** and you'll want to plan for that.

Although maps are slightly different, ferries are usually shown with the word "Ferry" or letters "FY" and a dotted line showing their route.

Airports are used when a driver must be dispatched to take over a truck in an emergency. Some owner/operators will fly home for holidays or other reasons. Flying is almost always cheaper than bobtailing your tractor. Airports usually have an airplane symbol.

Time Zones

You'll have to know about different **time zones** to figure the **time difference in another city or state.** A driver can load 40,000 pounds of pickled herring in Halifax, Nova Scotia, destined for Los Angeles. The trip will begin in the Atlantic time zone and will cross four other time zones: Eastern, Central, and Mountain. It will end in Los Angeles which is in the Pacific time zone. Each zone is one hour time difference. When it's 1 P.M. in Halifax, it's 9 A.M. in Los Angeles. Suppose the same driver gets a load in Los Angeles destined for

Atlanta. Atlanta is in the Eastern time zone. When it is 1 P.M. in Los Angeles, it is 4 P.M. in Atlanta.

Drivers must **add or subtract** these hours **to figure** their **ETA (Estimated Time of Arrival).** Your estimated travel time allows you to plan an arrival time. Your ETA is needed by your consignee so labor and space can be scheduled to receive your payload. Also, you don't want to break the world speed record to arrive at a warehouse only to wait a couple of hours for it to open.

Time zones will be shown as a broken line or a line of Ts. Some maps will have a clock face at the lower end of the line. With these you can easily see the difference in local time as you move across zones.

fig. 31-4
The time zone information on maps helps you figure out what local time is.

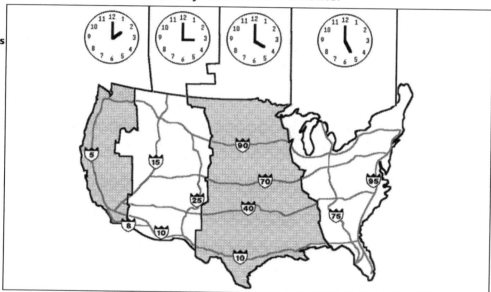

Ports of Entry and Weigh Stations

Finally, one of the newest important symbols for a long distance truck driver is the Port of Entry symbol. Drivers should **be prepared** ahead of time **for entry into another state.** Your **log book must be current** and any **permits** that **have to be shown** should be at hand. A port of entry will often have a scale and an inspection station. A trained driver plans ahead for what can be a time-consuming stop by finding and knowing where the next port of entry is located.

You can get still more information from your map. Dotted lines may be used to show a construction area. A tent symbol usually means a campground. Other symbols show capital cities, bridges, dams, and interchanges. A capital city could be your destination, or a place you would want to stop for services. On the other hand, it could just be a congested area you want to avoid. Either way, you'll want to know it's there. Whatever symbols are used will be explained on the map key.

Designated System

The interstate system and certain state highways make up the National Network of Designated Routes, or the Designated System. The purpose of the system is to provide heavy vehicles with reasonable access on and off the highway from terminals. Some states provide unlimited access to highways. Others control access by permit. Still others make only certain routes available to trucks, and mark those routes with signs. Truckers map books usually have details about the designated system in each state.

Trip Planning

Planning a trip means more than taking any road that gets you there. **Aim to find the shortest** and **smoothest** route. You should plan the **most efficient route** every time, loaded or empty. This is true whether you're an owner/operator or company driver. If you have your own company, of course you'll want to save every penny you can. As a company driver, you should have the same concern for your employer's bottom line. Running a trucking company is a real partnership between you and the boss. If the company goes belly-up, your job goes with it.

Therefore, how do you plan the most efficient route? Well, for starters, make sure your maps are up to date. Check the copyright date next to the publisher's name. If it's more than a year old, get yourself a brand new one. Many changes can occur in a year. You don't want to get caught in a construction area and sit there wasting time, money, and fuel. On the other hand, sometimes a map will indicate that a stretch of road is under construction or is a "proposed route." If the map is not brand new, that work may have already been completed.

CHOOSING A ROUTE

Most of the time, you want to avoid toll bridges, low tunnels, and underpasses. If you have your choice you'll **take a level road instead of a steep grade.** With a truck that costs over a dollar per mile to operate, you don't care to waste time, fuel, or cause undue wear and tear to the equipment. On the other hand, a **toll route might pay for itself if it is the most direct and efficient option.** The only way you can make the right choice is if you have a good map and know what it is trying to tell you.

Your best route does not generally include a scenic highway. These are roads that wind through canyons and valleys, offering gorgeous vistas and thousand-foot drops. They also offer narrow lanes, steep grades, and no shoulders.

On the map, a scenic highway or "historical road" might be shown as "ALT" or "alternate." Sometimes there will be the letter A after the highway number, followed by a dotted line. As a rule, truck drivers are out of place on scenic routes. Leave them to the honeymooners.

Besides maps, another excellent **source of road information is other drivers.** Talk to them about road conditions at rest areas and fuel stops. **Check with your dispatcher** and keep up to date with what's happening along your route. You can make that a give-and-take situation by telling your dispatcher about any road trouble you may have noted along the way.

THE WEATHER

Weather is always a major consideration in trip-planning. You naturally want to avoid killer blizzards, tornados, hurricanes, and floods. Certain freight must not be exposed to extremes of heat and cold, so you'll have to make suitable arrangements to protect it. **There are any number of weather conditions that you may have to plan for.** As with so much else in life, trip-planning is often a matter of your good judgment.

Luckily there is plenty of weather information available to the public. The National Weather Service will issue warnings about storms or other hazardous weather conditions on the rise. Whatever's cooking, it will be well publicized on radio, television, and in the newspaper. Weather information numbers are listed in the first few pages of the telephone book. You need not be caught in adverse weather.

Snow storms are just one of the many things you must plan your way around. With every area of the country there is something to watch out for. In the Rocky Mountain states, high winds are sometimes powerful enough to blow a truck right off a highway. Fog in the Northeast can be so dense that all traffic must come to a halt.

Just remember that **if** you do find yourself **caught by the weather,** don't try to wrestle with it. Instead, find a sheltered area near services and **wait it out.**

Figuring Mileage

Mileage means everything to a truck driver. Companies base cost and income on mileage, and most drivers are paid by the mile. You will also find that drivers tend to see their performance in terms of mileage. They talk a lot about miles driven, miles without an accident, paid miles, and deadhead miles. The challenge is always to improve mileage efficiency.

Most of the time, the most efficient route will be the most direct route. Yet there are times when the most direct route isn't really the best way to go. A highway that may seem to be a shorter distance from your destination could turn out to involve more mileage than you thought. This might be the case if it's a secondary road or full of curves and steep grades.

Such an example is the trip from Phoenix, Arizona, north to Holbrook, Arizona. From the map you would think that cutting straight across on Highway 87 would be shorter than taking the freeway. Not so. The freeway route is only 20 to 30 miles further and much smoother sailing. It also keeps you clear of local Phoenix traffic as well as smaller towns to the north. You will avoid those slow mountain curves and won't get stuck behind a long line of sightseers.

MAP SCALE

On a worst case basis, you'll have to **use the map mileage scale** and a straight edge or ruler **to figure** your **mileage.** All maps are drawn to scale. That is, an inch equals a certain distance, often 100 miles. The map scale will show how many fractions of an inch on the map stand for how much actual distance.

Mark off that fraction on your straight edge. Then use it to measure your route. For instance, say your map has a scale of one-half inch to ten miles. Your route takes up five inches on the map. Some simple arithmetic tells you your actual mileage is about 100 miles.

Your **map book may include** a chart on the **mileage between principal cities.** This gives you the most accurate mileage and driving time. To find the distance between two cities, run your finger down from the city until it meets the line running from the other city.

In other words, to find the mileage from Chicago to Los Angeles, locate Los Angeles on the chart and follow that column until it meets the column running down from Chicago. On a typical chart, the distance between those two cities is 2,113 miles.

Travel Time

Estimated driving time may also be given. Our map book gives an estimated driving time of 41 hours and 22 minutes for the trip just described. Of course, this driving time is using the most commonly traveled routes, within speed limits and under average conditions. Your own driving time will reflect any variations in those conditions.

If a town or city is not shown on a mileage and estimated driving time chart there is another method to find distance and figure out how long the trip will take. Most maps will show miles between dots. The dots will be located at crossroads or by towns and cities. Some maps will show miles between arrows. The miles and arrows will be the same color, usually red. By adding the mileage, you can figure the distance from any town or city to another.

Now that you **know the distance in miles** from Point A to Point B, you must **figure how long it will take you** to cover those miles. That will be your travel time.

Assume you will maintain an average speed of 40 mph. On a freeway you can average 50 mph. Yet after you add in fuel stops, rest stops, safety inspections, and traffic conditions, 40 mph is more like it. In heavy traffic or mountain areas it will drop to 35. Keep your estimate around the 40 mph figure until you have enough experience to figure your own actual driving time.

Now take the total distance and divide it by your average speed (40). The answer will be an estimate of the driving time for the trip. In other words, if you have a 160-mile trip, divide 160 by 40. Your driving time is four hours. To figure your ETA you'll have to add sleeper berth time, loading and un-loading, and anything else that will use up extra time.

All set now? It's really pretty simple. When you finish that first trip on your new job, find out from the dispatcher what the more experienced drivers have been averaging. That will give you something of a goal to work toward.

Chapter 31 Quiz

For Questions 1 through 5, refer to the map of a fictitious state on the next page.

1. What is the name of the capital city?
   A. Center City
   B. Burnsville
   C. West Place
   D. Capital City

2. What interstate goes through this state?
   A. 97
   B. 5
   C. 95
   D. 10

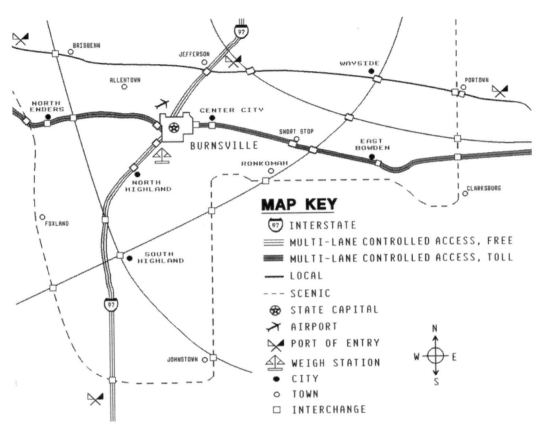

MAP KEY

97	INTERSTATE
≡	MULTI-LANE CONTROLLED ACCESS, FREE
▬	MULTI-LANE CONTROLLED ACCESS, TOLL
—	LOCAL
---	SCENIC
✪	STATE CAPITAL
✈	AIRPORT
⋈	PORT OF ENTRY
△	WEIGH STATION
●	CITY
○	TOWN
□	INTERCHANGE

3. On this map, _____ gives you a clue that this state is in the eastern part of the country.
    A. the compass
    B. the name of the state
    C. the number of the interstate
    D. there's nothing that

4. This state has a weigh station just outside of _____.
    A. Brisbenn
    B. Portown
    C. Burnsville
    D. Jefferson

5. The scenic route is the only east-west route through this state.
    A. True
    B. False

For Question 6, refer to the map below.

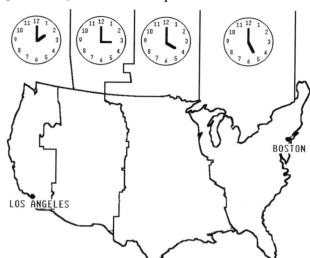

6. If it's 1 P.M. in Los Angeles, what time is it in Boston?
   A. 2 P.M.
   B. 3 P.M.
   C. 4 P.M.
   D. 5 P.M.

7. You should never take a toll route if there is ever another route you could take.
   A. True
   B. False

8. A map scale shows_____.
   A. how many fractions of an inch on the map stand for how much actual distance
   B. how much the map weighs
   C. what all the symbols mean
   D. which route is the most direct

9. If a town or city is not shown on a mileage and estimated driving time chart you can still figure out how long the trip will take.
   A. True
   B. False

10. If you have 400 miles to go, and you're traveling at a steady 40 mph, how long will it take you to complete the trip?
    A. 40 hours
    B. 4 hours
    C. 10 hours
    D. 5 hours

PREVENTIVE MAINTENANCE

The Importance of Preventive Maintenance

Whether you are an owner-operator or a company driver, you should be concerned with preventive maintenance for motor vehicles. Preventive maintenance is important in terms of overall safety and economy. The point of a preventive maintenance program is to **spot a minor problem before it turns into a major problem.** By fixing small problems instead of large ones, expensive repair bills can be prevented.

A preventive maintenance program is going to cost the truck owner or trucking company some money. However, in terms of overall expenses, it's like buying insurance. The company is making sure that expensive towing is rarely needed to rescue a vehicle that's broken down on a run. Plus, it's better to spend a little bit of money in the company's own Maintenance shop than a lot on roadside or outside repair bills.

The idea of saving a lot of money for major repairs by spending a little on a preventive maintenance program must certainly make sense to you. If you've ever owned a car, you've probably put out a little money for upkeep in order to save yourself the expense of a major repair bill. Spending a few dollars to top up the oil now and then is certainly smarter than spending thousands on a new engine because yours seized up for lack of proper lubrication.

Preventive maintenance helps **ensure you'll be driving a safe vehicle.** It's against regulations to take an unsafe vehicle out on the road, and you inspect that vehicle routinely to make sure it's safe. Of course you don't stop with merely inspecting the truck. You have to see that any defects which threaten the safety of the vehicle are repaired. A good preventive maintenance program takes care of minor defects before they become safety hazards.

There are different levels of service checks that help to make a motor vehicle safe for the open road. The checks range from the very basic to the more involved levels which include extensive maintenance work, engine and brake work. Some of these levels involve work that you, the driver can do. Others are jobs for the mechanics.

Driver's Daily Checks

By now you're probably convinced of the wisdom of fixing small problems before they become big ones. So how do you discover these problems? As you might have guessed, you **inspect your vehicle,** and inspect it often.

OBSERVATION SKILLS TEST

Part of preventive maintenance is simply being aware of changes in the condition of your vehicle. Just how aware are you? Did you pay close attention to the first illustration in this chapter? Did you spot any small problems that could develop into larger ones? Check the Observation Skills Test Grid at the end of the book to see just how aware you were.

Of course, you'll inspect your vehicle every time you take it out and bring it back in from a run, as **required by the regulations.** And, if these inspections disclose any defects that could threaten the safety of the vehicle, those should be repaired promptly. Plus, on your report, you'll have a chance to note any other defects you found. Chapter 25 covers these required inspections in more detail.

It may be part of your job to **inspect more thoroughly than regulations require.** You could be responsible for making **daily service checks** on the vehicles you will take out on the road. There is no need to wonder just what your daily service check should include. Your employer will provide you with a schedule of all the items you're expected to check, or it could be in your driver's manual. Often, you'll find this **includes the driver's daily inspection required by regulations.**

Depending on the company you work for, it may be part of your responsibility to **make minor repairs,** or the company shop may do it. You may be required to top up fluid levels, replace blown bulbs, tighten down fittings, and the like. This is no big chore when you are in the yard. But say you're making your check somewhere out on the road, miles from a truck stop? What if you find you're low on coolant, or have a light out? For this reason, it's good to have an emergency repair supply kit on hand. Have a few spare bulbs with you, and perhaps a grease gun. Then, if you use any of your emergency repair kit, don't forget to resupply it the first chance you get.

Your driver's daily service check instructions might read something like the following. This example procedure is listed in one carrier's driver's manual.

POWER UNIT
- Check fuel, oil, and coolant levels. Fill fuel tank to capacity. Add oil to line tractors only if more than one gallon low. Add oil to local diesel only when two quarts low. Coolant may be topped up with tap water in small amounts.
- Check ammeter for proper alternator operation.
- Check all gauges. Oil pressure at operating temperature and rpm must be 30 psi or above. Oil temperature must be between 140 and 250 degrees F. Coolant temperature must be between 150 and 195 degrees F.
- Parking brake should hold vehicle on any grade likely to be operated.
- Low air pressure warning devices should operate at all pressures at and below 60 psi.
- Speedometer should be accurate to within 5 mph of actual.
- Make sure horns work.
- Clean windshield. There should be no cracks over ¼ inch wide or damaged areas larger than ¾ inch.
- Make sure windshield wipers and washers work and add washer fluid if needed.
- Adjust rear view mirrors to show highway along both sides of vehicle.
- Trailer air supply valve knob should stay in when pushed.
- Cab should be equipped with seat belts and accident reporting kit.
- Emergency equipment should be within ready reach. The fire extinguisher shall have been tested within the last 12 months. The cab

should be equipped with spare fuses and three red emergency reflectors or triangles.

- If snowy or icy conditions are expected, there should be tire chains for at least one driving wheel on each side.
- Make sure both high and low beams on headlights work.
- Make sure brakes are adjusted properly.
- Check for proper operation of front clearance lights, identification lamps, and turn signals as required by Sec. 393 Part B, FMCSR.
- Check exhaust system for leaks, burns, charring, or damage to electrical wiring, fuel supply, or other combustible part of the vehicle.
- Service and emergency air hoses and connections must be secured against chafing, kinking, or other damage and must not drag on the frame, fuel tank, or deck plate. Tape must not be used to secure these components.
- No tire shall have fabric exposed through the tread or sidewall, nor less than $\frac{2}{32}$ inch tread depth. Front tractor tires must have at least $\frac{4}{32}$ inch tread depth.
- Check wheels for cracks, or missing or loose studs or nuts.
- Secure brake tubing against chafing, kinking, or other mechanical damage. Check for leaks.
- Brakes must have adequate brake lining on all wheels.
- Check for cracked or broken brake drums, diaphragms, or other air chamber leaks. Have missing, broken, or disconnected parts repaired before vehicle is operated.

fig. 32-1
Check to see you have the required lamps and reflectors, and that they are all operating.

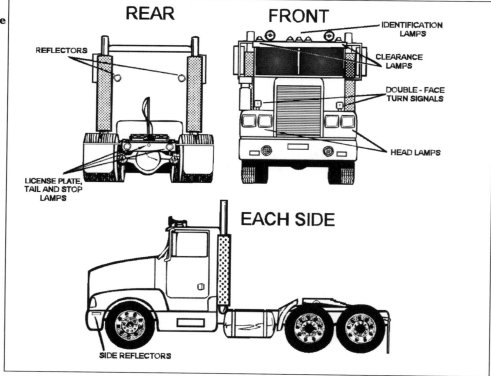

- Check steering for loose or missing nuts or bolts. Check for excessive play. Excessive play is present when too much movement is required at steering wheel before front wheels move from straight-ahead position. For trucks with manual steering, free play should not exceed $2\frac{1}{2}$ inches on a 20-inch steering wheel ($5\frac{1}{4}$ inches of free play is acceptable if you have power steering). For 22-inch steering wheels, the maximum free play is $2\frac{3}{4}$ inches with manual steering, $5\frac{3}{4}$ inches with power steering. Hard steering must be repaired before vehicle is operated.
- Fuel tank must be free of leaks, and have a securely attached cap with gasket.
- Check side marker lamps and reflectors for proper operation as required by Sec. 393 Part B, FMCSR.
- Battery must be covered unless in engine compartment or covered by a fixed part of the vehicle. Cable ends should be clean and fit tightly on clean terminal posts.
- Check rear tractor lamps and reflectors as required by Sec. 393 Part B, FMCSR.
- Check suspension for broken leaves and missing or loose U-bolts. Defects likely to cause an axle shift must be repaired before vehicle is operated.
- Lower half of fifth wheel must be secured and must not shift on frame. Cracks, breaks, loose or missing mounting brackets, or locking devices must be repaired before vehicle is operated.

TOWED UNIT

- Check lamps and reflectors at rear of towed unit for proper operation as required by Sec. 393 Part B, FMCSR.
- Check tires. No tire shall have fabric exposed through the tread or sidewall, nor less than $\frac{2}{32}$ inch tread depth.
- Check wheels for cracks, or missing or loose studs or nuts.
- Secure brake tubing against chafing, kinking, or other mechanical damage. Check for leaks.
- Brakes must have adequate brake lining on all wheels and be properly adjusted.
- Check for cracked or broken brake drums, diaphragms, or other chamber leaks. Have missing, broken, or disconnected parts repaired before vehicle is operated.
- Check right side trailer marker lamps and reflectors for proper operation as required by Sec. 393 Part B, FMCSR.
- There must be no bare, loose, dangling, chafing, or poorly connected electrical wires.

As you can see, this company's program of checks includes the inspection required by DOT regulations, and then some.

fig. 32-2
Required lamps and reflectors for towed units.

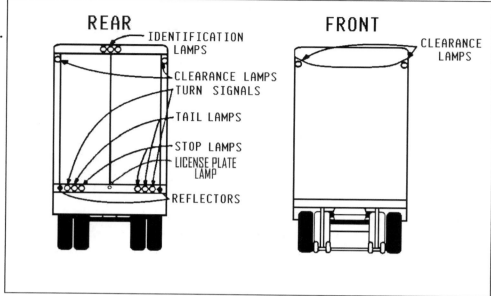

Types of Service Checks

We've talked about your role in finding small problems and getting them repaired before they become big, expensive ones. But that's not all there is to preventive maintenance. There's another aspect to PM. That is when you **give the vehicle service, before it needs repair.** It's **replacing parts before they wear out, or give out.** Here's where the Maintenance Department, and scheduled service, comes in.

There are **different levels of service** for the vehicle you may be driving. They range from taking care of the very basic needs to doing a major overhaul. The most basic is the A level of service. Next is the B level, and so forth.

A vehicle is scheduled for service on the basis of time, or miles, or a combination.

The vehicle you're driving may come due for service while you're out on the road. Your carrier will have given you instructions about what to do in such a case. You may be told to wait until you return to the terminal, or to get it done en route. You may be directed to a particular garage, or told to get the service at a truck stop on your route.

The following will give you a clear idea of what takes place in the different levels of service provided in a good program of preventive maintenance.

PRE-SERVICE CHECK

Before you bring in the truck for service, there are some checks and minor repairs you may want to (or be asked to) make. Many will be covered by the driver's daily service check we outlined in the last section. Here are some others.

Check the starter and charging systems. If your dashboard has a voltmeter, it will read around 11 to 15 volts all the time. If you have an ammeter, it should show a charge right after starting, and when lights and other electrically-powered accessories are in use. Once the engine is started, the alternator should be putting power back into the batteries. The maximum amount of charge should be around 75 amps and no more than 15 volts. You're not likely to see even these maximums unless it's really cold outside or the truck has been sitting for some time. If you do, something's wrong, which calls for further checks.

Inspect the batteries and cables for corrosion. This is probably the most overlooked part of the truck. Starting with the negative side, pull the cable end off the posts. Check for corrosion inside and out, and up inside the insulation cover. Bad cables should be replaced. The insulation will be swollen if there is corrosion under it. Then check the water level in the battery. Even "maintenance free" batteries can run dry. Fill batteries with distilled water. Use tap water only in an emergency. Put the cables back in place tightly, starting with the positive one. These simple steps just might solve the problem, and save some vehicle down-time.

If the batteries and cables are in good shape, and you still have a problem, it could be the regulator on the alternator. The voltage could be set too low. Adjusting the voltage regulator is a job for a mechanic, so your pre-service check of the starting system would end here.

Next, with the engine running, **check the air compressor and governor.** If you listen carefully to the engine, you can hear when the compressor is working, and when the governor cuts out. Your first check is to see that the air pressure builds from zero to 120 psi within five minutes at the most. The governor should cut out with a range of 115 to 130 psi. Stab and release the brakes until the compressor comes on. The governor should cut in again at 100 psi. Faulty operation calls for the attention of a mechanic.

Check the clutch for free play. Move the clutch pedal with your hand. It should start moving easily, then get harder and harder to move. The distance from the pedal's normal position to where it resists movement is the amount of free play, and it should be between one inch and $1\frac{3}{4}$ inch. The company you drive for may want the mechanic to make clutch adjustments.

Your daily service check may have turned up problems with wander in the steering. This could be due simply to a low front tire. You may be able to air up the tire and fix the steering problem with no need for further service.

With the engine stopped, check the engine compartment. **Look for cracked or worn belts.** Pull on them to see if they're too loose. **Look for exhaust leaks** around the exhaust manifold and turbocharger. A black streak is a sign of a leak. You'll want to see that this gets fixed for sure. Exhaust fumes leaking into the cab could make you sleepy or sick, and lead to an accident.

A-LEVEL SERVICE

The A-level service is the **most basic** type of service that can be done. It includes checks and adjustments which you could take care of without any trouble. However, a large carrier company is likely to have the A-level service done on a regular basis in the company shop.

The three primary tasks that are taken care of at this level of service check are:

- tire inspection
- brake inspection
- fluid level checks

The fluid levels which should be checked are the oil, water, power steering, windshield washer, and battery.

Brakes are inspected to ensure both the proper application and release. During a brake inspection, wheel seals can be checked to see that they are not starting to leak or seep. Brake drums can also be checked to make sure that they are not cracked.

An air pressure check is also included in the A-level check. Under DOT regulations, a tractor-trailer is not to lose more than three pounds of air pressure in one minute when the engine is turned off and the service and spring brakes are released. If there is an air leak, repairs can be made at this time.

Tires are checked for proper inflation, and also for tread depth and any uneven or unusual wear patterns. Tread depth must comply with federal safety regulations. Dual tires should also be equal in height to prevent one tire from doing all the work.

Other tasks which are a part of the A-level service include a check of the boxes: transmission and differentials. The vehicle is also checked for any leaks which may be present. The U-joints are checked and so is the emergency equipment: flares, the triangle reflectors, and the fire extinguisher.

B-LEVEL SERVICE

Now, let us take a look at the B-level service. To start with, **everything that takes place in the A-level service also takes place at the B level.** This additional service includes changing the oil, oil filter, and fuel filter.

Today's engines are for the most part equipped with two oil filters. One is the primary filter which is commonly called the full flow filter. The second filter is known as the "by-pass" filter. The full flow filter collects all of the larger pieces of debris that collect in the oil. The bypass filter is a finer filter than the one serving as the primary filter. Its function is to filter out the even finer bits and pieces of debris circulating in the oil system.

When the oil is being changed, a sample of the old oil may be sent to a laboratory for testing. The tests show the amounts of iron, aluminum, dirt, and other forms of debris found in the oil. This debris is scrapings from the engine, the result of wear and tear on various parts. Such tests can reveal much about the condition of the inside of the engine.

Fuel filters are changed one at a time and they should be changed on a regular basis. Their function is to filter out any water or other foreign matter which may be present in the fuel. Clean fuel helps protect the engine.

HIGHER LEVELS OF SERVICE

Other levels of service for the motor vehicle **begin with** the services included in the **A and B levels,** and go on from there. Advanced service levels **include engine tuning, brake change, and changing or rebuilding other components** when called for by wear or failure.

Tuning the engine calls for running the overhead. When this should be done varies, depending on the manufacturer. It involves adjusting valves and injectors. This service is necessary because of the wear and tear placed on the valve stems of the valves and rocker arms. If this adjustment is not made on a regular basis, the result will be a drop in fuel efficiency and possible damage to the engine.

A brake change must be taken care of whenever the lining on the brake shoes reaches $\frac{5}{16}$ or $\frac{1}{4}$ inch in thickness. In the case of trucks that do the same kind of runs day in and day out, the brakes are sometimes changed on a routine basis based on a predetermined amount of miles traveled.

With today's trucks, engines will run strong for a distance of anywhere between 300,000 to 500,000 miles or more. Transmissions and rear ends will generally hold up for a distance of 600,000 to 700,000 road miles.

When an engine is being rebuilt or when engine components are being changed, the radiator is removed and sent to a radiator shop where it will be cleaned both inside and out. This will insure maximum cooling power for the new engine. This is vital to the life of an engine as overheating a new engine can shorten the length of time it could be expected to operate by one half or more.

There are some parts which will go unchanged during this program of regular maintenance. These items include the alternator, starter, and water pump, just to name a few. This is because these components are not subject to much wear. An alternator could last the lifetime of the truck. It would only be changed if it were faulty.

Winterizing and Summerizing

Your vehicle should get special attention for adverse weather conditions. If you'll be driving in very cold weather, you should make sure you have tire chains in good condition. Know how to put them on. Also:

- check the antifreeze level
- make sure the heaters and defrosters work
- use windshield washer antifreeze

For very hot weather:

- double-check the engine oil supply
- check the antifreeze level
- double-check the condition and tightness of the water pump and fan belts
- double-check the condition of the coolant hoses
- check tire pressure

Cleaning the Truck

Keeping the truck clean is a small thing that can be a big help to you in doing inspections and preventive maintenance. It's easier to see early signs of wear on a clean truck. Visit a truck wash now and then. Take advantage of the free truck washes that are sometimes offered with a fill-up.

Keep the engine clean as well. Go that extra mile and get the engine and transmission steam-cleaned now and then. It's easier to spot leaks on a clean engine. Here's why. Before the cleaning, note any fluid leaks or spots. Then clean the engine. In your next inspection, you'll be able to see very easily any fresh deposits. A steam-cleaned engine will also clearly reveal bright spots and rust on the metal parts, signs of premature wear, or poor adjustment. Steam-cleaning isn't cheap, but it's cheaper than an engine overhaul. And that's the point of preventive maintenance.

Chapter 32 Quiz

For Questions 1 through 5, study the tractor sketched below. The arrows point to sites you would inspect as part of the driver's daily service checks. Match those sites, listed in Column A, with the checks you would be making at those points, listed in Column B.

Column A
Service Check Sites

1. _____

2. _____

3. _____

4. _____

5. _____

Column B
Service Checks

A. Check coolant level in radiator and add fluid if need be.

B. Check tread depth on tire.

C. Check steering wheel free play.

D. Check windshield wipers for proper operation and top up windshield washer fluid if needed.

E. Check high and low beams on the headlights for proper operation.

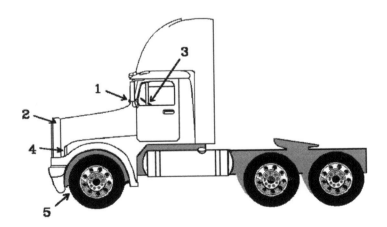

The Maintenance Supervisor for a large carrier is making out a service schedule for the company's trucks. His shop performs three levels of service, A, B, and C, the highest level of service. Five different services are listed on the schedule below. Our Supervisor has put Xs in the boxes to show which services are to be performed at which level, but he hasn't finished the schedule. Complete it by answering Questions 6 though 10.

	A	B	C
brake inspection	X	?	X
check rear end for leaks	X	X	?
change fuel filter	?	X	
run the overhead	X	?	X
change the alternator			?

6. Should a brake inspection be performed at level B?
   A. Yes
   B. No

7. Should the rear end be checked for leaks at level C, the highest level of service?
   A. Yes
   B. No

8. Should the fuel filter be changed at service level A?
   A. Yes
   B. No

9. Should service level B include running the overhead?
   A. Yes
   B. No

10. Should the alternator be automatically changed at level C, the highest level of service?
   A. Yes
   B. No

GETTING A JOB AS A PROFESSIONAL DRIVER

From the Other Side of the Desk

You have probably applied for jobs and gone through some of the steps required to find and get work. Even if you haven't, you know people who have. You have a pretty good idea of what it's like to look for work.

But you probably have not ever had to go through the process of hiring someone else. You have not had to read a stack of applications. You have not had to conduct interview after interview just to find out which of those applicants is best suited for the job.

This chapter will discuss job hunting from the perspective of what it's like to hire someone. Instead of telling you how to look for a job (something you probably already know how to do), **we'll show you how people get hired.** Then, we hope you'll see job hunting in a new light. You'll better understand why certain things are required and desired when you **look at yourself through the eyes of the decision maker** on the other side of the desk. So, for the rest of this chapter, you're not a graduate looking for a job. You're a manager looking for an employee. **Would you hire you?**

Getting Started

First, as a terminal manager or safety supervisor seeking to fill a position, you have to let prospective employees know you have a position available. You usually use one of the ways listed below:

- the want ads
- cold calling
- networking

THE WANT ADS

One way that you try to reach prospective employees is through the want ads in your local newspaper. Want ads often contain a lot of different information. You may list the skills, training, or experience needed to be considered for the job. You may list the duties the person who is hired will have to perform and how much the job pays.

fig. 33-1
When you run a want ad, you expect applicants to read it carefully and follow the instructions exactly.

DRIVERS — Experienced
ABC TRUCKING COMPANY
NEW AJO FACILITY
- Adding 300 new units
- Earn up to 28 cents per mile
- Annual pay increases
- Solo/Husband-Wife Teams welcome

New fully equipped double sleeper Kenworth & Peterbilts. Includes Button & Tuck interior, AM/FM Cassette Stereo, Air Ride, Jake Brake, Air Conditioning & Power Steering. No truck is older than 2 years.
- Full Time Rider policy for spouse
- Mileage, unloading, stop & layover pay
- Stock purchase program
- Many other mileage & safety bonuses
- Must be 23 years/older
- Applications will be accepted Monday between noon and 5 P.M.

ABC Trucking Company
123 Elementary Avenue
Ajo, AZ 85321

However, your ad at least tells what job is available and how to apply for it or how to find out more about it. The information on how to apply may be very brief or it may be quite detailed. It may be only a telephone number, or it may include dates, times, and the location for picking up applications.

You expect applicants to **follow** whatever **instructions** you put in your ad. If the ad says applications can be made on Monday between noon and 5 p.m., you will not see the dingbat who shows up on Monday morning or on Tuesday. If it says apply in person only, you will not be accepting phone calls. After all, you do not want to hire someone who can't follow the simple instructions in a little want ad. Such a person is unlikely to be able to follow complicated instructions on the job.

If an applicant heard about your company through an ad, you'll want to know so you can see how effective those ads are.

COLD CALLING

Although the want ads are a good way to attract applicants, you often fill a job without ever running a want ad. Sometimes, the very person you're looking for happens to call you or walk in the door at just the right time. They're cold-calling—simply **calling** on the telephone or **at the company in person** "cold," **without knowing if a specific job is available.**

Like many managers, you have a policy of taking applications even when you're not looking for a driver. For you, the **application is the first screening** for people you hire. If the application meets your standards, you put it on file. That can save you time later if you need to conduct interviews and find a new driver fast.

If you are looking for a driver, you have cold callers come in to fill out an application. That way, you can get a quick look at them. There are some you will eliminate right away, no matter how good their application makes them look. For instance, take a look at Figure 33-2.

fig. 33-2
A cold caller arriving at your company to fill out an application.

Unfortunately for this applicant, you see her arrive. There is no way in the world you are going to hire this person. If that's how she takes care of her car, you wonder how she'll take care of your equipment!

NETWORKING

Another way job seekers find out about jobs in your company is networking. **Someone you know tells you about someone they know who is looking for a job.** Some of the people who come in to fill out an application have a relative who works in the trucking industry, and that person was part of their network. People who work around trucks or drivers may have been part of their network too, even if they don't work directly in the trucking industry. For instance, maybe the job hunter heard about your company from a waitress who pours coffee for some of your drivers.

THE APPLICATION

The first contact you have with a job seeker is the application. Your secretary has taken the phone calls and given out the blank applications. Now you have to go through the completed applications to decide whom to interview.

The first thing you do is scan the applications quickly. You **throw away** the ones that are **incomplete or messy.** You don't want to hire drivers who aren't going to take their paperwork seriously. As a carrier, you can be fined if your drivers don't fill out their papers correctly! Someone who is sloppy enough to bring back an application with coffee stains all over it will probably make a mess of your equipment, too, so you just reject this applicant.

The next thing you do is look quickly to see that all sections on the application are filled out and that it is signed. You know that the **DOT requires** you to provide the **application,** and that it must get at least the information listed below:

- name, address, birth date, and social security number
- the applicant's addresses for the last three years
- the date the application is submitted
- the issuing State, number, and expiration date of license or permit issued to the applicant
- how much and what kind of experience the applicant has had in operating motor vehicles, including the type of equipment used
- all motor vehicle accidents the applicant has been involved in for the past three years, including the date and nature of each accident, and any deaths or injuries involved
- all violations of motor vehicle laws and ordinances, except those involving only parking, for which the applicant has been convicted or forfeited bond or collateral during the last three years

- a statement giving the details of any denial, revocation, or suspension of any license or permit, or a statement that no denial, revocation, or suspension has occurred
- the names and addresses of the applicant's employers for the last ten years, along with the dates of employment and reasons for leaving each job

fig. 33-3
Here's a portion of two applications. Which person would you interview?

An Equal Opportunity Employer
Application For Driving Employment

Please print plainly and complete all blanks

Date *March 31* 19 *90*

Name ___*John*___ ___*H.*___ ___*Carrier*___   Telephone *(602)242-7860*
   last   First   middle   area code   number

Position Applied For *Driver*_____   Soc. Sec. No. *423-78-1234*

Present Address *742 2nd Drive   Ajo   Az 85321*   How Long? *7 yrs*
               street   city   state & zip code

ADDRESS)   *Same as above*_____   How Long? _____
FOR   )   street   city   state & zip code
PAST)   *Same as above*_____   How Long? _____
FIVE)   street   city   state & zip code
YEARS)

(Attach sheet if more space is needed)

Are you under 23 or over 69 years of age? *No*   If yes, date of birth _____

Have you previously applied for employment with this firm? *No* When? _____

Names of relatives in our employ *None*   Who referred you? *Jack Higgins*

Rate of pay expected *The Going Rate*

An Equal Opportunity Employer
Application For Driving Employment

Please print plainly and complete all blanks

Date *3/31* 19 *90*

Name ___*Jamie*___ ___*L.*___ ___*Smith*___   Telephone *(602)543-8211*
   last   First   middle   area code   number

Position Applied For *Driver*_____   Soc. Sec. No. _____

Present Address *895 Ad.   Phoenix Az 852*   How Long? *1 yr.*
               street   city   state & zip code

ADDRESS)   *176 1st Street #44 Phoenix Az 85721*   How Long? _____
FOR   )   street   city   state & zip code
PAST)   _____   How Long? _____
FIVE)   street   city   state & zip code
YEARS)

(Attach sheet if more space is needed)

Are you under 23 or over 69 years of age? *Yes*   If yes, date of birth *1/14/72*

Have you previously applied for employment with this firm? *No* When? *Want Ad*

Names of relatives in our employ *No*   Who referred you? *Want Ad*

Rate of pay expected *?*

Plus, the applicant has to sign and date a statement that says, "This certifies that this application was completed by me, and that all entries on it and information in it are true and complete to the best of my knowledge."

Even though all applicants are required to sign this statement, you have learned from experience that sometimes people lie on their application. Because of that, your **company checks out all information on the application** from education and driving experience, to personal references and traffic violations. The ones who lie always get caught and never get hired.

You throw away any applications that are not signed, or that have information missing from one of the areas required by the DOT, but you still have a stack of applications to consider. You continue to narrow down the number of people you want to interview.

You look to see which applications are filled out neatly (printed or typed). You are impressed by the applicants who took the time to make their work look first rate. You are also impressed by applicants who sent a cover letter explaining things that weren't covered on the application.

You look at experience, but you don't reject people just because they haven't worked a lot in the industry. Some of your best drivers have come right out of school. You hired them because they were **eager and enthusiastic** about the job and because they took the time to be **neat and accurate.** If you have to choose between two applicants who are pretty evenly matched in training and experience, you will interview the one who has filled out the application neatly and completely.

The Interview

Now it's time for the next step in the hiring process. You've decided whom you want to interview, and your secretary has scheduled the appointments. During the interview, you want to be sure the applicant has the basic skills and training to do the job. You will be looking for some other things as well:

- How does the applicant look? Is this someone you would want your customers to meet every day?
- Does the applicant have the required documents to go to work?
- Is the applicant prepared for the interview? Has he or she learned anything about your company before coming in?
- How well does the applicant communicate? Is this someone you can count on to find or give the information needed to do the job well?

OBSERVATION SKILLS TEST

Think back to the picture at the beginning of this chapter. How many applicants were waiting for interviews? Which applicant do you think will get the job? Now turn to the Observation Skills Test grid at the back of the book to see how you did.

THE FIRST CONTACT

Of course, the **first contact** anyone looking for work has with your office is **with** your **secretary.** You've asked your secretary to take notes regarding the following items about these first contacts:

- phone manners
- personal manners and appearance
- what questions they ask

You are impressed by applicants who have good manners, a neat appearance, and who ask the right questions. One of the right questions is, "What does the company want from new applicants? Should I mail my application in, or bring it with me?" You are impressed by job seekers who are interested in what they can do for the company and not just what the company can do for them.

You have a list of things to check even before you actually talk to the applicant. Was the applicant:

- on time?
- clean and well groomed?
- neatly and appropriately dressed?

You don't expect or even want your applicants to wear suits and ties or dresses and high heels. That's not necessary since it's not how truck drivers dress for work. You do expect them to show up for the interview **dressed as if** they were **going to work that day.** You expect them to look and act as if they were meeting your customers. That means showing up on time, checking in with your secretary, and being **polite** not only to you but to your secretary and **to anyone** else **they come in contact with.** You aren't interested in someone who puts on a good face for the boss and is rude to everyone else.

REQUIRED DOCUMENTS

There are some documents that you **must have before you can put someone to work.** Anyone who is serious about the job will have them (or copies of them) available at the interview. They are:

- current CDL
- a social security card
- driving record current to the last 30 days
- proof of citizenship or right to work in this country (a green card)
- any other licenses or permits needed to do the job
- valid medical card

BEING PREPARED

If an applicant has shown up unwashed, sloppily dressed, without the license or driving record needed to do the job you're looking to fill, the interview will be very short. However, if the applicant still looks like someone you might want to hire, the interview will help you find out some more about this person.

You have learned that next to good driving skills, perhaps the single most **important attribute is attitude.** Someone with a positive outlook on the job and a willingness to learn new things can work out well.

NOW FOR THE INTERVIEW

First, you ask questions to find out how much the applicant knows about your company or the industry in general. You are impressed if the applicant took the time to **call the local motor truck association for information or go to the library and look up** the **things** that have been written in business or trade magazines **about the company.** That shows a willingness to go "above and beyond the call of duty" in order to do the best job possible.

Next, you encourage applicants to talk about **jobs held in the past**, even if they weren't in the trucking industry. You have been in the business long enough to know that there are many qualities of a good employee that show up in any job.

When applicants respond by putting down their last boss, telling you how stupid the people they had to work with were, or bragging about how they walked off the job when things didn't go their way, you know to keep on looking for someone else to hire.

Some applicants may be dreaming of becoming a solo over-the-road driver when all you have to offer right now is second seat driving or local deliveries. If someone is too good for anything but the best, you aren't interested. But if an applicant is **willing to start at the bottom and work up** as better jobs become available, then this just might be the person you hire.

During the interview, you encourage applicants to talk about their goals. These are some kinds of information you will be looking for:

- Have they really thought about what they want to do for a living, or are they just filling out applications?
- Are they sincerely interested in your company, or are they just killing time until a job opens up somewhere else?
- Do they really want the kind of work your drivers do?
- Do they plan to stay with one company as long as possible, or will they move from place to place if something else looks a little better?
- What do they hope to be doing in five years?
- Do their goals fit with your company's goals?

This stage of the interview will help you find answers to these questions.

COMMUNICATING

During the interview, you will be paying attention to how well the applicants communicate. You will be listening to what they say and how they say it. You will be evaluating their verbal skills as well as their body language.

Verbal Skills

You are looking for drivers who can **speak clearly and calmly** when dealing with the many situations that can come up in the course of the job. You aren't expecting speech makers, of course, but you do want someone who won't get flustered and confused whenever there is a little pressure. Many people are nervous in an interview, so now is a pretty good time to see how they do. You have learned from doing interviews that the better prepared an applicant is and the more interviews an applicant has been to, the more relaxed and effective that applicant is.

Body Language

You know that communication is more than words. You've seen plenty of applicants who had good references and sharp looking applications who came into your office and slouched in the chair. Or, they just couldn't seem to get their head off their chest and look you in the eye. Or, they crossed their arms and refused to unbend them during the entire interview. Those applicants rarely got hired. You knew that those types of body language said negative things about those applicants, things like, "I'm not really interested in being here," and "I'm not good enough to be here. There's something wrong with me," and "I'm hostile or frightened."

Your customers and others are aware of body language, even though they may not be able to identify certain types of behavior. You want drivers who say positive things about themselves and your company not only with their words, but with how they carry themselves. You will hire applicants who **sit up straight, hold their head up, look you in the eye, and appear relaxed and confident.** You want drivers whose manner says, "I'm proud of myself and my employer. We're a winning team!"

Tests

The last thing you discuss with the applicants is the tests they **must pass** in order to work for your company. Of course, since they have their CDL, they have already passed at least **the required commercial driver general knowledge and skills tests.** You check to make sure they have a Group A Combination Vehicles CDL without an air brake restriction. This tells you drivers are - licensed **to drive heavy tractor-trailer combinations equipped with air brakes.** The different codes on their license tell you that some even have endorsements for hazardous materials (code H), tank vehicles (code N), and doubles and triples (code T).

Driver applicants **must** also **meet DOT qualification requirements.** They must:

- be at least 21 years old
- read and speak English well enough to talk with the general public, understand highway signs, respond to officials, and fill out reports and records
- be able to operate the vehicle safely
- be able to tell whether cargo is distributed properly
- be able to secure cargo in the vehicles they drive
- meet the physical qualifications set by the DOT
- have a single valid commercial motor vehicle operator's license
- have notified you of any violations or certified that there are none to report
- not have been disqualified to drive a motor vehicle

Next are the **DOT physical,** a **drug test,** and your **company's own exam.**

THE DOT PHYSICAL

The DOT requires drivers to meet certain physical standards. Your company has no choice about these. People who do not meet them cannot be hired to drive. Most of your applicants will already have a current DOT medical card, but your company requires all new drivers to undergo a physical examination at your expense. You tell your applicants this.

THE DRUG TEST

You explain the law requires you to test all driver applicants for drug abuse. Your company has applicants give a urine sample which is tested for marijuana, cocaine, opiates like heroin, amphetamines (speed), PCP (phencyclidine), and other controlled substances, and for alcohol use. You also tell all applicants that the company retests every driver at random, as the law requires, and that drug tests are given following an accident or for reasonable suspicion.

THE COMPANY EXAM

Your company requires yet another written test of new drivers. It covers basic arithmetic and problem solving skills. Most of the applicants who make it through your thorough interviewing process have no trouble with this test, but you let the applicants know it's coming.

After the Interview

By the time you have read the applications and interviewed some of the job seekers, you have a pretty good idea who you want to be the next driver hired by your company. Sometimes there are two or more who are closely matched, and you have a tough choice. Which of these well-qualified applicants will you choose? However, sometimes an applicant will do one more thing that impresses you. Sometimes an applicant will **send a thank-you letter.**

You've heard a lot of people say that thank-you letters are old fashioned and that no one sends them any more, especially in business. But sometimes an applicant takes the time to send just a short note thanking you for the time you took to review the application and conduct the interview. You're glad somebody on that side of the desk appreciates the amount of work you do to help them get a job!

Of course, you aren't going to hire an unqualified person just because you got a thank-you letter. But courtesy counts. If you have to choose between two equally qualified people, you will choose the most courteous one.

fig. 33-4
Thank-you letters are still a good idea, and they can make the difference in getting a job.

ABC Trucking Company

April 1, 1996

123 Elementary Avenue

Ajo, AZ 85321

Attn: Ned Seer, Safety Supervisor

Dear Mr. Seer:

Thank you for the interview on Wednesday, March 31, 1996, regarding the position as driver trainee with your company. I appreciate very much the time you took to speak with me about your company and its plans for the future. I would like very much to work for a company like yours that has 100 percent customer satisfaction and accident-free operation as its main goals. If you need any more information about my qualifications or background, please call me at the number on my application.

I look forward to hearing from you about this position, and I wish you luck in finding a driver who fits your needs regardless of your choice.

Sincerely,

Lee Looker

Back to Your Side of the Desk

Well, that's it! You've seen what it looks like from the other side of the job-hunting process. You've seen some of the things you would learn to look for if you were the one getting ready to hire a driver. This experience has given you a better idea of how to make your application and your interview result in the job you want. Good luck!

Chapter 33 Quiz

1. The first contact a driver looking for work usually has with a company is with the _____.
    A. CEO
    B. the terminal manager
    C. the terminal manager's or safety supervisor's secretary
    D. the coffee shop waitress

Fill in the blank in Questions 2, 3, and 4 with the either A, B, or C from the following list.
    A. Networking
    B. A want ad
    C. Cold calling

2. _____ at least tells what job is available and how to apply for it or how to find out more about it.

3. _____ is hearing about a job or a job applicant from friends and acquaintances.

4. _____ is calling on the telephone or arriving at the company in person without knowing whether or not a specific job is available.

5. If an application is incomplete or too messy, the applicant will probably be_____.
    A. asked to try again
    B. called for an interview anyway
    C. rejected
    D. called in and offered help in filling it out

6. Managers always hire the drivers with the most experience.
    A. True
    B. False

7.   Applicants should dress for an interview as if they were going to work that day.
      A. True
      B. False

8.   Next to good driving skills, perhaps the single most important attribute of a driver is _____.
      A. mechanical ability
      B. a good attitude
      C. an expensive wardrobe
      D. polished public speaking skills

9.   Only driver applicants from out of state have to take a drug test.
      A. True
      B. False

10.   After the interview, it's a good idea for applicants to

      _____.
      A. call back every morning to see if the manager has made a decision
      B. send flowers
      C. send a thank-you letter
      D. wait for the manager to call

CHAPTER 34

THE DRIVER'S LIFE

It Takes a Little Extra Planning

It's quite an adjustment to start on a new job that requires you to "camp out" for sometimes weeks on the road. That gives you a great deal to plan and arrange for. First, there are the basics of food, exercise, hot showers, and other personal care to think about. **Things that are easy and convenient to do at home take a little planning to get done on the road.** You'll have to know where and how to obtain these necessities, and how to budget for them.

Then, throughout all of this, you must also see that things continue to run smoothly at home. That means finances and bill-paying must be organized. It also means keeping things sunny between you and every member of your household. When you're away from home, this takes a little extra planning and effort.

Managing Your Time

Your job on the road will include taking care of yourself, your truck, and your cargo. That's quite a bit to handle. It's a good idea to have a note pad and pencil handy to jot down your list of "Things To Do" as you think of them. You can divide the list into those three categories: self, rig, and cargo. Schedules will help you keep yourself organized on the road.

Most drivers are very careful with their time. They try to avoid the busy hours at the truck stops and cafes. After a while you will learn which truck stops are better and more efficient than others. If the little place where you were planning to have dinner is very crowded, you might be wiser to drive down the road and find another one. If you do have to wait in line for a shower or for a fuel island, use the time to do a tire and safety check. **Turn waiting time into productive time** whenever you can.

If you have your "To Dos" uppermost in your mind, or on your list, you can plan how to spend your stops so you can **get several chores done at one time.** Have to stop to make a check-in call? This would be a good time to top up your fuel supply as well. It will save you yet another stop a few hours later.

Managing Your Road Money

Most companies will have you use a fuel credit card. It will have a prearranged credit or mileage limit. Or, your employer may have select stations where you are to stop for fuel or service.

If you pay cash for fuel, you'll have to learn to **budget your money** so it will last the whole trip. Check your road atlas for the mileage you'll have to cover on your road money. When you're estimating how much fuel you'll need, always figure the highest possible cost per gallon, and take your lowest average miles per gallon. That way you'll be covered.

For example, if the trip will be 2,000 miles and you know your top fuel price will be $2.40 and your worst mileage is 5 mpg, use this formula:

- 2,000 miles divided by 5 mpg = 400 gallons of fuel; then
- 400 gallons X $2.40 per gallon = $960.00

So you'll have to set aside $960 for fuel. (It could end up costing you less, but you can't count on it until your trip is run.) If you're starting out with $1,100, that'll leave you $140 for other expenses.

Your other main expense is for food. If the trip will take you three days, and you allow $25 per day for meals, your food should cost you $75. Many drivers cut food costs nearly in half while enjoying greater nutrition by making some of their own meals. We'll discuss this more in a later section of this chapter.

SAVE YOUR RECEIPTS!

Make sure you **get a receipt** for every penny you spend. Your company must have a receipt in order to reimburse you. If for some reason you are not automatically given a receipt for a purchase, ask for one and don't leave until you get it. The receipt must list the products bought, showing the date and the name and address of the seller. Most trucking companies require the driver to sign the receipt as well.

Then carefully place your receipts for each trip in a separate zipper wallet or bag. Make this your custom and practice. Handle your receipts like money, for that is what they are once you have turned them in at the end of your trip.

EMERGENCY EXPENSES

There may certainly come a time when you'll have to arrange for more road money than you have on hand. You might have been fined for some reason, lost your cash, or had to pay for a new tire. In such an emergency, call your dispatcher and explain the situation.

Companies usually use a money service. The dispatcher will give you a code number to use with other identification in claiming your money at a money service location (usually a truck stop). When the clerk verifies your request, you'll get a check for the amount sent, less a service charge. You may cash the check at once or hold it until you need it.

Those drivers who carry large amounts of cash are living dangerously. Do not flash a big wad of bills up and down the highway. For your safety and peace of mind, we advise that you **carry traveler's checks** instead.

Physical Fitness

Exercise is one of the best things you can do for yourself. You don't need fancy designer workout gear to do it, nor do you need to take instructions from a movie star. Exercise is free and any driver can and should get some form of it. In fact, it would be hard to say too much about the body's need for daily exercise. That need is even greater when you've got a high-stress job and you're sitting on your caboose all day.

If you already get plenty of exercise, we don't need to tell you how much your body appreciates it. You are well aware of the difference it makes in both your physical and mental powers.

If you've been on the verge of getting more exercise, but haven't quite gotten around to it, there's no time like the present! Even if you spend only 20 minutes a day, it's a small investment for a very fine payoff.

With exercise, circulation is improved and the muscles are kept firm. The brain cells work at their best because your heart and lungs are strong and fit. The strong, healthy heart pumps the blood to the lungs. Your blood picks up oxygen from the lungs and carries it to the brain cells. (Sounds like another branch of the transportation industry!)

OBSERVATION SKILLS TEST

Do you recall the truck stop pictured at the start of this chapter? Will the driver be able to pay for his purchase with a credit card? How much do showers cost? Turn to the Observation Skills Test Grid at the end of the book to check your answers.

That oxygen supply to the brain is what **makes it possible for you to think and act quickly.** When you don't get a good supply of oxygen because you've been at a standstill for too long, your brain cells don't operate at their best. As a result you feel dull, weak, and slightly depressed. At such times your thoughts turn to a candy bar or a cola drink. That will certainly pick you up for a short time, but it's like kicking a dead horse. What your body really needs is a good workout. That will get the circulation going again.

What sort of exercise fits into a trucker's life? Clearly, it's got to be portable. You may enjoy swimming, weight lifting, or tennis. But if you can't easily get to a gym, you won't get to exercise very often.

Fortunately, brisk walking or jogging are excellent for keeping you fit. You can do that just about anywhere, any time you find some open space. Get into the habit. Look forward to it. Aim to get in a half-hour walk or run every day.

Slow, easy stretches will help keep you limber. They'll help you relax when you need to sleep. There are good stretching exercises you can perform while you're outside inspecting your truck. For some suggestions, buy yourself an exercise manual or video for a few dollars.

THE FOOD OF CHAMPIONS

Exercise and the right foods just naturally go hand in hand. Experts have been saying that it's not how much food you eat, but the kind that is important. If you choose the right foods, you can eat just about as much of it as you would like. So what is the food of champions? We're talking about **whole grains, lean meat, and lots of fresh produce.** That definitely does not include packaged "food" products full of chemical additives.

When you look at Figure 34-1, you may be surprised to see many of the foods you eat now in the EAT LESS list. Aim to **eat very little processed and more fresh food.** Look for foods that are **low in salt, sugar, caffeine, and fat.** You'll feel better for it. You'll get sick less often, recover faster when you do, and your work will simply be easier to do in general. It's a little tougher when you're on the road all the time, but it can be done.

Unless you've got one of those small refrigerators in your sleeper, get yourself an ice chest. That way you can stop at a supermarket for a good supply of juices, salad vegetables, low-fat dairy products, and sandwich fixings. Whenever you get a chance, stop at a produce stand or farmer's market along the road. One trick with eating right is always to have something healthful on hand so that you won't be tempted to make do with junk food. Junk food is just too handy, while a healthy diet takes a little bit of planning.

Learn to read the list of ingredients in the food you buy. Ingredients are listed in order from most to least. So when sugar is the first on the list, that means the product contains more sugar than anything else. By reading the ingredients on a box of doughnuts you see that you're getting mainly sugar, lard, bleached flour, and chemicals. Doughnuts don't sound quite so delicious now, do they?

Once you develop a taste for real food, you won't want anything to do with things like boxed doughnuts. The foods on the EAT LESS list will start to taste like what they are: greasy, sugary junk. You don't have to make all these changes overnight. Just do what you can, gradually. Start by exercising just a few minutes a day, until you feel you can and want to do more. Improve your diet by eating just a little less of this, a little more of that. Over time, lots of little changes will add up to big, important changes. Your body will reward you with greater health and alertness. But don't take our word for it. Find out for yourself!

Fatigue

Fatigue sets in when you deprive your body of its proper amount of sleep. Proper eating and exercise as just described will help your system ward off fatigue. Fatigue can easily overcome your senses when they are weakened by bad eating habits and the lack of exercise.

FOR ENERGY AND GOOD HEALTH

EAT MORE

  whole grains (oatmeal, whole wheat)
  low-fat and skim milk products (low-fat cottage cheese,
     mozzarella cheese, yogurt)
  unsalted nuts and plain (no butter, no salt) popcorn
  fresh or dried fruit
  fresh vegetables
  unsweetened juices
  lean meats, poultry, and fish

EAT LESS

  white bread
  sugary soft-drinks
  ice cream, whipped cream, American cheese
  candy bars, cakes, cookies, doughnuts, and pastry
  fried foods
  cold cuts, sausage, and bacon
  fatty cuts of pork (like ribs) and beef (like hamburger)

The best way to combat fatigue is to get the proper amount of sleep. Sleep is a vital human function. When your body is deprived of food and water your brain sends out specific signals–hunger and thirst–to cause you to meet these needs by eating food and drinking water. Similarly, your body's response to lack of sleep is sleepiness.

Don't ignore this signal! A brain deprived of sleep for a prolonged period will respond by shifting uncontrollably from being awake to being asleep. The sleepier you get the more often your brain makes these shifts. The periods of sleep can be very short, only a few seconds long, and are called microsleeps. Or, sleep periods can last for minutes. Short or long, you are unable to process or react to anything going on around you. At 60 miles per hour you are traveling 88 feet per second. If you fall asleep for even one second, many things you don't want to miss can happen in those 88 feet!

Sleep loss accumulates into sleep debt. A person who requires eight hours of sleep and gets only six is sleep deprived by two hours. Sleeping only six hours a night over four nights, the two hours of sleep loss per night accumulates into an eight hour sleep debt.

It is your responsibility to be well rested, sleep-debt free, before you are dispatched on a run.

THE CIRCADIAN CLOCK

You have a "clock" in your brain that regulates your bodily functions and behavior on a 24-hour basis, and this includes your sleep/wake patterns. For example, you may be programmed to sleep at midnight, wake up at eight A.M., and stay awake all day with one afternoon sleepiness period.

But when this circadian clock is tampered with, like being put in a new time zone, it does not adjust right away. This explains the problem of "jet lag." Also, your body's internal rhythms, like digestion and mood, don't adjust all at the same time.

Day/night reversal also upsets the circadian clock. Moving from day shift to night shift and back again forces the clock to readjust constantly. Combining the two changes–moving between time zones and changing work shifts–makes the problem even worse. You feel the results in restless sleep, sleepiness during wake periods, and poor performance.

Science shows there are two periods of significant sleepiness in every day: nightly, between three and five A.M., and in the afternoon, again at three and five. If you are scheduled to drive at night when your clock is set for sleep, you will be fighting sleepiness the whole time. And, if you try to get your sleep when your clock is set for wakefulness, you won't rest well. By the same token, if you can take a nap when your clock is set for sleepiness, you will be in tune with this natural rhythm.

The bottom line is to take sleepiness seriously. Be aware that if you must work when your body wants to sleep you will be at a disadvantage. Don't make the situation worse with a poor diet or lack of exercise, or worse yet, with alcohol and drugs that dull the senses and slow your reactions.

Your State of Mind

To a large extent, your **mental attitude reflects your physical condition.** It also works the other way around. Your **physical condition will reflect your mental attitude. Both will affect your driving.**

A truck driver's attention must be devoted to safety and to the task at hand. Therefore, when a personal problem gets you down, it must be dealt with as soon as possible.

Whether you call it being in the dumps, or having the blues, or feeling like you're boxed in with nowhere to turn, most of us know the feeling. The main thing to remember is that you can help yourself. So if you're just not able to get out from under your problem, do something about it!

What should you do? Well, that depends on the nature of the problem and how serious it is. Very often, some strenuous physical activity can put things in order, or at least restore your confidence and help you to cope. Then again, sometimes exercise just isn't enough.

Whatever's going on inside you, it's important to get it out in the open. If it's a family problem, or trouble brewing with a loved one, you should talk it out with that person. You know what they say, an unspoken complaint becomes a rock in the stomach. If for some reason it's not possible to talk things out with the party in question, talk to someone else. You may have a trusted friend, a relative or a minister who could help. If that doesn't work, a professional counselor might.

There are advantages to talking with a counselor. Sometimes it's easier to talk to a complete stranger. Sometimes we can be more honest. Look in the Yellow Pages under "counseling." There you will find local agencies that offer help for very little money or for whatever you're able to pay.

Counselors are generally very good listeners and skilled at helping people sort out their lives. Just remember that a lack of funds should never keep you from asking for professional help.

If you need a few days off to get yourself back together, talk to your boss. Let him or her know that the problem is affecting your ability to do your job. Bosses are reasonable, safety-minded people. They will appreciate your honesty. They will be glad that you're intelligent enough not to risk disaster on the road when you're not at your best.

THE JOB-RELATED PROBLEM
Now if it's a job-related matter, don't grumble about it to your family or to other truck drivers. Talk to someone in the company. If you don't know who that should be, ask your dispatcher to refer you.

Be honest about your problem. Don't worry about rocking the boat. Good drivers are a valuable resource and companies are very interested in keeping the ones they've got. They understand that these things will come up. After all, most employers are actually human!

DRUGS AND ALCOHOL
The worst thing you can do is to mask your feelings with drugs or alcohol. We're not talking about a situation in which you take your spouse out to

dinner and enjoy a bottle of good wine or a cocktail. We're talking about drinking or pill-popping on the road.

Never drink on duty. Don't even have any alcoholic drink four hours before going on duty; not beer, not wine, not liquor. A 12-ounce glass of beer or a five-ounce glass of wine affects you just as much as a $1\frac{1}{2}$ ounce shot of liquor. This is true for everyone. People who claim they can hold their liquor are just kidding themselves.

Drugs and alcohol can end up costing you just about everything you care about, including your entire career as a commercial driver. **Drugs and alcohol will wreck your health and distort your judgment.** When your judgment goes, you have become a bad driver. Even worse, you don't realize how bad you are. While you sit behind the wheel risking life and limb of yourself and others, the drug or the booze has given you a false sense of well-being. Once drugs and alcohol are in your system, there's nothing you can do to lessen their effects except allow enough time to pass for them to work their way out of your system. Coffee won't help, and neither will fresh air.

What it boils down to is this. There's no possible excuse for taking any drug or alcoholic beverage while you're on the job. No, not even to stay awake. If you're exhausted, it's sleep you need.

Remember, too, that **even legal drugs can affect your driving.** Many cold and allergy remedies will make you drowsy. If you're taking a prescription for any medical condition, be sure and **ask your doctor about side effects.**

Running Your Home from the Road

If you have someone at home while you're away, it may be that person who keeps the bills paid on time and the plumbing in good working order. But while you're on the road, concentrating on your job, it's easy to lose track of time. And, a plumbing problem just doesn't seem so urgent when you're hundreds of miles away from it. You need a system to support those at home so they can manage in your absence.

Perhaps you're still the head of the household, and everything stops until you arrive home. **You'll need a bill-paying system to keep current** on such things as rent or mortgage payments, utilities, and other obligations. If you live alone, you definitely need such a system.

There are several ways you can handle this. You can arrange with your bank to pay your bills out of your account. You can use online banking and pay bills electronically. Or you can carry your checkbook and stamped envelopes with you on the road, paying your bills as they come due.

Deposits and withdrawals away from home have become much simpler with the automatic teller machines. For a fee, money can be taken out or put in from most states in the country. You could deposit your paycheck in Sun Valley, Idaho, and have it credited to your checking account in Tampa, Florida. Or, you can arrange with your employer to have your paycheck deposited directly into your account.

Whatever your living situation, you might want to ask your bank, credit union, utilities, and other creditors what services they provide that could further simplify your handling of these practical matters.

As for household emergencies, perhaps you already know a doctor, plumber, electrician, and so forth whom you can depend on. If not, try to line up these people before you leave. Even if you don't have a problem now, you could still go around and get to know these people. Then if an emergency should happen while you're away from home, you'll know just a phone call will take care of it.

DON'T ADVERTISE YOUR EMPTY HOUSE
Drivers who live alone or whose family is also gone a lot usually get themselves a post office box for their mail. They also make sure they don't have a week's worth of newspapers piled up on their doorsteps, which only advertises that no one is home. Perhaps you have a neighbor, friend, or relative you can trust to check up on things for you.

To Keep the Home Fires Burning

With the long hours and the traffic and the many other hassles, drivers generally look forward to blessed relaxation once the trip is over. They're hoping for a home-cooked meal, a truly comfortable night's sleep, and a pleasant time with the family. But it doesn't always work out that way. You might walk in and find that your spouse is just as tired and in just as bad a mood as you are. You both might be ready to snap at one another. That's not what a tired driver wants.

Or there could be times when your family might have other things going that you don't know about. You might feel excluded. When you first get home, they might treat you like "company." Everybody seems a little nervous. There you are, home at last, but no one knows what to talk about.

Well, let's take the situation in hand and see how it can be improved. Here's just a few ideas that have helped keep more than one truck driver's marriage close.

When you first get back to the home front, remember that you're still geared up to the rhythm of the road. Therefore, make sure you're relaxed and comfortable before you tackle family business. Give yourself some time to adjust to your surroundings. If something important has come up during your absence, ask for a little delay in talking about it. Chores or repairs can wait a while.

Plan an outing with the family, and something fun or romantic with you and your spouse. After an absence, you need to do a certain amount of getting reacquainted with your loved ones. You won't accomplish that by just sitting at home staring at the television! Be creative. Ideas will come to you when you're out on the road. Make a list of your ideas and let your family vote on it. Then, don't get so busy you don't leave enough time to do it.

It doesn't have to involve spending your money. Just going off to visit Aunt Myrtle for the afternoon can be fun. Or invite friends over for a backyard picnic and some volleyball. Doing things together will strengthen your home ties. It will also give you pleasant memories to relive when you're out on the road.

Every so often, let your family members know how much they mean to you. Even if you assume they already know, tell them. When you're home all the time, it's a little easier to show them. When you're away from home, you have to make a point of telling them.

Take pictures on your trip so that you can show your family some of the places you see on your job. Send home funny postcards to let them know you're thinking of them. It doesn't matter what the message is. Mail a souvenir home, noting where it's from and when you were there.

Invite your wife or husband to go with you on a trip. The best way to understand the life of a trucker is to have a little taste of it. Most companies will give you a special guest permit a couple of times a year. After all, it's in the company's best interest that your home life be a happy one.

If you will notice, these suggestions are all ways of sharing your experiences. As much as possible, try to share your own working life with your spouse and family members. Don't forget to share in their experiences, too. Reserve some energy to take their problems and concerns seriously. Don't just turn your back on your family when you leave and then expect everything to be just fine when you suddenly reappear.

Every marriage or close relationship requires work and constant vigilance. It's just that **a driving career requires you to put in a little extra effort to make up for those long separations.** But then you're lucky, too. You get to enjoy all those happy reunions!

Chapter 34 Quiz

1. After making a purchase on the road, _____.
   A. look both ways and drive slowly onto the highway
   B. call your dispatcher
   C. do a safety inspection
   D. get a receipt

2. If a truck driver were to go to a counter, give the clerk a list of numbers, and show his company ID card, he would probably be _____.
   A. buying something for cash
   B. ordering a square meal
   C. receiving funds through a money service
   D. arranging for laundry services

3. The brain cells receive oxygen _____.
   A. only during sound sleep
   B. from the bloodstream
   C. only during physical exertion
   D. after a good meal

4. Truckers simply can't work a daily exercise session into their routine since they're not always near a gym.
   A. True
   B. False

5. When it comes to getting good nutrition, it's not how much food you eat but _____ that counts.
   A. when you eat it
   B. what kind of foods you eat
   C. how much you paid for it
   D. your table manners

6. The best remedy for an afternoon slump is _____.
   A. a candy bar washed down with a large cup of coffee
   B. a butterscotch sundae
   C. 20 minutes of fresh air and exercise
   D. milk and cookies

7. Married truckers can forget about household responsibilities completely and let their spouse handle all the problems.
   A. True
   B. False

8. Of the following, _____ is the healthiest meal.
   A. french fries, a cheeseburger, and pie
   B. a salami sandwich, root beer, and an ice cream sundae
   C. white toast, butter and jelly, fried eggs, sausage, and coffee
   D. a baked chicken breast, whole wheat rolls, salad, and fresh fruit in yogurt

9. Drugs and alcohol should be avoided _____.
   A. as often as possible
   B. until evening
   C. by all professional drivers who value their lives and their jobs
   D. by those who can't handle them

10. To keep your marriage close, _____.
    A. send your spouse expensive gifts
    B. stay away from home until your spouse cools down
    C. make sure that your spouse hears no gossip about you
    D. share your trucking experiences, and work to create new ones when you're together

CHAPTER 35

CONTINUING EDUCATION

We Never Stop Learning

This is the last chapter in this book, but it's certainly not the end of your education. In fact, **your education is really just beginning.** It's through working on the job that you'll develop the judgment and common sense that no good driver can do without. Those qualities are the result of experience, and of keeping your mind active. In a changing industry like trucking, you simply can't afford to stop learning at any point.

One reason people keep their mind active at work is because they just can't help it. They're not robots. A robot will do whatever it's programmed to do without any questions. It doesn't want to know why it does a certain thing. It doesn't want to know what the other robots are doing, and it has no ideas about how to improve job conditions and performance. It simply does what it has been programmed to do and that's that.

The human being is another matter. It's important that we challenge ourselves again and again. "Use it or lose it," they say. That can apply both to muscles and to brain power. With that in mind, we're going to conclude this book with some suggestions for continuing your formal and informal education.

Just as it was your decision to train for a new career, and your hard work and dedication that got you to this point, it'll be up to you to **continue growing and challenging yourself.**

Shindigs and Get-togethers

Let's start off on a slightly social note here. We want to make sure you have all the fun you're entitled to as a truck driver. Remember, just because you're having fun doesn't mean you're not learning things to improve your job performance.

Besides, seeing old friends and meeting new ones should be encouraged. Friendships are important. They add a pleasant glow to the truck driver's lonely hours out on the road. Maybe that's why people in the trucking industry are so fond of getting together. You'll find that there are countless excuses for doing so. One of the most exciting events for everyone is the annual "Roadeo."

THE ROADEO

The Roadeo is the annual Superbowl **competition of knowledge, truck driving skills, and safety habits.** The American Trucking Associations (ATA) has designed courses that reflect everyday trucking situations. That includes a serpentine course, backing to an offset dock, and parallel parking. All drivers who have been with a company, accident-free, for at least a year are eligible to enter. Contestants must take a written test which includes questions about the industry, equipment, and safe driving. They are also tested on their ability to inspect equipment.

fig. 35-1
The ATA Roadeo
challenges your
maneuvering skills.

First, a company's drivers compete with each other to see who will represent the company. For this competition, the company sets up a course similar to that used in the state and national competitions. There are eight different categories:

- straight truck
- three, four, and five axle competitions
- tanker
- car hauler
- flatbed
- twin trailers

The winners in each category then represent their company at the state roadeo. State winners go to the nationals where they face as many as 250 of the most skillful drivers in the country. Out of that contest, some talented driver will earn the title of "Best." Everyone looks forward to the Roadeo, and the public always enjoys seeing what a big truck can do. So round 'em all up and head 'em on out!

OTHER EVENTS

Except for December, there are **truck shows, maintenance sessions, and conventions** all over the country. They're often advertised in the trucking magazines, and subscribers sometimes receive free tickets. What better excuse to drop by and see what's going on, especially if you're going to be driving in that area? It's fun and you'll pick up some valuable pointers.

The following calendar is typical of what you might find in any given year:

JANUARY
- Arkansas Motor Carriers Association Convention in Little Rock

FEBRUARY
- Greater New York Truck Show

MARCH
- Mid-America Trucking Show in Louisville, Kentucky

APRIL
- New England Truck and Equipment Show in Boston

MAY
- Antique truck show in Maryland

JUNE
- International Truck Show in Las Vegas, Nevada

JULY
- New York State Truck Association Driving Championships in Schenectady
- Walcott Trucke'rs Jamboree, Iowa

AUGUST
- Classic truck exhibition in Belle Fourche, South Dakota

SEPTEMBER
- Vermont Truck and Bus Association Convention in Killington

OCTOBER
- National Truck Driving Championship Roadeo (various locations; contact your local state trucking association)

NOVEMBER
- Auto Internationale Show in Las Vegas, Nevada

There are always driving seminars and brush-up courses and classes offered to keep drivers current with new techniques and new laws. Check with your company. Read the bulletin board and any company flyers with such information. Ask around.

Professional Associations

Getting involved in an organization is another **good way to continue your education** in the trucking industry. Trade groups form for several reasons:

- political action
- research
- education
- social and networking

Trade groups interested mainly in **political action** form in order **to act together on a certain issue or issues and get laws written, revoked, or enforced.** They may try to bring public pressure to bear on lawmakers, or hire a lobbyist to promote their views directly. The Interstate Truckload Carriers Conference is such a group. Members are irregular route common and contract carriers. Representatives from this group often speak to government bodies about issues that concern the membership. They work to see that legislation on transportation is favorable to their business.

Other groups exist to **achieve a goal or promote their cause through education.** They might offer training or skill workshops only to their membership, or the general public may be welcome to attend. Or, they might conduct public awareness campaigns to inform people about an issue. An example of this type of group is the Citizens for Safe Drivers Against Drunk Drivers and Chronic Offenders. Its members want to decrease the number of traffic deaths caused by drunk drivers. Toward that end, they conduct public information and education campaigns.

Still others are devoted to doing research. Members of these types of groups feel they can best achieve their goals by **finding out more about a subject, and making the information available to others.** An example of such a group is the Automotive Market Research Council. This is a group of parts, components, and accessories manufacturers. Their goal is to improve how well industry can predict what automotive products the market will need in the future. They accomplish their goal through research into such areas as buying trends.

Yet another type of trade group is one made up of people who do the same work you do. There you meet with others who have the same kind of work-related problems and challenges. The group provides an organized way to **share information, trade solutions,** and **provide mutual support** and understanding. It also provides for **organized networking.** Chapter 33 shows networking being put to use by a carrier looking for a driver to fill an open position. In the same way, you might hear about a new and better job opportunity in casual conversation at a trade group function. And, that might be the only way you would ever hear about that opening.

Some organizations may combine several of these functions, or even all of them. Being involved in a trade group doesn't have to take up a lot of time. Your participation may simply be a check that helps fund the group. Or, you may want to be more actively involved.

Our examples were trade groups for carriers, manufacturers, and the general public. But what about professional associations for drivers? For starters, your home state has state chapters of the American Trucking Associations. Owner-operators may be interested in several of the associations for independent drivers. You'll read or hear about other organizations of interest once you're out on the job. Plus new groups that form will contact you to see if you would like to become a member. Maybe you'll end up starting your own group!

Career Changes

Right now, you're very focused on starting your career and getting your first driving job. But after a while, you'll start to be concerned about **your future in the industry.** You may drive for a certain length of time and then want to look into another aspect of the industry. Maybe you'd like to be a dispatcher. Maybe you'd be good at sales, or a management position. Perhaps you'll get your own truck and become an owner/operator.

If you set your sights on an administrative job, you'll need to know how to run a business as well as drive a truck well. At this point you may need to get more formal education. You can get the business education you need through a home study course or by taking business classes at a junior college. At the very least, you'll want to look for seminars on issues such as taxes, record keeping, and money management.

You might want to keep driving forever, but are interested in what another company might have to offer for your talents. As we said, you may find out about just such a job through a networking group, a trade group newsletter, or a trucking magazine.

OBSERVATION SKILLS TEST

The future is sure to bring changes in equipment. What about the fantasy truck that was pictured at the start of this chapter? How does its driver control the steering? The shifting? Turn to the Observation Skills Test Grid at the back of the book to check your answers.

Reading Programs

If you're already a confirmed reader, you understand how it enriches your life. For others, it may take a bit of dedication. However, reading and **keeping informed** is one of the extras that **separates the** really **professional driver from the truck jockey** who simply puts in time on the road.

You may be convinced that **staying current by reading** is a good idea. But you may be wondering where you're going to find the time. Here's one way to keep up with it. Make sure you've always got something around, in the cab or sleeper, to read during those little waiting periods on the job. It will sure beat twiddling your thumbs and watching the clock when you're waiting to unload or waiting out a traffic delay. And, it helps turn downtime into productive time.

FEDERAL MOTOR CARRIER SAFETY REGULATIONS

Throughout this book we have referred to the Federal Motor Carrier Safety Regulations (FMCSR). The FMCSR is updated periodically and you should keep up with the changes.

DRIVER'S MANUAL

Most companies have a **driver's manual.** It usually contains important company policies, **lists driver responsibilities,** and often includes information about **driver benefits.** It may describe the fuel bonus program and includes **tips on how you can become a better driver.** By all means, read your company's Driver's Manual.

TRADE MAGAZINES

Truckers enjoy reading about matters that concern their daily lives. There's a lot to choose from. To sample some of the **many trucking magazines available,** you can either go to one of the large library branches or you can see what's for sale down at the truck stop. You can use your computer to shop the Internet for books and materials. The book you're reading now, *BUMPER TO BUMPER, The Complete Guide to Tractor-Trailer Operations,* is listed on the Internet. There are magazines designed especially for the driver, some for the independent owner/operator, and others that are basically company-oriented.

They all help key you in to the **trucking industry** with **reports, articles, and interviews.** Even the advertisements are informative. You can almost always send away for more, free information on something that interests you. Plus, there are classified ads where companies may advertise for drivers. You will also find used trucks, mechanical parts, gadgets, and insurance deals for sale.

GENERAL INTEREST MAGAZINES

The general news magazines will often have **articles that pertain to the transportation industry.** In fact, *Readers Digest* reprinted an article about "killer trucks" that was very influential in the campaign to upgrade driver performance.

Try to read either a newspaper or news magazine on a regular basis. The economic and political news pertains to all of us, directly or indirectly. Be aware of the world in which you live. Understand how certain changes will affect you personally, along with the entire trucking industry. Observe public affairs.

THE TIME IS RIGHT

In closing, as we send you off to seek your fortune, let us repeat that this is a very favorable time for you to present your truck driving skills to the job market. There is a serious driver shortage that promises to get worse in the next few years. **Companies are snatching up all the good drivers they can find.**

If you prove to be a bright, skillful person (and we're betting that you will) you will find an employer who will value you. So keep yourself bright and skillful. Continue your education, and continue to grow throughout what we hope will be a long and happy career.

CHAPTER 35 QUIZ

1. If you have taken a formal training course in the last five years, you can be confident your knowledge is up to date.
   A. True
   B. False

2. When truck drivers gather for a barbecue or picnic, that can't be considered a learning experience because it's mostly for social reasons.
   A. True
   B. False

3. All drivers who have been with a company, accident-free, for at least a year are eligible to enter competition leading to the ATA national roadeo.
   A. True
   B. False

4. A knowledge test is part of the _____.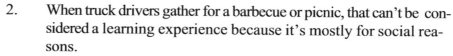
   A. FMCSR driver training program
   B. ATA truck roadeo
   C. range exercise course
   D. highway patrol sobriety test

5. Truck shows, maintenance sessions, and conventions are held all around the country, every month of the year.
   A. True
   B. False

For Questions 6, 7, 8, and 9, match the type of trade group in Column A with its function in Column B.

Column A Trade Group   Column B Function

6. political action   A. organized networking

7. education   B. conducts workshops and
                                       public awareness campaigns

8. research   C. influences lawmakers

9. social   D. conducts studies and shares
                                       the results

10. About the only time you can't read to continue your education is
     _____.
     A. when you're off-duty (not driving), waiting to unload at a ware-
         house
     B. when you're off-duty (not driving) during a lunch break at a
         truck stop
     C. when you're off-duty
     D. when you're driving

Get Your Own Copy!

Didn't get to keep the copy of *BUMPER TO BUMPER, The Complete Guide to Tractor-Trailer Operations,* that you received in the classroom? Order your own copy directly from us at a special price $44.36. That's a 20% discount off the list price and includes Priority Mail postage. You may reach us

by mail at
Mike Byrnes and Associates, Inc.
P. O. Box 8866
Corpus Christi, TX, 78468-8866
or by e-mail at
mbapub@aol.com
or visit us at our Web site
www.bumper2bumpertruckbook.com

Complete and mail the request blank, or, if you contact us online, provide the information requested below. You may send a check or money order for $44.36 (include sales tax where applicable) or charge your purchase to VISA or Mastercard.

- -

Fill out completely. Please print.

Name_____

Address_____

City_____State_____Zip_____Phone No. (___)_____

School Attended_____Date Graduated_____

School Director Name_____

School Director Signature_____

Your Signature_____Date_____

Charge my purchase to (Check One): ❏ VISA ❏ Mastercard

Account number _____ Expiration Date _____

Name as it appears on the card_____

Allow six to eight weeks delivery
Price subject to change without notice. Does not include sales tax where applicable.

The Observation Skills Test

Having good powers of observation is an important skill for a professional driver. There are so many things going on around you at all times that you must be aware of in order to drive safely, economically, and responsibly. If you are not observant naturally, it's a skill you can and should develop.

The Observation Skills Tests in your book help test your powers of observation and train you to be more observant. You may have completely ignored the first few tests. As you caught on, you probably began to pay more attention to them. By the end of the course, you likely "got" more of them than you missed. You learned to be observant.

THE OBSERVATION SKILLS GRID

This grid allows you to see graphically how observant you are and how well your observation skills have improved over the course of your studies. Every chapter begins with a large illustration that presents a puzzle or problem. Later in the chapter, you're asked a question about that illustration. If you were able to answer the question right away without looking at the answer, you give yourself a point or two for being observant (the number of points you earn are given here, along with the answer). Mark that point or points on the horizontal line that intersects the vertical line for that chapter.

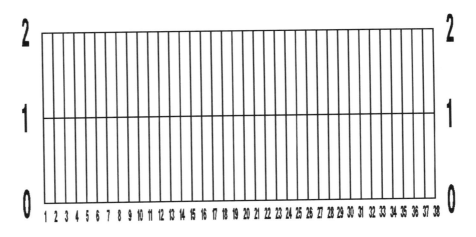

The numbers 1 through 35 at the bottom DO NOT correspond to the chapter numbers. Instead, they are the order in which you go through the book, since you may not read the chapters in the order they appear in this book. In other words, if you get a point for the first chapter you read, you mark it on the horizontal line where it intersects with the vertical line numbered 1. For the second chapter you read, mark your point on the vertical line numbered 2 where it intersects with the horizontal line, and so forth.

When you have finished the book, connect all the dots. You'll probably end up with a saw-toothed line that looks something like this:

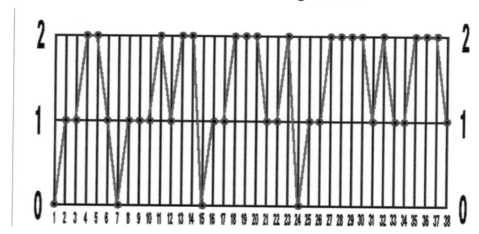

What does it mean? That's fairly simple. Count the number of points you have on the horizontal lines. These are the points you earned for being observant. Compare the results with the scale below.

OBSERVATION
POINTS

0 to 11

Being observant is not a skill you possess naturally. This doesn't mean you can't be a professional driver. It does mean you will have to work very hard to polish your observation skills. Pay particular attention to the techniques outlined in Chapter 19, Safe Driving. Make a point of using those techniques. At first it may seem forced or awkward. With practice, it will come naturally, and you will learn to be more observant.

12 to 24

You're a pretty observant person. Sometimes your attention might falter, but most of the time you're aware of what's going on around you. Take a look at the chapters where you missed the test. Do they have anything in common? Are there any particular situations in which you are less observant than others? It will be helpful to know that, so you can practice being more aware at those times.

25 to 35

You are very observant by nature. This skill will really help you to be a safe and professional driver.

Becoming Observant

Just doing the Observation Skills Tests may have helped you to develop your observation skills. But if this area needs more help, here's a technique you can use to improve. You can (and probably should) practice this now when you drive the family car. Later, use it when you drive your truck to keep your skills sharp.

Commentary Driving

As you drive, observe and identify obstacles in the road ahead. Identify them by describing them out loud.

The rules for commentary driving are as follows.

- Identify the obstacle with short phrases.
- Identify only the most important obstacles.
- Don't look at your instructor, co-driver, or passenger while talking.
- Don't explain the obstacle.

Answers to Observation Skills Tests

CHAPTER NUMBER AND TITLE	ANSWERS
1. Your Future in Trucking	What's missing in this picture? You, of course...there's no driver! Giver yourself one point on the grid if you even remembered what the picture was. Give yourself two points if you noticed the truck was in motion but there was no driver.
2. Dashboards and Gauges	The steering wheel cluster is missing from the instrument panel. Give yourself one point if you noticed "something" was missing. Give yourself two points if you were able to name any of the missing parts, for instance, the speedometer or tachometer.
3. Transmissions	There's two problems with the cab of this manually-shifted truck. The shift lever is on the wrong side of the cab. You'd have to climb over it to get to the driver's seat. Also, there is no clutch pedal. You earn one point for each of the two problems you noticed.
4. Air Brakes	A lower speed is posted for the curve. The driver of this truck should slow down—and fast! Give yourself one point for noticing the curve and the reduced speed sign. Give yourself another point if you noticed the driver's speedometer pegged at 55 mph.

5. Electrical

The battery showed signs of some common problems that impair battery performance. The battery cable was loosely connected, and it was frayed. Give yourself a point if you noticed either of those problems. Also, the battery case is cracked. Give yourself another point if you noticed that.

6. Engines

The Observation Skills Test picture was of an engine. Give yourself one point if you recalled the picture. How many oil filters did you notice (they were the only component labeled)? If you answered "two," give yourself another point.

7. Drive Train

Did you notice the tandem axles on this frame? Give yourself a point if you did. Give yourself another point if you noticed the black air bags that are part of the suspension system.

8. Steering

What tire was shown in the Observation Skills Test picture? Give yourself a point if you answered the front, passenger side tire. Improper alignment on this tractor has caused the front tire to wear unevenly. Give yourself one point if you noticed the uneven wear.

9. Tires and Wheels

Did you notice the underinflated front tire (it was so bad it was nearly flat!)? What about the mismatched tires on the tandems? One is clearly smaller than the other. Give yourself one point for each of the two problems you noticed.

10. Tractors

The tractor pictured is a single axle (one point), conventional (another point). Give yourself one point for each of the two classifications you were able to name.

11. Vehicle Management Systems

The driver performance report reveals this driver had an excessive amount of idling time, and too many incidences of speeding. Give yourself one point for recognizing the speeding problem, and another point if you recognized the idling problem.

12. Types of Trailers

The trailer is missing two important components. One, it has no landing gear to hold it up and is defying gravity, balancing on its rear axle. Two, it has no kingpin for the approaching tractor to hook up with. Give yourself one point for each of the two defects you noticed.

13. Specialized Rigs

The two types of trailers pictured are a single-drop and a double-drop with removable gooseneck. Give yourself a point for each one of the two trailers you were able to name.

14. Refrigerated Trailers

Give yourself one point if you answered that the reefer pictured had ribbed walls and floor. Give yourself another point if you were able to name the three kinds of frozen pizza being hauled: cheese, pepperoni, and sausage!

15. Coupling and Uncoupling

If the driver pulls this tractor away from this trailer, two things will happen. One, the trailer will fall to the ground, since it is not completely coupled to the tractor and has no support. Two, the supply lines will be torn off the trailer. Give yourself a point for each one of the two results you predicted.

16. Putting the Truck in Motion

The truck in the illustration is a cabover—the doghouse in the cab tells you that. And, it's a nine-speed transmission. You can tell by the shift pattern in the dash area. Give yourself one point for each one of the two questions you were able to answer correctly.

17. Driving Techniques

First you probably noticed an accident about to happen. The truck is attempting a right turn from the leftmost lane and a car is in the trucker's blind spot. If the car doesn't stop before truck completes this turn, the car will be hit. Give yourself one point for noticing that. Second, there's a problem with the electrical system. The tractor turn signal is working, but the trailer turn signal is not. Give yourself another point if you noticed that.

18. Backing

This driver failed to get out and look before backing, and faces two possible accidents. He's in real danger of backing into an overhead wire, or running over a board with a nail in it that lies in his path. Give yourself one point for each one of the two backing dangers you noticed.

19. Safe Driving

Give yourself one point if you noticed the no-passing zone that's coming up. The car in the foreground will be trying to return to the right lane quickly to avoid a head-on collision with the approaching car in the left lane (the truck driver should slow down and allow the car to get back into the lane). Give yourself another point if you noticed the potential collision.

20. Driving Challenges

Heading downhill, the driver of this vehicle is going way too fast. Give yourself a point for noticing that. Give yourself another point if you noticed the runaway ramp off to the right. This driver will probably need it to get his rig under control.

21. Handling Doubles and Triples

The driver of this combination rig started from the wrong lane to make this turn around the corner. As a result, the trailers will come up over the curve. Give yourself one point if you noticed. The female pedestrian has a "DON'T WALK" sign, so the male pedestrians will be crossing the street. Give yourself another point if you noticed.

22. Auxiliary Brakes

The driver of this rig has just crested a hill and is facing a downgrade. He'll need to do something to control his downhill speed. He's at top speed and at top rated rpm for his gear. Give yourself a point if you noticed either the speed, the rpm, or both. Give yourself another point if you realized he'd have to downshift, brake, use the retarder, or do something to control his speed.

23. Sliders

The trailer is heavily overloaded on the front axle. Give yourself one point if you noticed it. Some more of the lumber could be loaded towards the back of the trailer. Give yourself another point if you knew how to redistribute the weight to remedy the problem.

24. Economy Operating

This driver is driving at the right rpm for his speed, and that's economy driving. Give yourself one point if you were able to recall the speed and another point if you were able to recall the rpm the vehicle was being operated at.

25. Vehicle Inspection

The driver noted on her report that there was a problem with the brake lines to her trailer. Give yourself one point if you noticed it. Give yourself two points if you figured she'll put the truck back in the shop for repairs rather than taking it out.

26. The Log Book

There were lots of problems with the way this log was filled out. Here are just a few: the driver failed to sign it and the total hours don't add up correctly. Give yourself a point for each of these two problems you noticed. Did you also notice the driver has logged in as being in the sleeper and driving at the same time? If so, that was really being observant!

27. Cargo Documentation	The cargo documentation shows the load contained boxes of canned soup, cartons of TVs, and cartons of TV stands. Give yourself a point for being able to name the cargo. The soup cartons were opened, but the contents were all right; ten cartons of TV sets were damaged, and the TV stands were five cartons short. Give yourself another point if you were able to describe any or all of these problems with the load.
28. Loading, Securing, and Unloading Cargo	Two methods were used to secure the cargo in the trailer. One, the pallets were bound up with straps. Two, load locks were used to hold the stacks in place. Give yourself one point for each of the two methods you observed.
29. Accidents and Fires	The driver is smoking in spite of the warning sign. Give yourself a point if you noticed it. Meanwhile, the co-driver isn't paying attention to the fueling process and doesn't see that the fuel tank is full and running over. A fire is sure to develop. Give yourself one point if you noticed his carelessness.
30. Hazardous Materials	The driver was doing two very dangerous things while loading hazardous material. One, he failed to load the compressed gas cylinders properly. They should be loaded upright, held in the racks so they won't overturn. Two, he was smoking while handling a flammable material. Give yourself a point for each of the two violations you noticed.
31. Map Reading	The map was of a portion of the state of Arizona. Give yourself one point for noticing that. Give yourself another point if you recalled that the map showed two main routes between Phoenix and Holbrook.
32. Preventive Maintenance	The driver of this truck failed to see a couple of problems developing. Did you see them? Give yourself one point if you noticed the air line connection was loose, or that the electrical line was frayed. Give yourself another point if you noticed that the driver's side mirror was cracked.
33. Getting a Job as a Professional Driver	There were two applicants waiting for interviews. Give yourself one point if you answered that question correctly. Assuming their experience and abilities are about equal, the applicant in the long-sleeved shirt will likely get the job because of his neat, well-groomed appearance. Give yourself another point if that was your response.

34. The Driver's Life

The truck stop pictured accepted all major credit and fuel charge cards. Showers were free with fill-up, otherwise they cost three dollars each. Give yourself one point for each of the two questions you answered correctly.

35. Continuing Education

Did you see the steering in the right arm rest and shifting controls in the left arm rest? The shifting was done with pushbuttons, and the steering with a lever-type control. Give yourself one point for each correct answer. Right now, this futuristic truck is just the product of a creative imagination, but who knows?

Index